CHARTING THE CONSEQUENCES:
THE IMPACT OF CHARTER RIGHTS ON
CANADIAN LAW AND POLITICS

In 1990 Supreme Court Justice Bertha Wilson proclaimed that the Canadian Charter of Rights 'is and must continue to be a vital force in molding the lives of Canadians.' In this collection of original essays commissioned by the Centre for Constitutional Studies, University of Alberta, legal and political scholars evaluate the impact of the Charter on life in Canada since 1982.

Other works have focused on the jurisprudence of the Charter – its internal coherence or its implications for the role of courts. *Charting the Consequences* considers 'externalities' – the effect of the Charter and its jurisprudence on non-constitutional aspects of the law and on the dynamics of legislative power, provincial politics, and social movements. Specific contexts are examined, including certain provinces, economic rights, taxation, First Nations, sexual orientation, social movements, private law, access to justice, and political science. Patterns become manifest across contexts. First, the editors identify three strata of actors in society – ranging from the most powerful to the least powerful – who are affected by the Charter in differing degrees. Second, they expose how the actors' influences on Charter interpretation are determined, in some measure, by the magnitude of their social and political power.

Charting the Consequences offers a fresh perspective on the Charter. It will generate new thinking and scholarship among lawyers, political scientists, and public policy makers.

DAVID SCHNEIDERMAN is Executive Director, Centre for Constitutional Studies, University of Alberta. KATE SUTHERLAND is a doctoral candidate at Harvard Law School.

EDITED BY DAVID SCHNEIDERMAN
& KATE SUTHERLAND

Charting the Consequences: The Impact of Charter Rights on Canadian Law and Politics

Published in association with the Centre for Constitutional Studies, University of Alberta, by

UNIVERSITY OF TORONTO PRESS
Toronto Buffalo London

© University of Toronto Press Incorporated 1997
Toronto Buffalo London
Printed in Canada

ISBN 0-8020-0811-9 (cloth)
ISBN 0-8020-7181-3 (paper)

Printed on acid-free paper

Canadian Cataloguing in Publication Data

Main entry under title:

Charting the consequences : the impact of Charter rights
on Canadian law and politics

ISBN 0-8020-0811-9 (bound) ISBN 0-8020-7181-3 (pbk.)

1. Canada. Canadian Charter of Rights and Freedoms.
2. Law – Canada.   3. Canada – Politics and government –
1984–1993.*   4. Canada – Politics and government – 1993–   .*
I. Schneiderman, David, 1958–   . II. Sutherland, Kate.
III. University of Alberta. Centre for Constitutional
Studies.

KE4381.5.C54 1997   342.71'085   C97-930031-2
KF4483.C519C42 1997

University of Toronto Press acknowledges the financial assistance to its publishing
program of the Canada Council and the Ontario Arts Council.

Contents

Acknowledgments

In edited collections of this sort, there are many acknowledgments to make and persons to thank. We are grateful to the members of the Management Board of the Centre for Constitutional Studies, University of Alberta, for having supported the idea for this project and for entrusting us with its carriage: Dean Timothy J. Christian, Bruce P. Elman, Fil Fraser, Gerald L. Gall, Susan Jackel, Anne McLennan, Roderick C. MacLeod, J. Peter Meekison, Kenneth Norrie, June Ross, David Taras, and Allan Tupper. We are particularly grateful to the Alberta Law Foundation, who generously provided financial support both for the project and for the publication of this book. Christine Urquhart, Executive Assistant of the Centre for Constitutional Studies, deserves special thanks for assisting in the administration of the project and for helping to bring this book to completion. The enthusiasm and support of Virgil Duff, Executive Editor, University of Toronto Press, is greatly appreciated. During production of the book, Barb Porter of University of Toronto Press and Curtis Fahey were both a pleasure to work with. The contributors are deserving of our special thanks for patiently having endured delays and our editorial entreaties. We would like to acknowledge, as well, the respective institutional support that was provided by the Centre for Constitutional Studies, University of Alberta, and the College of Law, University of Saskatchewan.

DAVID SCHNEIDERMAN
KATE SUTHERLAND

Contributors

Joel Bakan	Faculty of Law, University of British Columbia
Richard W. Bauman	Faculty of Law, University of Alberta
John Borrows	Faculty of Law, University of British Columbia
Alexandra Dobrowolsky	Department of Political Science, Dalhousie University
Didi Herman	Department of Law, Keele University
Kathleen A. Lahey	Faculty of Law, Queen's University
Yves de Montigny	Faculté de droit, Université d'Ottawa
Mary Jane Mossman	Osgoode Hall Law School, York University
David Schneiderman	Centre for Constitutional Studies, University of Alberta
Michael Smith	Department of Geography, University of British Columbia
Kate Sutherland	Doctoral candidate, Harvard Law School
Ian Urquhart	Department of Political Science, University of Alberta

Introduction

Speaking *ex cathedra* on her last day sitting as a justice of the Supreme Court of Canada, Bertha Wilson proclaimed that the Charter had given Canadians 'a new awareness of rights and freedoms ... Our Charter is and must continue to be a vital force in molding the lives of Canadians.'[1] Ten years after the incorporation of the Charter into Canada's constitutional fabric, the Centre for Constitutional Studies at the University of Alberta decided to initiate a research project enquiring into whether the Charter indeed has shaped the lives of Canadians. We hoped to answer a basic question: what have been the effects of the Charter on various facets of Canadian law and politics? Essays were specifically commissioned from scholars across Canada and they are assembled here in this collection. Each article addresses a particular aspect of Charter life that, to date, has frequently eluded scholarly endeavour.

Much of the literature concerning the Charter addresses its developing jurisprudence. This is not too surprising a phenomenon. The enactment of the Charter in 1982 expanded the range of judicial responsibility, if not radically altering it. Primarily, the literature concerns both the transformation of the judicial role and the results of that transformation as played out in the case law. In contrast, our objective was not only to look at the jurisprudence but also to move beyond it, into the realm of what economists describe as 'externalities,' examining what effect, if any, the Charter and its jurisprudence have had on non-constitutional aspects of the law and on the dynamics of legislative power, provincial politics, and social movements. Our impression was that the impact of the Charter needed to be studied in specific institutional, juridical, political, and social contexts. We wanted to focus not only on how the Charter was transforming these contexts but also on the ways the Charter itself was being transformed in the process.

Another of our objectives was to go beyond some of the stale divisions that are readily identifiable in the scholarship – the opposition between Charter pessimists and Charter optimists.[2] As exhibited by the essays collected here, Charter scholarship is maturing – the research is more contextualized and focused. This perhaps can be explained not only by the passage of time but also by the increasing convergence of the oppositional stances of the past. Some of the strong sceptics, influenced in part by critical feminist and critical race literature, have come to acknowledge the pragmatic utility of rights discourse, while Charter optimists have been sobered by the slow pace of social change initiated by Charter litigation.

In order that we be able to understand the role of the Charter in Canadian law and politics, it was important that we not consider the 1982 Charter in freeze-frame. The Charter has insinuated itself into a variety of dynamic settings which pre-existed the Charter, and which have continued to evolve since 1982. As the articles in this book show, the Charter has had a significant impact on political dynamics – within the provinces of Quebec and Alberta and in the politics within and between First Nations. The Charter also has affected judicial values, academic practices, and the practices and politics of social movements. Still further evidence of the multifaceted nature of the Charter is the fact that these politics and practices themselves have helped to shape Charter jurisprudence.

While it may be too early to ascertain definitively the impact of the Charter in these various domains, some of the effects are identifiable. We have isolated the Charter's impact on three groups of actors, differentiated by the sum of their power and influence in Canadian society.

First, the essays suggest that powerful and dominant actors have been the most resilient to Charter influences. For example, both Yves de Montigny and Ian Urquhart suggest that, contrary to current assumptions, provincial powers under the Constitution Act, 1867 largely have been untouched by the Charter and that provinces have been able to resist some of the Charter's homogenizing influences.[3] Kathleen Lahey argues that the federal government mainly has been immune from the influence of the Charter in the development of tax policy. Finally, Richard Bauman concludes that business enterprises have not had to alter their practices in any significant way as a result of the Charter.

Second, what we call middle-power actors have felt more of the influence of the Charter. Kate Sutherland explains how the judiciary has mediated the Charter's impact in the development of the common law of torts. Alexandra Dobrowolsky suggests that academic disciplines – political scientists are the object of her study – have felt that influence, even if only by attempting to assimilate the Charter into pre-existing theoretical frameworks. Similarly, Mary

Jane Mossman examines the impact of the Charter on the legal profession and claims that, while that impact has been identifiable, it may not have been profound.

Finally, the least powerful actors in society perhaps have been most profoundly affected and shaped by the existence of the Charter. Joel Bakan and Michael Smith examine the impact of the Charter during the course of Charlottetown Accord negotiations, suggesting that the Charter altered both the public face and the internal dynamics of two key actors, the Native Women's Association of Canada and the National Action Committee on the Status of Women. John Borrows explores the tensions within the First Nations, particularly around issues of gender, while Didi Herman focuses on conflicts over rights discourse in the gay and lesbian communities.

This picture is filled out by an understanding of the case law discussed by the authors. Each of these communities of actors have had varying success in Charter litigation. The essays in this collection lead to the conclusion that those Charter claims that fit well with the dominant intellectual and political milieu – for example, claims by business enterprises – fared well. Those that did not fit – for example, claims based on grounds of poverty, sexual orientation, and race – did not do as well.

In short, the studies suggest that the least powerful actors have made the fewest gains in Charter interpretation and at the same time have had their politics and practices the most disrupted by the Charter. The fact that these social movements have been able to heighten their public profile by availing themselves of Charter language may produce some gains – such as larger membership or coalition-building – but further research will have to be done to bear this out. Paradoxically, the least powerful actors are least likely to give up Charter discourse as a ground for achieving social change. These issues are explored further in our conclusion. At this point, we offer a more detailed discussion of each of the essays.

Federalism, it is argued, encourages diversity. The Charter, in contrast, promotes a pan-Canadian version of equal rights-holders. This tension is heightened significantly in the context of the province of Quebec's desire to maintain and promote a distinct society. It is important, then, to determine whether and to what extent the Charter has impaired the ability of provincial governments to function in their legislative domains. Yves de Montigny canvasses the Supreme Court of Canada's record in this regard and concludes that the Charter, as interpreted by the Court, has not had a significant impact on the provinces' ability to legislate. Among the provinces, Quebec has seen its legislation challenged more frequently than that of other provinces, and those challenges have concerned the most symbolic of legislative endeavours – language laws. Yet, argues de Montigny, the Court has recognized a sphere for significant diversity and autonomy between provinces, even in the domain of language laws, a sphere that leaves the Quebec legislature largely free of the homogenizing influences of the Charter.

The operating assumption in much of the literature concerning the Charter is that it has taken root in most of Canada outside Quebec. Ian Urquhart tests this assumption in one jurisdiction by examining the uneasy relationship between the Charter and provincial politics in Alberta. His essay focuses on the responses of both the government of Alberta and public opinion in that province to the values being promoted under the Charter. The political reaction has been largely unenthusiastic and, at times, obstructionist, for example, in the legislative response to *Mahé*, which recognized the right of francophone parents to representation on public school boards. This stance of non-compliance has been aided by judicial self-restraint in Charter challenges which has minimized the Charter's impact in Alberta. With regard to public opinion, polling done in the period after the failure of the Meech Lake Accord suggests that Albertans' early enthusiasm for the Charter has peaked and that they view rights conservatively. Such conservatism is most marked in smaller communities, which have helped to elect recent Alberta governments. It is this unenthusiastic public response that helps to bolster the reluctant political response.

Although economic interests did not figure largely in the debates preceding the entrenchment of the Charter, the language of the document has enabled economic interests to figure large in Charter jurisprudence. Richard Bauman examines the role economic rights have played in Charter litigation, seeking an explanation of why courts have indirectly made room for economic rights despite their absence from most of the Charter text. In doing so he tests the assumptions of public choice theory, which argues that political behaviour can be explained in the same way as economic behaviour – on the basis of calculated, rational, self-interest. Public choice theory may be able to explain the absence of economic rights in the language of the Charter – they were left out, theorists would say, because politicians did not want to curtail their own spheres of influence – but it does not explain why courts have been amenable to finding economic rights in the Charter. Bauman concludes that the courts have been guided by no particular economic theory; rather, they have decided that the enumerated rights of the Charter have important economic aspects. For these reasons, business entities should remain confident that their interests are not being neglected under the Charter despite their having been left out in the first place.

Kathleen Lahey undertakes a detailed assessment of the Charter's impact on income tax law and policy. First, she examines what Charter challenges have been brought in the tax context and what have been the results of those challenges. Then she asks the fundamental question: have the Charter's guarantees materially affected the distributional impact of the Income Tax Act, or does the system continue to serve the interests of privileged groups? Lahey notes that the government has successfully defeated nearly every substantive equality claim that taxpayers have raised, and she goes on to indicate that even when taxpayers have been successful, Parliament has been quick to reverse those gains through statutory amendments. Ultimately, she concludes that the expectations and goals of equality-seekers have not been a dominant force in the shaping of income tax law and policy under the Charter, on the contrary, privileged groups have been effective in pressuring the courts to use the Charter to their advantage and to the detriment of historically disadvantaged groups. But Lahey indicates that the parallel growth in sophistication of Charter litigation and of tax-policy analysis has led to the emergence of a new area of Charter discourse, 'fiscal Charter litigation,' which has, in some measure, overcome the barriers to the promotion of equality through the application of Charter values to income tax policy. She emphasizes the importance of pursuing this avenue of Charter review in the future and expresses the hope that it will be possible to work collectively to develop a fiscal Charter jurisprudence that will promote the emergence of egalitarian institutions.

John Borrows explores the profound impact the Charter has had on First Nations identity and politics, finding that its influence has been most strongly felt in the area of Indian gender politics. He fears that this conflict within First Nations over the application of the Charter to their societies could threaten the gains that thus far have been made towards self-determination. But he argues that this need not be the case. He sees potential in the Charter to facilitate a dialogue between rights and traditions in First Nations communities which could lead to a transformation of rights discourse. Further, he argues that, given the compatibility of First Nations traditional values with some of the underlying principles of the Charter, rights discourse offers the opportunity to communicate with the oppressors in language they understand, thereby enlisting some measure of cooperation in making necessary change. Borrows admits the limitations and pitfalls of relying on the Charter but suggests nonetheless that its underlying principles can facilitate self-determination without overpowering First Nations societies' customs, laws, and traditions.

Didi Herman shifts focus from the standard broad inquiry as to whether the Charter is bad or good from the point of view of progressive politics, asking instead: have some groups made more out of the Charter than others and, if so, why? She attempts to answer this question with respect to the lesbian and gay rights movement by analysing several existing Charter perspectives which she terms 'debunker,' 'promoter,' 'reactionary,' and 'pragmatist.' She finds that each of these perspectives provides partial explanation for the successes and failures of rights strategies in the struggles of lesbian and gay activists, and that all raise important questions about the complex and contradictory effects of the Charter on these struggles. But no one perspective offers complete answers or useful guidance. Herman suggests an alternate approach to the Charter which she labels 'critical pragmatism.' Clearly the Charter is here to stay and, if lesbian and gay activists can use it to advantage, they should. But before they do so, the question of which of the different ways of pursuing rights claims is better or more progressive must be addressed. Herman concludes that the Charter's potential is different depending on who is invoking it and why; therefore, a comparative analysis of what different groups have and have not achieved through the Charter is required.

Joel Bakan and Michael Smith examine the relationship between Charter rights and social movements in Canada, focusing on the example of the strategies of the Native Women's Association of Canada (NWAC) and the National Action Committee on the Status of Women (NAC) during the debates leading up to the referendum on the Charlottetown Accord. Bakan and Smith acknowledge the potential rights discourse has to mobilize social movements, affirm marginalized identities, and attract wider support for progressive goals. But, they go on to enquire, to what effect? They argue that, in invoking rights discourse at all, social movements necessarily place themselves in the context of 'dominant ideological discourses of rights' and, in so doing, risk having their claims distorted through their translation into classical liberal terms by the media and other commentators. Often the effect of this distortion is to undermine rather than promote the movements' political goals. Bakan and Smith argue further that rights strategies can have as profound an effect on the internal politics of social movements as on the public perception of those movements' broader political agendas. They note that most contemporary social movements are divided among liberals, socialists, and radicals, and they suggest that rights strategies may advance the political goals of the liberals to the detriment of those of other factions, effectively excluding the latter from the movements with which they originally identified. Bakan and Smith conclude, then, that the risks of rights strategies go beyond the possibility of co-option and that closer consideration must be given to the natural and ideological constraints which prevent reinterpretations of rights from successfully challenging the dominant rights ideology.

Kate Sutherland explores the impact of Charter equality principles on private law decisions. In *Dolphin Delivery*, the Supreme Court of Canada made it clear that the Charter does not directly apply to the common law or to private litigation, but it left room for Charter influence on private law in stating that courts should nonetheless apply and develop the principles of the common law in a manner consistent with Charter values. The pairing of this pronouncement with the Supreme Court's subsequent embrace of substantive equality in *Andrews* has broadened the reach of this influence, probably well beyond what the Court intended. Sutherland illustrates its contours by turning to the example of the way Charter equality principles, at least with respect to gender equality, have been insinuated into the recent development of tort-law doctrine relating to consent, limitation periods, and the quantification of damages. Given, however, that the Charter is not explicitly invoked in these decisions, an inquiry into other factors which may be simultaneously effecting this trend in judicial decision making is necessary. For alternative and intertwining explanations, Sutherland looks to the influence that feminist legal scholarship has had on recent developments in tort theory and judicial education.

The Charter's impact on access to justice is assessed by Mary Jane Mossman, who studies two distinct but related themes. The first is the delivery of legal aid services; the second is the impact of the Charter's equality guarantees on the legal profession, in terms both of the changing demographics in legal education and of admission to the legal profession. As regards the first, Mossman finds that the Charter has had little effect in changing for the better the nature and scope of legal aid services in Canada. The Charter may have been more effective in changing the second aspect of access to justice, that is, the face of the legal profession. Here, Mossman concludes that the Charter has had a discernible impact on the discourse about admission policies to law schools and the practices of the legal profession by raising concerns about gender bias and systemic discrimination. But, given the resistance of the profession to change and the personal, career costs to complainants, it is too early to gauge the real impact of the Charter on the legal profession. Even as women and members of minority groups begin entering law schools and the legal profession in larger numbers, this resistance to change may not diminish.

The Charter has affected not only the courts, legislatures, and social movements but also the way in which society itself is studied. Alexandra Dobrowolsky discusses the impact of the Charter on political science, focusing on the literature produced by this discipline's Anglo-Canadian mainstream. While the Charter did not give rise to such collective actors as the women's movement, Aboriginal peoples, or gays and lesbians, it did provide a new vehicle by which their claims could be articulated. In the reaction of political scientists to these claims, Dobrowolsky identifies a number of different streams: the 'state-centred' approach to political science takes an institutional approach and emphasizes, for example, the design of federalism; the 'society-centred' approach concerns itself with societal factors, such as political and cultural influences or structural accounts which take class into consideration; and lastly, a conservative approach characterizes pejoratively the use of the Charter by collective actors. While the impact of the Charter is discernible in the various strains of thought, political scientists have not been able to abandon traditional models in favour of alternative paradigms which more fully appreciate the influence of the actors on the Canadian political scene.

Notes

1 Text of remarks by Justice Bertha Wilson, Supreme Court of Canada, 6 December 1990 (unpublished).
2 These are discussed in Didi Herman, 'The Good, the Bad, and the Smugly: Sexual Orientation and Perspectives on the Charter,' in this volume.
3 Their conclusions are somewhat in discord with those reached by Patrick Monahan and Marie Finkelstein, 'The Charter of Rights and Public Policy in Canada,' *Osgoode Hall Law Journal,* vol. 30 (1992), 501–46. This may be because of the latter's different focus: Monahan and Finkelstein are concerned largely with internal deliberative processes within government.

CHARTING THE CONSEQUENCES

1

The Impact (Real or Apprehended) of the Canadian Charter of Rights and Freedoms on the Legislative Authority of Quebec

YVES DE MONTIGNY*

Until 1982 Canadian political and constitutional history had been dominated by and had revolved around a single theme: federalism and the division of legislative powers that derives from it. In fact, the vast majority of debates that marked the country's first hundred years were based on the role that the central institutions (and, by extension, the provincial governments) should play in solving the problems that all modern states must face. Thus, depending on primary community allegiances, clashes between those who supported greater decentralization and those who defended a strong central government were inevitable. Within the context of this dialectic, it is not surprising to find that the only interest groups that appeared and influenced the course of events to some degree were the various levels of government and the provincial (and, to a lesser extent, the national) communities that they presumably represented.

Following the Second World War, however, this unidimensional perception of the Canadian reality came up against a new concern, one that was based on something other than strictly territorial considerations. In fact, the protection of fundamental rights, having universal appeal, transcended borders and was to give rise to a new dynamic in the relationships that had existed, until then, among political authorities. Yet this transformation did not take place over-night. On the contrary, the influence of the federal principle and its hold on the collective Canadian conscience was such that for many years it obscured all matters that could not be dealt with on the basis of the grid used as inspiration by those who had drafted the Constitution Act, 1867. The fact that most of the problems relating to the protection of fundamental rights were solved by bor-rowing from a 'division of powers' analysis is unquestionably one of the best illustrations of this phenomenon. Some members of the legal profession did

* This essay was translated from the French-language original by Isabel Milne.

attempt to break away from such logic by forging an 'implied bill of rights' based on the democratic values entrenched in the preamble of the Constitution Act, 1867; but, in the end, this theory was to meet with little success,[1] and it was essentially by associating infringements of fundamental rights with criminal law (falling under federal jurisdiction) that the courts came to invalidate the various provincial legislative measures of this type.[2]

The adoption by the provinces and the federal Parliament of legislation specifically intended to protect fundamental rights did not alter the dialectic in any way. Undoubtedly because such legislation did not question the sacrosanct principle of legislative supremacy, it had, on the whole, a rather limited impact on the evolution of the Canadian political system and was subject to restrictive judicial interpretation. As a result, it was not until the constitution was repatriated in 1982 that a major upset in the constitutional order took place. Formal integration of the protection of individual rights and freedoms in the country's constitution alongside the federal principle meant the concurrent enshrinement of a new vision of the relationships that were to consolidate the Canadian nation.

It is particularly important that this interpretation of events not be considered simply an *ex post facto* analysis of something that happened more than fifteen years ago. Indeed, Prime Minister Trudeau never concealed the role that the entrenchment of a charter of rights was designed to encourage. While giving citizens better tools to use against the growing threats to individual autonomy posed by frequent state interventions, he firmly believed that the Charter was bound to promote greater cohesion at the national level and to create stronger ties between each Canadian and the central institutions. This would happen because, first of all, by recognizing that all Canadians have the same rights, the Charter was going to give birth to debates and interest groups that would be little affected by provincial boundaries and traditional political allegiances. But, in particular, it would happen because these rights would ultimately be interpreted by a highly centralized institution whose decisions are binding on all Canadian courts.[3]

The fundamental importance of this latter point cannot be overemphasized. By giving rise, through the Charter, to debates that do not bring the unity of the country into question and by making the Supreme Court responsible for the interpretaton of individual rights by means of uniform, pan-Canadian standards, those in power were clearly implanting a substantial centripetal force in the federal system. This influence is undeniably more tangible when the Court invalidates a provincial legislative provision. In such an event, all the provinces indirectly lose the legislative authority to deal with issues such as censorship and job-hiring policies conditions by taking local circumstances into account. But its presence is felt just as strongly when a federal measure is at issue. If the central government loses, it is to another national institution which also has the power to impose a single standard from sea to sea.[4]

It was also not unreasonable to think that provincial laws and local regulations, because they better mirror the strength and homogeneity of the majority opinion in a region, were more likely than federal legislation to be interpreted as restricting the rights and freedoms of minorities. At least, this was a prediction supported by a study of American case law. According to H.J. Abraham, prior to 1980 the United States Supreme Court invalidated eight times more state laws than federal ones.[5]

Lastly, the essentially Canadian elements of the Charter of Rights cannot be ignored. The stated objective of entrenching in the constitution the right to take up residence and pursue the gaining of a livelihood anywhere in Canada (section 6) and the right to receive instruction in either of the official languages in all provinces (section 23) was to halt the trend toward balkanization and to instill in the country's citizens a feeling of allegiance that would encourage them to define themselves as Canadians first, before identifying themselves with their province of residence. Taking into account the fact that section 33 does not allow any derogation with respect to either of these rights, it is easy to see just how much importance the main framers of the Charter attached to the values conveyed by these rights.

In light of these factors, which did not augur well for the strengthening and development of Quebec's legislative powers, an initial overview of the judicial interpretation the Charter has received is in order. This essay offers such an overview. Its purpose is to assess the impact of the Charter on the equilibrium of the Canadian federalist system and on nationalist rhetoric.

Raw Results

Although the figures alone cannot provide a complete picture, it is useful to present them briefly by way of an introduction. In so doing, we hope to limit the debate somewhat and at the same time construct the backdrop against which the discussion that will follow must necessarily take place.

Of course, we do not claim that these statistics are absolutely accurate. Such absolute accuracy is not essential for our present purposes, and, in any case, there are different ways, all more or less arbitrary, of recording decisions when only the outcome is known.[6] Furthermore, we have confined ourselves to recording only judgments rendered by the Supreme Court, because it is at this level that the major directions of Canadian law are determined and that the full significance of uniform standards becomes evident.

When examining the case law concerning the Canadian Charter, it is striking first of all to note the relatively small number of appeals from Quebec heard by the Supreme Court. A quick calculation confirms that appeals originating in Ontario or even in British Columbia, for example, have been more numerous than cases originating in Quebec. While systematic use of the notwithstanding clause in Quebec legislation could account for the disproportion in the early years, the fact that this practice was discontinued almost nine years ago forces us to look for another reason.[7] Should these figures, then, be seen as the reflection of a certain feeling of estrangement among Quebeckers where the Canadian Charter is concerned, a feeling that could be explained by the political context in which the Charter was introduced as much as by the resultant decisions, which have not been very popular with the francophone majority? Such a possibility should not be dismissed, although an empirical study of the case law issuing from the Quebec courts does not admit of a firm conclusion in this regard.[8] It is also striking to note the frequency with which judgments rendered by the Quebec Court of Appeal have been reversed. In the country as a whole, appeal court decisions have been confirmed by the highest court two times out of three since 1982.[9] In Quebec, exactly the opposite happened in the first ten years the Charter was in force.[10] Perhaps this is not surprising since a number of studies have demonstrated that since 1867 Quebec's Court of Appeal has had its decisions (on all matters combined) overturned more often than confirmed.[11]

The final contextual element that cannot be ignored is the fact that the actions of the individuals responsible for administering the criminal and penal law are challenged in the courts more often than the laws they are called upon to enforce. Several studies[12] conclude that more than two-thirds of the cases indexed bring into question the conduct of the police officers and the various players in the judicial process. This phenomenon is easily explained by the fact that the attention of the courts is largely monopolized by legal-rights issues, a point that we will soon have the opportunity to revisit. What is more surprising, however, is that the leaves to appeal granted by the Supreme Court do not reflect this proportion and reverse the engines to the point that the Court is studying the validity of the legislation almost as often as the application of sections 7 to 14 of the Charter. It may well be that, in so doing, the Court is simply seeking to fulfil the role assigned to it, which is essentially to settle disputes that are apt to raise legal questions of national interest. But at the same time, it is increasing the risk of confrontation with the legislatures and with Parliament, and leaving itself open more frequently to criticism from those who challenge the democratic legitimacy of the positions it takes.

This being said, we can now present the breakdown of those decisions in which the validity of a legislative provision was attacked. Since the Charter came into force, the Supreme Court has invalidated about twenty federal legislative measures and only eight provincial ones.[13] This proportion, it should be noted, favours the provinces much more than that arrived at by analysing the case law from the country's various courts of appeal. Indeed, four professors from the University of Calgary[14] report that, between 1982 and 1988, the courts of appeal invalidated thirty-one provincial and thirty-two federal enactments.

Behind this relative advantage enjoyed by the provinces, however, lies a much more complex reality. First, the vast majority of federal provisions that were invalidated belonged to the domain of criminal law, a finding that is predictable, to say the least, given the frequency with which legal rights are invoked.[15] A brief listing of these provisions will make it easier to assess the overall impact of the Charter on federal legislation. Provisions that were declared invalid included sections of the Narcotic Control Act that created a 'reverse onus,'[16] authorized searches relying solely on a writ of assistance,[17] and provided for minimum sentences.[18] Also declared invalid were provisions of the Criminal Code setting out the conditions of therapeutic abortions,[19] creating constructive murder,[20] allowing for an offence punishable by imprisonment without giving the accused the opportunity to invoke due diligence as a defence,[21] expressly relieving the crown of the obligation to prove beyond a reasonable doubt that the accused had subjective foresight of the death,[22] and allowing an accused to be declared guilty of an attempt to commit a crime on the basis of an objective foreseeability test when a conviction for the crime itself requires proof of subjective foresight.[23] Still within the context of criminal law, the following sections of the Criminal Code were also deemed invalid: section 614, which provided for automatic detention of insanity acquittees at the pleasure of the lieutenant-governor;[24] section 276, which, with three clearly defined exceptions, excluded evidence of the complainant's sexual conduct with a person other than the accused;[25] sections 563(1) and (2), which granted the crown four times as many opportunities as the accused to intervene in the jury-selection process;[26] section 181, under which anyone who wilfully published a statement, tale, or news that he or she knew was false and that caused or was likely to cause injury or mischief to a public interest was guilty of a crime;[27] and, lastly, section 515(10)(b), insofar as it stipulates that the criterion of 'public interest' can justify a denial of bail.[28] Similarly, the procedure for issuing search and seizure warrants relating to the Combines Investigation Act was declared inconsistent with Charter requirements.[29] Along the same lines, it was concluded that sections 37.3(2)(c) and (d) of the Competition Act were inconsistent with section 7 of the Charter insofar as they obliged the person charged with misleading advertising to make a retraction before being able to plead due diligence.[30] It was also concluded that the procedure for determination of refugee status established in the Immigration Act, 1976 did not meet the requirements of fundamental justice set out in section 7 of the Charter.[31] It was decreed that the Lord's Day Act violated the freedom of religion protected by section 2(a) of the Charter.[32] It was deemed that section 33 of the Public Service Employment Act (R.S.C. 1985, c. P–33) by prohibiting public servants from expressing their support of a political party or candidate,[33] violated freedom of expression in such a way as to be inconsistent with section 1 of the Charter. Lastly, section 32 of the Unemployment Insurance Act, 1971 was condemned on the ground that it gave a benefit to adoptive parents that it did not give to other recipients of unemployment insurance.[34]

On the basis of this exceedingly short survey, we can make a number of observations. First, the vast majority of federal provisions that did not survive the Charter were essentially procedural in nature.[35] The provisions of the Lord's Day Act that prohibited for religious reasons all profit-seeking or commercial activity on Sunday were anachronistic to say the least and could have been overturned by the provinces in any event.[36] As for section 181 of the Criminal Code, it was hardly ever used. What is more, most of the texts that were censured by the Court were expressions of policies from another era, policies with which the government of the day did not necessarily identify. In this regard, the federal government had already replaced two of the provisions deemed contrary to the Charter by the time the Supreme Court heard the appeal[37] and had conceded that another provision was inconsistent with the Charter.[38] The impression that emerges is that the central authority came out of the situation rather well and saw few of its political decisions brought into question by the courts.[39] With the exception of the Morgentaler and Singh cases, as a result of which the federal government had to revise thoroughly its abortion and immigration policies, Supreme Court decisions have not given rise to any real conflict between the judicial branch and the political authorities. By focusing on legal-rights issues and tackling the method of proceeding rather than the objective sought, the Court is not straying far from its traditional role in criminal matters and its interventions are not causing much of a stir.

A summary review of provincial statutes that have been deemed inconsistent with the Charter tells a different story. For example, the provisions of the Quebec Charter of the French Language that restricted access to English schools to those children whose parents had received their elementary instruction in an English school in the province were declared of no force or effect,[40] along with the other provisions of the same Charter that made French the required language for commercial advertising and names of the firms.[41] Also rejected by the Supreme Court were the following provisions: a section of Quebec's Summary Convictions Act that allowed the prosecution to appeal an acquittal by way of *trial de novo*;[42] a subsection of the Motor Vehicle Act of British Columbia creating an absolute-liability offence;[43] a section of the Barristers and Solicitors Act that made citizenship an inescapable prerequisite for admission to the British Columbia bar;[44] rules of the Alberta Bar that prohibited the establishment of interprovincial law firms;[45] a rule of the professional association of dental surgeons of Ontario that prohibited some forms of commercial advertising;[46] and a city of Peterborough by-law prohibiting posters on public property.[47]

With respect to this jurisprudence, a few observations are appropriate. First, the majority of the provincial provisions affected were of a substantive, rather than a procedural, nature, in contrast to the kind of federal legislation affected by the Charter. Unquestionably, that is in part because legal rights have, to date, been the grounds for most appeals (and, consequently, judgments) bringing fundamental rights into question; and, although sections 7 to 14 of the Charter may have some effect in penal law and even in administrative law, it is first and foremost in the area of criminal law, an area under exclusive federal jurisdiction, that they are most frequently applied. Thus, it should come as no surprise that the provincial statutes deemed inconsistent with fundamental rights were more varied than the federal statutes that suffered the same fate, or that legal rights were used to invalidate only two of the seven defective provincial statutes while the other five were instead considered inconsistent with the fundamental freedoms of language rights, equality, and mobility.

It is also evident that all the provincial measures that did not find favour with the Supreme Court resulted from recent political decisions. In fact, they had all been enacted less than ten years before being declared of no force or effect by the highest court.[48] This is a crucial element when it comes to evaluating the impact of the Charter on the legislation introduced by the provinces and on the leeway allowed their respective governments.

Given the foregoing observations, there is no need for a lengthy demonstration to establish the fact that the provinces (or at least some of them) have felt the impact of the entrenchment of rights in the constitution more intensely than the federal authority. And it is just as certain that, of the ten Canadian provinces, Quebec has been most deeply affected, not only by the frequency with which its legislative measures have been nullified[49] but also by the highly symbolic and sensitive nature of the texts that have been struck down. Above all, the Charter has destroyed whole sections of the language regime gradually adopted by the province over the years. The destruction has been so great it has led some to claim that it is in Quebec that the profoundly individualistic character of the Charter, and the restraint the Charter imposes on the wishes of the majority, have been most clearly demonstrated.

By declaring the 'Quebec clause' unconstitutional with respect to the language of instruction, and by refusing to entertain the arguments put forward by the attorney general in defence of the provisions prescribing unilingualism in commercial advertising, the Supreme Court contributed to a further dismantling of the Charter of the French Language and, at the same time, added to the restrictions that the Constitution Act, 1867 already imposed on the National Assembly with respect to language-related enactments.[50] While Quebec can still regulate the use of languages[51] within its areas of jurisdiction, its freedom to act is nonetheless limited by the inclusion in the constitution of a Charter that enshrines the sacrosanctity of a number of language rights. Since 1982 the Quebec legislature has not had the option of denying access to English schools to children whose parents received their elementary instruction in English elsewhere in Canada. According to the Supreme Court, the 'Quebec clause' is the archetype of what the framers of the constitution wished to reform by adopting section 23 of the Charter of Rights, and to see it as reasonable in terms of section 1 of this same Charter[52] would therefore be completely out of the question. Given the impossibility of derogating from this provision by borrowing the mechanism provided for in section 33, we have to admit that Quebec lost an important lever for integrating new arrivals into its culture.[53]

The language guarantees inferred by the Supreme Court from the freedom of expression entrenched in section 2(b) of the Charter may at first glance appear less restrictive. In *Ford* the Court accepted the legitimacy of Quebec's traditional concerns with respect to language and appeared inclined to recognize the validity of a legislative measure aimed at making French clearly predominant over any other language.[54] Also, the legislature can avail itself of section 33 to override language requirements that may be derived from the fundamental freedoms.

Nevertheless, the scope of the new impediments implied by the decision rendered in *Ford* should not be underestimated. Although the legitimacy of any attempt to give the French language priority in commercial advertising seems to have been conceded, it will still be up to the government to establish the need for such a regime if it wants to make use of the regime in a different context. And even supposing that it manages to discharge this heavy responsibility, it will still have been obliged to seek endorsement of its policies by the judicial branch, an obligation it did not have to meet before the Charter came into force as long as such policies did not contravene section 133 of the

Constitution Act, 1867. Moreover, if the National Assembly were to think about prescribing some form of unilingualism in the exercise of one of its powers, it could achieve its objectives only by adhering to the mechanics of the notwithstanding clause, an exercise that is politically risky to say the least and one that will always expose the Quebec government to reproaches from the English-Canadian community. In this regard, the reactions to the use of not-withstanding clauses in Bill 178 in order partially to maintain unilingualism for public signs and names of firms are revealing. They provide eloquent testimony to the substantial obstacles that will inevitably be encountered by any government bold enough to use section 33 of the Charter to protect a measure it deems to be essential for development and protection of the French fact.

In summary, we may conclude that, of all the legislative powers Quebec enjoys, the ones that have to date been most directly affected by the entrench-ment of fundamental rights in 1982 are those that can be excercised with respect to language matters. Yet, this is not the only area in which the scope of Quebec's powers is threatened. Section 6(2)(b) of the Charter and the interpre-tation given to it in *Skapinker*[55] and in *Black*[56] further underlines the possible long-term effects of the Charter on Quebec legislative policies. In decreeing that section 6(2)(b) entrenches the right to move to another province in order to work there without taking up residence, and by using this line of reasoning to invalidate rules of the Alberta bar that prohibited members normally resident in Alberta from entering into a partnership with more than one law firm or with a member not normally resident in the province, the Supreme Court clearly showed its colours. Its broad interpretation of the freedom to move to, and the right to earn a living in, any province will no longer allow the legislatures to prohibit Canadian citizens and permanent residents from exercising any trade or profession whatsoever. Unless it can demonstrate that the employment rate in the province is lower than the national average,[57] or that the limit placed on the right set out in section 6(2)(b) is reasonable in a free and democratic society, the National Assembly will no longer be able to adopt a preferential hiring policy that takes local conditions into account.

The new constraints placed on Quebec lawmakers by the Charter of Rights and Freedoms are, of course, not limited to those stemming from language and mobility rights. In fact, all the substantive rights and all the procedural guaran-tees entrenched in the Constitution Act, 1982 restrict, to some extent, the freedom of the provinces to exercise the powers that the act of 1867 had conferred on them. This is precisely the object of any entrenchment of rights in a constitution, and it is essentially the objective that the National Assembly was pursuing in decreeing that sections 1 to 38 of its own Charter of Human Rights and Freedoms take precedence over all Quebec statutes, regardless of the date they came into force.[58] Insofar as the rights entrenched in the Quebec Charter correspond closely with those included in the Canadian Charter, it is reasonable to ask whether the guidelines prescribed by the Canadian Charter will have any significant effect on the design of Quebec's policies and their transcription into law. The conclusion offered here is that only the language and mobility rights, which have no equivalent in the Quebec Charter, are likely to give rise to any new constraints.

Some people will object that the resemblance between the two charters is more apparent than real and will further allege that simple differences in wording can sometimes lead to different results. This argument cannot be dismissed out of hand, and indeed it appears particularly credible when the exception clauses of section 1 of the Canadian Charter and section 9.1 of the Quebec Charter are compared. We will soon have the opportunity to address this subject briefly when we deal with the problems posed by the interaction between the two charters. For now, we will simply point out that the Supreme Court and the Quebec courts have not been receptive to this view and have, more often than not, equated the two instruments. Nowhere has there been a more striking illustration of their approach than in *Ford v. Quebec (A.G.)*[59] and *Irwin Toy Ltd. v. Quebec (A.G.)*.[60] In these two cases, the Quebec Court of Appeal and the Supreme Court of Canada both explicitly refused to interpret differently the concept of freedom of expression found in the two charters, and, what is perhaps more surprising, in the same breath they held that section 9.1 of the Quebec Charter was for all practical purposes the counterpart of section 1 of the Canadian Charter.[61]

It may well be that the invalidation of a legislative provision by the courts is politically more acceptable when it is initiated by the Quebec Charter. In this regard, perceptions are often so important that the reality and legitimacy of the instrument pursuant to which democratically enacted laws are set aside can have other than purely symbolic impact. Nevertheless, from a strictly legal standpoint, the only true threats the Canadian Charter poses to the integrity of the legislative authority of the provinces are those that derive from the language and mobility rights. This is especially true since the Supreme Court has appeared very sensitive to the potential risks to Canadian federalism of any attempt to make rights uniform, as we are about to see.

Qualitative Analysis

If there is one area in which the courts could reasonably be expected to take advantage of the Charter to achieve some uniformity in Canadian law, it is the domain of criminal law. Given the exclusive power of Parliament to define crimes and to exercise control over the procedure and evidence applicable to criminal matters, it was predictable that such federal statutes with prescriptions that varied from one province to the other would be attacked on the basis of the principles of equality implicit in the legal rights or, more directly, the equality rights entrenched in section 15. The Supreme Court, however, took great care not to allow this argument; on the contrary, it expressed the opinion that the Charter did not bring into question Parliament's legislative authority to give its criminal or other enactments special applications, whether in terms of locality of operation or otherwise. In so doing, it was, for all intents and purposes, reiterating the opinion it had already expressed on the same subject, but in the context of the Canadian Bill of Rights, in the *Burnshine* case.[62]

It was in the *Valente*[63] and *Lyons*[64] cases that the Supreme Court first showed its attachment to pluralism and the underlying diversity of federalism. In the first of these two decisions, Mr Justice Le Dain took into account provincial jurisdiction over the administration of justice and the resultant heterogeneity with respect to the powers and status of the courts to give meaning to the concept of judicial independence; he came up with a definition of this funda-mental guarantee based on its essential elements, which allowed him to accomodate provincial diversity.[65] In the second decision, the Court rejected the argument that the lack of uniformity in the various regions due to the discretion enjoyed by the crown would constitute the type of arbitrariness prohibited by section 9. Without going into the subject at great length, Mr Justice La Forest wrote that 'variation among provinces in this regard may be inevitable and, indeed, desirable, in a country where a federal statute is admin-istered by local authorities.'[66]

But ultimately it was in *Cornell*[67] that the Court clearly expressed an opinion on this issue for the first time. In that case, the appellant submitted that his right to equality before the law had been violated, because the Criminal Code provision under which he had been charged[68] was in force in Ontario but not (at the time of the offence) in British Columbia or Quebec. Since it deemed that the inequality resulting from non-universal proclamation and application of the provision at issue was justified by a valid federal objective,[69] the Court easily (and unanimously) concluded that section 1(b) of the Canadian Bill of Rights had not been violated, relying on the decision it had previously rendered in *Burnshine*.[70] What is even more significant for our purposes, however, is the fact that the highest court refused to recognize the right to equality before the law as a principle of fundamental justice. It is true that the offence giving rise to this proceeding had been committed prior to the date of coming into force of section 15, a situation that enabled the Court, in its reasons, to stress the fact that it would be acting against the clearly expressed intention of the framers of the constitution[71] if it were to accept the appellant's argument and allow him the right to equality before the law under section 7. Although it would have been better had the Court expanded somewhat on this aspect of the question, the effect of its decision was still to limit the scope of the debate to just the equality rights explicitly conferred by section 15.

It was therefore only logical that the Court would one day be faced with the question it had temporarily evaded in *Cornell*. And this is what was to happen in *R. v. Turpin*.[72] Accused of first-degree murder, the appellant in that case complained that section 429 of the Criminal Code took away his right to a trial without jury, while in Alberta a person charged with the same offence had that right.[73] Relying on the approach it had taken in *Andrews*[74] to deal with a challenge based on section 15 of the Charter, the Court first asked whether the provisions at issue infringed the appellant's equality rights. Because the appellant and any persons charged with an offence under section 427 outside Alberta are treated more harshly than persons charged with the same offences in Alberta, in that they are not allowed to be tried before a judge alone when they believe it to be in their interest, the Court did not hesitate to answer this first question in the affirmative. Later, however, the Court concluded that such differential treatment was not discriminatory because the distinction was not based on personal characteristics comparable to those in section 15. Expressing the opinion that it would be stretching the imagination to compare with a 'discrete and insular minority' persons accused of one of the crimes mentioned in section 427 of the Code, in all provinces but Alberta, Madam Justice Wilson (again on behalf of a unanimous bench) went on to add that the purpose of section 15 was to remedy the kind of discrimination suffered by those groups of persons who are socially, politically, or legally disadvantaged, and that the appellant's requests clearly did not fit into this context.

Keeping just to these statements of principle, one might conclude that the varied application of federal legislation across the country no longer created many difficulties with respect to the Charter. The Court, however, refused to commit itself any more than was necessary in *Turpin*, and caveats expressed at the end of the judgment certainly left room for speculation.[75] Less than a year later, the decision in *Sheldon*[76] provided a number of useful clarifications on the same subject. In this case, the accused alleged that the failure of the attorney general of Ontario to implement an alternative-measures program for adolescents found guilty of breaking a federal law, as section 4 of the Young Offenders Act authorized him to do, violated the accused's right to equality and placed him at a disadvantage compared with young offenders residing in other provinces where such programs were available. Expressing the view that the federal legislative provision in question imposed no mandatory obligation on the attorneys general of the provinces, the Court ruled that the decision by the Ontario authorities not to exercise the power they had been granted could not be constitutionally attacked. In other words, the failure to act, even when it is apt to create differences between provinces, cannot be considered 'the law' for purposes of a challenge on the basis of section 15 of the Charter. To find otherwise, added the Court, 'would potentially open to Charter scrutiny every jurisdictionally permissible exercise of power by a province, solely on the basis that it creates a distinction in how individuals are treated in different provinces.'[77] This is no doubt an observation that will appear superfluous to many; nevertheless, it has the advantage of establishing once and for all that the Charter has not subsumed the values of diversity conveyed by the federal principle. It will therefore never be possible to claim that the disparities resulting from the exercise by the provinces of their legislative powers can be subject to judicial control and Charter scrutiny.[78]

Since the accused had not challenged the constitutionality of section 4 of the Young Offenders Act as such, the Court would have been justified in not committing itself further. Contrary to all expectations, however, it proceeded to offer a detailed analysis of the conformity of this legislative provision with the Charter. Once more taking the approach advocated in *Andrews*, Mr Justice Dickson (again on behalf of a unanimous bench) first noted that, because of the discretion granted by the federal legislator to the provincial attorneys general, there were, in all provinces but one (Ontario, in this case), alternative-measures programs for adolescents found guilty of having violated a federal law in one of those provinces. The resultant distinction based on the place where an offence was committed was, in his view, comparable to a geographic distinction based on the province of residence of the young offenders, it being understood that adolescents who commit an offence generally do so in their province of residence. And, since the absence of an alternative-measures program in Ontario unquestionably placed young offenders residing in that province at a disadvantage, it was relatively easy to conclude that there was infringement of the right to equality.

Called upon to express an opinion on the discriminatory nature of this distinction, the Court reiterated the opinion expressed by Madam Justice Wilson in *Turpin*, deeming that the province of residence could not be considered a 'personal characteristic' in such a situation. While specifying that, in determining whether province-based distinctions arising from the application of federal law contravene section 15(1) of the Charter, a case-by-case approach was appropriate, the chief justice formulated a number of general principles of the utmost importance. He first pointed out that 'differential application of federal law can be a legitimate means of forwarding the values of a federal system,'[79] and he illustrated his point by referring to the administration of the criminal law. In this connection, he expressed the opinion that the question of how young people who have committed criminal offences should be dealt with was one 'upon which it is legitimate for Parliament to allow for province-based distinctions as a reflection of distinct and rationally based political values and sensitivities.'[80] This was especially so, he added, since the federal law in question was not wholly unconnected to child welfare — a matter of provincial jurisdiction. It was, however, in the following statement of principle that the Court conveyed its message most clearly: 'Differential application of the law through federal-provincial cooperation is a legitimate means whereby governments can overcome the rigidity of the "watertight compartments" of the distribution of powers with respect to matters that are not easily categorized or dealt with by one level of government alone.'[81]

That statement should help alleviate the concerns of those who felt that section 15 of the Charter posed a serious threat to the survival of the federal system in Canada and who fully understood the use that could be made of it by a Supreme Court bent on eliminating all traces of regionalism in the name of the protection of human rights.[82] Still, not all the danger has passed. It may well be, for example, that the effect of subjecting the Civil Code to the Charter[83] will be to undermine the special character of the Quebec legal culture by encouraging the courts to measure systematically the legal system that expresses this culture against the yardstick of common law. If that were to be the case, the rules of private law could be made uniform through the Charter only at the expense of solutions peculiar to Quebec. However, the guidelines established by the Supreme Court, to which we have just alluded, make such a scenario highly unlikely.

Lastly, the use that can be made of the exception clause to give effect to a decentralized approach to rights and freedoms should not be overlooked. Of course, the invalidation of a provincial law by the Supreme Court will, more often than not, be a reliable indicator of the approach the judicial branch will take toward other, similar provincial laws. But there is nothing to prevent a province using section 1 to justify novel political decisions, especially when it is possible to establish that the legislator was faced with distinct needs or had to come to terms with more limited resources. It is possible that judges, once they agree to be convinced by such evidence, will do so in a language that refers more to the complex problem of the interaction between the judicial and legislative branches than to the requirements of the federal system. The result, however, will be the same: each time a court acknowledges the validity of a law and agrees to rely on elected officials to decide controversial issues and mediate the demands of opposing groups or individuals, the provincial legislators acquire more room to manoeuver.[84]

If the Supreme Court had adhered strictly to the test it put forward in *Oakes*,[85] those who supported a flexible approach respectful of Quebec's distinctness would have had little reason to be optimistic. In that case, the Court decreed that, in order for a limit to be deemed reasonable within the meaning of section 1, two fundamental criteria must be met. First, the objective to be served by the measures limiting a Charter right or freedom must be sufficiently important to warrant overriding such right or freedom. At the very least, therefore, the objective must relate to societal concerns which are pressing and substantial in a free and democratic society. Once an objective is recognized as being sufficiently important, it falls to the party invoking section 1 to demonstrate that the means used are reasonable and demonstrably justified. Then it will be necessary to weigh the interests of society and those of individuals and groups, using a proportionality test with three components: the measures adopted must be rationally connected to the objective sought; the means chosen should impair the right or freedom in question as little as possible; and there must be a proportionality between the effects of the measures limiting a right or freedom and the objective that is recognized as sufficiently important.

On the whole, the courts were fairly easily convinced that the objective sought related to pressing and substantial concerns and that the measures adopted were rationally connected to that objective. Where things were spoiled was in the application of the second component of the proportionality test. There were many who regarded this minimal impairment requirement as the introduction of a necessity criterion, comparable to that found in several international documents and in the European Convention, but of which no mention is made in section 1 of the Charter. Needless to say, full respect of this condition would have left very little latitude to the various legislatures, and the attorney general of a province would have been hard pressed to convince the Court of the reasonableness of a given measure in the event that its equivalent in another province had already been invalidated.

Fortunately, it was not long before the Court changed its standard in order to make it more flexible. Unquestionably, it was Mr Justice La Forest who appeared most sensitive to this aspect of the problem and who was the first to reaffirm the merits of diversity.[86] That statement of belief was certainly not out of keeping with his conception of the relationships that should exist between the judicial and legislative branches or his deep conviction that elected officials are in a better position than anyone to make the necesssary decisions with respect to economic or social matters.

Yet it was definitely the opinion expressed by Mr Justice Dickson in *Edwards Books*[87] that contributed most to changing the direction of the analysis required by the exception clause by making somewhat more relative what he himself had written in the *Oakes* case. Allowing that lawmakers sometimes have difficult choices to make and that it is not up to the courts to indicate which legislative measure might be the most desirable, the chief justice also recognized the possibility that a single law might be limited in a variety of ways, each just as valid as the other.[88]

In the same connection, Mr Justice Dickson was subsequently to uphold sections 248 and 249 of Quebec's Consumer Protection Act, which banned all advertising directed at children.[89] Expressing the opinion that the government has a certain latitude in both the formulation of objectives and the choice of means when it must rely on social-science evidence that is not totally conclusive, he did not hesitate to recognize that these two legislative provisions imposed a reasonable limit on the freedom of expression. Since the matter involved what is commonly referred to as the 'minimal impairment' requirement, the chief justice clearly implied that the courts should show greater deference to the legislature when the latter is mediating between the claims of competing groups on the basis of conflicting scientific evidence. Strict application of the proportionality test put forward in *Oakes* would therefore be required only in cases where the state does not play this role of mediator but rather assumes its responsibility to prosecute criminals on behalf of society as a whole.[90]

The Court had the opportunity to reiterate this point of view in *McKinney v. University of Guelph*,[91] in which it was to decide whether mandatory retirement at sixty-five years of age impaired 'as little as possible' the right to equality without discrimination on the basis of age. Essentially repeating what was said in the *Edwards Books* and *Irwin Toy* cases, Mr Justice La Forest wrote on behalf of the majority:

... the ramifications of mandatory retirement on the organization of the workplace and its impact on society generally are not matters capable of precise measurement, and the effect of its removal by judicial fiat is even less certain. Decisions on such matters must inevitably be the product of a mix of conjecture, fragmentary knowledge, general experience and knowledge of the needs, aspirations and resources of society, and other components. They are decisions of a kind where those engaged in the political and legislative activities of Canadian democracy have evident advantages over members of the judicial branch, as *Irwin Toy*, supra, at pp. 993–94, has reminded us. This does not absolve the judiciary of its constitutional obligation to scrutinize legislative action to ensure reasonable compliance with constitutional standards, but it does import greater circumspection than in areas such as the criminal justice system where the courts' knowledge and understanding affords it a much higher degree of certainty.[92]

Considering this receptiveness, which was already noticeable when the Court expressed its opinion in *Ford*,[93] it could reasonably have been expected that the justices would be open to the distinctness of Quebec and its potential implications with respect to the regulation of language. There was, however, no question of this. Taking the view that the freedom of expression guaranteed by the Canadian and Quebec charters protects both 'commercial expression' and the freedom to express oneself in the language of one's choice, the Court decided in *Ford* that the provisions of the Charter of the French Language requiring that public signs, commercial advertising, and names of firms be in French only violated the fundamental freedom of those who wished to convey their message or identify themselves in another language. The greatest blow, however, came when the Court concluded that the attorney general had not established the need to require exclusive use of French in order to achieve the stated legislative objective. At most, the Court was prepared to recognize the reasonableness of measures intended to promote the French language in commercial advertising, such as provisions requiring the predominant use of French.

By recognizing the vulnerability of the French language in Quebec and in Canada, and the legitimacy of efforts that can be made to ensure its development, the Supreme Court certainly took a step in the right direction. What was surprising was its refusal to see in sections 58 and 69 of the Charter of the French Language a necessary means to defend and enhance the status of the French language. This position can undoubtedly be explained in part by its perception of the aim of the provisions at issue. Indeed, it may well be that exclusive use of French in commercial advertising is not required to ensure that the reality of Quebec society is reflected in its 'visage linguistique,' as the Court claims. However, the objective of the legislature was something quite different. It was, to use the exact words of the factum submitted to the Court by the attorney general, 'défendre et rehausser le statut de la langue française au Québec.' From this perspective, the desire to present a resolutely French image was not the ultimate objective but simply a way of inducing newcomers to conform and, consequently, of contributing to the vitality of the French language.

Yet it was probably the adoption of the necessity criterion that dealt the fatal blow to Quebec's claims. By demanding a perfect balance between the end and the means, and by compelling the attorney general to prove that the measures used limited the freedom of expression as little as possible, the Court was giving Quebec an impossible mission. Considering the many variables that enter into language planning, will it ever be possible to prove that one or another system is required in order to enhance the status of the French language and at the same time is the one that impairs freedom of expression as little as possible? Is the solution outlined by the Court (mandatory presence of French, or predominance of that language over all others) any more likely to meet these criteria? Are elected political authorities not in a better position than the courts to perform such assessments and make the necessary decisions?

These are some of the questions that the Court left unanswered and that seem not even to have occurred to it during its consideration of the case. This omission is not only curious, it is in strong contrast with the circumspection it showed earlier in *Edwards Books* with respect to the regulation of economic and social matters. Instead of ignoring its own warnings and taking the place of the legislature by putting forward its proposals, the Court would have been better advised to adhere to the same view it expressed in *Irwin Toy*.[94] After all, is the legislature that intends to promote the French fact in Quebec and in Canada not faced with assumptions just as varied, analyses just as divergent, and choices just as difficult as when it wishes to protect children from the most harmful effects of commercial advertising? If the Court had recognized this reality and adjusted its minimal-impairment criterion accordingly, it would probably have shown greater deference to the Quebec legislature, and the attenuation reflected in the Charter of the French Language with respect to the language of advertising and names of firms would have allowed it to conclude that Quebec had reasonably conformed to the constitutional standards.

Apart from the criticisms that can be levelled at the Court from the strictly legal perspective, it is the insensitivity shown by the Court with respect to the distinctness of Quebec that commands attention. The Court is not ignorant of the precariousness of the French fact in North America, but it refuses to draw all the inferences from this situation and, on the basis of a fundamental freedom that was not intended to govern the use of languages, even goes so far as to impose on the Quebec legislature new obligations and a procedure for conforming to them. In a way, this is something much more harmful in the long term that its earlier decision to invalidate the 'Quebec clause' in regard to education in *A.G. of Quebec v. Protestant School Board*.[95] In that case, the Court could at least rely on the manifest intention of the framers of the constitution and claim flagrant inconsistency between section 73 of the Charter of the French Language and section 23 of the Canadian Charter. The Court was, moreover, careful to note in its decision in *Ford*, the highly exceptional nature of the school board case, explaining that the latter was a unique example of a complete denial of guaranteed rights.[96] At the risk of caricaturing the situation, we could summarize the preceding development by saying that the 'Quebec clause' owes its invalidation to the Charter, while the prohibition of exclusive use of French in public signs and commercial advertising is due to the activism of the Supreme Court. This does not bode well for recognition of Quebec's distinctness by the courts; on the contrary, all indications are that the deference to legislators that the Supreme Court can show itself capable of will be of no benefit to the National Assembly when the latter's intention is to promote the distinctness of Quebec, or at least when, in order to do this, it regulates the use of languages.

In other words, the country's highest court is clearly inclined to recognize the virtues of both decentralization and diversity. But, true to the spirit of the Canadian Charter, it will not carry this logic to the point of conferring on Quebec greater latitude than the other provinces enjoy. Unless there is an unexpected and highly unlikely reversal of the situation, only explicit constitutional prescriptions in this regard will influence the course of events.

Conclusion

The Charter of Rights and Freedoms has not had the devastating impact on the legislative authority of Quebec (and of the other provinces) that some may have feared. All in all, few laws have been censured by the country's various courts. Upon completion of a detailed study, Professor Danielle Pinard even established that Quebec civil law had been very little affected by the inclusion in the Canadian constitution of an instrument intended to protect fundamental rights.[97]

That said, it is impossible to measure the real impact of the Charter solely against the yardstick of the judicial decisions stemming from it. Indeed, it may be assumed that the Charter (and the courts' interpretation of it) is on the legislators' minds even at the stage of policy development and therefore reduces their freedom of action in a way that is unquestionable but not easy to quantify. Also, the risks of acculturation, which stem from the fact that the Charter entrenches pan-Canadian values interpreted by a centralized judicial hierarchy, will always be present. For while it is true that fundamental rights are universal, they do not assume their full significance until they are interpreted and given effect within a specific political, economic, and social context. As Professor Henri Brun aptly wrote in 1985:

The Charter must leave room for recourse to a law, in the name of the right to be different, which, in the final analysis, is perhaps the only truly universal right. The constitutional judge must make sure that the judicial acculturation flowing from the Charter is limited to what is ineluctably imposed by the intrinsically centralizing influence of such an instrument in a federal country. The strongest proponents of the argument that interpretations of the Charter should draw upon the American Bill of Rights never fail to add that this should not, however, occur to the detriment of the Canadian cultural identity, a fragile identity characterized by, among other things, a greater trust in the state than in individual laissez-faire. What, then, holds true for the cultural relationship between Canada and the U.S. should even more so hold true for the cultural relationship between Quebec and Canada.[98]

As we have seen, the Supreme Court of Canada has not been insensitive to this aspect of the problem. It has been careful not to interpret substantive rights (and in particular section 15) by disregarding the federal principle, and it has also ultimately relied on an interpretation of section 1 that leaves room for diversity and regional autonomy. The decision rendered by the Supreme Court in *Ford*[99] is, incidentally, the best example of this approach. In this case, the Court deemed that the imposition of the French language in commercial advertising (provided it was not made the exclusive language) was a reasonable limit on the freedom of expression guaranteed by the Quebec and Canadian Charters. In explaining its decision, the Court emphasized that the legislative provisions in question were necessary to preserve the 'visage linguistique' of Quebec, given the vulnerability of the French language in Quebec and in North America as a whole. In doing so, it implicitly recognized the distinctness of Quebec. If a law requiring the use of English in commercial advertising was adopted by another province, it is unlikely that such a measure would be considered a reasonable limit on freedom of expression since the English language is not in a vulnerable position in Canada.

Perhaps because of its prudent attitude, and because of the respect for the underlying values of federalism that is evident from the use it has made of the Charter, this Court has not been at the centre of the debates regarding national status in Quebec. In fact, the decisions rendered by the courts on the basis of the Canadian Charter have been generally well received, especially since Quebec's Charter of Human Rights and Freedoms[100] would, in most cases, have led to similar results. It is therefore only in the area of language rights (or rights that may have a linguistic connotation, such as sections 2(b) and 15) that the Canadian Charter has left a bitter taste in the mouths of many Quebeckers. And it is precisely in this direction that Canadians will have to turn one day in order to remove the heaviest burden weighing down the Charter (and perhaps the constitution as a whole) in Quebec.

Notes

1 In the Supreme Court, this argument was endorsed by only a few judges and in a very limited number of decisions. See *Reference re Alberta Statutes*, [1938] 1 S.C.R. 100 at 138, and *Switzman v. Elbling*, [1957] S.C.R. 285 at 328. The

highest court eventually administered the *coup de grâce* to this judicial interpretation in *Dupond v. Montreal*, [1978] 2 S.C.R. 770 at 796.

2 See, as examples, the majority opinions expressed in the decisions mentioned in the preceding note, and in *Saumur v. City of Quebec*, [1953] 2 S.C.R. 299 and *Henry Birks and Sons (Montreal) Limited v. City of Montreal*, [1955] S.C.R. 799.

3 See, among others, D. Smiley, *The Canadian Charter of Rights and Freedoms* (Toronto: Ontario Economic Council 1981); P.H. Russell, 'The Political Purposes of the Canadian Charter of Rights and Freedoms,' *Canadian Bar Review*, vol. 61 (1983) 30; H. Brun, 'The Canadian Charter of Rights and Freedoms as an Instrument of Social Development,' in Clare F. Beckton and Wayne MacKay, eds., *The Courts and the Charter* (Toronto: University of Toronto Press 1985); A.C. Cairns, *Charter versus Federalism: The Dilemmas of Constitutional Reform* (Montreal: McGill-Queen's University Press, 1992).

4 It should be noted, however, that this is not always the case. Sometimes it can prove very difficult for the federal Parliament to fill the legislative void that a judicial declaration of unconstitutionality can create. This is precisely the situation that has prevailed since the Supreme Court declared null and void the provisions of the Criminal Code relating to abortion (*R. v. Morgentaler*, [1988] 1 S.C.R. 30). Until such time as a consensus is reached in Ottawa concerning a new law, the provinces will be responsible for dealing with this thorny issue through their power over health matters. Similarly, the provincial authorities have been given greater freedom of action in regard to the regulation of business hours, following the declaration by the highest court that the Lord's Day Act violated the freedom of religion (*R. v. Big M Drug Mart Ltd.*, [1985] 1 S.C.R. 295).

5 The figures noted by the author (valid in 1979) take into account 950 state laws, compared with 123 federal laws. See H. J. Abraham, *The Judicial Process*, 4th ed., (New York: Oxford University Press 1980), 296–7. Abraham's figures are cited by F. L. Morton and R. Knopff, 'Nation-Building and the Canadian Charter of Rights and Freedoms,' in *Constitutionalism, Citizenship, and Society in Canada*, eds. A. Cairns and C. Williams (Research Program of the Royal Commission on the Economic Union and Development Prospects for Canada, 1986), vol. 33:166.

6 For example, should decisions where the Court simply confirmed the appeal court judgment without giving its reasons be taken into account? And what about appeals that are grouped together and decided all at once by pronouncing on one of the cases and settling the others by reference to it? Also, some major decisions have been made on the basis of the Canadian Bill of Rights or of the language rights or religious freedoms recognized in the Constitution Act, 1867 and the Manitoba Act, 1870. Should they be excluded from the scope of our study

because the Charter was not explicitly considered, even if it can be surmised that it influenced the interpretation given to these various texts?

7   Far from weakening, it seems that the trend is becoming more pronounced. In 1993 alone, the Supreme Court rendered judgment in thirteen cases from Ontario but decided only two from Quebec. Moreover, this should not be considered an isolated incident. The figures for 1990, 1991, and 1992 were the following: 27–3; 10–4; and 18–4.

8   Professor Andrew D. Heard analysed the treatment given the Charter by the Quebec courts in an interesting article entitled 'Quebec Courts and the Canadian Charter of Rights,' *International Journal of Canadian Studies* (1993), 153. Relying on a quantitative study of Quebec case law, Heard concludes that the citizens of that province invoke the Charter with the same frequency as their compatriots from the other provinces, and that the courts find in their favour in proportions comparable to those observed elsewhere in Canada. Curiously, it even seems as though Quebeckers are more inclined to challenge the laws made by their own legislature than they are those made by the federal Parliament (a ratio of two to one), while the opposite is true in all the other provinces. Lastly, it is interesting to note that the decisions rendered by the Supreme Court are those most often cited by the Quebec courts when interpreting the Charter, in a much higher proportion than can be observed in the other jurisdictions. This is yet another reason for choosing to focus on the jurisprudence of the highest court.

9   In 1993, for example, the Supreme Court reversed the appeal court decisions in thirteen of the thirty-seven judgments it rendered based on the Charter, and in 1992 it did the same in twelve out of thirty-four decisions.

10   For 1992 and 1993, however, a reversal of this situation can be seen, while most appeals from decisions by Quebec's Court of Appeal were rejected. But it is difficult to draw any conclusions from this, especially since the number of appeals originating in Quebec and heard by the Supreme Court over these two years was relatively small.

11   A study by Peter McCormick, quoted by F.L. Morton, P.H. Russell, and M.J. Withey in a study entitled *The Supreme Court's First One Hundred Charter of Rights Decisions: A Statistical Analysis* (Calgary, Alta: University of Calgary, Research Unit for Socio-Legal Studies, Research Study 6.1, 1990), shows that only 45 per cent of the decisions handed down by the Quebec Court of Appeal were confirmed by the Supreme Court, a performance bettered by all but the New Brunswick and Prince Edward Island courts of appeal.

12   See F.L. Morton and M.J. Withey, 'Charting the Charter, 1982–1985: A Statistical Analysis,' *Canadian Human Rights Yearbook*, vol. 65 (1987), at 72; P. Monahan, *Politics and the Constitution: The Charter, Federalism and The Supreme Court of Canada* (Toronto: Carswell 1987) 38.

13 To arrive at this figure, we do not take into account decisions where the Court relied on the language and religion provisions of the Constitution acts from 1867 to 1982. In spite of the close affinity between such texts and sections 16 to 23 of the Charter, it did not appear relevant to us, for purposes of the present study, to deal with judgments that do not rely on the Constitution Act, 1982. Indeed, the perspective could be distorted if we took into consideration decisions that the Court would undoubtedly have rendered even in the Charter's absence. The cases excluded are the follwoing: *A.G. (Que.) v. Greater Hull School Board,* [1984] 2 S.C.R. 575; *Re Manitoba Language Rights,* [1985] 1 S.C.R. 721; *Bilodeau v. A.G. (Man.),* [1986] 1 S.C.R. 449; *R. v. Mercure,* [1988] 1 S.C.R. 234; *Quebec (A.G.) v. Collier,* [1990] 1 S.C.R. 260; and *Sinclair v. Quebec (A.G.),* [1992] 1 S.C.R. 579. We do, however, include municipal by-laws in the same category as provincial provisions.

14 F.L. Morton, G. Solomon, I. McNish, and D.W. Poulton, 'Judicial Nullification of Statutes Under the Charter of Rights and Freedoms, 1982–1988,' *Alberta Law Review,* vol. 28 (1990), 396.

15 In fact, 75 per cent of the appeals heard by the Supreme Court that involved fundamental rights were based on sections 7 to 14 of the Charter.

16 *R. v. Oakes,* [1986] 1 S.C.R. 103. The provision invalidated was section 8 of the Narcotic Control Act.

17 *R. v. Hamill,* [1987] 1 S.C.R. 301.

18 *R. v. Smith (E.D.),* [1987] 1 S.C.R., 1045.

19 *R. v. Morgentaler,* [1988] 1 S.C.R. 30.

20 *R. v. Vaillancourt,* [1987] 2 S.C.R. 636.

21 *R. v. Hess,* decision rendered on 4 Oct. 1990.

22 *R. v. Martineau,* decision rendered on 13 Sept. 1990.

23 *R. v. Logan,* [1990] 2 S.C.R. 731; *R. v. Sit,* [1991] 3 S.C.R. 124. The provisions at issue in these cases were sections 213(c) and 21(2) of the Criminal Code.

24 *R. v. Swain,* [1991] 1 S.C.R. 933.

25 *R. v. Seaboyer; R. v. Gayme,* [1991] 2 S.C.R. 577.

26 *R. v. Bain,* [1992] 1 S.C.R. 91.

27 *R. v. Zundel,* [1992] 2 S.C.R. 731.

28 *R. v. Morales,* [1992] 3 S.C.R. 711.

29 *Hunter v. Southam Inc.,* [1984] 2 S.C.R. 145.

30 *R. v. Wholesale Travel Group Inc.,* [1991] 3 S.C.R. 154.

31 *Singh et al v. Minister of Employment and Immigration* [1985] 1 S.C.R. 177.

32 *R. v. Big M Drug Mart Ltd.,* [1985] 1 S.C.R. 295.

33 *Osborne v. Canada (Treasury Board),* [1991] 2 S.C.R. 69.

34 *Schachter v. Canada* [1992] 2 S.C.R. 679.

35 We are aware that the distinction between a procedural provision and a substan-

tive provision can be arbitrary and must not be given too much significance. Nevertheless it is true that the 'what' and the 'how' cannot be confused; and although legislative measures do not always fit into one or the other of these paradigms, it is still possible to classify them according to whether they announce an objective or provide means that are to be placed at the disposal of those who will be responsible for ensuring implementation.

36 The fact that the act allowed the provinces to exempt some or all of their citizens from its application is, however, seldom mentioned.

37 The provisions in question were section 10(1)(a) of the Narcotic Control Act, which allowed a peace officer to search a dwelling-house relying on a writ of assistance (*R. v. Hamill*); and section 146(1) of the Criminal Code, which prevented the accused, who had had sexual intercourse with a person of the female sex under fourteen years of age, from clearing himself of a crime by pleading that he believed in good faith that this person was fourteen years of age or older (*R. v. Hess*).

38 See *Schachter v. Canada.*

39 The same conclusion could be reached by considering the jurisprudence of the appeal courts. Indeed, in 'Judicial Nullification,' Morton, Solomon, McNish, and Poulton, show that, out of forty-eight federal acts deemed by the courts to be inconsistent with the Charter, thirty-five were deemed inconsistent on the ground that they violated legal rights. Furthermore, half the offending provisions were found in the Criminal Code; the Narcotic Control Act also figured prominently in the list of acts most often affected. Also according to these authors, it appears that 88 per cent of the federal enactments that did not find favour with the appeal courts were procedural in nature. Lastly, the invalidated federal provisions were not of recent vintage, two-thirds of them having been enacted prior to 1970. This again corresponds to our conclusions regarding decisions rendered by the Supreme Court.

40 *A.G. (Que.) v. Quebec Protestant School Boards*, [1984] 2 S.C.R. 66.

41 *Ford v. Quebec (A.G.)*, [1988] 2 S.C.R. 712.

42 *Corporation professionnelle des médecins v. Thibault*, [1988] 1 S.C.R., 1033.

43 *Re B.C. Motor Vehicle Act (British Columbia)*, [1985] 2 S.C.R. 486.

44 *Andrews v. Law Society of British Columbia*, [1989] 1 S.C.R. 143.

45 *Black v. Law Society of Alberta*, [1989] 1 S.C.R. 591.

46 *Rocket v. Royal College of Dental Surgeons of Ontario*, judgment rendered on 21 June 1990.

47 *Peterborough (City) v. Ramsden*, [1993] 2 S.C.R., 1084.

48 Once again, the jurisprudence of the Supreme Court simply confirms the trends that are evident from the indexed decisions of the country's courts of appeal. Indeed, Morton, Solomon, McNish, and Poulton clearly demonstrate in 'Judicial

Nullification' that 84 per cent of the provincial legislative provisions invalidated by the highest provincial courts had been enacted since 1970 (compared with 34 per cent for federal provisions).

49 Three of the eight provincial legislative provisions invalidated by the Supreme Court originated in Quebec. In the following years, however, the highest court has endorsed several Quebec enactments that had been challenged on the basis of the Charter. Thus, in *R. v. Lippé* ([1991] 2 S.C.R. 114), the validity of the Quebec system of part-time municipal judges received confirmation. Similarly, in *Sinclair v. Quebec* ([1991] 3 S.C.R. 134), the Court unanimously agreed that the Act respecting the cities of Rouyn and Noranda did not violate the right to vote, the freedom of association, or the equality rights set out in sections 3, 2(d) and 15 of the Charter. Lastly, in *P.(D.) v. S. (C.)* ([1993] 4 S.C.R. 141), it was the opinion of the Court that the criterion of the child's best interests, provided for in article 30 of the Civil Code of Lower Canada, was not vague within the meaning of section 7 of the Charter, in spite of the broad discretion it confers on the courts.

50 Section 133 of the Constitution Act, 1867 already prescribed the use of the French and English languages in legislation and before the courts, both in Quebec and at the federal level. It was, in fact, pursuant to this constitutional guarantee that sections 7 to 13 of the Charter of the French Language, which made French the language of legislation and justice, were scrapped. See *A.G. of Quebec v. Blaikie*, [1979] 2 S.C.R., 1016, and *A.G. (Quebec) v. Blaikie*, [1981] 1 S.C.R. 312. See also *A.G. (Quebec) v. Collier* and *Sinclair v. Quebec*.

51 In *Devine v. Quebec (A.G.)*, [1988] 2 S.C.R. 790, the Supreme Court clearly recognized that jurisdiction with respect to language was ancillary in nature and, consequently, that it was possible (from the point of view of the division of powers) for Quebec to govern the use of French and English in local commercial operations.

52 Attempting to show the reasonableness of the regime instituted by the Charter of the French Language with respect to access to English schools, the attorney general of Quebec had based his arguments on the physical mobility (migration) and linguistic mobility (assimilation) of individuals and the fact that other free and democratic societies with a socio-linguistic situation comparable to that of Quebec had adopted stricter language-related measures than Bill 101. The Supreme Court, however, rejected his arguments, on the ground that they flouted the clearly demonstrated will of the framers of the constitution: 'The framers of the Constitution unquestionably intended by s. 23 to establish a general regime for the language of instruction, not a special regime for Quebec; but in view of the period when the Charter was enacted, and especially in light of the wording of s. 23 of the Charter as compared with that of ss. 72 and 73 of Bill 101, it is apparent that the combined effect of the latter two sections seemed to the framers like an

archetype of the regimes needing reform, or which at least had to be affected, and the remedy prescribed for all of Canada by s. 23 of the Charter was in large part a response to these sections.' See *A.G. (Quebec) v. Quebec Protestant School Board* at 79–80.

53 It should be made clear that the purpose of section 23 is not simply to enable children to receive instruction in the minority language. Section 23(3)(b), in fact, clearly states that the right to minority-language instruction includes, when numbers warrant, the right to publicly funded educational facilities. In *Mahé v. Alberta*, [1990] 1 S.C.R. 342, the Supreme Court interpreted this provision using a sliding-scale approach. Expressing the view that the term 'educational facilities' could not refer uniquely to physical structures, it concluded that s. 23(3)(b) granted the minority some degree of management and control over those aspects of education that may affect language and culture. Where warranted by a sufficient number of children, this right may lead to the existence of an independent school board. Where this is not the case, the linguistic minority may at least demand proportional representation within the school board. What is more, these representatives should have exclusive power to make certain decisions concerning minority-language instruction and the facilities in which it is provided, especially in regard to 'a) expenditures of funds provided for such instruction and facilities; b) appointment and direction of those responsible for the administration of such instruction and facilities; c) establishment of programs of instruction; d) recruitment and assignment of teachers and other personnel; and e) making of agreements for education and services for minority language pupils' (at 377). We have deemed it unnecessary to expand on this aspect of language guarantees where education is concerned because the provinces are not directly affected by it. As the Court itself explains, 'the management and control accorded to s. 23 parents does not preclude provincial regulation. The province has an interest both in the content and the qualitative standards of educational programs. Such programmes can be imposed without infringing s. 23, *in so far as they do not interfere with the linguistic and cultural concerns of the minority*' (at 380). The portion we have italicized, however, implies that perhaps not all the ramifications of this new constitutional guarantee have been explored yet.

54 Here is how the Court expressed its view on this matter: 'In the opinion of this Court it has not been demonstrated that the prohibition of the use of any language other than French in ss. 58 and 69 of the *Charter of the French Language* is necessary to the defence and enhancement of the status of the French language in Quebec or that it is proportionate to that legislative purpose. Since the evidence put to us by the government showed that the predominance of the French language was not reflected in the "visage linguistique" of Quebec, the governmental response could well have been tailored to meet that specific problem and to

impair freedom of expression minimally. Thus, whereas requiring the predominant display of the French language, even its marked predominance, would be proportional to the goal of promoting and maintaining a French "visage linguistique" in Quebec and therefore justified under the Quebec *Charter* and the Canadian *Charter*, requiring the exclusive use of French has not been so justified. French could be required in addition to any other language or it could be required to have greater visibility than that accorded to other languages. Such measures would ensure that the "visage linguistique" reflected the demography of Quebec: the predominant language is French.' See *Ford v. Quebec (A.G.)*, at 779.

55 *Law Society of Upper Canada v. Skapinker*, [1984] 1 S.C.R. 357.

56 See n. 45.

57 See section 6(4) of the Charter.

58 Unless, of course, the legislature derogates from these rights by making a precise statement to that effect, as it may do under the Canadian Charter. This primacy of the Quebec Charter over ordinary laws dates only from 1 Jan. 1986, when section 52 of the Quebec Charter in its current form came into force.

59 See n. 41.

60 [1989] 1 S.C.R. 927.

61 The Court did not accept the argument put forward by the attorney general of Quebec to the effect that section 9.1 left the lawmaker greater latitude than section 1 and authorized only a judicial review of the legislative purpose. Here is how it dealt with this matter: 'What this would mean is that it would be a sufficient justification if the purpose or object of legislation limiting a fundamental freedom or right fell within the general description provided by the words "democratic values, public order and the general well-being of the citizens of Québec." It cannot have been intended that s. 9.1 should confer such a broad and virtually unrestricted legislative authority to limit fundamental freedoms and rights. Rather, it is an implication of the requirement that a limit serve one of these ends, that the limit should be rationally connected to the legislative purpose and that the legislative means be proportionate to the end to be served' (*Ford v. Quebec* at 771). Yet this reading of section 9.1 is not the only plausible one. Without going as far as the attorney general of Quebec, some authors have claimed that Quebec's exception clause is more permissive than its equivalent in the Canadian Charter because it does not include any criterion similar to the minimal impairment requirement of section 1. In this regard, see F. Chevrette, 'La disposition limitative de la Charte des droits et libertés de la personne: le dit et le non-dit,' *Revue Juridique Thémis*, vol. 21 (1987), 461.

62 *R. v. Burnshine*, [1975] 1 S.C.R. 693.

63 *Valente v. The Queen*, [1985] 2 S.C.R. 673.

64 *R. v. Lyons*, [1987] 2 S.C.R. 309.

65 'It would not be feasible, however, to apply the most rigorous and elaborate conditions of judicial independence to the constitutional requirement of independence in s. 11(d) of the Charter, which may have to be applied to a variety of tribunals. The legislative and constitutional provisions in Canada governing matters which bear on the judicial independence of tribunals trying persons charged with an offence exhibit a great range and variety. The essential conditions of judicial independence for purposes of section 11(d) must bear some reasonable relationship to that variety ... The standard of judicial independence for purposes of section 11(d) cannot be a standard of uniform provisions. It must necessarily be a standard that reflects what is common to, or at the heart of, the various approaches to the essential conditions of judicial independence in Canada' (*Valente* at 692–4).

66 *Lyons* at 349.

67 *R. v. Cornell*, [1988] 1 S.C.R. 461.

68 The provision in question was section 234.1 of the Criminal Code, under which a police officer could order a person suspected of being intoxicated to provide a roadside breath-sample for analysis.

69 This objective was identified by the court as being to give the governor-in-council authority to proclaim section 234.1 of the Code in a particular province only with the agreement of that province, because of the impact section 234.1 would have on provincial law-enforcement priorities and on effectiveness and the allocation of resources in the field of highway traffic control, where there is division of powers.

70 See n. 62.

71 Section 32(2) of the Charter provides that section 15 was to take effect only three years after the coming into force of the Constitution Act, 1982, that is, on 17 April 1985.

72 [1989] 1 S.C.R., 1296.

73 It is section 430 of the Code that allowed for this exception. That provision was subsequently amended to provide all Canadians with the opportunity to be tried by a judge alone when charged with an offence included in section 427.

74 *Andrews v. Law Society of British Coumbia*, [1989] 1 S.C.R. 143.

75 In particular, we have in mind this caution voiced by Madam Justice Wilson: 'I would not wish to suggest that a person's province of residence or place of trial could not in some circumstances be a personal characteristic of the individual or group capable of constituting a ground of discrimination' (*Turpin* at 1,333). In the same connection, it is surprising to note that Madame Justice Wilson refused to express an opinion on the issue of whether equality of application of the criminal law to all persons in Canada was a principle of fundamental justice within the meaning of section 7, an issue that, it could reasonably be believed, had been resolved once and for all by *Cornell*.

76 *R. v. Sheldon*, [1990] 2 S.C.R. 254.

77 Ibid., at 285.

78 In this regard, the comments of the Court could not be more explicit: 'Obviously, the federal system of government itself demands that the values underlying s. 15(1) cannot be given unlimited scope. The division of powers not only permits differential treatment based upon province of residence, it mandates and encourages geographical distinction. There can be no question, then, that unequal treatment which stems solely from the exercise, by provincial legislators, of their legitimate jurisdictional powers cannot be the subject of a s. 15(1) challenge on the basis only that it creates distinctions based upon province of residence ... To find otherwise would be to completely undermine the value of diversity which is at the foundation of the division of powers' (ibid., at 288).

79 Ibid., at 289.

80 Ibid., at 291.

81 Ibid.

82 See, in this regard, J. Woehrling, 'Le principe d'égalité, le système fédéral canadien et le caractère distinct du Québec,' in *Québec-Communauté française de Belgique: Autonomie et spécificité dans le cadre d'un système fédéral*, ed. P. Patenaude (Montreal: Wilson and Lafleur 1991), 119.

83 It is common knowledge that in *SDGMR v. Dolphin Delivery Ltd.*, [1986] 2 S.C.R. 573, the Supreme Court indicated that a legislature could infringe a right or freedom only within its own legislative jurisdiction; consequently, the Charter is not applicable to common law, at least not with respect to purely private relationships. The situation is, however, quite different in Quebec, where the common law is largely codified. If the Court's line of reasoning in this case is adhered to, there is every reason to believe that the Civil Code is subject to the Charter. Moreover, Madam Justice Wilson explicitly recognized this point in *McKinney v. University of Guelph*, [1990] 3 S.C.R. 229. The result is that private law is theoretically subject to greater constitutional limits in Quebec than it is in the common-law provinces. But it may well be that the distinction is more apparent than real, given that, according to the Supreme Court itself, the courts must explain and develop the principles of common law in a manner consistent with the fundamental values enshrined in the constitution.

84 Professor Katherine Swinton clearly perceived this close relationship between arguments based on democratic theory and those formulated in regard to the federal principle within the context of the Charter: 'The language of section 1 of the Charter, at least, seems to permit arguments based on diversity to be made as justifications for the limitations on rights. The question for the courts is whether and when such arguments should be persuasive. The answer turns, not surprisingly, on the question we cannot escape in Charter interpretation – on the one

hand, the kinds of interests that enter into the section calculus and, especially, the degree to which the courts should accept arguments based on community considerations; on the other hand, and often interrelated with the first issue, the degree to which the courts should defer to the legislature. These questions do not directly speak of the value of federalism, but the answers to them have important ramifications for the territorial diversity protected by that system of government.' See *The Supreme Court and Canadian Federalism* (Toronto: Carswell 1990), 342.

85 *R. v. Oakes*, [1986] 1 S.C.R. 103.

86 It was in *Jones v. The Queen* ([1986] 2 S.C.R. 284) that he first drew attention to the complex interaction that exists between the need to preserve diversity in a federal system and the deference the courts must sometimes show to the legislatures. At that time he wrote: 'Some pragmatism is involved in balancing between fairness and efficiency. The provinces must be given room to make choices regarding the type of administrative structure that will suit their needs unless the use of such structure is in itself so manifestly unfair, having regard to the decisions it is called upon to make, as to violate the principles of fundamental justice,' (ibid. at 304).

87 *R. v. Edwards Books and Art Ltd.*, [1986] 2 S.C.R. 713.

88 The following excerpts from the written opinion of Mr Justice Dickson give a good idea of the substance of his remarks. Called upon to determine whether the exemptions regime provided for by the Retail Business Holidays Act of Ontario was justifiable in relation to the various types of retail businesses, the chief justice first wrote: 'Legislative choices regarding alternative forms of business regulation do not generally impinge on the values and provisions of the Charter, and the resultant legislation need not be tuned with great precision in order to withstand judicial scrutiny. Simplicity and administrative convenience are legitimate concerns for the drafters of such legislation.' Then, a little farther on, he added: 'The courts are not called upon to substitute judicial opinions for legislative ones as to the place at which to draw a precise line.' In concluding, he expressed the view that 'it is not the role of this Court to devise legislation that is constitutionally valid, or to pass on the validity of schemes which are not directly before it, or to consider what legislation might be the most desirable' (Ibid., at 772, 782, and 783).

89 *Irwin Toy Ltd. v. Quebec (A.G.)*, [1989] 1 S.C.R. 927.

90 'When striking a balance between the claims of competing groups, the choice of means, like the choice of ends, frequently will require an assessment of conflicting scientific evidence and differing justified demands on scarce resources. Democratic institutions are meant to let us all share in the responsibility for these difficult choices. Thus, as courts review the results of the legislature's delibera-

tions, particularly with respect to the protection of vulnerable groups, they must be mindful of the legislature's representative function ... In other cases, however, rather than mediating between different groups, the government is best characterized as the singular antagonist of the individual whose right has been infringed. For example, in justifying an infringement of legal right enshrined in ss. 7 to 14 of the Charter, the state, on behalf of the whole community, typically will assert its responsibility for prosecuting crime whereas the individual will assert the paramountcy of principles of fundamental justice. There might not be any further competing claims among different groups. In such circumstances, and indeed whenever the government's purpose relates to maintaining the authority and impartiality of the judicial system, the courts can assess with some certainty whether the "least drastic means" for achieving the purpose have been chosen, especially given their accumulated experience in dealing with such questions' (ibid., at 993–4).

91 See n. 83.
92 See *McKinney v. University of Guelph* at 304–5.
93 See n. 41. The author represented the attorney general of Quebec in the Supreme Court in that case.
94 See the extract cited in n. 90.
95 See n. 40.
96 'In the *Quebec Association of Protestant School Boards* case, the minority-language educational rights created by s. 23 of the Canadian Charter were, as the court observed, of a very specific, special, and limited nature, unlike the fundamental rights and freedoms guaranteed by other provisions. They were well defined rights for specific classes of persons. In the opinion of the Court, the effect of ss. 72 and 73 of Bill 101 was to create an exception to s. 23 for Quebec, that is, to make it inapplicable as a whole in Quebec. There was thus what amounted to a complete denial in Quebec of the rights created by s. 23. The extent of the denial was co-extensive with the potential exercise of the very specific and limited rights created by s. 23. Such an exception to s. 23, as the Court characterized it, was tantamount to an impermissible attempt to override or amend s. 23. An exception of such effect could not be a limit within the meaning of s. 1 of the Charter' (*Ford v. Quebec* at 772–3).
97 See 'Les dix ans de la Charte canadienne des droits et libertés et le droit civil québécois: Quelques réflexions,' in *Ottawa L.R.*, vol. 24 (1992), 193.
98 'The Canadian Charter of Rights and Freedoms as an Instrument of Social Development,' in Beckton and MacKay, *The Courts and the Charter*.
99 See n. 41.
100 R.S.Q., c. C–12.

2

Infertile Soil?
Sowing the Charter in Alberta

IAN URQUHART*

... the better way to protect the rights of the citizens of our province, and frankly of the country, is to continue with the way we are doing it today and leave that responsibility to the elected representatives.

– Alberta Premier Peter Lougheed, September 1980

Ten years after Premier Lougheed's declaration that Alberta did not want to give the Canadian judiciary the responsibility for interpreting a constitutionally entrenched bill of rights, the same outlook continued to inspire key figures in the province's Progressive Conservative government. Solicitor General Dick Fowler lashed out at the 'old fogies' on the Supreme Court of Canada who dared to dictate to elected officials how their legislative responsibilities should be exercised. 'You have a body that is, in fact,' Fowler charged, 'not account-able to the public of Canada creating laws in this province. In my view, in a democratic, parliamentary system, I think that the people who are elected should make the laws.'[1] More recently, during a heated legislative debate on Canada's Young Offenders Act, prominent members of Premier Ralph Klein's cabinet heaped more scorn on the Charter. Their viewpoint was perhaps best expressed by Municipal Affairs Minister Steve West's comment: 'There's no changes that should be made to the Charter. It should be scrapped once and for all.'[2] Such antipathy towards constitutional review by the courts is a long-standing feature of Alberta political life. Since William Aberhart's Social Credit movement swept into power in 1935, provincial governments have regarded

* Research funding for this article was supplied, in part, by the Centre for Constitutional Studies at the University of Alberta. The author wishes to thank Anne Kaplan for her able research assistance and David Schneiderman and David Stewart for their comments on an earlier draft of this article.

the judiciary, particularly the federally appointed judiciary, with suspicion. The courts, along with the federal power of disallowance, helped destroy Premier Aberhart's efforts to bring social credit monetary doctrine to life during the Great Depression of the 1930s.[3] Forty years later, as a new generation of political leaders, flush with petrodollars, plotted Alberta's future, the courts again were perceived as threats to provincial policy-making powers. The decisions in the *Canadian Industrial Gas & Oil* and *Central Canada Potash* cases, while aimed directly at Saskatchewan, were viewed more generally as federally sanctioned attacks upon the provincial powers over natural resources which were the crucial foundations of Alberta's new-found wealth.[4] Calls for a 'representative constitutional court' for Canada joined demands for strengthened provincial natural-resource powers as key planks in Premier Lougheed's constitutional-reform platform.[5] For its part, the Charter of Rights and Freedoms came to be regarded as another expression of the central government's interest in constraining the legislative room for manoeuvre granted provinces in Canadian federalism.

This essay uses the provincial government's distrust of the Supreme Court and the Charter of Rights and Freedoms as its point of departure. Two general subjects interest us. First, we will examine whether the provincial government has tried to temper, if not circumvent altogether, the Charter's impact upon provincial legislation. Rhetoric aside, have successive provincial governments embraced or shunned the Charter? Second, we will examine public opinion towards the Charter of Rights and Freedoms. Much has been made in the political-science literature about the political purposes of the Charter. Foremost in this respect is the work of Alan Cairns, whose many writings on the changing constitutionalism of Canadian society since 1982 are premised on the idea of the Charter as 'an instrument to change our civic self-conceptions, strengthen the pan-Canadian against provincial communities, and manipulate our psyches.'[6] However, few studies have offered empirical support for the argument that the Charter has in fact transformed Canadian political culture, or, more specifically, that it has taken root in the mass public of English Canada to the extent that it has among the elites of social groups who have received consitutional recognition in the Charter.[7] This is exactly the question explored in the following analysis. Our purpose, in short, is to determine whether the stance successive Alberta governments have taken towards the Charter enjoys support within the general public.

Interpreting the Charter: Legislative Conservatism and Judicial Deference

In May 1985, nearly one month after the equality provisions of the Charter of Rights and Freedoms came into effect, Bill 42, the Charter Omnibus Act, was introduced into the Alberta legislature. The legislation modified sixty-two separate sections of forty-eight pieces of provincial legislation in order to harmonize existing provincial statutes with the rights entrenched in the Charter. During the debate on second reading, Neil Crawford, the province's attorney general, outlined the government's philosophy on the harmonization issue. He explained that obvious conflicts between the Charter and provincial statutes were the targets of the Omnibus Act; for example, inappropriate uses of gender-specific language would be changed. However, in the words of the attorney general, 'exotic arguments' were not entertained by the government nor recognized in the act.[8] Essentially, the government turned over to the public the responsibility for ensuring that provincial legislation respected the Charter. If citizens felt that the Omnibus Act did not go far enough to accommodate the Charter, they could challenge provincial legislation in the courts. Sensitive to the accusation that the government was deliberately refusing to acknowledge the legislative ramifications of the Charter, Crawford insisted that the reach of the Charter remained an important topic to debate in Alberta but that the courts were a preferred venue for such a debate. He also emphasized that his government would not promise to interpret whatever defeats of provincial legislation judicial review might deliver as signals that the government should abandon its policy direction and preferences. While the government might have to repeal sections of legislation which offended the Charter, Crawford advised the house that 'there would also be circumstances where amendments would suffice and where a legitimate legislative objective might be realized in some other way. That would be a proper area for consideration by the Assembly in cases where that would arise.'[9] This statement about the legitimacy of legislative responses to judicial defeats tempered the accuracy of one New Democratic Party MLA's observation that, when it came to the Charter, the Lougheed government had adopted a 'wait for the courts to decide' approach.[10]

The possible public-policy ramifications of this approach depended upon two factors: the attitudes of the courts towards their enhanced responsibilities of constitutional review and, when legislation was struck down, the reaction of the provincial government to judicial nullification of Alberta legislation. In regards to the courts, how willing would they be to use the Charter to strike down legislation? While Charter-based challenges to legislation have been received far more favourably by the courts than Canadian Bill of Rights-based challenges ever were, the success rate of Charter challenges remains rather low.[11] This is no less true in Alberta, where the courts generally have tended either to reject Charter claims outright or to rely upon the umbrella of section 1 to shelter provincial legislation that trespassed upon the constitution's guarantees.[12]

Against this general tendency to reject Charter-based challenges, the greatest number of Charter victories have been recorded at the Court of Queen's Bench.[13] In total, provisions of six pieces of provincial legislation have been struck down on Charter grounds by Court. In one of these cases, *Kask v. Shimizu*, the Court's judgment was reversed by subsequent Queen's Bench rulings in *Singh v. Dura*[14] and *Ankema v. Bernier Kitchen Cabinets*.[15]

In a seventh case, *R. v. Mahé*, although the Court of Queen's Bench found that the provincial School Act violated minority-language education rights, this decision in fact exemplified the reluctance of the courts to stipulate legislative courses of action to government. The Court did not agree with the francophone parents who launched this Charter challenge that a separate francophone-controlled school board was necessary in order to realize section 23 rights. Nor was the Court prepared to dictate to the province the threshold where the 'wherever sufficient numbers of children warrant' provision of section 23 would come into effect. Furthermore, the Court felt that cost was a legitimate factor for the province to consider when it came to respecting section 23 rights. The deferential posture assumed by the Court, despite its finding that the School Act violated the Charter, is captured well in its statement that, 'the courts should not become involved with preparing or drafting methods of achieving the desired objective. The courts have attempted to provide guidance by interpreting the Charter, but must not interfere by decreeing methods or becoming involved in ongoing supervision or administration.'[16] On balance, the first verdict in *Mahé* delivered only a hollow legal victory to francophone parents; it did not push the government to introduce the public-policy changes the parents sought.

Dissatisfied with the trial judge's interpretation of section 23, the francophone parents appealed the Queen's Bench verdict to the Alberta Court of Appeal. The appeal was dismissed, a result symptomatic of the Court of Appeal's unwillingness to uphold Charter rights against provincial legislation. In *Mahé*[17] the Court of Appeal agreed that the section 23 right to effective instruction in French had been violated, but it declared that this right could be limited legitimately by the number of students, by the costs of providing second-language instruction, and by section 1 of the Charter. Moreover, although the Court maintained that there were sufficient numbers of students in Edmonton to trigger the right to effective instruction in French, it would not agree that these numbers were sufficient to trigger the management rights extended by section 23(3)(b). The most that the Court was prepared to offer the appellants was the rather empty acknowledgment that 'some of the arguments of the appellant about the meaning of the Constitution have been accepted.' Like the Court of Queen's Bench, the Court of Appeal would not push the province to adopt specific legislation in light of its findings. The Court considered injunctive or other drastic relief to be inappropriate. 'In my view,' wrote Justice Keran, 'it would be imprudent for the court to go further at this time than to say what has here been said. Now that the law is explained, Alberta can act.'[18] A more satisfying legal result would not be obtained by francophone parents until the Supreme Court ruled on this issue in March 1990.

The Court of Appeal's tendency to view Charter claims unsympathetically was also demonstrated in its reversal of three of the Queen's Bench decisions that struck down provisions of provincial legislation. The Court of Appeal reversed the Queen's Bench judgment in *Neale* that twenty-four hour driver's licence suspensions violated the section 7 right to liberty.[19] Here, the Court of Appeal rejected the wide interpretation of the right to liberty offered in the initial judgment. It would not endorse the lower court's conclusion that the right to liberty included freedom of movement, including mode of movement by automobile. In a second case, *R. v. Maier*,[20] the Court of Appeal reversed a ruling by the Court of Queen's Bench that the province's mandatory seat-belt legislation violated the right to liberty and agreed with an earlier provincial court decision that sufficient evidence existed to demonstrate the life-saving importance of seat-belts. In *Budge v. Workers' Compensation Board (No. 2)*,[21] the Court of Appeal rejected the claim that a provision of the Workers' Compensation Act denying employees the right to sue for injury arising from employment violated the section 7 and section 15 rights of an employee's dependants. Section 7 did not protect, in the Court's opinion, economic rights and this provision of the act did not constitute discrimination on 'enumerated or analogous' grounds.

Only in one case – *Black v. Law Society of Alberta*[22] – did the Court of Appeal depart from its tendency to narrow the scope of Charter victories obtained in Queen's Bench rulings. And only in two cases – *Grier v. Alberta Optometric Association*[23] and *Edmonton Journal v. Alberta*[24] – did it adopt a more liberal interpretation of Charter rights than that of the Court of Queen's Bench. In *Grier*, whereas the Court of Queen's Bench had held that commercial speech was not protected by the Charter's right to freedom of expression, the Court of Appeal found that the professional association's blanket prohibition on advertising prices was contrary to section 2(b) and that, since the regulation in question deprived the public of important information, it was not a reasonable limit upon this right. In the *Edmonton Journal* case, after the Court of Queen's Bench had ruled that the Judicature Act's ban on the publication of divorce proceedings did not violate the publisher's section 2(b) right, the Court of Appeal employed the constitutional-exemption doctrine to suspend the enforcement of the act's prohibition in this case.

The Supreme Court of Canada has upheld the Charter claims of Albertans against provincial legislation in only three cases. In all three, however, the Supreme Court has crafted a more expansive interpretation of Charter rights than that taken by the lower courts. In *Black*,[25] the Supreme Court agreed with the Court of Queen's Bench that the Legal Profession Act violated the Charter's mobility rights, but it applied this conclusion to both rules 75(b) and 154 of the Law Society of Alberta. In *Edmonton Journal v. Alberta*,[26] the Supreme Court ruled that section 30 of the Judicature Act violated section 2(b) since it was a blanket prohibition on publication. Since this act denied completely the section 2(b) right it could not be justified under section 1. In its ruling in *Mahé*, the Supreme Court rewarded the persistence of francophone parents with a more sympathetic interpretation of section 23's minority-language education guarantees. Although the Supreme Court did not agree with the appellants that a separate francophone school board had to be established in Edmonton, it ruled that the city's francophone parents must be guaranteed representation in institutions that administered minority-language instruction and that they must be given management and control over minority-language instruction and facilities.

Judicial interpretations, characterized as they have been by their reluctance to accept Charter claims, have worked to minimize the impact of the Charter upon the established pattern of public policy in Alberta. But provincial-policy consequences of Charter review also depend, as Attorney General Crawford inferred during the Omnibus Act debate, on the response of governments to judicial decisions. The range of policy responses governments may make to judgments that strike down legislation will be shaped, in the first instance, by the breadth of the constitutional constraints raised by Charter review.[27] The qualitative variety of constitutional constraints has been identified by F.L. Morton, G. Solomon, I. McNish, and D.W. Poulton, who make a useful distinction between procedural and substantive nullifications of legislation. Procedural nullifications focus upon how government pursues a particular policy objective and offer legislators the opportunity to fine-tune the offending legislative or regulatory initiatives; substantive nullifications reject the main objects of legislation and restrict a government's choice of responses to either policy abandonment or, if applicable, use of the section 33 override.[28] However, a government's ultimate response to a court's decision depends upon more than if Charter review is broad or narrow, procedural or substantive. Government reactions depend as well upon factors completely unrelated to the scope and nature of the verdict; they depend upon the ideological outlook of the governing party and the constituencies that sustain it in office.[29] Government responses to Charter review also will be shaped by estimations of the political costs and benefits flowing from either accepting or rejecting judicial decisions.

In Alberta, this attention to the nature of the governing party's ideological agenda and political support helps to explain the provincial government's wide-ranging responses to Charter review. Rainer Knopff and F.L. Morton use Alberta's reaction to the Queen's Bench verdict in *R. v. Maier* to illustrate what they regard as a worrying tendency in post-Charter Canada – the emergence of an oracular courtroom, one where 'constitutional interpretation is the exclusive preserve of judges, whose opinions must be accepted as authoritative by everyone else.'[30] After the trial judge's verdict that mandatory seat-belt legislation violated section 7, the province stopped prosecuting those who ignored the province's mandatory seat-belt legislation. Prosecutions resumed only after the Court of Appeal reversed the trial judge's ruling. The province's behaviour, specifically its decision to stop enforcing the law on the word of one trial-level judge, supposedly signalled the politicians' acceptance of the assumption that government policies were completely 'at the mercy of judicial opinions.'[31] Yet, Alberta reacted far less compliantly to the Supreme Court's verdict in *R. v. Mahé*. The province's behaviour in this second case reflected a marked unwillingness to yield to the judiciary. When the Supreme Court of Canada declared in March 1990 that provincial legislation did not respect minority-language education rights, Education Minister Jim Dinning promised prompt action. While non-committal about when the province would introduce amendments to the School Act, Dinning felt that a legislative response before the end of the 1990 spring session of the legislature was 'a reasonable objective.'[32] This objective was never met. Instead of an early response to *Mahé*, the Alberta government procrastinated. Legislation responding to the Supreme Court's decision was not passed by the Alberta legislature until the fall of 1993, three and one-half years after the Supreme Court's decision!

In the interim between the Supreme Court judgment and the passage of Bill 8, the School Amendment Act, 1993, the ideological basis for the government's delay in responding to the Supreme Court's ruling was revealed on several occasions. Sprinkled throughout this period are statements from members of the Progressive Conservative Party which underlined their general antipathy towards the legislative entrenchment of bilingualism in Canada and the need to revise the province's School Act in particular. Premier Donald Getty, in widely publicized comments made before the Edmonton Rotary Club, described enforced bilingualism as an irritant in Canada. Calling for 'bilingualism by choice, not law,' Getty suggested that removing the legislative basis for bilingualism – 'a punitive, unwelcome law' – would actually encourage many more Canadians to support bilingualism.[33] In 1993 the legislative debate on Bill 8 was distinguished by several statements from Progressive Conservative back-benchers and one cabinet minister which emphasized their discomfort over the bill's linguistic provisions. Ty Lund, the member for Rocky Mountain House, warned the legislature about the consequences of this measure:

No one has ever built a province by having two separate languages, and English is the official language in Alberta. I really have a problem with it from that point of view. I think it's not going to be building; it's going to be divisive. If parents want their children to learn French, we have a very good French immersion program in this province, and that, in my opinion, should fill the bill. Furthermore, the cost of doing this in a time of restraint, the cost of setting them up and then the costs of operating are going to be prohibitive. So I really have trouble with this, but because it's the ruling of the court, and this government has always obeyed the law and we have to do it now, I guess I will simply hold my breath and hold my nose and vote for this Bill.[34]

Lund's uneasiness with the bill was shared not only by other back-benchers but also by at least one member of cabinet, Dr Steve West, the minister of munici-pal affairs. Like Lund, West felt that the provision of French-immersion pro-grams should satisfy francophones, an option the Court had rejected explicitly. West argued that the *Mahé* ruling actually fuelled discrimination in the prov-ince since it gave one special interest group special rights which could not be claimed by the majority. He ended his commentary on the linguistic provisions of the bill with a call for the courts to take their cue from the result of the referendum on the Charlottetown Accord, a referendum that, for West, demon-strated that Canadians did not want to travel any farther down the path of duality. Following this rather dubious interpretation of Charlottetown, West concluded: 'I wish the courts would look at that as a social direction for the future and understand that the statement made in that referendum was to look at the French language issue, the duality of this country, and not to split this country any further by segmental rights.'[35]

The slow provincial response to the Supreme Court's decision in *Mahé* suggests that the legislative conservatism which animated the government's Charter Omnibus Act was also at work on those rare occasions when the government was called upon to react to Charter rulings. This second form of legislative conservatism had roots in the nature of the judgments themselves. Provincial procrastination in responding to *Mahé*, for example, was facilitated by the nature of the constitutional constraint framed by the Supreme Court. While the Court made it very clear that Alberta had failed to honour its obliga-tions under section 23 of the constitution and that the province 'must delay no longer in putting in place the appropriate minority language education scheme,'[36] it did not declare the School Act unconstitutional.[37] Instead, the Court restricted itself to making a declaration regarding the concrete minority-language education rights of Edmonton francophones. 'Such a declaration will ensure that the appellants' rights are realized while, at the same time,' wrote Chief Justice Dickson, 'leaving the government with the flexibility necessary to fashion a response which is suited to the circumstances.'[38] The flexibility that the Court offered the province goes some distance in explaining the legislative conservatism which characterized the government's response to the judgment in *Mahé*.

To the extent that successful Charter claims establish a range of policy alternatives for governments to consider, we must look to more than simply the nature of the constraints fashioned by Charter review in order to explain the actual behaviour of governments. The policy direction governments take in response to judicial decision making depends as well upon political circumstances outside the judicial arena. In Alberta, we have noted already several examples of the antipathy the governing Progressive Conservative Party has shown towards the Charter generally and the decision of the Supreme Court in *R. v. Mahé* in particular. Later we will consider whether these examples of legislative conservatism in respect to the Charter coincide with the pattern of political support for the Charter exhibited by Albertans. First, however, we will map out the general attitudes of Albertans towards the Charter.

Abstract Fans, Concrete Foes? Albertans and the Charter

The introduction to this essay noted that relatively little attention has been devoted to detailing the pattern of mass political support for the Charter of Rights in Canada. Discovering this pattern is particularly important for evaluating the unifying power of the Charter, either within Canadian society as a whole or merely within 'English Canada.' The plausibility of the claim that the Charter is performing this unifying function at the level of mass politics depends first of all upon our ability to identify widespread, popular acceptance of the Charter and the abstract rights guaranteed there. General appraisals of the Charter should offer this type of evidence. In isolation, however, general appraisals are insufficient since they may mask the contradictory tendencies in public sentiment which may emerge once general or abstract opinions are placed in more specific contexts. Richard Johnston, in his study of public opinion and public policy in Canada, found that Canadian public opinion is home to many contradictory majorities. Take, for example, the issue of deficit reduction. Using data obtained from the Decima Quarterly Report, Johnston noted that when Canadians were asked for their general opinion about which means, tax increases or spending reductions, should be used to reduce govern-ment deficits, they were much more likely to prefer spending reductions. Yet, when asked about cutting specific services, a greater reluctance to cut ap-peared. The dissonance between these patterns led Johnston to conclude that 'much of the opposition to specific service cuts must come from respondents who favour cuts in the abstract.'[39] Contradictory majorities of this sort were the rule, not the exception, in the attitudinal data Johnston examined. Studies of attitudes towards civil liberties reveal a similar pattern: support for rights in the abstract may waver and weaken in the face of conflicts with other values.[40] Therefore, to gauge more accurately public support for the Charter in Alberta, we will also explore attitudes towards the concrete policy changes which could be demanded by judicial review of the Charter. Are Albertans fans of the Charter? If they are in the abstract, do they retain their enthusiasm when they are asked to comment upon the public-policy changes that the implementation of these claims to rights may demand?

Our portrait of Albertans' attitudes towards the Charter relies upon two databases: the Attitudes Toward Civil Liberties and the Canadian Charter of Rights Survey (Charter Attitudes survey) conducted by York University's In-stitute for Social Research in 1987; and the Attitudes Toward Constitutional Reform in Alberta survey conducted by the Angus Reid Group in 1991 for Alberta's select special committee on constitutional reform. In one respect, the Angus Reid study is preferred since it surveyed a large sample of Albertans (N=1200). However, since its focus was the general issue of constitutional reform, only two questions were asked about the Charter specifically. A strength of the other database, the Charter Attitudes survey, is its comprehensive ques-tioning about the attitudes of Canadians towards civil liberties and the Charter. Its weakness, for the purpose of this essay, arises from the fact that only 186 residents of Alberta were included in its national general-population sample of 2,084.

The Charter Attitudes survey reveals that an overwhelming majority of Albertans (81.1 per cent) felt that the Charter was a good thing for Canada. Albertans also demonstrated strong support for the importance of equality in Canadian society. In answer to questions touching on issues of gender equality, the 'push' for equality rights, and the contribution equal treatment could make to reducing Canada's problems, healthy, if not overwhelming, majorities of Albertans acknowledged the importance of equality. Ninety-five per cent of the respondents felt that it was very or somewhat important to guarantee equality between men and women in all aspects of life; 68 per cent disagreed with the suggestion that we have gone too far in promoting equality rights in Canada; and 64 per cent felt that we would have fewer problems if people were treated more equally. On these issues, the views of Albertans were consistent with those of other Canadians.[41] This fact offers an indication that, at the level of mass politics, the Charter and its guarantees of equality rights were viewed warmly by Albertans.

Yet the picture of a pro-Charter public is muddied by responses to three other equality questions posed by the Charter Attitudes survey. A slight majority of Albertans (52.7 per cent) agreed with the following statement: 'This country would be better off if we worried less about how equal people are.' Some of those who felt this way had disagreed with the suggestion that we have pushed equal rights too far. When asked specifically about government's responsibility for increasing equality in society, the opinions of Albertans hardened against a more expansive interpretation of equality rights. More Albertans believed that laws guaranteeing equal job opportunities for minorities 'sometimes go too far' (37.1 per cent) than felt the need to make those laws stronger (24.1 per cent). Finally, nearly 70 per cent (69.4 per cent) of Albertans did not believe that it was the government's job to guarantee that all Canadians had equal opportunity to succeed. The composite picture framed by these questions is marked by ambivalence. Some respondents who felt that the Charter was a good thing or that guaranteeing equality between men and women was important set these sympathies aside when other dimensions of their attachment to equality were probed.

The picture is muddied still further by the data presented in the 1991 Angus Reid survey. This later survey offers us the opportunity to see if general attitudes towards the Charter remained as positive as the Charter Attitudes survey reported them to be. Both surveys asked questions about general attitudes towards the Charter: whether the Charter was a 'good thing or a bad thing' or whether it had had a 'negative effect or a positive effect.' As table 1 illustrates, by 1991 Albertans had lost much of their initial enthusiasm for the Charter. The percentage of survey respondents who viewed the Charter positively dropped significantly between 1987 and 1991.

This suspicion of the benefits of the Charter also appeared in replies to the second Charter question posed by the 1991 Argus Reid survey. As table 2 details, when asked whether the rights guarantees in the Charter should be expanded or limited, respondents were more likely to recommend the latter. This pattern is especially interesting because the question was presented in the context of the courts overturning provincial legislation. As with the preceding question, the responses to the query regarding future changes to the Charter stand in sharp contrast to the tenor of opinion Albertans offered in 1987.

The steep decline in public sympathy for the Charter may have had many causes. One of the most likely contributors was the fact that the Angus Reid

TABLE 1
Effect of the Charter of Rights, 1987, 1991

	Good thing / Positive	Bad thing / Negative	Unsure / Refused	(N)
1987 Charter Attitudes	81.9%	8.3%	10.7%	169
1991 Angus Reid	43.0%	35.0%	22.0%	1200

Question (1987): In general, do you think the Charter is a good thing or a bad thing for Canada?
Question (1991): Now I would like to talk briefly about the Canadian Charter of Rights and Freedoms. Since the Charter was adopted in 1982, some people say that it has had a negative effect by giving too much power to the courts, allowing them to overturn legislation passed by elected representatives. Others say that the Charter has had a positive effect, by upholding the individual rights of Canadians even if it means ruling against some existing legislation. What do you think?

TABLE 2:
Future changes to the Charter, 1991

Expanded	39%
Limited	47
Unsure/ Don't Know	14
(N)	1200

Question: There are various opinions about possible future changes to the Charter of Rights and Freedoms. Some people feel the current Charter should be expanded or enhanced in some areas, even if it means that the courts could over-rule provincial legislation. Others think that the Charter should be limited to make sure that courts and judges cannot over-rule laws passed by elected representatives. What do you think?

survey was conducted in the post-Meech Lake Accord/pre-Charlottetown Accord period. The debates over constitutional change waged during this period made it clear that the Charter was regarded as a vehicle that could take specific social groups to lands where they would enjoy greater constitutional status. The erosion of support for the Charter also may have been rooted in a second, related factor – public concern about the more concrete policy consequences that either must or could flow from an expansive interpretation of Charter rights. This possibility is suggested by the generally negative responses to the 1987 questions about the role of governments and legislation in increasing equality. Of great interest in the same connection were three questions posed by the Charter Attitudes survey that placed claims to rights recognition within

TABLE 3
Access to abortion, percentage by province

	Nfld	PEI	NS	NB	Que	Ont	Man	Sask	Alta	BC
Hospital committee	42.9	21.4	39.7	40.5	26.4	32.0	30.7	34.8	29.0	27.0
Dr's permission	33.9	60.7	47.6	38.1	67.0	42.5	37.3	39.4	52.9	47.6
On demand	21.4	10.7	11.9	17.9	2.7	24.1	28.0	24.2	16.1	24.2
(N)	56	28	126	84	364	522	75	66	155	252

Question: In your view, should a woman have to go through a hospital committee to get an abortion, or is it enough that any doctor is willing to approve it, or should there be abortion on demand?

concrete, public-policy contexts. These questions, which involved the issues of access to abortion, homosexual teachers, and the mandatory retirement of university professors, are worthy of analysis not only for the concrete contexts they provided but also because the provincial government had been called upon to respond to the claims associated with each of them.

The Charter Attitudes survey posed two questions on the subject of abortion, one asking if abortion is never, sometimes, or always justified and another asking whether and in what manner abortion should be regulated. Responses to the second question are considered here (see table 3). In comparison with other provincial population samples, Albertans occupied something of a middle ground on this issue; they were much more willing to tolerate abortion on demand than Quebec residents but far less disposed to this alternative than Manitobans. A majority of Albertans endorsed the view that an abortion should require the approval of a doctor. Table 4 details the provincial breakdowns of opinion on the question of homosexuals teaching in schools. The structure of opinion in Alberta, like that in all provinces with the possible exception of Quebec, certainly could not be described as liberal. However, Albertans were less illiberal than Canadians in most provinces – higher approval ratings and lower disapproval ratings were found only among Quebec and Ontario respondents. When it came to the issue of the mandatory retirement of university professors, nearly one-half of the Albertans who returned the mail-back component of the Charter Attitudes survey felt that mandatory retirement was acceptable. The general pattern of opinion on these questions reinforces the conclusion suggested by our earlier discussion of the mass public's enthusiasm for the Charter of Rights. A significant current of Alberta opinion tended to view rights guarantees quite conservatively.

TABLE 4
Allow homosexuals to teach school, percentage by province

	Nfld	PEI	NS	NB	Que	Ont	Man	Sask	Alta	BC
Approve	26.7	36.7	36.4	25.7	49.1	46.6	39.1	40.5	45.7	42.4
Qualify, Approve	4.0	–	3.7	6.7	9.6	3.1	2.3	6.0	3.2	3.0
Disapprove	65.3	53.3	54.9	65.7	36.7	44.5	57.5	50.0	45.7	49.8
Qualify, Disapprove	–	–	1.2	1.0	1.8	.5	–	–	–	1.0
(N)	75	30	162	105	436	622	87	84	186	297

Question: Do you approve or disapprove of allowing homosexuals to teach school in (respondent's province)?

TABLE 5
Requiring professor to retire at age 65, percentage by province

	Nfld	PEI	NS	NB	Que	Ont	Man	Sask	Alta	BC
Age Discrimination	24.5	31.8	30.4	22.1	18.8	38.0	32.8	34.5	32.2	39.0
Making room for younger	69.8	59.1	56.9	69.1	69.7	41.4	51.7	41.8	49.6	41.3
(N)	53	22	102	68	218	374	58	55	115	172

Question: Complete the following sentence in the way that best reflects your view: Requiring professors to retire at age 65 is: 1) an unjustified form of age discrimination. 2) an acceptable way of making room for younger professors.

Legislative Responses, Partisanship, and Political Geography

This profile of public opinion in Alberta is important to understanding the legislative conservatism which the province's governments have shown towards rights claims generally and Charter claims in particular. The limited reach of the Charter Omnibus Act, as well as the lengthy delay in responding to the Supreme Court's decision in *Mahé*, resonated well with an important segment of provincial public opinion. This is not to suggest that the government is a slave to public opinion. Proponents of state-centred theory suggest that, on occasion, states act autonomously and formulate goals and policies independently of interest groups and classes.[42] However, for Alan Cairns, the pre-eminent Canadian architect of state-centred theory, this summary of the intersection between states and societies is too simplistic. For him, the term 'state autonomy' describes well only a small portion of state-society relationships. Symbiosis and interdependence are labels more aptly suited as generalizations.[43] According to this imagery, public opinion on policy questions may bear the imprint of governments' efforts to mould it to conform to the government's agenda. This view gains strength from Richard Johnston's work: 'Public opinion thus does not act as a self-directed force, requiring only that someone pull the lever on the adding machine ... Instead, opinion is something to be evoked and mobilized.'[44] Consequently, when examining the fit between public opinion and Alberta's legislative responses to Charter decisions, we are open to the possibility that government has helped to create the structure of provincial opinion.

The Omnibus Act and the response to *Mahé* are not the only examples of conservatism which stand out in the province's record of responding to demands for the recognition and legislative promotion of rights. Each of the issues introduced at the end of the previous section – access to abortion, homosexuals teaching in the province's classrooms, and the mandatory retirement of university professors – has been a focus of recent political conflict in Alberta. Each has sparked demands that the province use its legislative and regulatory powers to give a broad and generous interpretation to the rights of women to secure an abortion, of homosexuals to teach in the province's classrooms, and of the aged to continue to work. Following the striking down of the Criminal Code's abortion section by the Supreme Court in *Morgentaler*,[45] Alberta for the most part ignored the demands from the province's feminist community for greater access to this medical procedure. Decriminalization of abortion did not necessitate, from the government's perspective, liberalization of access.[46] Most recently, Premier Klein has bowed to caucus pressure and announced that he will allow Progressive Conservative MLAs a free vote on the question of whether or not the government should withdraw funding for all abortions other than those performed because of physical danger to the mother.[47]

Regarding the treatment of homosexuals, the government has balked at a variety of demands to extend the protections offered by the Individual's Rights Protection Act (IRPA) to this segment of the population. The minister of labour ignored the Alberta Human Rights Commission's recommendation that a new protected ground, sexual orientation, be added to the IRPA. On occasion, the government seemingly has not thought it necessary to advance well-reasoned or compelling explanations for its failure to extend these protections. The Canadian Human Rights Advocate reported in 1987 that Labour Minister Ian Reid explained that homosexuals were excluded from the IRPA because they did not have distinctive physical characteristics. Religion, however, was included as a protected ground since some religions had identifiable dress such as turbans![48] More recently, the Charter of Rights has been used explicitly as the basis for arguing that sexual orientation must be added to the IRPA's list of protected categories. Delwin Vriend, a teacher at a private Christian college in Edmonton, was fired for his homosexuality. When Vriend approached the Alberta Human Rights Commission to complain about his treatment by the King's College, he was told that the commission would not hear his case because sexual orientation was not included as a protected ground under the IRPA. Turning to the courts, Vriend argued successfully at the Court of Queen's Bench that subsections 2(1), 3, 4, 7(1), 8(1), and 10 of the IRPA were inconsistent with the equality provisions of the Charter found in section 15(1). 'When his employment was terminated because of his personal characteristics,' wrote Justice Russell 'he was denied a legal remedy available to other similarly disadvantaged groups. That constitutes discrimination contrary to s. 15(1) of the Charter.'[49] The judge ruled that sexual orientation must be read into the IRPA; the offending sections should be interpreted, applied, and administered as if they contained the words sexual orientation.[50] Although the minister responsible for the Human Rights Commission agreed that protection for homosexuals should be included in the IRPA, this opinion, like the liberal view on abortion access, was unpopular within the Conservative caucus. Bowing to caucus sentiment, the justice minister announced that the province would appeal the decision.

On the issue of mandatory retirement, when the province amended the IRPA in order to bring the act's provisions into step with Charter guarantees, it appeared to outlaw mandatory retirement by amending the IRPA's definition of age.[51] However, the province also borrowed the approach found in section 1 of the Charter and added a provincial version of a reasonable and justifiable limits clause to the IRPA. Contraventions of the act, such as mandatory retirement, would be deemed not to have occurred if the alleged contravention 'was reasonable and justifiable in the circumstances.' This approach was later affirmed by the Supreme Court of Canada in *Dickason v. The Governors of the University of Alberta.*[52] There the Supreme Court of Canada ruled that the Court of Queen's Bench and an Alberta Human Rights Commission board of inquiry were mistaken in concluding that mandatory retirement was unreasonable and unjustified in light of the IRPA's right for protection from age discrimination. Mandatory retirement was deemed to be a reasonable and justifiable limitation under section 11(1) of the IRPA.[53] These additional examples of the province's reluctance to offer a more generous legislative response to demands for the recognition of rights fit well with the nature of public opinion on the issues of abortion, homosexuality, and mandatory retirement. Given the patterns of public opinion in Alberta, the government's conservative legislative responses arguably were sustained to some extent by considerable mass support.

What political or socio-economic variables are related to these patterns of public opinion on the issues of access to abortion, homosexual teachers, and mandatory retirement? To explore this question, ten variables in the Charter Attitudes survey were selected: provincial-party affiliation, community size, gender, present religious preference, education level, ethnic or cultural group, satisfaction with standard of living, employment status, union membership, and total family income. The first two of these variables, party affiliation and community size, were designated as political variables. Given the small size of the Alberta sample in the Charter Attitudes survey, provincial-party affiliation was split into a dichotomy. Respondents who declared themselves independents or affiliated themselves with a provincial political party were divided into two groups, Progressive Conservative (PC) identifiers and non-Progressive Conservative identifiers. Are provincial PC partisans more likely than those who were either independents or affiliated with another party to exhibit a conservative attitudinal profile towards the rights claims of homosexuals, the aged, and those who advocate more liberal access to abortion?

Community size was also treated as a political variable since it has become an increasingly important gauge for measuring the likelihood of Progressive Conservative electoral success. Since its rebirth in 1967 the geographic nature of Progressive Conservative support has changed dramatically. Urban Alberta propelled Peter Lougheed and the Conservatives to their first electoral victory in 1971; rural residents, particularly those in southern Alberta, remained loyal to the Social Credit party until the mid-1970s. By the late 1980s, the faithfulness of the Conservatives' urban supporters was in question. In Edmonton, first New Democrats and then Liberals displaced the Conservatives as the dominant provincial political party in the city. In Calgary, while the Conservatives continued to supply most of that city's legislative members, electoral contests became more competitive and the opposition parties established beachheads. The collapse of Tory fortunes in Edmonton and signs of weakness in Calgary led Keith Archer to conclude that the Conservative Party 'was increasingly relying on small town and rural support to maintain itself in power.'[54] This shift in the geographical support for the Progressive Conservatives has been symbolized by a number of events – among them, Premier Getty's personal defeat in the affluent riding of Edmonton-Whitemud in the 1989 election, his subsequent decision to re-enter the legislature by running in a by-election in the rural riding of Stettler, and the failure of the Progressive Conservatives to

TABLE 6
Significance levels of selected political and socio-economic variables

	Access to abortion	Homosexual teachers	Mandatory retirement	
Community	–	.023	.057	p =
Size	–	.171	.256	Cramer's V
Prov. Party	.060	.064	–	p =
Affiliation	.197	.142	–	Cramer's V
Religious	.033	–	–	p =
Preference	.256	–	–	Cramer's V
Employment	–	.000	–	p =
Status	–	.309	–	Cramer's V
Total Family	–	.000	–	p =
Income	–	.254	–	Cramer's V

elect a single member of the legislature from Edmonton in the 1993 election.[55] The increasing importance of rural Alberta to the survival of the Conservatives as the governing party was also arguably at the core of the government's decision to introduce 'single-municipality' and 'multi-municipality' electoral divisions by way of responding to British Columbia Supreme Court Justice McLachlin's judgment in *Dixon* that section 3 of the Charter demanded 'relative equality of voting power.'[56] Is the particular geographical pattern of political support upon which the Progressive Conservative Party increasingly relies also related to the attitudes of Albertans towards Charter rights? Do the attitudes of Albertans vary according to community size? Are rural Albertans more likely than their urban cousins to exhibit attitudes consonant with the legislative directions taken by government?

Table 6 presents a summary of the statistically significant relationships uncovered by this analysis. It shows clearly that the political variables, party affiliation and community size, fared well against the assorted socio-economic variables. On the issue of access to abortion, the religion variable produced the strongest, statistically significant relationship; provincial-party affiliation came next. Those who did not claim any religious preference were much more likely to support abortion on demand but, because of small cell sizes, these relationships should be interpreted very cautiously. This same caution applies to evaluating the relationship between employment status and the homosexuality issue. Full-time workers were more likely to approve of homosexuals serving as teachers than part-time workers or retirees, and family income produced the strongest relationship. People from households with incomes of less than $20,000

TABLE 7
Future changes to the Charter, by region and community size

	Calgary	Edmon.	North	Central	South	< 10,000	10,000– 100,000	> 100
Expand	44	46	38	35	35	35	37	45
Limit								
Unsure	42	45	46	48	53	50	51	44
/DK	14	9	15	17	12	15	12	12
N=1200								

per year were more likely to disapprove than were members of households with incomes of more than $20,000. But the relationships between the political variables and this issue were quite strong also. On the final issue, mandatory retirement, only community size produced a strong, statistically significant result.

The importance of the rural/urban cleavage to understanding variations in public support for the Charter of Rights is also suggested by the data in the 1991 Angus Reid survey. The summary of the survey results provided to the select special committee on constitutional reform presents the responses to the Charter questions by gender, age, birthplace, education level, household income, region, and community-population size. Table 7 shows that respondents from smaller population centres were more likely to urge limiting Charter rights than those from the province's two major metropolitan centres.[57]

The significance of provincial-party affiliation and community size to the nature of the opinions expressed by Albertans suggests that party politics plays a significant part in the government's tendency to respond conservatively to the Charter and rights issues. Calls for limiting rights, such as those cited earlier by Progressive Conservative back-benchers and cabinet ministers, have a certain appeal among PC party identifiers and to the small cities and rural areas which have become increasingly important to the electoral survival of Progressive Conservative governments.

Conclusion

In this examination of Charter politics in Alberta we have tried to accomplish several goals: detail the government's legislative response to the Charter and Charter review, examine public attitudes towards the Charter and its equality guarantees, and explore the relationship among the government's legislative responses, public opinion, and Progressive Conservative political support. Several conclusions stand out. First, the government's responses to the Charter and to judicial review of its guarantees have been quite conservative. The government has been reluctant to give the Charter's guarantees a broad, expansive interpretation and modify provincial statutes accordingly. In this respect, the province's stance has been aided by the self-restrained approach the judiciary has taken towards exercising the task of judicial review. Not only have the courts saved provincial legislation either by denying that rights were violated or by citing section 1, but, at least in the case of *R. v. Mahé*, they have refused to use their discretion to dictate the substantive measures government must take in order to respect the Charter's guarantees. This refusal to take a more activist stance helps us to understand why conservatism typifies the province's reaction to the Charter.

Judicial deference to legislators, however, is not entirely responsible for the nature of the government's reaction. The province's conservatism also has roots in public opinion and the nature of the governing party's political support. The pattern of public support for the Charter is quite striking when considered in light of the Charter's penultimate political purpose – forging a stronger sense of Canadian citizenship. Albertans view the Charter with a considerable amount of ambivalence and send mixed signals about the extent to which the Charter is fulfilling its political role. On the surface, there is widespread enthusiasm for the Charter and some dimensions of equality, but the possible public-policy ramifications of respecting equality-rights guarantees inspire generally negative responses. Moreover, the Angus Reid data suggests that the mass public's initial enthusiasm for the Charter has disintegrated markedly since 1987. In 1991 significant percentages of Albertans were Charter skeptics, especially when their support for expanding or limiting rights was placed in the context of the courts' ability to overturn provincial legislation. The political geography of support for rights within the province, when combined with the distinctive attitudes of Progressive Conservative partisans, promises to fuel this scepticism. At the very least we should expect these factors to keep rights issues at the centre of political conflict in the province for some time to come.

Notes

1 Roy Cook, ' "Old fogies" on Supreme Court rewriting the law, Fowler says,' *Edmonton Journal*, 15 Sept. 1990. The specific target of Fowler's anger was the Supreme Court's ruling that the constructive-murder clause of the Criminal Code

violated the Charter of Rights and Freedoms. One month later, Culture Minister
Doug Main reiterated the view that judicial interpretation of the Charter was
preventing politicians from giving Canadians the kind of country they wanted.
In his opinion, the Charter should have been removed from the constitution.
See Lynda Shorten, 'Main thinks Charter is in Canada's way,' *Edmonton Journal*,
18 Oct. 1990.

2 Diana Coulter, 'Charter blamed for youth crime,' *Edmonton Journal* 22 April 1994.

3 The Social Credit Act, the Credit of Alberta Regulation Act, the Bank Taxation
Act, and the Accurate News and Information Act were all declared *ultra vires* the
province by the courts.

4 *Canadian Industrial Gas & Oil Ltd. v. Government of Saskatchewan et al.* (1977),
6 W.W.R.; *Central Canada Potash Ltd. et al. v. Government of Saskatchewan et al.*
(1978), 6 W.W.R. See also John Richards and Larry Pratt, *Prairie Capitalism:
Power and Influence in the New West* (Toronto: McClelland and Stewart 1979),
especially chapter 11.

5 Alberta, *Harmony in Diversity: A New Federalism for Canada* (October 1978), 11.

6 Alan C. Cairns, 'A Defence of the Citizens' Constitution Theory: A Response to
Ian Brodie and Neil Nevitte,' *Canadian Journal of Political Science*, vol. 26
(1993), 261–2. See also the work of Peter H. Russell, 'The Political Purposes of the
Canadian Charter of Rights and Freedoms,' *Canadian Bar Review*, vol. 61 (1983),
30–54; Rainer Knopff and F. L. Morton, 'Nation-Building and the Canadian
Charter of Rights and Freedoms,' in *Constitutionalism, Citizenship and Society in
Canada*, eds. Alan Cairns and Cynthia Williams (Toronto: University of Toronto
Press 1985).

7 One of the few published studies examining the attitudes of citizens towards the
Charter is Paul M. Sniderman, Joseph F. Fletcher, Peter H. Russell, and Philip E.
Tetlock, 'Political Culture and Double Standards: Mass and Elite Attitudes
Towards Language Rights in the Canadian Charter of Rights and Freedoms,'
Canadian Journal of Political Science, vol. 22 (1989), 259–84.

8 The phrase was used by the Hon. Neil Crawford, the province's attorney general.
See Alberta, *Hansard*, 29 May 1993, 1,225.

9 Ibid.

10 Gurnett, ibid., 1,227.

11 Focusing on the Supreme Court, Morton, Russell, and Riddell note that Charter
claimants have won 33 per cent of the cases heard by the Supreme Court between
1982 and 1992. See F.L. Morton, Peter H. Russell, and Troy Riddell, 'The First
Decade of the Charter of Rights, 1982–92: A Statistical Analysis of Supreme Court
Decisions,' paper presented to the annual meeting of the Canadian Political Science
Association, University of Calgary, 12 June 1994.

12 This observation does not presume that all Charter cases or decisions have comparable implications for public policy.
13 In another case, *Vriend v. Alberta (A.G.)*, the Court of Queen's Bench ruled that sections 2(1), 3, 4, 7(1), 8(1), and 10 of the Individual Rights Protection Act violated section 15(1) of the Charter and that the words 'sexual orientation' should be read into the IRPA. The following legislation was struck down by the Court of Queen's Bench: Law Society of Alberta rule 154 made pursuant to the Legal Profession Act (a violation of section 6[2]), in *Black v. Law Society of Alberta*, [1984] 57 A.R. 1; Alberta Rules of Court, rule 593(1) (a violation of sections 6[2] and 15), in *Kask v. Shimizu*, [1986] 69 A.R. 343; Motor Vehicle Administration Act. R.S.A. 1980, c. M–22, s. 110 (a violation of the section 7 right to liberty), in *R. v. Neale*, [1985] 62 A.R. 350; Highway Traffic Act, R.S.A. 1980, c. H–7, s. 65(3)(a) (a violation of the section 7 right to liberty), in *R. v. Maier*, [1989] 94 A.R. 163; Workers Compensation Act, R.S.A. 1980, c. W–16, s. 18 (a violation of sections 7 and 15), struck only in the case of *Budge v. Workers' Compensation Board (No. 2)*, [1987] 80 A.R. 207; Maintenance and Recovery Act, R.S.A. 1980, c. M–2, s. 23(1)(b) (a violation of section 15), in *Milne v. AG Alberta*, [1990], 75 Alta. L.R. (2d) 155 and *L.M.S.M. & M.T.S.M. v. D.S.*, [1990], 107 A.R. 152.
14 [1987] 80 A.R. 347 (Q.B.). This reversal was upheld by the Court of Appeal. See [1988] 86 A.R. 268 (C.A.).
15 [1987] 80 A.R. 354 (Q.B.).
16 *R. v. Mahé*, [1985] 39 Alta. L.R. (2d) (Q. B.) 243.
17 *R. v. Mahé*, [1987] 80 A.R. 161 (C.A.).
18 Ibid., 189.
19 *R. v. Neale*, [1986] 71 A.R. 337 (C.A.)
20 *R. v. Maier*, [1990] 101 A.R. 126.
21 *Budge v. Workers' Compensation Board (No. 2)*, [1991] 111 A.R. 228 (C.A.).
22 *Black v. Law Society of Alberta*, [1985] 68 A.R. 259 (C.A.). Whereas the Court of Queen's Bench had found that rule 154 violated section 6(2), the Court of Appeal ruled that both Law Society rules 75(b) and 154 violated the freedom of association guarantee found in section 2(d).
23 *Grier v. Alberta Optometric Association*, [1985] 62 A.R. 146 (Q.B.); [1987] 79 A.R. 36 (C.A.).
24 *Edmonton Journal v. Alberta*, [1987] 78 A.R. 375.
25 *Black v. Law Society of Alberta*, [1989] 96 A.R. 352 (S.C.C.).
26 *Edmonton Journal v. Alberta*, [1989] 103 A.R. 321 (S.C.C.).
27 Ian T. Urquhart, 'Federalism, Ideology, and Charter Review: Alberta's Response to Morgentaler,' *Canadian Journal of Law and Society*, vol. 4 (1989), 160.

28 'Judicial Nullification of Statutes Under the Charter of Rights and Freedoms, 1982–1988,' *Alberta Law Review*, vol. 2 (1990), 414–15.
29 I have used this logic elsewhere to help understand the reaction of the Alberta government to the Supreme Court's decision in *Morgentaler et al v. The Queen*, [1988] 1 S.C.R. 30. See Urquhart, 'Federalism, Ideology, and Charter Review.'
30 Rainer Knopff and F. L. Morton, *Charter Politics* (Scarborough. Ont.: Nelson Canada 1992), 177.
31 Ibid., 178.
32 Allen Panzeri, 'Dinning hopes to bring in francophone bill quickly,' *Edmonton Journal*, 28 March 1990.
33 'Notes for Remarks by the Honourable Don Getty, Premier of Alberta,' 9 Jan. 1992, 13–14. Health Minister Nancy Betkowski disassociated herself from the premier's remarks. She was the only member of the Getty cabinet to do so.
34 Alberta, *Hansard*, (27 Sept. 1993), 497.
35 Ibid., 499.
36 *R. v. Mahé*, [1990] 72 Alta. L.R. (2d) 297 (S.C.C.).
37 The Supreme Court concluded that regulation 490/82, which stated that approximately 20 per cent of class time must be spent on English-language instruction, was a prima facie infringement upon section 23 and was not saved by section 1 of the Charter. The Court did leave open the possibility, however, that Alberta could in the future argue that some minimum amount of English instruction was a reasonable limitation on the section 23 right.
38 *R. v. Mahé*, [1990] 72 Alta. L.R. (2d) 297 (S.C.C.).
39 Richard Johnston, *Public Opinion and Public Policy in Canada* (Toronto: University of Toronto Press 1986), 210.
40 Sniderman, Fletcher, Russell, and Tetlock, 'Political Culture and Double Standards.'
41 The relationship between province and the variable 'treated more equally, have fewer problems' was significant to less than the .001 level. However, the Cramer's V, the measure used here to gauge the strength of this relationship, was not particularly strong (.096). The relationships among province and 'the Charter as a good or bad thing,' 'gender equality,' and 'pushing equal rights too far' were not significant to less than the .05 level.
42 Alexandra Dobrowolsky, 'The Charter and Mainstream Political Science: Waves of Practical Contestation and Changing Theoretical Currents,' in this volume.
43 Alan C. Cairns, 'The Embedded State: State-Society Relations in Canada,' in *State and Society: Canada in Comparative Perspective*, ed. Keith Banting (Toronto: University of Toronto Press 1985), 78–9.
44 Johnston, *Public Opinion and Public Policy in Canada*, 226.
45 *Morgentaler, Smoling, and Scott v. The Queen*, (1988), 37 C.C.C. (3d) 449.

46 This policy response is detailed in Urquhart, 'Federalism, Ideology, and Charter Review.'

47 Tom Arnold, 'Klein OKs free vote on abortion,' *Edmonton Journal*, 19 July 1995, A1.

48 'Update: human rights items,' 3 *Canadian Human Rights Advocate*, vol. 3 (1987), 13 – as quoted in Alberta Civil Liberties Research Centre, *Annotation of the Individual's Rights Protection Act* (Calgary: May 1992), 30.

49 *Vriend v. Alberta (A.G.)* [1994] 6 W.W.R. 431.

50 Marina Jimenez and Corinna Schuler, 'Gays must be protected – judge,' *Edmonton Journal*, 13 April 1994, A11.

51 Originally, age was defined as any age between forty-five and sixty-five years; in 1985 this was amended to mean eighteen years or older.

52 *Dickason v. The Governors of the University of Alberta*, 127 A.R. 241.

53 For a criticism of the Supreme Court's decision in *Dickason*, see Shirish P. Chotalia, 'The Supreme Court and Mandatory Retirement: Sanctioning the Status Quo,' *Constitutional Forum*, vol. 4 (1993), 67–70.

54 Keith Archer, 'Voting Behaviour and Political Dominance in Alberta, 1971–1991,' in *Government and Politics in Alberta*, eds. Allan Tupper and Roger Gibbins (Edmonton: University of Alberta Press 1992) 131.

55 Since the 1993 election one Edmonton MLA, Julius Yankowsky, has joined the Conservatives after leaving the Liberal Party caucus. A second Edmonton Liberal MLA, Andrew Beniuk, has been thrown out of the Liberal caucus for his very public criticisms of newly elected Liberal leader Grant Mitchell. Beniuk sits as an independent Liberal in the legislature.

56 *Dixon v. British Columbia (Attorney General)*, [1989] 4 W.W.R. 393. For a discussion of Alberta's response to this decision see Rainer Knopff and F. L. Morton, 'Charter Politics in Alberta: Constituency Apportionment and the Right to Vote,' and David J. Bercuson and Barry Cooper, 'Electoral Boundaries: An Obstacle to Democracy in Alberta,' in *Drawing Boundaries: Legislatures, Courts, and Electoral Values*, eds. John C. Courtney, Peter MacKinnon, and David E. Smith (Saskatoon: Fifth House Publishers 1992).

57 Although these relationships were statistically significant they were not as strong as the relationship between age and future changes to the Charter. This latter relationship was significant to the .001 level. Nearly one-half of the respondents under thirty-five years of age advocated expanding Charter rights while nearly two-thirds of those fifty-five years or older recommended limits.

3

Business, Economic Rights, and the Charter

RICHARD W. BAUMAN

It is a curious phenomenon in Canadian constitutional law that business firms, whose *raison d'être* is purely economic, have succeeded in sustaining claims under the Canadian Charter of Rights and Freedoms.[1] After all, economic rights are not supposed to be included in or protected by the Charter. The business firm is an economic vehicle, devoted to economic goals and guided by economic rationality. What rights could possibly matter to the firm except economic types of rights? The present essay explores this constitutional conundrum, asking how the evolving interpretation of the Charter has provided private firms with a fresh range of opportunities to assert their interests against the vicissitudes of government regulation.

Particularly in the period leading up to the adoption of the Charter in 1982, participants in the process of entrenchment were careful to point out that the purpose of the Charter was to enunciate, protect, and enforce basic, inalienable 'human' rights and interests. According to the liberal-democratic theory underlying the Charter, fundamental freedoms necessary to the flourishing of each individual Canadian were guaranteed by the Charter and were worthy of the utmost protection by the guardians of the Charter, generally the judiciary.[2] Other rights, such as economic or commercial rights, certainly should continue to be legally protected in statutory or common-law form, but they do not necessarily deserve constitutional status.[3]

In light of this distinction between human and mere economic rights, an observer, situated in 1982, might understandably have concluded that the Charter would be of little assistance to business in terms of seriously affecting the

* An earlier version of this essay was presented at a faculty seminar at Duke University's School of Law in November 1994. In revising the text, the author had the benefit of insightful comments from participants in the seminar, especially Laura Underkuffler, as well as from David Schneiderman.

relationship between commercial enterprises and the various levels of government in Canada. From the evidence afforded by Parliamentary debates, public hearings, and stories in the financial and legal press covering events in the period preceding the enactment of a Charter regime, there was only minor controversy over how business enterprises might be served, one way or the other, by the rights contained in the Charter. Such controversy became marked only after the Charter came into force. Then, within a few years, the debate intensified, especially once it became clear who was able to invoke Charter guarantees and what this meant for the scope of permissible government regulation of business activities. During these years businesses grew increasingly mindful of their constitutional capacities, while critics of business firms as bearers of Charter rights grew more and more dismayed.

At the same time that business enterprises have used the Charter to advantage, the Supreme Court has rejected the suggestion that economic rights per se are protected under various Charter guarantees. Just as property rights were expressly excluded from the draft of the Charter that finally was adopted, so too economic rights were denied express recognition or protection under the Charter. Although, as we shall see, it is a delicate matter to separate property rights from economic rights, one difference between these two classes of rights is that efforts have been made periodically to insert the former into the Charter. No similar groundswell of support has appeared in relation to economic rights.

The history of the Charter to date makes it clear that in many instances business enterprises have benefitted significantly from the suits to enforce the Charter. Yet businesses have not simply stood idle and watched Charter litigation unfold; they have actively launched many applications to have laws or regulations reviewed by the courts. While the Supreme Court has declared that, except in special circumstances, section 7 of the Charter was not intended to benefit commercial firms, this is not the end of the matter. If one examines the whole context in which rights under the Charter have been invoked and elaborated, it becomes evident that there have been many instances, both in the Supreme Court of Canada and in courts below, where economic rights have been vindicated through successful Charter challenges to government actions. Business interests have not been disregarded or subordinated. On balance, they have so far been well served in the course of Charter history.

It is surprising that there has been relatively little systematic review of the degree to which economic rights have received, indirectly at least, a powerful boost through Charter litigation. Nor has there been significant commentary on why economic rights, especially those possessed by business enterprises, should not be raised to an express level of constitutional solicitude. The muted treatment of such themes in Canadian law contrasts with the situation in the United

States, where sweeping arguments have been articulated about the economic elements of the American Bill of Rights, and where there is a burgeoning literature calling for a reorientation of Supreme Court doctrine to ensure stricter scrutiny of legislation that affects property and economic rights.[4]

The first part of this essay recalls how representatives of business responded to proposals for a Canadian Charter and how some of those same organizations have continued to voice concerns during the subsequent decade of Charter jurisprudence. The second part begins by surveying the arguments in favour of explicitly including economic rights in the Charter and then explains, using public choice theory, why this has not happened. In the third section, we review Charter jurisprudence, primarily as developed by the Supreme Court of Canada, to determine the extent to which economic interests have been factors in the adjudication of Charter disputes. It turns out that economic rights have not been ignored. Although they do not form a separate rubric in the structure of the Charter, economic rights nevertheless play an important incidental role in how enumerated rights are understood and applied. The fourth section ex-amines the disparity between what public choice theory would predict about the Supreme Court as a policy-making body and the approach the Court has actually taken. Contrary to the expectations of public-choice theory, economic rights have not been given minimal protection under the Charter; instead, the Court, apparently guided by no particular theory, has discovered the vital eco-nomic aspects of Charter rights and freedoms. The Court has not been so restrictive in its interpretation, nor has it been so self-abnegating, as public choice theory might have forecast.

The conclusion of this essay is that the private-business sector should be confident that its interests are not suffering from neglect under the Charter. Far from simply providing another opportunity to justify government incursions into the 'private' market-place, the Charter offers mixed results in relation to commerce. Some of these consequences are disavantageous to economic enterpise, many are signally favourable. By affirming that constitutional claims can, in some instances, include economic elements, the Supreme Court of Canada has made the Charter an important source of power by which business can influence public policy.

Business Reviews the Charter

It is fair to say that, in the discussions from 1980 to 1982 surrounding the adoption of the Charter, there was relatively little discussion of the need to protect the economic rights of business against government intervention, limitation, or destruction. Property rights attracted far more attention. In presentations before the special joint committee on the constitution, nobody clamoured for entrenching, for example, freedom of contract. Such references as there were to economic rights took a different tack. One member of Parliament proposed adding to the constitutional-amendment package a limit on any government's ability to incur a deficit.[5] Another context in which economic rights were discussed was with a view to guaranteeing the economic and social rights of individuals. One presenter criticized the draft Charter for failing to stipulate the right to work, the right to unionize, the right to an adequate standard of living, and the right to protection from unemployment.[6] Even groups that one might have guessed would affirm the need to entrench rights associated with commerce failed to push vigorously on this issue. In their appearance before the special joint committee, leaders of the Alberta Chamber of Commerce opposed outright the adoption of the Charter at that juncture, calling for patriation of the constitution first and consideration of entrenched rights later.[7]

One of the few voices raised in favour of including economic rights in the Charter was that of the Business Council on National Issues (BCNI), an interest group claiming to represent 150 large firms across the country. It has been called the 'voice of Canadian business,' although it denies that it is a 'lobby group' representing the 'narrow interests that have been traditionally associated with business.'[8] The BCNI recommended the insertion of property rights, the explicit extension of Charter rights to 'corporate persons,' and the addition of 'mobility rights' designed to break down barriers to interprovincial trade. The last proposal took the form of a right to be enumerated in the Charter that would guarantee the movement of 'goods, services, capital, and entrepreneurship freely within Canada.'[9]

As pointed out above, there was during the same period considerable discussion of the advisability of including property rights in the Charter.[10] In this latter context, the concept of 'property' dominating the debates was based heavily on rights associated with real property. According to proponents of entrenching property rights, the primary goal was to set up a constitutional impediment to the taking of land by a government without adequate compensation or due process. In the end, of course, property rights were not included among the fundamental freedoms or legal rights contained in the Charter.[11] Among the reasons for this decision was the fear among several provinces that their jurisdiction over 'property and civil rights in the province,' including expropriation matters, would be curtailed by the proposed Charter right.[12] Calls for the insertion of property rights resumed soon after the adoption of the

Charter, and they have continued down to the most recent round of constitutional changes.[13] There have been some legislative attempts to amend the Charter by adding property rights, though these initiatives have failed to muster the support necessary to succeed.[14]

In reviewing the discussions in question, it is apparent how rights of property and economic rights are intimately related. Depending on the meaning assigned to each of these expressions, the rights referred to may not just overlap but even be treated as the same. For example, in its widest extension, the term 'property rights' may subsume economic rights. The owner of the subject matter of property may be defined by the economic incidents which are associated with that subject matter, including the right to use it productively; the right to lease or sell it; the right to occupy it exclusively; the right to let it fall into disuse or to destroy it; and the right to a remedy when the use of that subject matter is interfered with by someone else. It is also possible, conversely, to describe a firm's economic rights in largely proprietary terms. The firm's contracts with its suppliers, customers, or employees constitute something the firm 'owns' and something that it can choose to assign to another party; the firm may have a property interest in its products, its image, its trade secrets, its trademarks, and its client lists; the firm's business opportunities can be analogized to rights in property for the sake of determining when an opportunity has been unjustly usurped by a competing firm. On this understanding also, interferences with a corporation's ability to raise capital may amount to a restriction on its property rights, for the firm has created the shares it proposes to distribute. Similarly, corporate-taxation measures that require remittance of a portion of the firm's income to the government could be construed as interfering with what belongs to the firm as its property, that is, its profits. Because of the elasticity of the definitions that may be used to capture what constitutes either a property right or an economic right, it is often difficult to determine, in a constitutional context, precisely which specific rights are ultimately eligible for entrenchment.

Close attention should be paid to the kinds of examples used by speakers and legislators who have addressed the entrenchment of property rights. Most often, the rights in question have to do with the ownership and use of real property, or land and its appurtenances. The principal concern motivating those in favour of constitutionalizing property rights has traditionally been the capacity of government to expropriate private property without, first, having to establish a public purpose for the transaction. Other concerns for such people are that government is not constrained constitutionally by having to pay compensation to the former owner of the property, and that there is no constitutional right entitling the owner of the property proposed for expropriation or anyone else to a hearing before the expropriating authority. Though this is the dominant scenario cited in favour of protecting property rights through the Charter, what might eventually constitute a 'taking' that is covered by the constitutional guarantee can be quite different from a complete expropriation of an owner's land. Governmental measures, such as a change in land-use designation that diminishes the market value of privately held land, may arguably entitle the owner to sue the government for infringement of a Charter guarantee.[15] The owner need not be in the business of real estate development in order to claim an unconstitutional interference with property rights. Even the owner of a house in an area affected by a regulatory change that has an impact on the market value of the house could presumably claim the benefit of an entrenched right to the possession and enjoyment of property. Another example of an expropriation that does not involve the dispossession of the owner is the denial of permission by the government to exploit subsurface mineral rights because the claims in question are located within provincial-park boundaries.[16]

At any rate, the political process by which property rights were eventually omitted from the Charter involved widespread input from the federal government, provincial governments, and diverse groups which made submissions debating the merits of various draft proposals that, at some points, included property rights among the enumerated legal rights. With the rejection of property rights, one might have expected that courts would be careful not to import into the realm of Charter protection any claims that amounted to constitutional protection for the property rights of the claimants. Owing to the close association of property rights with economic rights, courts might similarly have refused to interpret the Charter in a manner that would tend to constitutionalize economic rights. As will become clear later in this discussion, that is not what courts have done.

A review of the Parliamentary discussions in the 1980–2 period reveals scant consideration of the extent to which business firms and entire industries might be affected by the advent of the Charter. In general, such discussion as there was revolved around whether property rights should be included in the Charter and how this would protect both foreign and domestic corporations from nationalization, as well as how it would protect family businesses.[17] Within the Special Joint Committee responsible for considering the draft Charter, various amendments were proposed to clarify or to limit the availability of the Charter to different classes of constitutional claimants, but there was no general discussion of the degree to which business would be aided or hampered by the operation of the Charter.[18] It was only in the aftermath of the constitutional changes made in 1982 that the financial and daily press began to feature articles on the importance to business of the new constitutional environment created through the Charter.

By 1985, owing in part to the landmark decisions of the Supreme Court on the standing of corporations to sue under the Charter, it had become more widely recognized that the Charter provides leverage against undue and unnecessary government regulation, that is, where the state intrudes into a sphere of economic activity best left to the control of market forces.[19] Such a recognition reinvigorated the movement to seek explicit protection of property rights in the Charter, a goal that some groups kept constantly in their sights throughout the 1980s.[20] As it did in 1981, the BCNI in 1992 continued to press for entrenchment of property rights, with the proviso that both the 'precise nature' of such rights and underlying rationale be spelled out by the special joint committee appointed to develop a package of constitutional reforms.[21] Before the federal government withdrew its proposal for entrenching property rights, there was a significant amount of public debate reviewing the merits of such a change.[22] Critics of the Supreme Court of Canada's tendency to grant standing to corporations to assert various Charter rights also argued against the proposals to add property rights to the Charter.[23]

Part of the critique of the Supreme Court's approach to Charter adjudication in the 1980s particularly has focused on the extent to which corporations have been permitted to bring constitutional challenges. Before 1982, of course, corporations had regularly resorted to the courts to impugn legislation on federalism grounds. Some of the very earliest cases that reached the Privy Council arose from a corporation alleging that a law was *ultra vires* the legislature which enacted it.[24] Throughout the century or so of jurisprudence on disputes over the respective jurisdiction of the federal Parliament and the provinces, there was little question about the standing of a corporate litigant to launch a federalism challenge. The most contested cases over a litigant's standing involved individuals or public interest groups seeking a judicial declaration of a law's invalidity.[25] In federalism cases, so long as a corporation is affected by the application of a law, the corporate party can bring an action challenging the constitutionality of the legislation. This willingness of Canadian courts to entertain corporate actions in the division-of-powers context evidently carried over into Charter adjudication with relative ease. Although there was some academic discussion as to whether the Supreme Court would ultimately permit corporations to bring Charter applications, and some criticism of the Court's eventual approach to the issue, a significant number of Charter claimants have been corporations.[26]

It appears that Supreme Court doctrine regarding corporate standing under the Charter can be divided into two phases. In the first, the Court entertained challenges with little inquiry into the justification for corporate standing. In a second phase, however, dating roughly from 1989 to the present, the Supreme Court has become more sharply aware of the theoretical dimensions and practical consequences of permitting corporations to launch Charter challenges. Chris Tollefson has offered a useful scheme that puts the Supreme Court's various approaches into relief against an historical background of corporate conceptions. His analysis shows the difference between the phases and the unsettled state of the law resulting from Supreme Court justices choosing one conception over another.[27]

The following discussion does not fix on the corporation-as-constitutional-claimant. To be sure, the debate about who should be allowed to bring Charter cases is important and the statistics on the matter are interesting to interpret.[28] The reach of the analysis in this essay, however, is broader. Whether or not a claimant is a corporation, certain economic rights or interests may be invoked and invite judicial elaboration. The claimant may be an individual in business or simply a taxpayer. The business may be a sole proprietorship or a family enterprise, such as a prairie wheat farm. The individual may assert economic rights as an employee, alone or as a member of a trade union. Or the claimant may be the union itself, or a partnership, a professional association, or a business corporation. The question of which types of business organization or relationship may lead to a constitutional challenge is purposely left open in the ensuing analysis. There is no single paradigm for what 'business' means. It will depend on the context created within each part of the discussion. Rather than concentrate on the particular status of the party that asserts constitutional rights, the focus of this article is on how the Supreme Court conceives of the economic aspects of rights which belong to that party. Of course, in particular cases to be discussed, the type of enterprise at the centre of the Charter challenge will be noted. When the term 'firm' is used generally, it can refer to any commercial enterprise ranging from a large, multinational corporate conglomerate to Joe's Confectionery, the small neighbourhood shop that may or may not benefit from the Charter victories won by its larger and more resourceful business competitors.[29]

Another stage in the evolution of the Charter's impact on businesses can be traced from the delayed implementation of section 15 and its guarantees against various forms of discrimination. While business generally welcomed the Charter as a rampart against regulatory control, private enterprises and business groups also came to fear that, through the application of section 15, courts would be empowered to set standards which would interfere with a firm's freedom to conduct its own business affairs (for example, in employment situations or in voicing political opinions and preferences).[30] This would be another form of undesirable official intrusion into the realm of private business conduct. Furthermore, business was concerned that the Charter would be used by litigious 'special interest' groups, sometimes referred to as the 'court party,' which have narrow purposes and specific political agendas. These groups derive their constitutional identity from the recognition of various differences and interests in sections 15 to 29 of the Charter. Appeals to the Charter have helped such groups 'reverse the decisions of democratically elected representatives.'[31] When Rainer Knopff and F.L. Morton defined what is meant by the 'court party,' which collectively has been successful in using the Charter, they included various 'citizen' interest groups as well as 'important elements within state bureaucracies, law schools, the broader intellectual community, and the media.'[32] Conspicuously missing from this list are business firms or groups that have employed Charter politics. 'Court party' as a pejorative ideological term has passed into journalistic usage.[33]

In the third part of this article, decisions illustrating both these expectations are described. That is, businesses have used the Charter on numerous occasions to resist government control and regulation. Constitutional challenges have become an important strategic device for businesses as they have made political gains through the process of Charter review. In addition, business organizations have been made uneasy by the proliferation of Charter jurisprudence that imposes judicially created standards of conduct on private enterprise. These developments might encourage business groups to seek further changes in the contents of the Charter, just as during the preparation of the constitutional-amendment package in 1992 business firms urged profound reform of the economic-union provisions in the Constitution Act, 1867.[34]

Arguments about the Express Protection of Economic Rights under the Charter

Other writers have lucidly advocated ways of interpreting the Charter so that the social-welfare rights of individuals could be protected through its equality or section 7 guarantees.[35] The relative lack of success so far in judicial recognition of such individual social rights has dispirited some Canadian constitutional commentators. Charter critics, for their part, have questioned this constitutional strategy and see the Charter as a dead end: ordinary political processes, they claim, still offer the best chance for progressive lawmaking.[36]

The purpose of this section is to review the strongest plausible reasons for incorporating another form of rights – economic ones – in the Charter. Many of the arguments are associated with public choice theory, a body of academic work based on an economic understanding of politics. If public choice reasons are unable to justify entrenching economic rights, it is difficult to imagine that any more robust defence of entrenchment could succeed. Whether these reasons are cogent and realistic, given our brief experience with the Charter, are issues deferred until later in the essay.

Why Economic Rights Should Be Included in the Charter

In Canada, there is only a smattering of literature about the merits of incorporating economic rights explicitly into the Charter. In the United States, however, arguments to this effect have been advanced by such well-known constitutional scholars as Richard Epstein and Cass Sunstein of the University of Chicago Law School. One of their key ideas is that economic rights deserve the same respect given to rights which are already constitutionalized. By protecting economic rights to a lesser degree, we have created the impression that those rights do not contribute to human dignity and to such liberal virtues as autonomy. When it is said that protecting ideas is more important than protecting wealth, the implication is that economic rights should remain subsidiary and vulnerable to unfettered government regulation.[37] The advocates of entrenching economic rights dispute this subordination. From their point of view, the freedom of individuals to make economic choices, to organize their lives around particular economic priorities, or to participate in the market-place through their labour, their production, or their entrepreneurial investments, is just as important as their freedom of expression or freedom of association. Ringing phrases have been used by the Supreme Court of Canada to characterize the vital interests served by the utmost legal protection of a person's conscientious beliefs, privacy, expressive opportunities, or associational rights. Similar language could be applied to a person's freedom to select economic goals and adopt the means to achieve those goals. As we shall see, in *Irwin Toy* the Court framed its purposive analysis of freedom of expression in terms of the values of self-government, truth in the market-place, and individual autonomy and self-fulfilment.[38] Economic liberties can serve precisely the same values. Freedom from interference by government with commercial contracts for supplies or labour, with economic exchanges, and with the maximization of personal utility through productive and consumer behaviour can equally contribute to the achievement of these goals. The ideals of economic markets and political democracy, of constitutionalism and the rule of law, can be conceived as intertwined.[39] Failure to honour any one of these promotes disrespect for the others.

Another argument in favour of constitutionalizing economic rights is that their preservation is necessary to protect non-economic freedoms. This conception of one right as more fundamental than other constitutional rights has been uttered repeatedly in American constitutional debates over the past two centuries.[40] It appeals to the political consequences of the destruction or diminution of economic rights. Proponents of economic rights are fond of describing how the lack of respect for free-market economic liberties in nations formerly under communist regimes undermined all political freedoms as well.[41] Where the state effectively controls economic decision-making through a centralized bureaucracy, freedoms such as the right to hold and express certain beliefs, or the right to associate with whomever one chooses, quickly become meaningless, because one fears that economic opportunities will be withheld. Citizens' interest in criticizing the government will be chilled. It does not matter in what glowing terms freedom of expression is nominally entrenched in a constitutional document. When citizens feel that their economic rights are not secure against government action, they will not use their political freedom to the full extent. That this is a real, and not just a notional possibility, has been recognized in the United States, where courts have developed the doctrine of unconstitutional conditions.[42] This doctrine prohibits government from attaching conditions to social benefits (such as employment or welfare) permitting the withholding of such benefits if the recipient tries to exercise a constitutional right. For example, the government cannot make social benefits conditional on the recipient's non-exercise of freedom of expression.[43]

A third argument in favour of inserting economic rights into the Charter is that their exercise is an important model for how constitutional rights generally should be used responsibly. When people use their right to vote, their right to express themselves freely, or their right to peaceful assembly, such enjoyment can often result in significant externalities. In the words of Jonathan Macey, 'there is a strong proclivity towards irresponsibility in the expression of non-economic rights.'[44] For example, there is no direct political or other cost to individuals who spoil their ballot, vote for an outrageous, 'flaky' candidate, or support a referendum proposal that runs counter to those individuals' own economic interests. An individual voter may feel that one vote makes no difference at all to the democratic outcome and may simply use the opportunity to register a whimsical or insincere choice. If voters are asked in a referendum to decide whether to impose additional taxes and use public funds to pay for a costly recycling program, an individual voter may 'put ideological considerations ahead of economic interests' and vote in favour of the proposal, despite that individual's own self-interest, calculated on a cost-benefit comparison.[45] The voter gets the satisfaction of expressing an ideological commitment to a clean environment, knowing that a solitary vote will almost surely make no difference in the final result.[46] Macey points out, as an aside, that a better way to involve individuals in the process of environmental decision making might be to structure the costs in terms of the price individual consumers pay for goods, the production, use or disposal of which have an environmental impact. If consumer demand reflected a real commitment to a cleaner environment, market prices could be increased to cover the cost to industry of investing voluntarily in pollution abatement.

Another example of the potential for irresponsible use of Charter rights is the Holocaust revisionist. This person can take advantage of a constitutional right to express the 'truth' behind the story of six million Jewish victims of the Nazi extermination policy. This right can be exercised at relatively little cost to the speaker, who may claim that it is worthwhile to say unpleasant or hurtful things even if individuals or groups are harmed thereby. Such was the justification claimed by the accused in *R. v. Zundel*, whose conviction for 'spreading false news' was overturned by the Supreme Court of Canada, because the law under which he was charged was found to be constitutionally infirm.[47] As Stanley Fish has pointed out, it is arguable that there is no such thing as 'free' speech, either in the sense that speech can be without consequences or in the sense that it can take place in some pure form without limitations: 'independently of a community context informed by interest (that is, purpose), expression would be at once inconceivable and unintelligible.'[48] Exercises of freedom of expression can have both the purpose and effect of injuring groups identified by the speaker. The general level of tolerance and liberality in a society sinks when intolerant speech becomes accepted as part of the norm.

Debates about the boundaries that governments are entitled to draw around the different varieties of expressive activity would be improved if they took into account economic models of analysis. Incorporating economic rights into the Charter would remind citizens that legislation, including the choice of rights to include in the Charter itself, has both costs and benefits. As the Charter stands now, the fundamental freedoms set out in section 2 can be invoked to legitimate conduct that largely defies the need to take into account negative consequences of the conduct. To many individuals, the freedoms of expression and association are 'pure' goods, any qualification or restriction of which is suspect. If economic liberties were placed in the Charter, they would contribute an important salutary lesson. Specifically, they would show that the costs or consequences of individuals' activities should be internalized by those who exercise those rights.

The argument that constitutional arrangements should have some reference to individual self-interest and responsibility is not necessarily cynical. It is based on a vision of how individual preferences shape social choice. Individuals are self-regarding and maximizing in the sense that they always seek the greatest possible benefit and the least cost through their decisions. This assumes that individuals have formed preferences that they can identify, compare, and rank.[49] The underlying theory purports to be realistic: we should not assume that legislators always act purely out of some rarefied sense of public interest and, setting aside any thought of their own individual aggrandizement, engage in rational, democratic deliberation. Lawmakers act, at least in part, opportunistically. Their own preferences are formed exogenously and remain unaffected by their own role in the political decision-making process. Self-interest can be distinguished from mere selfishness. Even altruism can be explained as an economically rational, self-regarding action under some circumstances.

Public choice analysis provides an alternative means to explain why legal changes occur. This form of explanation is not rooted in a conception of legislators' public spiritedness or their willingness to find compromises. It also does not deploy arguments based on party discipline or how power is wielded through legislative committees; instead, the political process is conceived as primarily organized around interest groups jostling with one another for a division of the spoils. Public choice theory has been criticized for its 'cynical descriptive conclusions about behavior in government.'[50] Reading this literature, one might be inclined to see its ideal illustrator in Honoré Daumier, its consummate chronicler in Henry Adams, and its perfect debunker in Gore Vidal. Public choice theorists are normally careful to point out, however, that their conception is not idealized or romanticized. It has been defended on moral grounds, with reference to the need for appropriate constitutional rules.[51] Interest-group politics can itself be carried to a corrupting extreme. Therefore, the constitution should be used to constrain the excesses of self-seeking behaviour.

Critics argue that public choice is simply a formal model for which supporting empirical studies are either lacking or ambiguous. Advocates of public-choice theory, in contrast, regard it as an illuminating explanation that incorporates the complex variables necessary to explain public-policy formation.[52] Although not the only model adopted for use in basic textbooks on Canadian public policy, it has its vigorous adherents.[53] It should also be noted that, although public choice is frequently identified with 'reactionary legal economic ideology,' it is not inevitable that public choice assumptions will be harnessed for a conservative program of legal reform.[54] Writers of different political stripes, including leading proponents of so-called 'analytical Marxism,' have used public choice methods to help clarify the principles of Marxist philosophy and economics.[55]

Why Economic Rights Have Been Excluded from the Charter

Proponents of public choice theory such as Richard Epstein, Cass Sunstein, and Jonathan Macey have tried to explain, by reference to a coherent model of government regulation, why economic rights have not been accorded their due in a constitution. In their model of explanation, the legislative process is itself treated as analogous to a microeconomic system.

According to public choice theory, economic rights are constitutionally subordinated because legislators are motivated by the same motives as citizens acting in the private sphere. Individual citizens, interest groups, and legislators are all, it is assumed, actuated by an instrumental predilection and self-interested goals. In public choice literature, the resulting behaviour has been labelled 'rent-seeking.'[56] Legislation is treated as a commodity, in which there is an active market of supply and demand.[57] Ordinary public statutes, so-called private bills, and even constitutional enactments are treated as goods available for purchase by interest groups that compete with one another for political gains. Legal changes, through the drafting, adoption, repeal, or amendment of statutes or regulations, are achieved by means of an exchange process. In return for legislation favourable to the most cost-effective interest groups, lawmakers obtain, for example, campaign contributions. This is the most overt, but not perhaps the most common, form of currency used in the exchange process. The straight sale of influence may attract criminal sanctions for bribery. Other means used include the spending by interest groups directly on campaigns in support of a particular party or candidate; an interest group can reciprocally agree to support the party in power and its policy now, with an understanding that it is owed a favour in the future; or the interest group can give the legislator valuable resources in the form of information or through using its own position to influence public opinion. There are several types of currency that are involved in this 'subtle and complicated exchange process.'[58] The primary motivation for legislators is their desire for re-election.

This economic model for explaining political action contrasts with models that assume that lawmakers are guided largely by ideological considerations in making public policy. Public choice theorists depreciate ideology, or individual beliefs about what is in the public interest, as a significant factor influencing political outcomes. This is not to deny that ideologically committed behaviour may occur, but public choice treats it as relatively unimportant.[59]

In the public choice model, representative government, in which legislators are supposed to be agents for the voters who elect them, involves relatively high information and transaction costs. Information costs may include procurement costs, analysis costs, and evaluative costs.[60] In these circumstances, serious collective-action problems face members of a democracy. Individual citizens are afflicted by both rational ignorance and rational apathy, for rarely will they find it worthwhile to inquire closely into wealth transfers effected by legislation that results from interest-group bargaining. Specialized agencies, such as the broadcast and print media, arise to gather, interpret, and transmit information needed for political decision making.[61] Legislation is essentially a matter of transferring wealth from one group to another. Even though it would be in the public interest for every citizen to acquire as much information as possible about who gains and who loses under proposed legal changes, it will generally not repay an individual to invest in information costs to discover the impact on that individual of proposed legislation. It will also be extremely expensive for individual citizens concerned about a proposed measure to organize themselves into an effective group to oppose the measure.[62] Groups that already have been formed for some 'private service' will find it less costly to engage in political lobbying than an assortment of individuals who will find that it costs them more than one dollar to resist having one dollar taken from them.[63] Moreover, not all interest groups face the same level of information and transaction costs. As Anthony Downs points out, 'inequality of political influence is a necessary result of imperfect information, given an unequal distribution of wealth and income in society.'[64] Those with better representation, lower costs, and easier access to the political process can be expected to obtain wealth transfers that benefit them, at the expense of groups that face under-representation and higher costs. Groups that successfully manoeuvre for legal changes must reward legislators, who thus act as brokers. They are conceived as brokering between well-organized and concentrated interest groups, which stand to gain concretely from the legal change, and diffuse individuals, who each must contribute a little to fund the transfer.[65]

Two of the most significant assumptions of public choice theory are that, first, governments generally will adopt laws that benefit the most effective interest groups; and second, because this process costs the public more than it benefits the interest groups concerned, it makes society worse off. On the Kaldor-Hicks standard of cost-benefit analysis, this process interferes with economic efficiency.[66] Individual citizens pay the freight because they are highly disaggregated and will not find it cost-effective to resist having their wealth taken away. It would make no sense for an individual taxpayer to spend one dollar for information about the costs and benefits created by proposed legislation, when the law will impose a cost of only eighty cents on that taxpayer. Even if some taxpayers form their own interest group, they will themselves have to bear the information and transaction costs associated with resisting measures that transfer wealth obtained from taxes. If they succeed, the benefits are widely distributed: the group must share the benefits with all taxpayers, not just members of the interest group. Again, the individual's share of the costs might far outweigh that person's proportionate share of the benefits. The individual might pay one dollar to support or oppose legislation that results in a personal benefit of only a fraction of a cent.

One of the implications of this model is that legislators will be rationally inclined to divert as much activity as possible through the public sector, for it is in this realm that they can ensure the flow of benefits to themselves. Under this scheme, their services are in more demand in the committee room or on the floor of the legislature than if firms could rely simply on the market as the locus of their transactions.[67] This helps explain why economic rights have been given less protection in the Charter than other types of rights. For among the main beneficiaries of this arrangement are the legislators themselves. By affording economic rights less protection, legislators are able to make themselves the important intermediaries in the competition to bid on legal and regulatory reforms. If economic rights were entrenched in the Charter, this brokering role would slip away from legislators. Their ability to effect wealth transfers would be hindered by constitutional limitations. The cost to interest groups of pressing for wealth transfers is reduced when there is no constitutional protection. Having obtained a legislative victory, those groups do not have to incur the further cost of ensuring that the legislation will be upheld by a court on a challenge under the Charter. When legislation affecting economic rights is not subject to Charter scrutiny, legislators also are not constrained by the need to attach some plausible purpose to the law or regulation that will ensure it passes the proportionality tests that will be required under section 1 of the Charter should a court find that an entrenched right has been violated.

It is illuminating to see how public choice theory places the protections that are guaranteed under the Charter into this same framework. It serves the legislators' interests that courts are able to guard political rights solicitously. Freedom of expression has been interpreted in a way that favours political speech as one of the most valuable forms of expression. Moreover, the courts have carefully scrutinized legislative limits on campaign expenditures and the ability of interest groups to make financial contributions to political campaigns has been jealously protected by the courts under the rubric of section 2(a) of the Charter.[68] This is consistent with public choice theory, for political incumbents are better able to use their notoriety to gain access to the media and to enlist financial support from interest groups which will expect some sort of favourable treatment or support of their policies in the long run. Public choice theory would predict that, where the courts have struck down measures designed to limit such forms of regulation in the name of enhancing democratic values, the legislators will not be altogether disappointed and will emphasize the constitutional impediments to passing replacement regulations.

Other freedoms enumerated in the Charter can be interpreted in similar fashion. Both freedom of peaceful assembly, provided in section 2(c) of the Charter, and freedom of association, section 2(d), connote values and protect activities that have a bearing on the political situation in which economic liberty is not given the same protection. From the legislators' perspective, it is useful to empower the courts to strike down measures that hinder the formation and actions of political-interest groups. Facilitating this kind of association serves the ultimate goal of creating a market for legislators' influence and votes. The easier it is for groups to form and have access to the political process, the more legislators stand to benefit from the wealth transfers over which they preside. The costs of entry to the political market-place are reduced for interest groups. Meanwhile, because groups interested in protecting economic rights do not have the same constitutional advantages, the costs of protecting economic rights in the private sector are forced up. Those who wish to use their wealth through the market-place must incur greater costs if they wish to mobilize politically to protect what they have gained from being recouped by legislators. They have to bear the increased information and transaction costs required when non-economic rights under the Charter are invoked by interest groups favouring redistribution of wealth created in the private sector.

Public choice theory also tries to account for why the courts acquiesce in an arrangement under which legislators stand to benefit from interest-group bargains. Several explanations have been offered by theorists of this persuasion.[69] One of the most interesting is that of Jonathan Macey. His account depends on a notion of 'judicial' culture, in which it is argued that judges seek to maximize their prestige within the legal community. This community includes fellow judges, the bar, and the law school.[70] A judge who accords a great deal of respect to economic rights will be viewed especially critically by legal academics. Law professors help shape judges' reputations by favourable articles, citations in casebooks, and discussions in class. According to Macey, when the fateful case of *Lochner v. New York* was decided by the U.S. Supreme Court, and labour legislation was struck down for interfering with the freedom of employment contracts, the desirability of protecting economic rights was in the ascendant.[71] During the New Deal, a different legal culture or consciousness influenced the Supreme Court's decision to deny constitutional protection to economic liberties.[72] The legal culture prevailing since the 1930s views economic rights as warranting less protection than other rights. The upshot of this approach is that, as the legal culture changes, one can expect that judges' views on the protection of economic rights should reflect those changes. Indeed, Macey discerns within U.S. law schools hopeful signs of a 'growing acceptance' of an economic theory of regulation. 'The tide may slowly be turning.'[73]

In summary, public choice theory is an attempt to understand the economic foundations of legal and political activity. The theory offers insights into why economic rights have largely been denied entrenchment. Public choice analysts argue that this omission makes the Charter less effective than it should be. In the absence of constitutional protection for economic rights, legislators are prone to make decisions about the distribution of wealth on an ad hoc, incoherent basis.[74] It is always tempting to bow to the pressure from interest groups and transfer wealth away from those who have made gains from their activities in the market. The constitutional system envisioned by public choice theorists does not necessarily entail that only those parties who are already well-off would benefit from constitutional protection. It is not inconsistent with public choice for a constitution to guarantee that everyone has not only an entitlement to some economic rights but also some actual economic wherewithal.[75] It would be anathema, of course, to such theorists if there were a constitutional requirement that everyone's resources be levelled so that wealth was shared equally.

Economic Rights That Might Be Guaranteed

Public choice theory has been invoked to justify prescriptive advice proffered to governments which are managing the transition from largely command economies to regimes based on private property and markets.[76] Creating a 'private' realm or operating civil society is seen as both a precondition of democratic government and a necessary basis for an efficiently functioning economy. Among the rights that have been discussed as necessary for ensuring that such constitutional changes have the most desirable economic results are the following.

Property rights invariably head the list. Protection of this interest has both real and symbolic importance to such rights advocates.[77] Freedom of contract is also frequently mentioned as worthy of an explicit constitutional guarantee. This freedom can work in two different ways. The scope of the guarantee might include contractual relations generally, so that neither an existing nor a future contract can be validly impaired or affected. Or the guarantee can protect private parties against government interference only in respect of contracts already made. That is, the government is able to regulate contracts, but it has to do so in advance, in the sense that only future contracts can be caught by the legislation.[78]

Another form of economic freedom (both contractual and associational) permits citizens to create private institutions such as corporations or other kinds of business enterprises, labour unions, management groups, social clubs, charitable organizations, and churches. These institutions are valuable collective agencies that countervail the potentially dominant power of government over an individual's life. Constitutional guarantees should be put in place to ensure that a government can only minimally constrain both the creation of such institutions and also any economic activities that those groups pursue. A Charter guarantee of freedom of contract might expressly prohibit a government from imposing wage and price controls, as was done in Canada in the 1970s.[79] This was a comprehensive regulatory scheme, administered by a central agency, that covered nearly all economic activity in the private sector. It is more debatable whether economic rights in the Charter should prohibit minimum-wage legislation or price-control legislation for particular products or services. Some public choice theorists concede that there may be good grounds for permitting minimum-wage laws.[80]

A further economic right that might be embedded in the Charter would be the freedom to enter the market place. This would include markets in the form of occupations or professions, trades and industries, and geographic regions. Some level of protection along these lines is already contained in the Charter, in the provisions of section 6, though public choice theorists imagine much larger scope for such freedom of entry. Setting up an economic freedom to enter markets would require governments to justify any laws that create barriers. To sustain such legislation, a government would have to show the rationality of the relevant requirements. This freedom would apply broadly, not just to freedom of individuals to pursue a living, but also to their freedom to invest capital, move goods, equipment or a manufacturing plant, offer services, or diversify their operations anywhere within Canada. Other economic rights that might plausibly be enumerated in the Charter include a prohibition on government monopolies, a principle of non-discrimination against private enterprises, a ban on tariffs and duties, the requirement of a balanced budget, and constitutional restrictions on the government's taxing power.[81]

According to public choice strategy, among the economic rights that should not be entrenched are social-welfare entitlements, such as a right to fair compensation, a right to social security, and a right to a safe and environmentally clean workplace. The problem with these kinds of rights is that they impose positive duties on a government, and it is unrealistic to expect that a government will always have the ability to ensure that such rights are satisfied. If the major mechanism for constitutional enforcement is judicial review, courts are ill-equipped and usually not disposed to oversee institutions to the degree necessary to ensure compliance with these positive social rights. The argument goes that, if some rights in a constitution are unenforced, then this threatens the enforcement of them all.[82] Moreover, strict enforcement of such positive rights might undermine, rather than reinforce, the operation of private markets.

It is also important from the perspective of public choice that the Charter should apply strictly to government actions and not to the private, lawful activities of citizens. The separation between public-political life and the realm of civil society is vital to ensure that government does not overstep its proper role. As much as possible, business should be carried on independently of governmental constraints. Constitutional rights should not be enforced against private organizations. If it is thought wise to make private institutions observe Charter values, then special legislation should be enacted to achieve this result. Courts should not be permitted to enforce such observance directly through the application of the Charter alone.

Judicial Treatment of the Economic Aspects of Charter Rights

The purpose of this part of the discussion is to determine the extent to which the Supreme Court of Canada has recognized or denied economic rights as falling within Charter protection. A number of rights or freedoms guaranteed in the Charter turn out to have significant economic incidents or features. Other rights have been construed as purely political or social in nature. Any economic meaning they may arguably have borne has been rejected by the Court. Examining at least several samples of Supreme Court jurisprudence in this light will help us understand whether there is any coherent theory or policy underlying the Court's approach to the constitutionalization of economic rights.

An attempt early in the history of Charter jurisprudence to establish an economic right was roundly rejected by the Supreme Court of Canada. Section 6(2)(b) guarantees every Canadian citizen or permanent resident of this country the right 'to pursue the gaining of a livelihood in any province.' On its face, this provision could be construed as guaranteeing an economic right to work. That right would apply wherever that person happens to reside. But, as the Supreme Court of Canada clarified in *Shapinker*,[83] section 6(2)(b) must be interpreted in context, as a right relating to the 'mobility' of a claimant. Section 6(2)(b) does not create a 'free-standing right' disengaged from the mobility elements that otherwise mark section 6.[84] The claimant could not establish an 'independent constitutional right to work as a lawyer' in Ontario that took precedence over the provincial legislation imposing a citizenship requirement.[85] This failure to link section 6 to economic rights did not, however, stop the Supreme Court from later using mobility rights as a basis for striking down laws that inhibited interprovincial economic activities. In *Black v. Law Society of Alberta*, an attempt was made to establish a Calgary law firm in which all the lawyers were members of the Alberta bar.[86] Some of these lawyers lived in Calgary, while the rest lived in Toronto. All the Calgary firm partners were at the same time members of a Toronto law firm. When the Law Society of Alberta adopted rules which, among other effects, prohibited lawyers residing and practising in Alberta from entering into partnerships with lawyers not ordinarily resident in Alberta, the proposed law firm invoked the Charter.

The Supreme Court in *Black* held that the Law Society rules in question infringed the Charter. *Shapinker* was distinguished on the ground that no mobility element was present in the earlier case: there the applicant for admission to the Ontario bar was already a resident of that province. While many of the lawyers in the proposed firm in *Black* would practise law from their Toronto offices, the Court nevertheless held that they had a right to pursue their livelihood through association with an Alberta firm. Actual 'physical' movement of individuals from one province to another is not a precondition for the application of section 6(2)(b). As long as the pursuit of a livelihood or business is obstructed by provincial regulations, that guarantee applies.

In discussing the background purpose of mobility guarantees in *Black*, Justice La Forest emphasized the 'economic concerns' that not only underlie this provision in the Charter but also are manifested in section 121 of the Constitution Act, 1867. From Justice La Forest's perspective, section 6 guarantees play a role in 'state concerns for the proper structuring of the economy.'[87] The mobility guarantees ensure that qualified non-residents are given the same access to vocational fields as residents.[88] Section 6 is essentially aimed at removing economic disadvantages that may be created by provincial regulatory barriers.

An important economic right of business firms is to be secure against unwarranted or unauthorized incursions into the firm's records. In another early case, *Hunter v. Southam*,[89] the corporate owner of a newspaper chain, successfully challenged the constitutional validity of parts of section 10 of the federal Combines Investigation Act, under the authority of which officers of the Combines Investigation Branch had conducted a comprehensive search of the files contained in Southam's offices in Edmonton. The purpose of the government inquiry was to obtain documentary evidence in relation to a possible anti-competitive trade practice prohibited by the Combines Investigation Act. One of the key policies underpinning that statute is preserving healthy competition in Canadian industry. The offence motivating the inquiry was framed in economic terms. In *Hunter* the Supreme Court struck down subsections 10(1) and 10(3) of the act on the ground that they infringed the right guaranteed by section 8 of the Charter to be secure against 'unreasonable search or seizure.' As Chief Justice Dickson noted in *Hunter*, common-law rights of individuals protecting them from government searches and seizures were historically 'based on the right to enjoy property and were linked to the law of trespass.'[90] But the fact that section 8 constitutionally entrenches this particular right makes it invulnerable to ordinary legislative enactments. Moreover, Dickson noted that the ambit of section 8 is not restricted to 'the protection of property.' Instead, it guarantees a 'broad and general right.'[91] Reframed in positive terms, section 8 amounts to an entitlement to a 'reasonable' expectation of privacy, whether or not that expectation arises out of the possession of property.[92] As the reasoning in *Hunter* makes clear, rights incidental to property are not banished from, or ignored in, the Charter. They are capable of reappearing through the freedoms and rights that are enumerated. In addition, the Supreme Court in *Hunter* predicated its analysis on the assumption that the claimant in that case, Southam Inc., a media conglomerate operating throughout Canada, had standing to bring its application under the Charter. The Court did not address the issue as to whether a business firm's expectation of privacy, in relation to its books, correspondence, memoranda, or other records, differs from ordinary individuals' interest in keeping their home, their papers, and their effects secure against government invasion. As Chief Justice Dickson put it, when the Court resolves a section 8 challenge, it weighs in the balance the 'public's interest in being left alone by government.'[93]

In all cases involving the interpretation of Charter guarantees, the Court invariably begins by conceiving the enumerated freedom or right in distinctly human terms. For example, even though the litigant in *Hunter* was a corporate giant, the Court couched its conception of the privacy interest protected by section 8 in terms of how the overweening state should be limited in its power to intrude into the personal affairs of the individual who may find it difficult to stand up to the formidable state apparatus. Similarly, in *The Queen v. Big M Drug Mart*, the Court described at some length the fundamental values, as they apply to natural persons, which are protected through the Charter guarantee of freedom of religion.[94] The case raised the issue of a corporation's standing to challenge the validity of the federal Lord's Day Act under the Charter. At stake in this appeal was the 'freedom of conscience and religion' provided in section 2(a) of the Charter. The Sunday observance legislation made it an offence to carry on the sale of goods on a Sunday. The Supreme Court treated the corporate status of the accused as irrelevant to whether someone charged with this offence could argue the law was unconstitutional. It did not matter that Big M Drug Mart could not practise or adhere to a particular religion. Chief Justice Dickson did not see the protection contained in section 2(a) as limited to persons capable of holding religious beliefs.[95] In his view, it is 'the nature of the law, not the status of the accused, that is in issue.'[96]

Among the rights important to business enterprises are what days and hours to open and whether employees can be required to work on certain days. The Supreme Court's analysis in *Big M Drug Mart* sent out important signals about the extent to which Charter rights and freedoms could be invoked by commercial enterprises in making decisions about how to conduct business. The case was as much about the right to engage in commerce on a Sunday as it was about whether the impugned statute could be upheld as a valid exercise of federal jurisdiction over criminal law or as a statute with a secular, rather than a religious or sectarian, purpose. The practical effect of the decision was profound. With one stroke, the result in *Big M Drug Mart* reshaped labour regulation, removed any trace of federal jurisdiction over limiting days for store openings, and removed a source of illegitimate state coercion of business activities that were otherwise 'lawful, moral and normal.'[97] *Big M Drug Mart* vindicated the economic rights of business firms to operate on Sundays, if they so chose. Although ostensibly the case protects freedom of religion, the nub of the decision was the Court protecting businesses against religious-based forms of discrimination and coercion that the state had enacted. In *Big M Drug Mart* there was no argument raised by the accused that the legislation created disadvantages for large businesses, in that smaller retailers were able, under provincial Sunday closing laws, to obtain exemptions from the prohibition on Sunday sales. That kind of economic advantage came to the fore in the later case of *R. v. Edwards Books and Art Ltd.*[98]

In *Edwards Books* the Supreme Court considered a challenge to Ontario's Retail Business Holidays Act, which, in its definition section, regulated retail sales on days designated as 'holidays.' The majority of the Court found that the Act violated section 2(a) but nevertheless should be upheld under section 1 as a reasonable limit. In his analysis, Chief Justice Dickson discerned that the provincial business closing law was enacted with a secular, rather than a religious, purpose. But the law had the effect of imposing substantial burdens on retailers who observed Saturday, rather than Sunday, as a religious holiday. Even though this may amount only to an 'indirect' form of coercion by the government, the rights afforded by section 2(a) may still be infringed so long as the burden is not 'trivial or insubstantial.'[99] The litigants in *Edwards Books* based their Charter challenge on the impact of the legislation on non-observing and Saturday-observing retailers. As Dickson noted in his reasons, the goal of all the litigants in *Edwards Books* was to open on Sundays in order to make money.[100] It was not any religious burden on the actual litigants in *Edwards Books* that determined whether section 2(a) had been infringed. The Court looked instead to the economic burden imposed by the retail closing law on the retailer who, being Jewish or Seventh-day Adventist, observes Saturday as a religious holiday.

The latter will be at a competitive disadvantage created by the legislation. A reciprocal burden is created for consumers who are Saturday-observers.

Despite its ruling in *Edwards Books* that the Ontario business-holidays legislation was valid, the Supreme Court had to return to virtually the same issue in 1993 in *Hy and Zel's Inc. v. Ontario (Attorney General).*[101] This case arose because of persistent defiance of the holiday closing law by some retailers (one of whom had been a party also to the challenge in *Edwards Books*). After *Edwards Books*, that legislation had undergone changes. When the provincial attorney general applied for a court order requiring several retailers to observe the law and close their shops on Christmas Day and Boxing Day, the subject retailers, along with some of their employees, sought a judicial declaration that the business-holidays law was unconstitutional. *Big M Drug Mart* and *Edwards Books* originated out of criminal proceedings, while *Hy and Zel's* was a civil suit.[102] Since the constitutional challenge was brought by incorporated enterprises, this difference in the type of proceedings was emphasized by the majority of the Supreme Court in deciding *Hy and Zel's*. In *Big M Drug Mart*, according to Chief Justice Dickson, the corporation had sought to vindicate the freedom of religion of persons capable of enjoying such rights. The majority judgment in *Hy and Zel's*, written by Justice Major, similarly conceived of the challenge as an attempt by a corporation to sue on the basis, not of its own rights, but of the rights of others under the Charter. In proceedings where a corporation faces a criminal charge, that corporation's challenge to the validity of the law creating the offence can be entertained by the courts. In a situation where the proceedings are based on a request for a civil remedy, a corporate challenger to the validity of legislation must persuade the court that standing should be granted. In the latter instance, the challenger is in the same position as any 'public interest' litigant in respect of the Charter. Standing will not be granted automatically. Arguments will have to be raised and evidence adduced to convince the court that standing to proceed on the merits of the constitutional issues should be granted.[103]

Justice Major reviewed the criteria for standing to be given to such a constitutional challenger in those cases where courts retain such discretion. One criterion is that 'there must be no other reasonable and effective way to bring the Act's validity before the court.'[104] The majority of the Supreme Court held that the challengers in *Hy and Zel's* failed to establish this point. There was a lack of evidence before the Court in *Hy and Zel's* and the majority feared that a decision was requested without adequate factual material.

Another instance in which the Supreme Court recognized that the Charter protects economic interests is found in *R.W.D.S.U. v. Dolphin Delivery Ltd.*[105] The constitutional claim in this case took the form of a union seeking protection for secondary picketing which had been enjoined by the British Columbia Labour Relations Board. The Supreme Court agreed that the picketing in question was a form of expression falling within section 2(b) of the Charter, which guarantees 'freedom of expression.' The purpose of the expression by the striking union in this case was 'to bring economic pressure on the person picketed.'[106] As the Supreme Court later confirmed, *Dolphin Delivery* shows that section 2(b) covers 'expression having an economic purpose.'[107]

The economic rights of trade unions under the Charter were also considered in the so-called *Labour Trilogy*. In each of these three cases, unions challenged legislation unilaterally limiting collective rights that ordinarily the unions enjoyed and could bargain over.[108] The gist of the three cases can be illustrated by looking at *Reference re PSERA*. For the majority, Justice Le Dain held that the freedom of association guaranteed in the Charter embraces neither the right to bargain collectively nor the right to strike. These are not fundamental rights protected by constitutional entrenchment. Accordingly, they can legitimately be affected by ordinary legislation.[109] The judges forming the majority of the Court were unimpressed with arguments that freedom of association lies at the root of modern labour relations and that at least some of the activities pursued by modern unions are protected by that freedom. In Chief Justice Dickson's dissenting judgment in *PSERA*, a much less restrictive or formal approach was taken. Dickson argued that section 2(d) does not merely protect the 'status' of an association but also can be invoked to protect particular group activities.[110] His judgment analyses which collective activities or means used by unions are 'essential' to their purposes and thus are shielded by section 2(d). The fact that trade unions pursue largely economic ends did not, for Dickson, make a difference as to whether the unions could rely on section 2(d).[111]

The Supreme Court has also reviewed the contexts in which different forms of expression, including commercial expression, are constitutionally sheltered. In *Ford v. Quebec (Attorney General)*, section 2(b) of the Charter was relied on by a business firm.[112] In this case, the commercial claimant had been penalized under Quebec's Charter of the French Language for failing to ensure that advertising was exclusively in the French language and the firm's name was displayed in its French version alone. The contested provisions in the language law were aimed specifically at commercial conduct. On the basis of U.S. constitutional law, and in light of some provincial appellate decisions in Canada, there was some doubt whether commercial advertising, for example, qualified as a form of expression that fell under section 2(b).[113] The rationale for denying constitutional protection to commercial forms of expression included the idea that the Charter is not concerned with the 'economic sphere.'[114] In developing regulatory policy, governments should not be hampered by entrenched commercial rights. Instead, the freedoms contained in section 2 are aimed at furthering the processes of democratic government.[115]

The Supreme Court in *Ford* resolved this issue by holding that the ambit of section 2(b) is not limited to political expression. Commercial expression also falls within the scope of section 2(b) for at least a couple of reasons. First, the Court explained that this is what a 'large and liberal interpretation' of Charter rights and freedoms demanded. Second, in the Court's view, constitutionalizing commercial expression serves the interests of not only speakers and advertisers but also recipients of messages.[116] Consumers exposed to advertisers' messages are enabled to make 'informed economic choices.' This ability enhances their 'individual self-fulfilment and personal autonomy.'[117] Because such values are furthered by commercial expression, it deserves constitutional protection. Of course, it is often difficult to link these purposes to the economic goals pursued by firms. The upshot of *Ford* does not really concern a commercial firm's self-fulfilment: advertising is about improving brand recognition, market demand, and the overall profitability of the enterprise. It would be stretching or abusing the metaphor whereby firms are figuratively treated as people to claim that a firm's self-fulfilment is enhanced by the unrestricted ability to flog its products or services to the consuming public. Justice McLachlin has recently declared in *RJR-MacDonald Inc. v. Canada (Attorney General)*, in which the federal government's restrictions on tobacco advertising were struck down, that the claimant's 'motivation' is irrelevant to the inquiry into whether section 2(b) has been impaired.[118] As McLachlin candidly admits, the primary goal shared by litigants in some of the key cases decided by the Supreme Court in respect of freedom of expression is the firm's shareholders' desire to profit from the corporation's business activity, whether the expression sought to be protected is closely linked to the core values of freedom of expression or not.'[119] 'Irrelevancy' of motivation in this context means that, while it may be true that the firm's economic motivation does not mean that its constitutional claim is subject to a lesser degree of protection, the courts will indeed protect, through an application of section 2(b), the profit-maximizing interests of the firm's owners. To that extent, the economic motivation of the firm is directly relevant.

Despite the emphasis placed by the Court in *Ford* on the protection of commercial expression, the reasoning in that case was not intended to delineate completely the extent to which governments are constitutionally able to regulate advertising.[120] The justificatory arguments, related to the reasonableness of the violation of Charter rights in *Ford*, were directed at the purposes of the French-only laws generally, not at the governmental goals to be achieved through regulating commercial expression. The permissible scope within which a government can impose limits on commercial advertising was tested directly in

Irwin Toy Ltd. v. Quebec (A.G.).[121] This same issue had been addressed obliquely in *Ford*. At stake in *Irwin Toy* was the constitutional validity of provisions in Quebec's Consumer Protection Act that regulated advertising directed at children under thirteen years of age. All the judges who decided the case in the Supreme Court of Canada held that the legislative measures violated the freedom of expression guaranteed by section 2(b) of the Charter. Nevertheless the majority found that the infringement was a reasonable limit on the Charter right under section 1.

The usefulness to business of section 2(b)'s freedom of expression was emphasized again in *Rocket v. Royal College of Dental Surgeons of Ontario*.[122] This case involved a challenge to Ontario regulations under the Health Disciplines Act that limited both the media and content of advertising that dentists could use. The two dentists who brought the action had been disciplined for engaging in an illegitimate advertising campaign. The Supreme Court held that the regulatory restrictions infringed the dentists' freedom of expression in a manner that could not be justified under section 1. The impugned regulations were struck down. *Rocket* provided the Court with an opportunity to enlarge on its views about Charter protection for commercial expression, particularly with respect to advertising by members of a profession. Justice McLachlin indicated in *Rocket* that, when the Court examines whether a law can be upheld under section 1, the fact that the type of expression in question is commercial becomes an important factor. In her reasons, McLachlin noted that, where the expression in question is 'primarily economic,' it might be easier to persuade a court that the restriction in justifiable.[123] However, in *Rocket*, the Court found that the dentists' expression was also useful for informing current and potential patients about the dentists' services. The advertising would enable consumers better to compare different dentists. The section 1 analysis thus becomes a crucial context in which courts have to weigh the primarily economic interests of advertisers against the 'public interest' in promoting consumers' access to relevant information.[124] Where the consumers are viewed as constituting a 'vulnerable' group, such as potential patients for dentists when advertising is unregulated, then the Court will also tend to be more deferential to government attempts to establish a balance through legislation limiting what representations dentists can make to the public.[125] With these strictures in mind, the Court in *Rocket* determined that the challenged regulations were unreasonably broad and were declared invalid.

Another part of the Charter invoked by business is section 7. That section guarantees to 'everyone' the 'right to life, liberty and security of the person and the right not to be deprived thereof except in accordance with the principles of fundamental justice.' In *Irwin Toy*, the firm that brought the constitutional challenge alleged, first, that it was subject to penal proceedings under the Consumer Protection Act, and, second, that the advertising regulations were so vague as to constitute a denial of its section 7 rights. A preliminary issue raised on this matter was whether a corporation could take advantage of section 7. Chief Justice Dickson in *Irwin Toy* (writing in concert with two fellow justices) concluded that 'a corporation cannot avail itself of the protection offered by s. 7 of the Charter.'[126] Among the factors supporting this interpretation is Dickson's view that section 7 does not protect some kind of 'economic liberty.'[127] He noted that the wording of section 7 specifically does not refer to 'property,' unlike the formulation used in the Fourth and Fifteenth Amendments of the American Bill of Rights. The drafters of the Canadian guarantee used the expression 'security of the person' instead. Dickson also carefully pointed out that this does not mean that 'security of the person' cannot have an 'economic component.'[128] However, because section 7 refers to the security of the *person*, Dickson concluded that a corporation's economic rights are not protected by that section. This leaves open the possibility, acknowledged by Dickson but not finally settled in *Irwin Toy*, that an individual's economic rights can be protected through the invocation of section 7. In the words of Dickson, it would be 'precipitous' to exclude so early in Charter history the various economic interests that may conceivably be recognized as embraced by section 7. These include an individual's rights enumerated in international covenants, such as 'rights to social security, equal pay for equal work, adequate food, clothing and shelter.' Dickson also saw the possiblity of protecting 'traditional property – contract rights' under this rubric.[129]

The application of section 7 to a corporation was revisited in *Thomson Newspapers Ltd. v. Canada (Director of Investigation and Research, Restrictive Trade Practices Commission)*.[130] Justice L'Heureux-Dubé reaffirmed that a corporation cannot invoke the guarantee protecting 'life, liberty and security of the person.' She also held that, because the individual officers were ordered to be examined as representatives of the firm, they too were excluded from protection under section 7. As witnesses in their own capacity, they can claim the benefit of section 7 but, in the circumstances in *Thomson*, any deprivation of their rights was in accordance with the principles of fundamental justice.[131] The Supreme Court summed up the principle about the general unavailability of section 7 to corporations in *Dywidag Systems International, Canada Ltd. v. Zutphen Brothers Construction Ltd.*[132] The only exception to the principle that section 7 cannot be claimed by a corporate firm is contained in *Big M Drug Mart*, which provides that a corporation charged with a criminal offence may defend itself by arguing that the law providing for the offence is unconstitutional.[133] This did not conclude the matter, since the availability of both section 7 and section 11(d) of the Charter to a corporation charged under the false advertising provisions of the Competition Act was recanvassed in *R. v. Wholesale Travel Group Inc.*[134] In that instance, the majority of the Supreme Court of Canada held that the corporate accused had standing to challenge the statutory provisions creating the offence and the penalty. If the provisions are invalid because they violate one or other right under the Charter, then they should be struck down. Chief Justice Lamer went on to note that it is constitutionally relevant that the provisions in the Competition Act do not distinguish between individual and corporate defendants. If the provisions have been framed to apply expressly to corporations, then a corporation may *not* be entitled to raise the Charter arguments that were raised in *Wholesale Travel.*[135] Because the provisions in the Competition Act applied to any accused, whether a human being or a corporate firm, this latter scenario did not arise. The accused in *Wholesale Travel* was entitled to raise section 7 arguments because the rights of defendants generally under the relevant sections of the Competition Act would be affected by the Court's review of the validity of those sections in light of the Charter.

Chief Justice Lamer also noted in *Wholesale Travel* that, where a firm has been able to argue successfully that its section 7 rights have been infringed, the Court, in conducting the requisite section 1 analysis, will take into account the fact that the accused is a corporation.[136] In such a case, against the 'public interest' would be balanced, not the individual's interest in liberty or security of the person, but the 'financial interests' of the corporation. The rationale for this is that a corporation cannot be imprisoned. The most effective sanction against it is in the nature of monetary loss. Even where a corporation is 'closely-held,' with only a couple of individuals holding shares in the firm, those persons standing behind a corporation as shareholders, officers, or directors should not be allowed to invoke section 7 as if it were the human beings' liberty or security that was at stake.

Justice L'Heureux-Dubé wrote a dissenting judgment in *Hy and Zel's* that is notable for her views on several points regarding the ability of corporate firms to sue under the Charter. First, she was of the opinion that whether a corporation is entitled to invoke section 2(a) has not yet been 'conclusively resolved.'[137] She reviewed the decisions of the Court since *Big M Drug Mart* and found that significant scope remains for argument whether a corporate firm can, in a Charter challenge, invoke rights that the litigant, because it is not a natural person, does not itself possess. While the reasoning in *Irwin Toy* appeared generally to deny corporations the use of section 7, because the rights therein protected apply only to human beings, the Supreme Court in *Wholesale Travel* did permit the corporation to invoke section 7. Not only was L'Heureux-Dubé more sceptical in *Hy and Zel's* than the majority of her colleagues on the Supreme Court about the certainty of the law regarding corporate litigants' assertion of Charter rights, she also parted ways with them on the applicable rules governing judicial discretion to grant standing. In her view, applicants are entitled to standing in cases where those parties can establish that they are 'exceptionally prejudiced' by the impugned law's effect on their 'personal, proprietary or pecuniary rights.'[138]

The principle that the Charter applies only to government activity is contained in section 32(1). The Supreme Court in *Dolphin Delivery* affirmed that the Charter is supposed to apply only to government's powers over the individual. 'Private' actions are not covered by Charter protections. The government can, of course, use its regulatory powers to control such private activities. In addition, certain private conduct may infringe individual rights protected by provincial human rights legislation. What constitutes a part of government for the purposes of the application of the Charter can be a contested issue, as in *McKinney v. Unversity of Guelph*.[139] When a body is non-governmental, then a provincial human rights scheme, enacted through ordinary legislation, may apply. If the provincial rights legislation fails to extend protection against discrimination, as required by the equality guarantees in section 15(1) of the Charter, then the provincial legislation is itself constitutionally infirm. In *McKinney*, the majority of the Supreme Court ultimately upheld Ontario's Human Rights Code provision on the basis that a section 1 analysis established the impugned provision as reasonable and justifiable. Mandatory retirement at a stipulated age is not constitutionally impermissible.

Another illustration of the way in which the Charter can touch 'private' or 'commercial' activities is found in *Lavigne v. Ontario Public Service Employees Union*.[140] In that case, a member of the public-service union objected to some of the uses made by his union of dues paid by members. In particular, he objected to purposes unrelated to collective bargaining, including union contributions to political parties and protest campaigns. He argued that the compulsory check-off of dues from his wages, along with the purposes he found objectionable, infringed his Charter right to freedom of association under section 2(d). The Supreme Court of Canada found that the compulsory check-off arrangements were subject to Charter review, even though no legislation directly required them. The institution in question, a community college, was found to be a part of government. Moreover, a majority of the Court held that the compulsory check-off violated section 2(d) of the Charter, because it 'compelled' an individual's association with others and thus undermined the goal of self-fulfilment and self-realization.[141] The argument that, when a government agency engages in 'commercial' or 'private' transactions, the Charter should not apply, was rejected by the majority. In the words of Justice La Forest, government should be bound by Charter principles especially when it 'enters the market-place,' if only to strengthen the general acceptance and respect for 'fairness' and 'tolerance.'[142]

It may be that common-law rules generally can be scrutinized with respect to their consistency with the Charter, in order to ensure that the development of the common law reflects the values contained in the Charter. This approach was adopted by the Supreme Court of Canada in *R. v. Salituro*, a criminal case involving a husband who forged his wife's signature on a cheque jointly payable to them and then cashed it.[143] At the core of the case was the established common-law rule making the wife an incompetent witness for the prosecution. In the Supreme Court, Justice Iacobucci re-examined the policy grounds for the common-law rule and found them both obsolete and not in keeping with 'the values in the Charter.'[144] This position coheres with earlier Supreme Court jurisprudence to the extent that, as Justice McIntyre said in *Dolphin Delivery*, 'the Charter is far from irrelevant to private litigants whose disputes fall to be decided at common law.'[145] In *Salituro*, Iacobucci determined that the best remedy was simply for the Supreme Court to declare that the common-law rule would henceforth be changed in circumstances where the spouses involved were irreconciliably separated.

The general principle animating *Salituro* is that a court can alter the common law, in both criminal and civil law contexts, to bring it into conformity with Charter values. These last-mentioned values are broader than the specific enumerated rights under the Charter. In *Salituro*, the value appealed to by the Court was the apparently sweeping one that 'individual choices should not be restricted unnecessarily.'[146] This is extremely broad and abstract: it amounts to a substantial judicial licence to rewrite the common law. For example, courts could, by invoking this value, re-examine specific rules of contract or tort law and determine that they are inconsistent with the constitutional value of non-discrimination, freedom of expression, or the liberties provided in section 7. Then, having reached this determination, the individual judge could unilaterally alter the common-law rule. If the Charter is used to revise the common law, including for example, the myriad of rules underlying business transactions, market-based conduct, and assessment of risks, it could have far-reaching effects on the activities of Canadian firms.

Where economic rights are involved, a consistent pattern emerges from Supreme Court jurisprudence. On their initial encounter with the task of elaborating a Charter guarantee, members of the Court tend to conceive of the guarantee in terms of the importance it bears to fundamentally liberal notions about the conditions under which humans flourish. State action that interferes with or undermines these conditions is viewed as presumptively bad. In other words, the Court fleshes out the background of political principle against which the case before it is to be considered. Only when this conceptual context has been articulated, when the stage has been set for a 'purposive' interpretation of the guarantee in question, will the Court apply its intellectual framework to litigants who invoke the particular Charter right against a specific law or regulation. It does not matter, for the most part, that the litigant itself is not a human being. Nor does it matter that the legislation in question is predicated on economic goals or policies. The Court proceeds on the basis that the constitutional challenge may nevertheless benefit someone whose human interests are at stake and are threatened by the impugned law. That is enough.

In the process of striking down legislation that infringes human rights, economic rights can be strengthened. A firm can test the constitutional validity of laws that restrict or inhibit its economic operations. If successful in challenging the regulatory scheme, the firm has made it more difficult and costly for the government to impose regulations on business of the type represented by that firm. The government is forced either to draft and adopt new measures to replace the invalid scheme, taking into account Charter standards, or to abandon the field as an area into which it is unconstitutional to intervene.[147] Where proposed legislation is considered by a legislative committee, interest groups, including business firms or representatives, can appeal to Charter decisions as part of their strategy to influence the choice of policy or to affect public opinion surrounding the proposed measures.[148] The same results were common under the division-of-power cases with which the Supreme Court has been dealing for over a century. And just as federalism disputes had side effects for the legal environment of business, so successful Charter attacks can have serious commercial consequences.

The Supreme Court of Canada has not spoken on the matter of economic rights, or on many other issues, univocally. If it is accurate to describe the Court as evolving its jurisprudence on corporate claims under the Charter in successive phases, there may be a multitude of variables at work,[149] – not least of which is the fact that the Court's membership has changed significantly since *Big M Drug Mart* was decided. It is difficult to reconcile the denial of constitutional protection of economic rights of unions with the availability of equivalent rights to commercial firms. The Court may not have deeply appreciated at the outset that enumerated rights would present issues of economic policy. Much of the debate about which kinds of interests are protected by the Charter has been channelled through disagreements about what kinds of claimants should be allowed to bring Charter challenges. This academic debate seems lately to have influenced the Court's approach. If *Hy and Zel's* is a useful indication, the doctrine of standing, used by the Court as a technical lever to control both the eligible parties and the nature of the claims they assert, will become an increasingly important factor in how economic rights are treated under the Charter. This is a strategic rather than a theoretically powerful approach, based as much on prudence as on a justification by reference to principle. It permits the Court to deal with substantive issues obliquely, rather than have to engage the matter on its merits.

In adjudicating economic claims, the Supreme Court does not appear to have been animated by any particular grand theoretical assumptions or guidelines. What the decisions have revealed is a mixed assortment of values and ideals, all of which are susceptible to a liberal or a libertarian spin. At any rate, public choice theory is not lurking in the background of the Court's encounters with claims to economic protection under the Charter. Instead, the Court has been vigilant on some occasions, and resistant on others, about upholding economic elements of enumerated rights. There has been no ruthless consistency. Through it all, the Court appears to have been following a middle course, so that, in the words of Justice Sopinka, the Charter has been interpreted in a way that proves it is 'neither the boon nor the bane of Canadian business.'[150]

The Value of Public Choice in Treating Economic Rights under the Charter

The preceding survey of the different contexts in which Supreme Court of Canada decisions have affected, directly or indirectly, the economic rights of business firms prompts several questions. Does public choice analysis illuminate the constitutional doctrine developed by the Court so far? To what extent does this study reveal the strengths or inadequacies of public choice theory as explanatory of Canadian constitutional developments?

Public choice theory does little to explain the political process by which the Charter was drafted, discussed, and adopted. The exclusion of both property rights and economic rights from the Charter is surprising, unless one assumes that interest groups ordinarily favouring such protection were either relatively weak or disorganized. Or the explanation may not be so surprising, considering that among the most powerful interest groups were the participating provincial governments. Their vested interests in protecting, to the greatest extent possible, legislative jurisdiction over 'property and civil rights in the province' may have been the most important factor in determining the exclusion of economic rights. This is a very broad source of provincial power that covers, not just property matters, but such items as contractual transactions and the regulation of trades and industries within the province.[151] The public choice explanations examined above do not generally take adequate account of the role of provincial administrations as interest groups. This reality of a federal division of lawmaking power, where a component province resists rights under the Charter that may be used to diminish its power, does not fit easily into the public choice schema which views interest groups as essentially self-maximizing private parties.

There are other problems with the public choice model as it relates to economic rights under the Charter. First, the importance of ideology and political partisanship is underestimated, or not well accounted for, in the public choice portrait of the legislative process. That is, a legislator sometimes might oppose a powerful interest group because of background political principle or party allegiance, notwithstanding it would be in the legislator's self-interest to defer to the group's pressure. The public choice characterization of all legislation as the product of rent-seeking has been called a 'caricature' of political processes by authors otherwise attracted by the theory.[152] Granted, some regulation-making is undoubtedly influenced by interest-group pressure: a good example is the recent proposal in the Alberta legislature, introduced as a private bill, that would have created a corporation for the provision of medical services by a prominent eye specialist and other doctors in his clinic. If passed, the bill would have entitled the corporation to charitable status and other tax benefits.[153] This is rent-seeking with a vengeance. By contrast, other statutes may be more reflective of some conception of the public interest. Even in the case of private bills (not to be confused with private members' bills), the legislative committee is often required to consider criteria chosen to ensure that a valuable public policy is furthered by the private piece of legislation.[154] The consultative process preceding the introduction of the Charter in 1982 makes it difficult to accept that any particular interest groups set the agenda, so far as economic rights were concerned. The history of attempts at constitutional reform since that date reinforces this perception. Among the issues most vocally addressed by business representatives, such as the BCNI, has been a provision in the constitution that would strengthen the 'economic union.'[155] In 1982, the BCNI supported this concept through a right or as freedom that could be included in the Charter, either as a separate right or as a component of, for instance, section 6.[156] A decade later, the idea resurfaced as a proposed amendment to the Constitution Act, 1867.[157] In either event, the guarantee would have been a judicially enforceable limitation on a government's ability to make laws that interfered with economic efficiency.[158] If it were placed in the Constitution Act, 1867, the provision would have empowered the courts to strike down laws without having to entertain arguments about whether, under section 1 of the Charter, the law was justified as an attempt, for example, to correct market failure or to promote some public value that goes beyond economic efficiency. Notwithstanding the BCNI's pressure to have this kind of justiciable right adopted, in one form or the other, the guarantee has not yet been incorporated into the constitution.

Although writers such as Sunstein view democratic practices as necessarily interconnected with profound respect for private property and economic rights, their writing also tends to portray legislatures as forums of rent-seeking and erratic behaviour. Democracy, conceived as simple majority rule, is deeply flawed. Some public choice theorists view democracy as a potentially dangerous system against which society requires constitutional and judicial safeguards. Hence, part of Richard Epstein's call for the constitutionalization of economic rights involves a return to the conservative doctrine associated with the high-water mark of *Lochner*, in which the Supreme Court used the due process clause to invalidate a New York law imposing maximum working hours for bakers. In other words, these writers manifest both a distrust of majoritarian governance and a faith in courts as principled arbiters of what the law should be.[159] Judges can be counted on to be more politically virtuous than elected representatives. To this extent, public choice can be called on to aid in the campaign for conservatively activist courts.[160] Not all writers who see the value in public choice analysis are enamoured with the prospect of a return to the judicial orientation associated with the *Lochner* era, when governmental regulation of business was viewed as constitutionally suspect.[161] Other constitutional scholars, such as Ronald Dworkin, argue that *Lochner* was wrong when it was decided and there is no reason now to rehabilitate it. As against Macey's claim that the values that underpin economic rights are experiencing a rebirth, Dworkin points out: 'It is now generally agreed, after all, that freedom of contract is not a basic liberty: governments regularly restrict the power of contract not only to protect economically vulnerable citizens from bad bargains they might be forced to accept, but also to protect the community from the effects of contracts with injurious social or economic consequences, including, for example, contracts that restrain trade and competition.'[162]

Macey's arguments that the 'judicial culture' is changing and that economic rights are commanding more respect because the public choice theory of legislation is gaining adherents in the law schools are both difficult to verify. Mark Tushnet, for example, who has also written about the cultural setting of the law school, has conceded that the economic understanding of law reached its apex in the 1980s but that interest in it as 'the law of the future' has since declined.[163] There is no question that much literature has been spawned on the economic underpinnings of the U.S. constitution. But it would be a grand overstatement to say that there is significant agreement with Epstein's proposal that courts reverse the so-called revolution of 1937 and return to the constitutional premises of *Lochner*. Tushnet describes economic models as having become 'tamed, normalized, and compartmentalized' within the law schools.[164] In Canada, any debate on this issue has been filtered through questions about which rights particular types of litigants are able to invoke. There are few signs that the Supreme Court of Canada will do much more than make incremental progress in identifying the economic activities or interests protected under enumerated rights and freedoms. The Court does not appear to conceive of itself as a vigilant supervisor of the political exchanges that lie in the background of legislation.

Public choice theory depends on assumptions about the fragmentation of political interests. Its proponents find it difficult to attach any meaning to notions of the common good, or a single public interest. In this aspect of their conception of modern politics, public choice theorists claim illustrious forebears. They point to affinities with James Madison, who warned of the 'dangerous vice' of 'faction' in *The Federalist Papers*.[165] Indeed, one public choice theorist views much American political theory as stemming from images of the 'Madisonian Nightmare.'[166] Madison wrote of the 'instability, injustice and confusion' that factional politics introduces into deliberative assemblies.[167] His recommended cure for this natural tendency goes to the effects rather than to the causes of the problem. Factions are most powerfully influential when the state is small and the politicians are few. Therefore Madison insisted on institutional arrangements, including a large republic governed by a great number of representatives, a dispersal of power between a national government and the states, and checks and balances among the different arms of government.

Madison's advice about factionalism can be as readily applied to courts as to legislators. Because of the small size of the nine-member Supreme Court of Canada, factionalism is more liable to creep into its deliberations than, for example, those of the House of Commons. On the premises of public choice theory, the Supreme Court as a policy-making body is treated the same as a popular assembly, in that the motivation of its members is similarly rent-seeking. If this is true, then explicitly protecting economic rights through Charter review would not solve the problem of immunizing those economic rights from redistributive decision-making on self-interested grounds. The problem would merely be shifted from one political venue to another. Judges would not so obviously as elected politicians or bureaucrats be subject to the motives of self-aggrandizement, but public choice theory has tried to account for judicial behaviour on this topic. Whether courts enforce the interest-group bargains consolidated in legislation should depend on what is in it for the judges. Public choice analysis rejects the suggestion that judges will afford the level of protection to economic rights that is consistent with their ideological beliefs.[168] Instead, judicial preferences are explicable on grounds of economic rationality. Macey has offered something of this sort, but even his remarks on the 'judicial culture hypothesis' require a notion of dominant legal consciousness. He explains that judges refuse to protect economic rights because, in part, they are anxious about their professional reputation and that this involves an economic calculation. Even more important, Macey asserts that the best explanation for the treatment of economic rights is that 'this treatment best reflects the views of the legal culture from which these justices came.'[169] This reference back to the ideological matrix in which decision-making is grounded appears to be a real weakness in Macey's account of why courts tend to defer to legislators. It reverts to assumptions that are eschewed generally by public choice constitutionalism.

Rigorously followed, public choice theory can no more account for the rational, deliberative capacity of courts than for the same virtue in respect of legislatures. If economic rights are unprotected in the Charter, then it is difficult to see why judges should do anything to protect economic interests. This failing has disposed Cass Sunstein to propose a model of reinvigorated liberal constitutionalism. He has described afresh what he thinks constitutional interpretation and adjudication ought to involve, especially in cases where the impugned laws have changed existing entitlements.[170] The terrors of Madisonian factionalism and the prevalence of rent-seeking self-regard are taken as part of his baseline. To overcome the dangers inherent in politics as conceived by public choice, Sunstein recommends a 'republican' system of institutions, in which a great deal of confidence in placed in the processes of public deliberation. Democratic action is viewed as changing individual preferences, rather than taking them for granted, so that political outcomes are not assumed to be simply interest-driven. In his projected model, outlined in *The Partial Constitution*, Sunstein assigns to the courts a strongly deferential role, so that if the legislature enacts measures that redistribute wealth, judges should have only limited scope to overturn them. Sunstein counsels judicial restraint on the primary ground that, once democracy becomes truly deliberative, there is little reason for courts to strike down the political outcomes.[171] Furthermore, in his attempt to reconcile deliberative democracy with public choice assumptions, Sunstein appears to backtrack on the need for the entrenchment of economic rights in all constitutions. While he continues to urge constitutional protection of property rights in a system 'emerging from (say) Communism,' Sunstein argues that the same level of protection may be unnecessary closer to home because 'in the Anglo-American culture, the institutions of private property and civil society are firmly in place. A democratic justification for aggressive protection of property rights seems implausible under current conditions.'[172]

In Sunstein's ideal scheme, legislatures will be so trusted to reach the rational result that it would be hard to imagine why economic rights would have to be entrenched in the first place. Sunstein seems to offer more than a complement to public choice: his theory, as elaborated in *The Partial Constitution*, radically departs from many of the fundamental assumptions of public choice constitutionalism.

A final criticism of the public choice defence of economic rights in the Charter is the extent to which public choice advocates underestimate the power that courts would gain to oversee business-government relations. The entrenchment of economic rights could create an untameable judicial urge to review legislation favourable to commercial firms. Business representatives that take solace in the degree of judicial recognition of constitutionalized economic interests should be aware of the threat posed by entrenching economic rights outright in the Charter. Unless those economic rights are narrowly specified or restricted, business might find that courts are endowed with extraordinary powers to roll back advantages to which firms have become accustomed. If judges are empowered, through the express protection of economic rights, to test the validity of any government act tainted by rent-seeking behaviour, the ensuing constitutional review would embrace more than just regulatory or social welfare legislation. Courts could conceivably become involved in scrutinizing and invalidating income-tax deductions and exemptions, tariffs and duties on goods traded internationally, governmental subsidies and financial guarantees, loans to private firms, government-procurement policies, public-works contracts, and any other activities which, in the judgment of the court, are likely to have been influenced by a particular interest group. When a judge discerns that a law impairs economic efficiency, this by itself might become a ground for declaring it a violation of the Charter. The impugned law may be an entire statute, or merely a part of a statute, depending on whether the court is persuaded that the trace of interest-group influence marks the whole regime or merely some details contained in it. Under section 1, courts would then consider the reasonableness of such a violation. This spectre of increasing the scope of judicial review over government-business relations would be an unwelcome side effect to business of extending the constitutional protection of economic rights. Yet it is not far-fetched.

Conclusion

There are several salient lessons to be drawn from the foregoing analysis. First, it should be clear that economic values and interests play a role in the interpretation of Charter rights and freedoms. As Judge Easterbrook has concluded in regard to the U.S. Supreme Court, the 'common perception' that the Court has dropped out of the business of business regulation is wrong.[173] Enumerated rights, as elaborated and applied by the Canadian Supreme Court, often have economic aspects or components that determine whether a law has infringed those rights. In addition, the economic character of the interest violated by the law can be a factor influencing the Court's decision about whether the law can be saved after all, under section 1.

At an abstract level, the insights of public choice theory appear promising to the extent that they might explain the politicians' exclusion of property and economic rights from the Charter. Public choice constitutionalism also provides an array of reasons for repairing this gap. But on neither account is the promise fulfilled. On its own premises, public choice fails to reflect how the Supreme Court of Canada has recognized the significance of claims to governmental interference with economic activities. Economic rights of firms and individuals have achieved a foothold in Charter jurisprudence to a degree that would puzzle the public choice analyst. As David Schneiderman has pointed out, 'in these cases the court has simply recognized that the discourse of economic exchange' predominates in Canadian society.[174]

From the point of view of business, the availability of Charter protection against governmental regulation has been valuable. There have been undoubted victories for business in the courts. Whether this amounts to a notorious abuse of the original purposes of the Charter is debatable. It is difficult to settle this issue because just what were the original purposes itself requires an interpretive exercise steeped in controversy. Moreover, any judgment on the matter depends on whether one believes that economic activities, including the use of whatever form of business planning or device is lawful, are central to the values of autonomy and self-realization that underlie the Charter.

Giving economic interests further recognition or increased weight under the Charter will probably present business with a mixture of gains and losses. While this might enable courts to scrutinize closely the regulatory environment which presses down on firms' activities in the market-place, it may also have the effect of inviting judges to review government acts or policies that are designed to stimulate business development or reward or favour individual enterprises. The externalities caused by such heightened judicial oversight may be difficult for business firms to absorb.

Finally, it should be said that, in construing various provisions in the Charter, the Supreme Court has succeeded in breathing life into guarantees favourable to commercial firms. The Court has been less generous about recognizing the economic rights of organized labour or individual employees. This illustrates one of the dangers of broadly constitutionalizing economic rights: there is no way to tell in advance which rights will be found to be essential for any particular claimant. One of the lessons of public choice theory is that, with a dearth of or only minimal constitutional protection, economic rights will least inhibit the resolution of one of the key issues of ordinary, non-constitutional politics: how wealth should be redistributed through governmental action. On balance, justice requires that economic rights continue to be left out of the Charter, and, further, that the Supreme Court of Canada re-examine how its doctrines so far have distributed economic rights unequally.

Notes

1 Part I of the Constitution Act, 1982, being Schedule B to the Canada Act 1982 (U.K.), 1982, c. 11.

2 One should keep in mind the extent to which an administrative tribunal also has the power to determine the constitutional validity of its constitutive statute: see *Cuddy Chicks Ltd. v. Ontario (Labour Relations Board)*, [1991] 2 S.C.R. 5 and its companion case, *Tétrault-Gadoury v. Canada (Employment and Immigration Commission)*, [1991] 2 S.C.R. 22.

3 For a discussion of the difference between constitutional rights, which tend to be framed in abstract guarantees or standards, and legal rights, which are concrete and do not require reference to any background political morality, see Ronald Dworkin, *Taking Rights Seriously*, rev. ed. (Cambridge, Mass.: Harvard University Press 1977), at 90–4 and 105–23.

4 With some effect, to judge by some of the opinions of Justice Scalia: see, for example, *Nollan v. California Coastal Commission*, 483 U.S. 825 (1987); *Pennell v. City of San Jose*, 485 U.S. 1 (1988) (Justice Scalia in dissent); and *Lucas v. South Carolina Coastal Council*, 112 S.Ct. 2886 (1992).

5 See the speech of Blaine Thacker MP in *House of Commons Debates*, 15 Dec. 1981, at 14,105.

6 See the remarks of Nick Schultz (associate general counsel of the Public Interest Advocacy Centre) in the *Proceedings of the Special Joint Committee on the Constitution of Canada* (18 Dec. 1980), 29:20–1, 24–33.

7 See ibid., 12 Dec. 1980, 27:47.

8 See Andrew Cohen, *A Deal Undone: The Making and Breaking of the Meech Lake Accord* (Vancouver and Toronto: Douglas and McIntyre 1990), 220. The disclaimer is contained in Business Council on National Issues, *National Priorities: A Submission to the Royal Commission on the Economic Union and Devlopment Prospects for Canada* (Ottawa: The Council 1983), 76.

9 *Proceedings of the Special Joint Committee,* 7 Jan. 1981, 33:134–5, 144, 153–4.

10 For illustrative views and exchanges, see ibid., 18 Nov. 1980, 7: 105–6 and
    27 Jan. 1981, 46:17–30.
11 See Alexander Alvaro, 'Why Property Rights Were Excluded from the Charter of
    Rights and Freedoms,' *Canadian Journal of Political Science*, vol. 24 (1991),
    309, and Richard W. Bauman, 'Property Rights in the Canadian Constitutional
    Context,' *South African Journal of Human Rights,* vol. 8 (1992), 344.
12 Provincial opposition to the entrenchment of property rights was emphasized by
    Jean Chrétien, then minister of justice, in discussing the issue before the Charter
    was adopted: see *House of Commons Debates*, 26 Jan. 1981, 6,545. It was
    reiterated by Chrétien's successor, Mark MacGuigan, during debates arising out
    of a Conservative Party motion to amend the Charter by adding protection of
    property rights: see ibid., 29 April 1983, 25,003–4.
13 See Government of Canada, *Shaping Canada's Future Together: Proposals*
    (Ottawa: Minister of Supply and Services Canada 1991), 3.
14 See Alvaro, 'Why Property Rights Were Excluded.'
15 An illustration of the extent to which an owner's property rights can be subordi-
    nated is found in *Hartel Holdings Co. v. Calgary*, [1984] 1 S.C.R. 337. In her
    judgment for the Court, Justice Wilson noted how the provincial-planning
    legislation in question 'has gradually moved away from the situation in which
    the rights of the property owner were given paramount consideration towards
    the situation in which planning flexibility and the public interest are given
    paramountcy': see ibid., 353.
16 See *The Queen in Right of British Columbia v. Tener*, [1985] 1 S.C.R. 533.
17 See, for example, *House of Commons Debates,* 10 March 1981, 8,081–2.
18 An amendment proposed by Svend Robinson MP was aimed at making section 7
    unavailable to corporate claimants: see *Proceedings of the Special Joint Commit-
    tee*, 23 Jan. 1981 44:7–11.
19 See 'Business may benefit most from Charter of Rights,' *Globe and Mail*,
    5 Jan. 1985, B1, B3; 'Rights Charter gives edge to corporations,' *Calgary Herald*,
    5 Jan. 1985, D15; and 'Rights Charter favours corporations: expert,' *Vancouver
    Sun*, 7 Jan. 1985, B9.
20 See 'The missing link: let's get property rights into our Charter before Canada
    Day rolls around again,' *Vancouver Sun*, 29 June 1985, A6, and 'Property rights
    change gets support of Board,' *Calgary Herald*, 5 Oct. 1985, F4. The board
    referred to in the latter article was the Calgary Real Estate Board.
21 See Business Council on National Issues, *Canada's Constitutional Future: A
    Response by the Business Council on National Issues to the Government of
    Canada Proposal 'Shaping Canada's Future Together'* (Ottawa: The Council
    1992), 6–7.

22 See, for example, 'Property, personal rights could collide: proposal gains backing of real estate lobby, but denounced by the poor,' *Globe and Mail*, 25 Sept. 1991, A10, and 'Property rights plan under fire: critics warn of "unintended" effects on zoning rules, native claims, women,' *Globe and Mail*, 2 Oct. 1991, A5.

23 See Allan Hutchinson and Andrew Petter, 'Charter's core values don't belong to property owners,' *Canadian Lawyer*, vol. 10, no. 6 (September 1986), 23 and 42.

24 See, for example, *Citizens Insurance Company of Canada v. Parsons* (1881), 7 A.C. 96.

25 See Peter W. Hogg, *Constitutional Law of Canada*, 3rd ed. (Toronto: Carswell 1992) 1,263–64.

26 On the issue of corporate standing, see the relatively early literature, including William D. Moull, 'Business Law Implications of the Canadian Charter of Rights and Freedoms,' *Canadian Business Law Journal*, vol. 8 (1984), 449; Wallace Rozéfort, 'Are Corporations Entitled to Freedom of Religion Under the Canadian Charter of Rights and Freedoms,' *Manitoba Law Journal*, vol. 15 (1986), 199; and Gerald D. Chipeur, 'Section 15 of the Charter Protects People and Corporations – Equally,' *Candian Business Law Journal*, vol. 11 (1986), 304. For a sample of the critique of the Supreme Court's willingness to hear corporate claimants, see Andrew J. Petter, 'The Politics of the Charter,' *Supreme Court Law Review*, vol. 8 (1986), 473.

27 Chris Tollefson, 'Corporate Constitutional Rights and the Supreme Court of Canada,' *Queen's Law Journal*, vol. 19 (1993), 309.

28 See F.L. Morton, Peter H. Russell, and Michael J. Withey, 'The Supreme Court's First 100 Charter Decisions: A Statistical Analysis,' *Osgoode Hall Law Journal*, vol. 30 (1992), 1. Andrew Petter had warned in the mid-1980s that the greatest benefit from the use of the Charter would accrue to business corporations and well-heeled individuals: see Petter, 'Politics of the Charter,' 482–3. Dale Gibson has disputed whether the effect of corporate claims under the Charter has not been exaggerated, since only a small proportion (12 per cent) of Charter challenges have been initiated by corporations: see Dale Gibson, 'The Deferential Trojan Horse: A Decade of Charter Decisions,' *Canadian Bar Review*, vol. 72 (1993), 449.

29 For many years Joe's Confectionery operated in Elk Point, an eastern Alberta village in which I spent part of my re-imagined idyllic youth. Joe's served the same commercial and social functions as Lake Wobegon's Chatterbox Café and Mayberry's Snappy Lunch.

30 See 'Businesses wary of equality clause,' *Vancouver Sun*, 16 April 1985, C2.

31 Rainer Knopff and F. L. Morton, *Charter Politics* (Scarborough, Ont.: Nelson Canada 1992), 79.

32 Ibid.
33 See George Koch, 'Rise of the "Court Party": activists are abusing the Charter for partisan ends,' *Alberta (Western) Report*, 18 Nov. 1991, 10–11.
34 See Constitution Act, 1867 (U.K.), 30 & 31 Vict., c. 3, s. 121.
35 See, for instance, Martha Jackman, 'Poor Rights: Using the Charter to Support Social Welfare Claims,' *Queen's Law Journal*, vol. 19 (1993), 65.
36 For a survey of different views evincing greater or lesser hope on this score, see the papers collected in *Social Justice and the Constitution: Perspectives on a Social Union for Canada*, eds. Joel Bakan and David Schneiderman (Ottawa: Carleton University Press 1992).
37 For arguments that freedom of expression is more important that property rights, see Alexander Meiklejohn, *Free Speech and Its Relation to Self-Government* (New York: Harper 1948), 2.
38 *Irwin Toy Ltd. v. Quebec (Attorney General)*, [1989] 1 S.C.R. 927.
39 See Cass R. Sunstein, 'On Property and Constitutionalism,' *Cardozo Law Review*, vol. 14 (1993), 907.
40 See James W. Ely, Jr, *The Guardian of Every Other Right* (New York: Oxford University Press 1992), 26, and James M. Buchanan, *Property as a Guarantor of Liberty* (Aldershot, Hants: E. Elgar 1993).
41 See Bernard H. Siegan, 'Constitutional Protection of Property and Economic Rights,' *San Diego Law Review*, vol. 29 (1992), 162.
42 Sunstein, 'On Property,' 915–16.
43 See Laurence Tribe, *American Constitutional Law*, 2nd ed. (Mineola, N.Y.: Foundation Press 1988), 681–2, and Kathleen M. Sullivan, 'Unconstitutional Conditions,' *Harvard Law Review*, vol. 102 (1989), 1, 413. The doctrine has been explained as a response to a collective action problem in Richard A. Epstein, *Bargaining With the State* (Princeton: Princeton University Press 1993), 79: 'As a single unified entity, the state may be able to make offers to widely dispersed individuals who find themselves faced with a prisoner's dilemma game. Each person acting alone may think it in his interest to waive some constitutional right, even though a group, if it could act collectively, would reach the opposite conclusion. By barring some waivers of constitutional rights, the doctrine of unconstitutional conditions allows disorganized citizens to escape from what would otherwise be a socially destructive prisoner's dilemma game.
44 Jonathan R. Macey, 'Some Causes and Consequences of the Bifurcated Treatment of Economic Rights and "Other" Rights Under the United States Constitution,' in *Economic Rights*, eds. Ellen Frankel Paul, Fred D. Miller, Jr, and Jeffrey Paul (New York: Cambridge University Press 1992), 149.
45 Ibid., 150.

46 Judge Learned Hand eloquently described the value of the individual vote thus: 'Of course I know how illusory would be the belief that my vote determined anything; but nevertheless when I go the polls I have a satisfaction in the sense that we are all engaged in a common venture. If you retort that a sheep in the flock may feel something like it; I reply, following Saint Francis, "My brother, the Sheep."' (*The Bill of Rights* [Cambridge, Mass.: Harvard University Press 1958], 74).

47 [1992] 2 S.C.R. 731.

48 Stanley Fish, *There's No Such Thing as Free Speech ... And It's a Good Thing, Too* (New York: Oxford University Press 1994), 108.

49 Such assumptions are controversial: see Amartya Sen, 'Rational Fools: A Critique of the Behavioral Foundations of Economic Theory,' *Philosophy and Public Affairs*, vol. 6 (1977), 317.

50 Steven Kelman, '"Public Choice" and Public Spirit,' *Public Interest*, vol. 87 (1987), 93.

51 See Geoffrey Brennan and James M. Buchanan, 'Is Public Choice Immoral? The Case for the "Nobel" Lie,' *Virginia Law Review*, vol. 74 (1988), 179.

52 For a survey of opinions on the usefulness of public choice theory, see Daniel A. Farber and Philip P. Frickey, *Law and Public Choice: A Critical Introduction* (Chicago: University of Chicago Press 1991), 13–21.

53 Public choice provides the dominant model used in William T. Stanbury, *Business-Government Relations in Canada: Influencing Public Policy*, 2nd ed. (Scarborough, Ont.: Nelson Canada 1993), especially 100–13. A more pluralist presentation of basic explanatory models is contained in G. Bruce Doern and Richard W. Phidd, *Canadian Public Policy: Ideas, Structure, Process* (Toronto: Methuen 1983), 137–61, in which public choice takes its place alongside models based on 'rationalism,' incrementalism, and class analysis.

54 This description of public choice as one type of right-wing legal economics is contained in Mark Kelman, 'On Democracy-Bashing: A Skeptical Look at the Theoretical and "Empirical" Practice of the Public Choice Movement,' *Virginia Law Review*, vol. 74 (1988), 201.

55 See, for example, Jon Elster, *Making Sense of Marx* (Cambridge: Cambridge University Press 1985). For an attempt to reconstruct public choice models so as to produce radically different empirical strategies, see Patrick Dunleavy, *Democracy, Bureaucracy and Public Choice: Economic Explanations in Political Science* (New York: Prentice Hall 1992).

56 See Jonathan R. Macey, 'Transaction Costs and the Normative Elements of the Public Choice Model: An Application to Constitutional Theory,' *Virginia Law Review*, vol. 74 (1988), 472 n. 4: 'Rent-seeking refers to the attempt to obtain

economic rents (i.e., rates of return on the use of an economic asset in excess of the market rate) through governmental intervention in the market. An example of rent-seeking is a firm's attempt to secure government-granted monopolies. Such monopolies allow a firm to increase its prices above competitive levels. The resulting profits represent economic rents from government regulation.'

57 See George Stigler, 'The Theory of Economic Regulation,' *Bell Journal of Economics and Management Science*, Sci. vol. 2 (1971), 10–13; Robert D. Tollison, 'Public Choice and Legislation,' *Virginia Law Review*, vol. 74 (1988), 339; Jerry Mashaw, 'The Economics of Politics and the Understanding of Public Law,' *Chicago-Kent Law Review*, vol. 65 (1989), 123; and Richard A. Posner, *Economic Analysis of Law*, 4th ed. (Boston: Little, Brown 1992), 524–28.

58 See Stanbury, *Business-Government Relations*, 112–13.

59 See Farber and Frickey, *Law and Public Choice*, 23–4, and Mancur Olson, *The Logic of Collective Action: Public Goods and the Theory of Groups* (Cambridge, Mass.: Harvard University Press 1965), 162. A variegated approach to the influence of ideology in legislative voting is described in Tollison, 'Public Choice and Legislation,' 351–3, where the author remarks that the 'issue, then, is not whether ideology matters at all to political behavior, but how much and under what conditions.'

60 See Anthony Downs, *An Economic Theory of Democracy* (New York: Harper and Row 1957), 210.

61 Ibid., 212.

62 Thus, individual consumers, despite their numbers, tend not to be as well represented by organized interest groups as producers, manufacturers, or retailers: see Farber and Frickey, *Law and Public Choice*, 24.

63 See Tollison, 'Public Choice and Legislation,' 342–3.

64 Downs, *Economic Theory of Democracy*, 141.

65 See Tollison, 'Public Choice and Legislation,' 343.

66 See Richard A. Posner, *The Economics of Justice* (Cambridge, Mass.: Harvard University Press 1981), 91–4. The Kaldor-Hicks concept of efficiency depends on overall wealth maximization, taking into account both the benefits accruing to the two parties to a bilateral transaction and the harm (if any) caused to third parties. For a good explanation of why he prefers the Kaldor-Hicks view of efficiency over its rivals, which include Paretian efficiency, see Posner, *Economic Analysis of Law*, 13–16. Pareto-optimality as the standard of efficiency requires economists to make a number of 'restrictive assumptions' (such as zero transaction costs and zero redistribution costs) which remove the economic analysis 'far from real life': Werner Z. Hirsch, *Law and Economics: An Introductory Analysis*, 2nd ed. (San Diego: Academic Press 1988), 7. Posner characterizes Kaldor-Hicks efficiency as 'less austere' and more commonly used than the Paretian model (14).

67 Public choice analysts tend to use U.S. examples to support their generalizations, and therefore, the committee process of the U.S. Congress, so important a feature of national politics, is treated as the norm.

68 On campaign expenditures, see *National Citizens Coalition v. Canada (Attorney General)* (1984), 11 D.L.R. (4th) 481 (Alta. Q.B.) and, on campaign contributions by third parties, see the decision of Justice MacLeod in *Somerville v. Canada (Attorney General)* (unreported decision of 25 June 1993, Alta. Q.B.).

69 For a survey, see Macey, 'Causes and Consequences,' 162–6.

70 Ibid., 167–9.

71 198 U.S. 45 (1905).

72 See *West Coast Hotel v. Parrish*, 300 U.S. 379 (1937).

73 Macey, 'Causes and Consequences.'

74 Sunstein, 'On Property,' 917–18.

75 Ibid., 917.

76 See Dennis C. Mueller, 'Choosing a Constitution in East Europe: Lessons from Public Choice,' *Journal of Corporate Economics*, vol. 15, no. 2 (1991), 325.

77 Sunstein, 'On Property,' 923–4.

78 This is the approach in U.S. constitutional law: see ibid., 924. If a right against interference with contractual relations had been set out in the Charter, this might have protected the acquirors of Toronto's Pearson Airport, under the deal with the outgoing Conservative federal government that was rescinded as one of the first official acts of the Liberal administration which took power in October 1993.

79 See the Anti-Inflation Act, S.C. 1974–75–76, c. 75.

80 Sunstein, 'On Property,' 925.

81 Ibid., 926–9.

82 Ibid., 919–20.

83 *Law Society of Upper Canada v. Shapinker*, [1984] 1 S.C.R. 357.

84 Ibid., at 379–80 (per Estey J.).

85 Ibid., at 383.

86 [1989] 1 S.C.R. 591.

87 Ibid., at 612.

88 Ibid., at 618.

89 [1984] 2 S.C.R. 145.

90 Ibid., at 157.

91 Ibid., at 158.

92 Ibid., at 159. Section 8 has also been invoked to protect an individual's bodily integrity: see *R. v. Dyment*, [1988] 2 S.C.R. 417. In *Dyment*, Justice La Forest noted that the purpose of the guarantee against unreasonable search or seizure transcends the need merely to prevent 'governmental intrusions on property,'

104 Richard W. Bauman

(see ibid., at 426). La Forest also noted that 'privacy is at the heart of liberty in a modern state' and that 'grounded in man's physical and moral autonomy, privacy is essential for the well-being of the individual' (ibid., at 427).

93 [1984] 25 S.C.R. at 159. The Supreme Court has subsequently made clear that 'individuals and corporations alike' have privacy rights that should not lightly be trammelled by the government: see *Canadian Broadcasting Corporation v. Lessard*, [1991] 3 S.C.R. 421 at 444 (per Cory J.). Where the premises in question belong to a media corporation, according to Cory, the firm is 'entitled to particularly careful consideration' because the media are especially important in maintaining a democratic society (see ibid.).

94 [1985] 1 S.C.R. 295.

95 Ibid., at 314.

96 Ibid.

97 Ibid., at 337 (per Dickson C.J.).

98 [1986] 2 S.C.R. 713.

99 Ibid., at 758–9.

100 Ibid., at 761–2.

101 [1993] 3 S.C.R. 675.

102 In *Hy and Zel's*, the attorney general brought applications under the provision in the *Retail Business Holidays Act* that contemplate court orders to ensure compliance with the statute. The retailers initiated a suit seeking, among other remedies, a declaration that the whole or part of the legislation was invalid.

103 The most recent authoritative statement of the Supreme Court of Canada's doctrine on judicial discretion to grant standing is *Canadian Council of Churches v. Canada (Minister of Employment and Immigration)*, [1992] 1 S.C.R. 236. For a critical review of recent decisions on standing, see June M. Ross, 'Further Restrictions on Access to Charter Review: A Comment on *Hy and Zel's Inc. v. Ontario (A.G.)*,' *Constitutional Forum*, vol. 5 (1994), 22.

104 [1993] 3 S.C.R. at 690.

105 [1986] 2 S.C.R. 573.

106 Ibid., at 588 (per McIntyre J.).

107 See *Ford v. Quebec (Attorney General)*, [1988] 2 S.C.R. 712 at 764.

108 In *Reference re Public Service Employee Relations Act (Alberta)*, [1987] 1 S.C.R. 313, the Court examined provincial legislation that prohibited strikes and imposed compulsory arbitration in respect of disputes involving three public-service unions. In *P.S.A.C. v. Canada*, [1987] 1 S.C.R. 424, section 2(d) was invoked by the union representing federal public-sector employees objecting to federal legislation imposing special restraints on wage increases, thus precluding collective bargaining on this issue. In *R.W.D.S.U. v. Saskatchewan*, [1987] 1 S.C.R. 460, unions representing workers in the dairy industry challenged special

provincial laws temporarily denying union rights to strike and employer rights to impose a lock-out in that industry.

109 See *Reference re Public Service Employee Relations Act (Alberta)* at 390–1.

110 Ibid., at 363–4.

111 Ibid., at 367–8.

112 See n.107.

113 See, for example, *Re Klein and Law Society of Upper Canada* (1985), 16 D.L.R. (4th) 489 (Ont. Div. Ct.). In contrast with Klein, the Court in *Re Grier and Alberta Optometric Association* (1987), 42 D.L.R. (4th) 327 (Alta. C.A.), decided that commercial expression was protected by section 2(b).

114 See *Klein* at 532 (per Callaghan J.).

115 See ibid., at 539.

116 *Ford*, at 767.

117 Ibid.

118 [1995] S.C.J. No. 68 (Q.L.), at para. 171.

119 Ibid.

120 *Ford*, at 767.

121 [1989] 1 S.C.R. 927.

122 [1990] 2 S.C.R. 232.

123 Ibid., at 247.

124 Ibid.

125 Ibid. at 248–9.

126 *Irwin Toy* at 1,002–3.

127 In *Edwards Books*, in a brief disquisition on the section 7 issue, Chief Justice Dickson stated that the 'liberty' in that part of the Charter does not extend to 'an unconstrained right to transact business whenever one wishes': see [1986] 2 S.C.R., at 786.

128 *Irwin Toy*, at 1,003.

129 Ibid.

130 [1990] 1 S.C.R. 425. See also *Thomson's* companion case, *Stelco Inc. v. Canada (Attorney General)*, [1990] 1 S.C.R. 617.

131 Justice Wilson took a different approach in *Thomson* and found that, because the officers were themselves made subject to the RTPC's orders, section 7 applies. If section 17 of the Combines Investigation Act were struck down as violating section 7, then of course the corporation itself would benefit from this result. In her analysis, Wilson held that the rights to liberty and security of the person were violated in this instance and that this violation contravened the principles of fundamental justice: see [1990] 1 S.C.R., 431.

132 [1990] 1 S.C.R. 705.

133 See ibid., at 709 (per Cory J.).

134 [1991] 3 S.C.R. 154.
135 Ibid., at 181 (per Lamer C.J.).
136 Ibid., at 182. Chief Justice Lamer had made this same point before in *Reference re B.C. Motor Vehicle Act*, [1985] 2 S.C.R. 486, 518.
137 [1993] 3 S.C.R., at 699.
138 Ibid., at 703. This formula is derived from *Smith v. Attorney General of Ontario*, [1924] S.C.R. 331. For the majority in *Hy and Zel's*, Justice Major held that *Smith* was superseded by the much more recent Supreme Court decisions on the availability of public-interest standing: see [1993] 3 S.C.R. at 694. In Justice L'Heureux-Dubé's view, the criteria for standing laid out in *Smith*, in regard to declaratory actions, survive and are merely supplemented by the later case law.
139 [1990] 3 S.C.R. 230.
140 [1991] 2 S.C.R. 211.
141 Ibid., at 318–19 (per La Forest J.).
142 Ibid., at 315.
143 [1991] 3 S.C.R. 654.
144 Ibid., at 675.
145 [1986] 2 S.C.R., at 603.
146 [1991] 3 S.C.R., at 674.
147 See Patrick Monahan and Marie Finkelstein, 'The Charter of Rights and Public Policy in Canada,' *Osgoode Hall Law Journal*, vol. 30 (1992), 501.
148 See Leslie A. Pal, 'Advocacy Organizations and Legislative Politics: The Effect of the Charter of Rights and Freedoms on Interest Lobbying of Federal Legislation, 1989–91,' in *Equity and Community: The Charter, Interest Advocacy and Representation*, ed. F. Leslie Seidle (Ottawa: The Institute for Research on Public Policy 1993), 119. On the significant influence of corporate lobbyists, see Michael M. Atkinson and William D. Coleman, *The State, Business, and Industrial Change in Canada* (Toronto: University of Toronto Press 1989), 87–8.
149 See Tollefson, 'Corporate Constitutional Rights.'
150 From an address by Justice Sopinka to the Canadian Chamber of Commerce, Ottawa, as reported in *Financial Post*, 7 Aug. 1989, 10.
151 The general contours of the provincial power in this regard were established in a series of Privy Council cases inolving the insurance industry: see *A.G. Canada v. A.G. Alberta* (Insurance Reference]) [1916] 1 A.C. 588, *A.G. Ontario v. Reciprocal Insurers*, [1924] A.C. 328, and *Re Insurance Act of Canada,* [1932] A.C. 41.
152 See Farber and Frickey, *Law and Public Choice*, 68.
153 See Bill Pr6, *Gimbel Foundation Act*, 2nd Sess., 23rd Leg., Alberta, 1994.
154 For example, in Alberta, private bills that provide an exemption from general legislation are supposed to be enacted only in instances where the lawmakers are

satisfied that the reason for the request is not to seek a privileged position for one party in relation to its competitors. In addition, the criteria guiding the legislative committee's deliberations provide that the assembly's first priority is to the population as a whole and there must be some overwhelming public-policy justification for enacting an exemption through special legislation.

155 For data supporting the view that such barriers have interfered with economic efficiency and integration, see Thomas J. Courchene, *Economic Management and the Division of Powers* (Toronto: University of Toronto Press 1986), 212–3. For a discussion of the various types of barriers that can arise, see Robert Howse, *Economic Union, Social Justice, and Constitutional Reform: Towards a High But Level Playing Field* (North York: York University Centre for Public Law and Public Policy 1992), 17–34.

156 For an account of how section 6 might have been used to overcome interprovincial barriers, see Tanya Lee and Michael Trebilcock, 'Economic Mobility and Constitutional Reform,' *University of Toronto Law Journal*, vol. 37 (1987), 268.

157 See *Shaping Canada's Future*, 55, for the revamped 'common market' clause.

158 See David Schneiderman, 'The Market and the Constitution' in *Constitutional Politics*, eds. Duncan Cameron and Miriam Smith (Toronto: James Lorimer 1992), 59.

159 See Mark Tushnet, 'Idols of the Tribe: Public Choice Constitutionalism and Economic Rights,' in *Liberty, Property, and the Future of Constitutional Development*, eds. Ellen Frankel Paul and Howard Dickman (Greenwich, Conn.: JAI Press 1990), 23. Tushnet views public choice theory as the conservative version of the constitutional theory expounded in John Hart Ely, *Democracy and Distrust* (Cambridge, Mass.: Harvard University Press 1980).

160 This campaign made great strides during the 1980s: see David Kairys, *With Liberty and Justice for Some: A Critique of the Conservative Supreme Court* (New York: New Press 1993).

161 See Frank H. Easterbrook, 'The Constitution of Business,' *George Mason University Law Review*, vol. 11, no. 2 (1988), 54: 'The objection to review of economic legislation is that there is neither constitutional warrant for the beast nor any way to tame it.' See also Robert Bork, 'The Constitution, Original Intent, and Economic Rights,' *San Diego Law Review*, vol. 23 (1986), 829: 'Viewed from the standpoint of economic philosophy, and of individual freedom, the idea has many attractions. But viewed from the standpoint of constitutional structures, the idea works a massive shift away from democracy and toward judicial rule.'

162 Ronald Dworkin, 'Mr. Liberty,' *New York Review of Books*, vol. 41, no. 14 (11 Aug. 1994), 20n4.

163 Mark Tushnet, 'Idols of the Right: The Law-and-Economics Movement,' *Dissent* (Fall 1993), 480.

164 Ibid., at 482.
165 See Alexander Hamilton, James Madison, and John Jay, *The Federalist Papers*, No. 10 (New York: Bantam Books 1982), 42.
166 See William N. Eskridge, Jr., 'Politics Without Romance: Implications of Public Choice Theory for Statutory Interpretation,' *Virginia Law Review*, vol. 74 (1988), 280.
167 *Federalist Papers*, No. 10:42.
168 This claim has been made by Laurence Tribe to explain why the U.S. Supreme Court no longer protects economic liberty: see *American Constitutional Law*, 678–9.
169 Macey, 'Causes and Consequences,' 168.
170 Cass R. Sunstein, *The Partial Constitution* (Cambridge, Mass.: Harvard University Press 1993), 15–40.
171 Ibid., at 145–9.
172 Ibid., 143. Even with respect to renewed economic systems in central and eastern Europe, it would be advisable to survey and perhaps try out more policy options than simple entrenchment of economic rights. For innovative reform suggestions that contrast with the prescriptions of public choice, see *A Fourth Way? Privatization, Property, and the Emergence of New Market Economics*, eds. Gregory S. Alexander and Grazyna Skapska (New York: Routledge 1994).
173 See Easterbrook, 'Constitution of Business,' 55.
174 David Schneiderman, 'Being Large and Liberal,' in *Freedom of Expression and the Charter*, ed. David Schneiderman (Toronto: Thomson Professional Pub. Co. 1991), xl.

4

The Impact of the Canadian Charter of Rights and Freedoms on Income Tax Law and Policy*

KATHLEEN A. LAHEY

When the Charter of Rights was adopted in 1982, many Canadians had high hopes that the Charter guarantees of equality – especially sections 15 and 28 – would contribute to the promotion of genuine equality of all persons in Canada by providing a constitutional framework within which outmoded stereotypes, assumptions, and norms could be scrutinized for their discriminatory impact on disadvantaged groups.

Looking back over the last decade or so, one must conclude that the expectations and goals of equality seekers have certainly not been the dominant force in shaping income tax law and policy under the Charter. Indeed, it is becoming obvious that traditionally privileged groups have placed a great deal of pressure on the courts to employ the Charter to promote their interests at the expense of the historically disadvantaged. The result has been that, even when progressive values have emerged at all in fiscal Charter discourse, they have been easily distorted and twisted to support the status quo rather than forming a basis for rethinking income tax law or policy.

That there was considerable resistance to the application of Charter values to the Income Tax Act comes as no surprise. Equality theorists in the United States had predicted that members of disadvantaged groups might well find that they could lose more than they could gain as the result of Charter litigation.[1] Early Canadian studies suggested that dominant groups were making more active use of the Charter in litigation, and at the expense of members of historically disadvantaged groups.[2] An analysis of sex-equality litigation demonstrated that this was certainly true in relation to gender claims, as men

* Funding for this study was provided by the Centre for Constitutional Studies, University of Alberta, and by the Social Sciences and Humanities Research Council of Canada. The author wishes to thank Daina Groskaufmanis, Cynthia Tape, Joanne Prince, and Marguerite Russell for their assistance in the completion of the essay.

brought and won substantially more Charter challenges than women in the first few years after section 15 of the Charter came into effect.[3]

The present study of the impact of the Charter on income tax law and policy has grown out of this critical perspective[4] and has been conceived with a few basic questions in mind. First, just what Charter challenges have been brought to the Income Tax Act and what have been the results of those challenges? What groups have made use of the Charter, and who has won? Second, how have privileged groups attempted to capture and harness fiscal Charter jurisprudence to serve their own needs and to block the claims of disadvantaged and privileged taxpayers? Have the Charter guarantees materially affected the distributional impact of the Income Tax Act in any way, or does the income tax system continue to serve the interests of privileged groups?

The results of this study are presented in seven sections. The first section describes what equality seekers had expected from Charter review of income tax law and contrasts that with the 'numbers,' outlining the types of substantive income tax provisions that have actually led to Charter litigation and the distribution of 'wins' and 'losses.' In the remaining sections, fiscal Charter litigation and changes in income tax policy are examined in detail. These sections relate generally to six basic areas of income tax law: exemptions from income taxation; special categories of income; registered plans; anti-avoidance provisions; the taxation of persons who live in families; and the taxation of divorced and separated taxpayers.

The principal conclusion of this study is that three important factors have operated to shield the fundamental values reflected in income tax legislation from disruption by Charter challenges. One is the insistence that fiscal legislation should be subjected to a lower level of scrutiny under the Charter than other types of legislation, the argument being that the revenue-raising function of taxation is so central to the existence of the state that legislators are permitted more latitude in drafting taxation legislation. Although the courts have insisted that income tax legislation is subject to the same level of scrutiny as other types of legislation, they have actually paid Parliament greater deference on income tax policy than on other matters. A second factor has been the persistence of conservative and superficial definitions of equality in Charter litigation. Despite assertions in cases such as *Andrews v. Law Society of British Columbia*[5] that equality must be given a substantive meaning, courts at every level – including the Supreme Court itself – have found ways to uphold provisions in the Income Tax Act that allocate tax liability on the basis of factors such as sex, age, ability, or marital status, usually by 'reframing' these distinctions so as to base them not on personal characteristics but on differing income levels.

A third factor has been the interplay between equality litigation and the parliamentary process. The Charter is really set up to give Parliament the last word on the meaning of 'equality.' Thus, even claimants who have lost in court have sometimes 'won' in Parliament when the Income Tax Act has been amended to adopt their perspective. The opposite is true as well: if the government of the day is unhappy with a court decision, it can mobilize the entire legislative process to contain or override that result with 'reform' legislation. Not surprisingly, Parliament has intervened in tax policy issues most frequently on the side of the privileged; indeed, in recent years, it has not once intervened on the side of the historically disadvantaged.

Hopes and Realities

Even before section 15 of the Charter came into effect in 1985, it had become clear on the basis of the United States experience that the Charter would probably not have much impact on income tax legislation. The one area where a difference in outcome was expected, however, was that of sex discrimination. Section 15 of the Charter had been strongly influenced by the Equal Rights Amendment (ERA) movement in the United States. Though the ERA was never adopted in that country, Canadian women were hopeful that the Canadian ERA would help eradicate discrimination on the basis of sex, even when that discrimination was embodied in income tax legislation. This section outlines the nature of these hopes and what has become of them.

Women's Hopes

Canadian women had been aware since the early 1970s that the Income Tax Act had been constructed around fundamentally masculinist and hierarchical visions of women. In its 1970 report, the Royal Commission on the Status of Women recommended that the Income Tax Act be amended to eliminate structural barriers to women's participation in wage labour.[6] Some of the commission's recommendations were eventually adopted.[7] However, by the 1980s the combination of male attacks on the validity of the child-care expense deduction[8] and continued pressure to provide some tax benefits to married couples[9] had brought to an end any hope that income tax reform might benefit women.

When the sex-equality guarantees in the Charter of Rights were drafted, women began to think that there was still some room for change. Between 1982 and 1985, women legal scholars devoted a great deal of energy to studying the potential impact of the Charter of Rights on various areas of law in

Canada. One of the most ambitious non-governmental projects was the Statute Audit Project carried out by the Charter of Rights Educational Fund (CREF), which made recommendations to the parliamentary committee on equality rights on income tax legislation. CREF looked at the Income Tax Act specifically from the perspective of women and low-income taxpayers and called for numerous changes.

Things began to look very bleak after the parliamentary committee released its report. Not only did the report largely ignore CREF's recommendations,[11] the government of the day rejected even the limited recommendations the committee had made with respect to disabled and cohabiting taxpayers[12] and systemic discrimination,[13] and it also began the process of turning the definition of substantive equality upside down by taking the position that the only taxpayers who were disadvantaged by the provisions of the Income Tax Act were married persons.[14]

Political Realities

Since the Charter of Rights came into effect in 1985, taxpayers have raised Charter issues in approximately 300 income tax appeals.[15] The most striking thing about these challenges is that the government has won almost every case. Eight taxpayers won substantive cases on the merits of the tax provisions in question,[16] but only two taxpayers have won their appeals on Charter grounds – Linda Lazarescu (the Tax Court of Canada ruled that the taxpayer did not have to include child-support payments in her own income),[17] and Marcelle Mercier (the Tax Court invalidated the eighteen-year age limit in the equivalent-to-married credit).[18] Because the Lazarescu decision more than likely will be treated from now on as having been overruled by the Supreme Court decision in *The Queen v. Thibaudeau*, only one Charter challenge to the Income Tax Act has succeeded to date.

Virtually all of the Charter issues raised in taxation cases have been raised by individuals – only one substantive Charter issue has been raised by a corporation,[19] and only one by a union.[20] However, the vast majority of Charter issues have been raised by men. Seventy per cent of the 104 substantive appeals have been brought by men, and in another six cases Charter issues were raised by husband-and-wife couples. Only 24 per cent of the Charter issues were raised by women litigants acting independently. The fact that the two substantive challenges that have succeeded were brought by women is not significant, since the *Lazarescu* case is probably irrelevant now and the issue raised in *Mercier* is not particularly germane to the status of women in Canada.

Literally every structural feature of the Canadian Income Tax Act has been brought under review in Charter challenges. Tax protesters and Native persons have attempted to invoke the Charter to buttress claims for at least partial tax exemptions; the tax consequences of bunched income[21] have been challenged in a variety of ways;[22] taxpayers have challenged the validity of anti-avoidance and collection provisions; and the creation of special categories of income, as well as the allocation of tax benefits to special groups of taxpayers, have been brought into question. The taxation of the family has received considerable attention. Several cases have revolved around the extent of women's separate economic and legal identity;[23] means-tested tax benefits and family-income rules have been challenged under section 15 of the Charter; the alimony, child support, child tax credit, and child care expense deduction provisions have all attracted numerous challenges, as have various provisions relating to the tax unit, concepts of dependency, age limits or requirements, disability credits, and sales-tax credits. The rules relating to registered retirement plans have also been litigated extensively.

Taxpayers have invoked several different constitutional theories in these cases. They have argued that various provisions of the Income Tax Act violate section 7 of the Charter, on the ground that security of the person includes economic security; they have attempted to invoke the legal rights of section 8 in various ways; they have appealed to the equality guarantees in sections 15 and 28 of the Charter; and they have attempted to prove that even provisions of the Income Tax Act that appear, on the surface, to be neutral in fact have a discriminatory impact on some members of disadvantaged groups. Especially in light of the Supreme Court decisions in *The Queen v. Symes*[24] and *The Queen v. Thibaudeau*,[25] however, it has become clear not only that section 15 of the Charter is much weaker than equality seekers had initially believed, and that the 'reasonable limits' provision of section 1 is much more powerful, but that a *de facto* lower level of scrutiny surrounds provisions of the Income Tax Act. The result is that, for the time being, Parliament has a huge scope for action in relation to Charter challenges to the Income Tax Act, and this fact alone threatens to frustrate many of the hopes that members of disadvantaged groups – especially women, women with children, and lesbian and gay couples – have had for the future. Parliament has already demonstrated a willingness to be guided by litigation brought by members of privileged groups such as men and married heterosexuals in formulating legislative amendments that buttress the tax benefits received by those groups. Given the unique role that the Income Tax Act plays in giving the government unlimited resources to defend its own legislation against Charter challenges, it seems particularly unfair that the

Supreme Court has come to exhibit so much deference to Parliament in this regard.

Exemptions from Income Taxation

Two important groups of taxpayers have sought authority in the Charter of Rights for their claims to exemptions from income taxation – tax protesters who would ordinarily be liable for income taxation, and Native persons who felt that they were unfairly denied the benefit of the tax exemption for status Indians under the Indian Act. Both groups have been disappointed by the courts' interpretation of the Charter.

Tax Protesters

Income tax legislation has attracted repeated constitutional challenges since it was first introduced in North America.[26] With the adoption of the Charter of Rights, political protesters have claimed partial exemption from income taxation on the basis that, as taxpayers, they could not be forced to give financial support to government activities that they felt were invalid. To date, such claims have been brought, on the one hand, by taxpayers protesting military expenditures, and, on the other, by taxpayers who have opposed government funding of abortion services.

The leading case on military protests to income taxation was brought by Jerilynn Prior. Prior had refused to pay 10.5 per cent of her taxes to the federal government and instead paid them to the Peace Tax Fund of Victoria, British Columbia. In the appeal she launched against her reassessment, the Tax Court of Canada held that any violation of her right to freedom of conscience and religion as guaranteed by the Charter of Rights was demonstrably justifiable in a free and democratic society.[27] The taxpayer then commenced an action in the Federal Court – Trial Division, seeking a declaration that to require her to pay the full amount of her income tax did violate her Charter rights. At that time, she included section 15 of the Charter in the grounds for her application. The crown countered with an application to dismiss the taxpayer's statement of claim as disclosing no reasonable cause of action.

The Court granted the crown's application on the basis of section 1 of the Charter, and this result was upheld by both the Federal Court of Appeal and the Supreme Court of Canada.[28] The Federal Court reasoned that the taxpayer could not show that she had been compelled to act contrary to her conscience, because the mere payment of tax did not identify her with the military or with other functions of the government, and that the Charter could not override the taxation provisions of the Constitution Act, 1867.[29] The Court further noted that it did not have jurisdiction to grant the remedy sought by the taxpayer, because allowing her to pay part of her tax liability to a non-governmental organization would require the Court, in essence, to amend the rate provisions of the Income Tax Act or to create a tax-credit scheme.

Several military protesters subsequently launched challenges to the Income Tax Act on the same grounds as Prior.[30] In each case, the minister of national revenue brought an application to quash the appeal for failure to state a reasonable cause of action, and in each the Court granted the minister's application, describing one appeal a 'purported appeal' because it had so little merit in law.[31]

Those who understand the importance of abortion services to the status of women have been, ironically, grateful for the way the courts approached the Prior cases. When Gerard O'Sullivan withheld $50 from his tax payable, declaring that it was 'to be held in trust in solemn protest against the use of taxpayers' money to pay for the murder of the unborn,' the courts consistently held that the government of a secular state could not enforce any one set of religious beliefs, could not permit ardent believers to incite co-religionists to commit illegal or anti-constitutional acts in the name of religion or God, and could be restrained only from forcing the taxpayer to participate personally in the provision of abortion services. The courts drew a distinction between requiring the taxpayer to contribute to general government revenues, which it held to be constitutional, and requiring personal participation in practices to which the taxpayer objected.[32]

Indian Act Exemption

Native persons who fall within the scope of the Indian Act have always been exempt from taxation of personal property situate on the reserve.[33] This exemption was originally granted in order to ensure that treaty entitlements would not be eroded indirectly by taxation. Over time, the courts have given this exemption wide application. The Charter cases involving the exemption have dealt with two distinct types of issues. Some have considered challenges to the types of income streams to which the courts have applied the exemption; others have considered challenges to the circumstances in which Native persons have been denied the legal status of 'Indian,' which is a precondition to eligibility for the exemption.

Nineteenth-century jurisprudence in the United States established that exemptions from taxation for Native persons are to be interpreted liberally: Indian treaties 'must ... be construed, not according to the technical meaning of [their] words ... but in the sense in which they would naturally be understood by the Indians.'[34] In Canada, the foundation case of *Nowegijick v. The Queen*[35] adopted this liberal approach, and the later case of *Williams v. The Queen*,[36] which involved a claim for exemption of unemployment-insurance benefits, established the 'connecting factors' test for determining whether the taxation of particular types of income would 'erode' the entitlement of the Indian qua Indian on a reserve. These connecting factors include residence on the reserve, amount of work time spent on the reserve, physical location of the employment entity on the reserve, and allocation of federal funds to the operation of the entity pursuant to treaty obligations.[37]

In subsequent litigation, it became clear that, notwithstanding the Williams case, the scope of the treaty exemption was going to have significant limits – limits that were not 'naturally understood by Indians.'[38] Thus, the taxpayer in *Brant v. M.N.R.*[40] invoked section 15 of the Charter in order to communicate to the Tax Court of Canada why he felt that his employment income and his family-allowance payments should be exempt from income tax. The taxpayer resided on the reserve but worked as an auditor for the local branch of Revenue Canada, Customs and Excise, which was located off the reserve. The Court did not set out the taxpayer's argument in detail, but he apparently argued that drawing a distinction between his income (which consisted of salary and family-allowance payments) and Williams's unemployment-insurance payments violated his rights under section 15 of the Charter of Rights because the lack of employment opportunities on the reserve forced him to accept employment elsewhere.[40] He may also have argued that much of his work time was directed towards persons and businesses located on the reserve or towards non-status Native persons who lived off the reserve.

The Tax Court of Canada rejected Brant's appeal to section 15 of the Charter. Despite the clear indication in *Andrews v. Law Society of British Columbia*,[41] the fountainhead of all Charter equality jurisprudence, that the equality provisions should be applied in a manner that promotes the elimination of disadvantage, the Court found several reasons to support its decision. It rejected the taxpayer's contention that he belonged to a discrete and insular minority characterized by personal features such as race or ethnic origin, and instead concluded that the only relevant group to which he belonged was a disparate and heterogenous group of Indians linked together merely by the fact that they chose to work off the reserve. Somewhat inconsistently, the Court also stated that section 15 of the Charter entitled the taxpayer only to treatment equal to that accorded to other Indians who resided on the reserve but worked off the reserve.[42] Finally, the Court contended that denial of the exemption did not violate Brant's equality rights because the use of the exemption to redress the admitted economic disadvantage of 'Indians' would overshoot the actual purpose of the Charter equality guarantees.

Notwithstanding the ruling in *Williams*, the Court drew no distinction between Brant's employment income and his family allowance. This is surprising, for there are strong similarities between family-allowance payments and unemployment insurance benefits. Both are payments that have a clear social-welfare purpose, and both meet the 'connecting factors' test as articulated in *Williams*. Because Brant lived on the reserve, the activities that gave rise to the receipt of family-allowance payments took place on the reserve, where the children in relation to whom the payments were made lived. The fact that unemployment-insurance benefits are paid out of general government revenues was not fatal to Williams's claim for an exemption, and there is no reason to think it fatal in Brant's case. Nor was the location of the government bank against which the cheques were drawn problematic in Williams's appeal.

The taxpayer in *Brant* did not strongly argue disparate impact, although such an argument would flow from data on the economic status of Aboriginal persons in Canada and the history of how the reserve system has affected Aboriginal persons who are status Indians. For example, Statistics Canada has reported that North American Indians have the second-lowest average income in Canada; as a group, their income is only 52 per cent of that of the total population.[43] The persistent reduction of the size of reserves over the centuries, the lack of economic opportunities off the reserve, the erasure of Aboriginal economic structures and cultures, the disparate policing to which many Native communities are subject, and the pressure towards assimilation into the Euro-Canadian economy are all factors that explain why a wide definition of 'personal property situate on the reserve' is necessary to prevent further erosion of treaty entitlements of Indians qua Indians and to counter systemic discrimination.[44]

The courts have also refused to consider the contention that denial of tax exemptions as the result of the status rules violate the Charter. In the 1974 case of *A.-G. Canada v. Lavell*,[45] the Supreme Court of Canada had ruled that former section 12(1)(b) of the Indian Act, which provided that status Indian women who married non-status persons lost their status when status Indian men did not, did not discriminate against Aboriginal women because it treated all Aboriginal women alike. This decision powerfully influenced the final drafting of section 15 of the Charter of Rights, because women in Canada understood that the definition of equality used by the Court in that case could drastically limit the potential for change under the new section 15. A parallel appeal resulted in strong criticism of the old section 12(1)(b) of the Indian Act by the International Court of Justice, which reached a conclusion about its impact on Aboriginal women opposite to that of the Supreme Court in *Lavell*.

The *Lavell* decision has also come under unrelenting attack from scholars, and the federal government subsequently reversed the position it took in *Lavell* by enacting Bill C-31, which provides a mechanism for reinstatement of at least some of the Native persons who lost their status under the old section 12(1)(b).[46] All of these reactions signal that the definition of equality used in *Lavell* has been discredited.

Yet, notwithstanding the disrepute into which the old status rules have fallen, they have retained their vitality under the Income Tax Act. In *Gros-Louis v. M.N.R.*,[47] the minister had reassessed the taxpayer for income tax liability on the basis that she had lost both her status under it and her tax exemption under it when she married a non-status person. The taxpayer appealed that reassessment to the Tax Court of Canada on the basis that it violated her section 15 equality rights. The Court dismissed the taxpayer's appeal, reasoning that section 15 of the Charter, which did not come into effect until 17 April, 1985, could not be applied retroactively to the taxpayer's appeal because it involved her 1982 taxation year. However, the Court went on to state in *obiter dictum* that the Canadian Bill of Rights did not support the taxpayer's appeal because of the Supreme Court ruling in *Lavell*. It seemed to be quite unmoved by the barrage of criticism that had been heaped on *Lavell*, as well as insensitive to the impact that ruling has had on Aboriginal women in Canada.

While many of the status problems caused by old section 12(1)(b) of the Indian Act have been resolved, at least for some people and some of their descendants, many other Aboriginal persons have suffered irreparable harm as the result of the out-marriage rules. Women who have lost status as a result of the old section 12(1)(b) have lost not only their claims for tax exemptions but also any claims they may have had to property on the reserve, because provincial courts have held that they do not have jurisdiction over land governed by the federal Indian Act.[48] Fortunately, *Gros-Louis* is not a binding precedent, and future Charter challenges to the impact of the status rules will not be bound by it.

Special Categories of Income

The Income Tax Act is filled with special rules, special categories, special distinctions, and a myriad of special regimes. Not surprisingly, these complex rules have had a magnetic attraction for would-be Charter challengers who feel aggrieved by the way the rules have affected them. Invariably, all of these challenges have failed. This section examines one of the most influential of such cases, the OPSEU decision, as well as others involving a variety of taxation issues – the use of special categories of income in the Income Tax

Act, special-source rules, timing problems arising out of the use of the cash method of accounting for non-business income, and retroactive changes to special rules which have resulted in bunched income for some taxpayers.

Business versus Employment Income

Early on in Charter litigation, *OPSEU v. National Citizen's Coalition Inc.*[49] established a conceptual basis for placing the provisions of the Income Tax Act beyond review under the Charter of Rights. The appellant, the Ontario Public Service Employees Union, brought a challenge in provincial court to the difference in tax treatment given to taxpayers who earn income from employment as compared to those whose income is from sources characterized as 'business.' This challenge arose out of the fact that taxpayers who earn income from business could deduct charitable donations in calculating their income from that source, while taxpayers who were employees instead of entrepreneurs could not. The union and the other appellants, who were officers of the union, complained that employees were thus precluded from making tax-deductible donations to the National Citizens Coalition, an organization that advocated certain political views. The appellants contended that the Income Tax Act thus violated their freedom of expression, freedom of association, and right to equal benefit of the law.

This was the first serious attack on the different tax treatment given to employment and business incomes. Instead of contesting the issue on the merits, however, the minister applied to the court for an order striking the statement of claim for failure to state a reasonable cause of action. The court of first instance, the Ontario High Court of Justice, granted the application in strong terms, agreeing with the minister that the allegations contained in the statement of claim did not even show the possibility of a Charter violation because the mechanical provisions of the Income Tax Act were beyond Charter review. The Court contended that using the Charter to weigh and balance 'the nuts and bolts of taxing statutes' came close to 'trivializing' it. The Ontario Court of Appeal upheld this analysis, finding that employed taxpayers constituted the great majority of the working population and so could not be considered to be a 'discrete and insular minority' of the type section 15 was intended to protect, and that the limitations on deductions from employment income did not place any direct restriction on the appellant's freedom of expression or association.

Largely because of the disposition of the OPSEU appeal, no other challenges to income categories have succeeded. In *Douglas v. M.N.R.*,[50] the Federal Court–Trial Division held that section 8 of the Income Tax Act, which precluded an employee from deducting rent paid while working in another city, did not violate the taxpayer's equality rights. In *Petrin v. The Queen*,[51] the Court ruled that an appraiser who was an employee could not deduct dues paid to a professional association, even though he could have deducted them if he had been self-employed. The Tax Court of Canada has followed OPSEU in at least three decisions,[52] and, in one of them, directly quoted the Ontario High Court of Justice in saying that such appeals came close to trivializing the Charter by using it to challenge the 'nuts and bolts' of the Income Tax Act.

Special Source Rules

Although the distinction between employment income and business income is fundamental to the Income Tax Act, it is not the only area where income from differentiated sources of income are given differential treatment. Other special-source rules have been tested in Charter challenges as well. For example, in *Botosan v. M.N.R.*,[53] the Tax Court of Canada held that section 32 of the Income Tax Act, which applied only to sales agents who earned commissions from the sale of insurance contracts other than life-insurance contracts, did not violate the taxpayer's equality rights under the Charter.[54]

The courts have also rejected taxpayers' attempts to invoke special-source status in order to gain exemptions for various kinds of receipts. In *Fischer v. M.N.R.*,[55] the taxpayer had argued that the inclusion in his income of union pension benefits received from a fund located outside Canada violated section 15 of the Charter because he had never claimed his contributions to the fund as deductions when calculating his taxable income in prior years. This argument was summarily dismissed by the Court, which found that the taxpayer had not only failed to offer any credible evidence but had made his contention in ignorance of the provisions of the Income Tax Act that specifically covered his situation.

Timing of Income

The courts have also refused to apply section 15 of the Charter to problems of timing of income that arise out of the cash method of accounting, which is the only accounting basis on which employee taxpayers are permitted to report their income. Whether bunched income has arisen from back pay from employment or from social-benefit payments such as unemployment insurance, taxpayers are forced to treat it as income in the year of actual receipt. Court challenges invoking the Charter as support for the practice of shifting the income into the taxation year in which the work or unemployment that gave rise to the payment occurred have not been successful.

Thus, in *Markham v. M.N.R.*[57] the Tax Court of Canada held that the tax-payer, who was a salaried lawyer at the federal Department of Justice, had to include a retroactive pay raise in her income for 1986, even though her legal entitlement to the additional increment arose in mid-1985. The taxpayer had argued that shifting the increment into the 1986 taxation year meant that she paid a higher rate of tax on that amount than she would have had to if it had been included in her 1985 income, and hence that her equality rights had been violated. The Court dismissed the appeal on the basis that there was nothing discriminatory about section 5(1) of the Income Tax Act, which had been interpreted by the courts as requiring employed taxpayers to report their income on a cash basis. The Tax Court of Canada came to the same conclusion with respect to unemployment-insurance benefits which had been received two years after the relevant period of unemployment.

Retroactive Changes in Rules

From time to time, Parliament has given some taxpayers relief from the tax consequences of bunched income, for example, old section 61 of the Income Tax Act permitted taxpayers to purchase income-averaging annuity contracts (IAACs) to soften the tax impact of income bunching. When Parliament essentially abandoned the policy objective of smoothing out bunched income, its action was challenged in *Huet v. M.N.R.*,[58] in which the taxpayers contended that the retroactive repeal of section 61 violated their rights under sections 7 and 15 of the Charter. The Tax Court of Canada and the Federal Court-Trial Division both rejected this appeal on the basis that, although retroactive, the legislation had been validly enacted and did not violate any Charter rights.[59]

Even when linked with issues relating to age or economic class, retroactive changes in anti-bunching rules have easily withstood Charter challenge. In *Stewart v. M.N.R.*,[60] the taxpayer had deregistered some of his registered retirement plans when his wife became ill. He mitigated some of the tax impact of that deregistration by using the forward-averaging provisions that were in effect at that time. When the forward-averaging rules were phased out as part of the 1988 tax-reform process, the taxpayer challenged the change in the rules on the ground that those changes discriminated against him on the basis of age. The Tax Court of Canada rejected that appeal, finding that the legislation did not discriminate or infringe any vested rights but had simply increased his tax burden, making him feel that the changes were unjust and unfair because of the particulars of his financial situation. In *Vosicky v. The Queen*,[61] the taxpayer had argued that the reduction of the rate at which forward-averaging credits were calculated from 34 to 29 per cent violated section 15 of the Charter.

Although the Court rejected this aspect of the taxpayer's appeal because he had not given proper notice of constitutional question in his appeal, it did note that the reduction affected all taxpayers the same 'irrespective of their financial means' and therefore did not infringe the Charter.

Registered Plans

Registered plans offer taxpayers limited opportunities to defer current income-tax liability to future years. Unlike IAACs, however, they are usually available only to fund retirement, although they can also be used to shift income into a later pre-retirement year simply by deregistration. Registered-plan rules contain numerous special-source rules and can also be thought of as embodying tax relief for the bunching of income earned by taxpayers before they go into retirement.

The registered-plan rules have attracted a great deal of Charter litigation. Some of these Charter challenges have attacked the limits placed on the amounts of income that can be shifted to future years; other challenges have attacked the limits on the kinds of income that can be so shifted or the period of time over which deferral is permitted. The courts have consistently rejected all three kinds of challenges, largely because the registered-plan rules themselves appear, on their face, to be neutral with regard to characteristics such as sex, race, and so on. In some of these cases, the courts have also ruled that registered-plan rules cannot be reviewed under either section 7 or section 15 of the Charter because they are economic provisions.

Period of Deferral

In *Gerol v. A.-G. Canada*,[62] the taxpayer sought a declaration from the court that the compulsory maturity date in the rules governing registered retirement savings plans, which deemed all his RRSPs to be deregistered in the year he turned seventy-one, was null and void because it violated his Charter rights under sections 2(a), 7, and 15. He had some $96,000 in RRSPs in the year he turned seventy-one, and all that deferred income was included in his taxable income in that one year, which resulted in a large increase in his tax burden for that year.

The taxpayer's appeal was dismissed, largely because the Court concluded that, far from having an adverse effect on the taxpayer, the RRSP rules had conferred tax benefits on him. The Court reasoned that the age distinction which determined the maturity date of the benefit scheme could not itself be seen as discriminating against the taxpayer, even though it did use age as a marker. It also found that the age-limit on the deferral period for RRSPs was reasonable, because the purpose of the overall RRSP scheme, which was to create retirement income for individuals, was valid.

The *Gerol* decision does depart in one important regard from the trend of other Charter challenges to income tax legislation. The Court did reject the taxpayer's claim that the mandatory-maturity rule violated his rights to security of the person, reasoning that security of the person refers only to the physical and personal integrity of the individual. However, in stating that security rights did not include the right to unrestrained conduct in business affairs, or to complete economic freedom, it noted that the right to security of the person might include 'certain economic freedoms.' This statement is important, because it goes somewhat against the trend in most of the other taxation cases that have looked at security of the person, all of which have tended to dismiss that claim completely. For this reason, *Gerol* offers a starting point for developing arguments about the extent of the economic freedoms that are included in security of the person. Especially when linked with a disparate-impact analysis, the limited recognition of economic freedoms suggested in *Gerol* might be helpful in appropriate cases.

Source Rules

Registered plans place restrictions on both the types of income and the amounts of income that can be deferred to future taxation years. These restrictions vary from plan to plan and from year to year, but the source rules generally preclude taxpayers from deferring anything but 'earned income' to future years.[63] The definitions of 'earned income' have frequently been challenged under the Charter, as have other limitations on eligible types of income.

The leading case on this point is *Kasvand v. The Queen*,[64] in which the taxpayer had claimed deductions for contributions to her RRSP against family-allowance payments, investment income, and various pension and superannuation payments, all of which were excluded from the statutory definition of 'earned income.' The taxpayer pleaded sections 7, 8, and 15 of the Charter, arguing that elderly and disabled taxpayers disproportionately depend on the very types of income that were excluded from the definition of earned income and thus did not have an equal opportunity to spread income tax liability over time. The Federal Court of Appeal rejected this contention on the basis that the source rules relating to RRSPs applied equally to all taxpayers – elderly and disabled taxpayers were subject to the same limits as young and able-bodied taxpayers who had earned income – and so distinctions made with regard to the sources of income did not constitute 'discrimination' within the meaning of section 15(1) of the Charter.[65]

In the *Kasvand* and *Rosen* cases, the courts found that the definition of earned income did not discriminate on the basis of age because the computation of earned income was not premised on age or any other purely personal characteristic of the taxpayers but solely on the nature of their sources of income. This reasoning is startlingly circular. Most of the kinds of income received by the taxpayers in these kinds of cases – superannuation payments, Old Age Security (OAS) payments, Canada Pension Plan payments, pension incomes, and RRSP income – could be received only by taxpayers over the age of sixty-five. Thus, the exclusion of those kinds of income from the definition of earned income produced a *de facto* differentiation on the basis of age, for the simple reason that persons under that age could not legally receive such income. The assertion that the definition of 'earned income' in the legislation applied equally to all taxpayers without distinction based on age, infirmity, or lack of resources therefore ignored the obvious reality that only older taxpayers could be affected by rules that exclude retirement-types of income. While a court might well chose to justify such a distinction under section 1 of the Charter, it is alarming that in *Kasvand* and *Rosen* the courts failed to find that such an age-linked provision violated section 15(1) of the Charter because it discriminated on the basis of age.[66]

Contribution Limits

Taxpayer challenges to the RRSP contribution limits in the Income Tax Act have been no more successful than other types of challenges to the registered-plan rules. In *Kurisko v. The Queen*,[67] the Federal Court of Appeal held that section 8(1)(m) of the Income Tax Act, which limited a federally appointed judge to a registered pension plan deduction of $3,500 for the 1982 taxation year, did not violate the Charter. Given the employment and economic status of most judges in Canada, that result seems to be quite appropriate. So, too, is the result in *Walsh v. M.N.R.*,[68] in which the Tax Court of Canada held that the one-year lag in the size of the RRSP contribution limits relative to actual earned income in the taxation year in question did not discriminate against the taxpayer as an entrepreneur.

The courts have fairly automatically rejected registered-plan challenges on two grounds: because they deal with mere economic legislation that is beyond the reach of the Charter, and because the taxpayers affected by those rules did not appear to be members of a 'discrete and singular minority.' These crude rationalizations have prevented the courts from reaching the class and gender issues embedded in some of the registered-plan cases that have been brought.

Admittedly, the taxpayer in *Gaal v. M.N.R.*[69] did not provide much in the way of expert evidence or documentation on the disadvantaged economic and biological status of women who are on maternity leave, but the Court appeared to dismiss her appeal rather peremptorily. The taxpayer in that case had argued that her low RRSP contribution limit violated her equality rights because, as a woman on maternity leave, she had a disparately low income.[70] Especially as retirement funding becomes increasingly privatized and as the social, economic, and fiscal barriers to retirement funding for the poorest segments of the population become better understood, courts may come to realize that, when bare economic survival is at stake for aging and aged Canadians, it is no longer adequate to dismiss such Charter challenges with the general assertion that these rules create benefits rather than disadvantages and so are beyond the reach of Charter review.[71]

Anti-Avoidance Provisions

Every substantive element of the Income Tax Act is supported by specific and general anti-avoidance provisions. These rules add another layer of distinctions to the act and increase again the range of outcomes that can be generated by seemingly simple scenarios. Thus, it is not surprising that they have attracted numerous Charter challenges. These challenges have related to four issues: the constitutional status of taxable-benefit rules in general[72]; the rules dealing specifically with restricted farm losses; the rules relating to the personal tax liability of corporate directors for unremitted corporate-withholding taxes; and the constitutional status of other anti-avoidance provisions, some of which involve the exercise of administrative discretion. None of these Charter challenges has succeeded, but the contexts in which they have been brought and the reasons for their failure merit some consideration.

Taxable Benefits

Although numerous provisions in the Income Tax Act bring taxable benefits into income, there are more specific provisions which bring various cash and non-cash benefits into taxable employment income and these are applied with a high degree of frequency.[73] Indeed, all of the taxable-benefit cases relate to taxable employment benefits.

In *Chaldean v. M.N.R.*,[74] the taxpayer received $63,000 from his employer to compensate him for the decrease in the value of his home that resulted from the employer's closure of a mine. The taxpayer did not in fact sell his house, nor did he report the $63,000 as income of any kind. When the minister treated the $63,000 as a taxable employment benefit, the taxpayer appealed to the Tax Court of Canada on the basis that inclusion of that amount in his income violated his equality rights under the Charter. The Court upheld the minister's reassessment for three reasons: first, because the taxpayer had not in fact incurred any loss, having not actually sold his house; second, because if the taxpayer had suffered a loss, he would have received treatment identical to that given taxpayers who were in similar circumstances; third, because even if the taxpayer's equality rights had been violated, the violation was a reasonable limit on the taxpayer's equality rights in a free and democratic society.

   Laflamme v. M.N.R.[75] differed from *Chaldean* in that one of the facts that led to the minister's reassessment of the taxpayer was the existence of a family relationship between the parties. The minister had included some $21,000 in the taxpayer's income in *Laflamme* on the basis of section 15(2) of the Income Tax Act, which included shareholder loans in taxable income from property. The taxpayer appealed the reassessment on the basis that section 15(2) of the Income Tax Act violated his Charter equality rights, especially because the reassessment was in part triggered by the fact that the taxpayer's father controlled the corporation. The Court rejected this argument, reasoning that all taxpayers who receive loans from corporations controlled by specified relatives are treated the same under section 15(2) of the Income Tax Act, and, in consequence, Laflamme could not claim to have experienced discrimination.

   It is not quite so clear that the taxpayer's appeal in *Morin v. M.N.R.*[76] was resolved correctly. Morin, who had been granted permanent-disability status, continued to be employed but the only income he received was from a pension under a wage-loss-replacement benefit policy. The premiums of the policy were paid by the employer, and the plan was described as a sickness, disability, and rehabilitation plan. The taxpayer took the position that the payments from the policy were tax exempt under section 81(1)(d) of the Income Tax Act.[77] The minister reassessed the taxpayer on the basis that the payments were taxable under section 6(1)(f) of the act because the plan fell within the definition of sickness, accident, or disability insurance or of an income-maintenance plan and therefore could not be considered to be payments under a pension plan. The Court agreed with the minister, holding that the payments were taxable benefits as described in section 6(1)(f) and were not pension payments because they were not paid under a plan the purpose of which was to provide for payment on retirement. The taxpayer appeared to have simply contended that the mere differences in treatment – quite apart from the taxpayer's status as a person with a permanent disability – violated his equality rights.[78]

Restricted Farm Losses

Section 31 of the Income Tax Act limits deductions for business expenses incurred by hobby farmers to a maximum of $5,000 in each taxation year. Section 31 was enacted in order to prevent such farmers, who are quite capable of incurring net losses from their farming operations each and every year, from obtaining tax subsidies for what is in essence a costly lifestyle choice. The test of whether section 31 applies to a taxpayer revolves around whether the taxpayer had a reasonable expectation of profit from his or her farming activities, the inference being that, if such expectation is not reasonable, then the costs giving rise to farming losses are non-deductible personal and living expenses.

Several taxpayers have challenged section 31 of the Income Tax Act under section 15 of the Charter. In contrast with the vast majority of fiscal Charter challenges, two of these taxpayers won their appeals – but on the tax merits, not on Charter grounds.[79] In the one appeal in which the Court actually discussed the section 15 claim, it stated in *obiter dictum* that section 31 of the Income Tax Act does not offend section 15 of the Charter because farmers who are prevented from deducting losses by section 31 do not constitute a discrete and singular minority.[80] In an interesting departure from the usual tone of such opinions, however, the Court emphasized that it found it difficult to see how subjecting an important piece of fiscal legislation in appropriate cases to the scrutiny of the judiciary could be described as 'trivializing' the Charter.

Directors' Personal Liability

Section 227.1 of the Income Tax Act imposes personal liability on corporate directors who do not exercise due diligence to ensure that their corporations remit withholding taxes. As in the restricted farm-loss cases, these taxpayers have had some success on the merits but the courts have rejected all of their Charter arguments, whether based on sections 7, 11, or 15 of the Charter.[81] In most of these rulings, the taxpayer's Charter claims were dismissed in peremptory fashion. The court did elaborate on its reasons for dismissing the taxpayer's appeal in *Byrt v. M.N.R.*[82] In that case, the Court explained that section 227.1 of the Income Tax Act did not infringe section 7 of the Charter because the taxpayer's liberty to seek directorships had not been impaired by the imposition of personal liability for unremitted source deductions, and that the same provision did not infringe section 15 of the Charter because the additional duties borne by directors, as compared with non-directors, did not constitute discrimination.[83]

Other Anti-Avoidance Provisions

Charter challenges to the validity of other anti-avoidance provisions have also failed. In *Krag-Hansen v. The Queen*,[84] the Federal Court–Trial Division held that the minister's power to deem corporations to be associated with each other for purposes of calculating their total small-business deduction did not infringe the Charter. In *Kostiuk v. M.N.R.*,[85] the Tax Court of Canada held that section 160 of the Income Tax Act, which imposed on the transferee of a property joint and several liability for unpaid taxes of the transferor, did not violate section 15 of the Charter. The Court allowed the taxpayer's appeal in *Kostiuk* in part, reducing the amount of the assessment to reflect the taxpayer's actual equity in the property. But it did not reach the real heart of the issue in this case, which was the taxpayer's contention that the amount of her liability should be reduced even further to reflect the interest her mother held in the property under provincial matrimonial legislation. The minister had treated the taxpayer's father as the sole owner of the property, since he was the only one on title. The Court dismissed that part of the taxpayer's argument on the basis that the mother's interest was at best a mere personal right to require a court to determine the ownership of family assets, and not a right that could be recognized as consideration in a transaction such as the one in question.

Fortunately, the *Kostiuk* decision has been somewhat counterbalanced by the court's reasoning in *Holizki v. The Queen*,[86] in which a husband raised exactly the same objection to the application of the section 74(2) attribution rules as they existed in the mid-1980s. He contended that shares, the disposition of which had given rise to a capital gain which the minister had then attributed to him, had actually been acquired by his wife for good and adequate consideration under the doctrine of resulting trust. The Court relied on the Supreme Court decision in *Pettkus v. Becker*[87] in concluding that, when the husband initially acquired the shares in question, he had held them on resulting trust for his wife. Thus, the ultimate transfer and disposition did not fall within the scope of section 74(2) of the Income Tax Act. However, the Court did not address the taxpayer's Charter argument under section 15, preferring instead to treat the wife's interest in the shares as a matter of property law rather than as an issue of sex discrimination under the Charter.

The courts' handling of Charter challenges to the various anti-avoidance provisions discussed in this section is incomplete. As in the challenges to registered-plan legislation, the courts have often settled for a superficial and formulaic dismissal of Charter issues and have failed to grapple meaningfully with the fundamental problems raised.

Taxation of the Family

The taxation of the family involves profound policy issues. The central one arises out of the fact that, in predominantly common-law jurisdictions such as Canada, there has been considerable pressure historically to view women not as autonomous and self-dependent individuals in their own right but merely as members of married couples or families.[88] Added to this pressure is the tendency, borrowed from social-benefits theory, to fashion tax-benefit provisions in such a way as to promote the ideal of horizontal equity – according to which, families or married couples with the same amounts of total income are treated alike. These two forces have tended to obscure or treat as irrelevant the very real differences between women and men both within the family structure and in the larger society, with the result that the distribution of tax benefits has reinforced women's social and economic disadvantage in comparison with men.

Unfortunately, the fragmented nature of income tax legislation has made it difficult for women lobbyists or litigants to uncover this dynamic. Thus, the record of Charter litigation revolving around issues touching on families, tax benefits to families, and other types of provisions of concern to women as a class have failed virtually across the board. Although it is becoming possible now to demonstrate how it is that the structure of the Income Tax Act fundamentally operates to nullify the recognition of women's legal personality, that insight has yet to have much impact on the outcome of Charter litigation over specific provisions which affect women negatively.

Women's Legal Personality

It has only been during this century that women's legal personality has come to be recognized in Canada. Canadian women did not obtain equal voting rights until 1954,[89] Native women did not receive the right to vote federally until the 1960s, and the last legal barriers to married women's ownership of property have yet to fall.[90] Women's lack of social and economic autonomy has also disappeared slowly. Successive waves of legislation designed to redress women's poverty as a class, beginning with equal-pay legislation in the 1950s and extending through the enactment of human-rights legislation and the Charter of Rights sex-equality guarantees, have so far done little to change the two most important determinants of women's disadvantaged status: the heavy responsibilities that women bear for reproductive labour and non-waged work, and the extremely low incomes that women receive relative to men.

It may appear at first glance that income tax policy does not have much to do with women's economic or legal status. However, income tax policy does contribute in numerous ways to women's continuing poverty as a class, poverty that can be eliminated only when the tax system ceases to intensify it and becomes either neutral towards women's low incomes or part of the solution. And at the level of technical discourse, the rush in tax policy to treat women as being subsumed within the tax unit or the benefit unit is seriously eroding what gains in social, economic, and political status women have been able to achieve in the last two decades.

The most important way in which tax policy had contributed to women's poverty is the emergence of the hybrid taxation-unit rules, which, taken as a whole, operate to reinforce and perpetuate women's economic dependency within 'the family.' The married tax credit, the provisions regarding the child care expense deduction, the spousal RRSP rules, and all the transferable tax credits that benefit married persons – primarily men who have economically dependent wives – either create conditions in which women's most rational economic choice is to perform non-waged work in the home or, on the basis of restrictive and unfair 'family income' tests, withhold important tax benefits that are crucial to redress women's economic status.[91] For example, section 3(f) of the Income Tax Act operates to deny the child care expense deduction to all members of families in which one of the adults – usually the wife – earns no income at all. This creates an economic incentive for women to perform non-waged child-care work themselves, instead of working outside the home in the many ways that, even when such employment is non-waged, contribute to women's economic autonomy.[92]

Tax policy on the taxation unit contributes in a more general way to women's poverty as a class through the aggregate allocation of the tax burden and tax benefits. In a 1988 study of the impact of the taxation system as a whole, I found that women's share of pre-tax income – which was only 31.5 per cent of all incomes to begin with – shrank to a post-tax share of only 26.8 per cent. The difference of nearly 5 percentage points is due directly to the operation of the total tax system. While indirect taxation produced most of that skew, it is clear that the sex-specific allocation of tax benefits in the income tax system, which is otherwise slightly progressive, has regressive results when analyzed by sex.[93]

A growing number of Charter challenges have focused on the issue of women's legal personality. Unfortunately, the prevailing view that is emerging is that the spousal unit – whether constituted through formal marriage or through mere cohabitation – is more significant on the policy level than is the status of the women in those units. The clearest evidence of this trend is found in the majority judgments of the Supreme Court of Canada in *The Queen v. Thibaudeau*,[94] in which each of the male judges who sat on the Court in that case concluded that the relevant unit of analysis for purposes of ruling on the constitutionality of including child-support payments in women's incomes was the divorced family 'unit.' Justice Cory and Iacobucci stated that the 'inclusion/ deduction system,' which is 'geared to operate at the level of the couple,' was designed to promote 'the best interests of the children': 'If anything, the legislation in question confers a benefit on the post-divorce "family unit."' 'The fact that one member of the unit might derive a greater benefit from the legislation than the other does not, in and of itself, trigger a s. 15 violation.'[95] Although Cory and Iacobucci purported to disagree with Justice Gonthier's narrow approach to the application of section 15 in this case, their reasoning, which lay at the heart of the majority's section 15 analysis in *Thibaudeau*, is indistinguishable from Gonthier's conclusions on the same issue: 'The group contemplated by the legislation consists of separated or divorced couples ... That is not the group to which the respondent claims to belong: she claims she is a member of the smaller group of custodial parents having some financial self-sufficiency and consequently receiving maintenance solely for the benefit of their children ... So far as the children of the family unit are concerned ... separated or divorced parents still form an entity.'[96]

The two women justices on the Supreme Court hotly disputed this characterization of the central issue in *Thibaudeau*. Justice McLachlin linked the issue directly to the language of section 15, contending that it was individual women and not 'the fractured family' who were protected by section 15 of the Charter: 'Its opening words state: "Every individual is equal before and under the law and has the right to the equal protection and benefit of the law." It is no answer ... to say that a social unit of which the individual is a member has, viewed globally, been fairly treated.'[97] Given that men's attempts to obtain deductions for alimony and child-support payments predated the recognition of women's legal personality in Canada by several decades, it is absolutely stunning that the majority of the members of the Supreme Court did not move decisively to strike down this now-outdated artefact of married women's legal disabilities.

The question of women's legal personality is by no means unique to the Thibaudeau case. As income tax policy in Canada has more overtly moved to adopt the marital unit as the benefit unit, increasing numbers of women have found themselves legally disabled from receiving tax benefits simply because of their marital status – the very same factor that had led to their foremothers being legally disabled more generally under the English common law. For example, the taxpayer in *Collins v. M.N.R.*[98] found that, although her family-allowance payments were included in her own income and thus subject to federal taxation at the marginal rate of 26 per cent, she could not deduct her child-care expenses herself because her husband had been deemed by section 63 of the Income Tax Act to have paid them. And because his federal marginal rate was only 17 per cent, the taxpayer argued, the net value of that deduction to the family as a whole was substantially reduced, to the extent of some $400 for the taxation year in question. The taxpayer's real complaint was that she was prevented by virtue of her marital status from claiming the deduction directly, and that even if she had had the lower income, which would have entitled her to claim it despite the fact she was married, her entitlement would have been calculated by reference to her marital status. Yet, because of the artificial reasoning that has come to characterize Charter equality discourse on the bench, she was forced to frame her arguments in terms that the Court would consider. The Court dismissed her husband's aspect of the appeal out of hand by saying that no one can appeal on the basis that their tax is too low. It refused to look at the family-allowance issue in the historical context of compensation for discrimination against married women, instead treating it and the issue of child-care expenses as merely involving questions of vertical equity – the allocation of income tax liability by reference to different (gender-neutral) levels of incomes.

Relying on the highly formulaic 'tests' of 'discrimination' that the judiciary has fashioned out of the language of section 15 of the Charter, the Court reasoned that neither the family-allowance provision nor the provision for the child-care-expense deduction 'discriminated' directly against the taxpayers because neither made any distinctions on the basis of sex or 'family status'; rather, both provisions allocated tax liability on the basis of differences in levels of personal incomes. The Court also reasoned that neither provision indirectly discriminated against the taxpayers because any disparate impact they generated related merely to 'family status,' and families cannot be likened to a 'discrete and insular minority' that has historically suffered disadvantages such as would render it vulnerable to discriminatory legislation. Because these provisions distinguished merely on the basis of income levels and not on the types of families involved, neither of them could be considered to have 'discriminated' against the taxpayers within the meaning of section 15.

Poulter v. M.N.R.[99] reflects the same analytic distortions. The taxpayer, a non-married mother who lived with a man, lost her entitlement to the child tax benefit because she became a deemed spouse when the definition of 'spouse' was expanded to include heterosexual cohabitants after the 1992 taxation year. Before 1993 she had been considered to be a non-married taxpayer in terms of the cut-offs to family income; after 1992, the treating of her cohabitant's income as family income pushed her over the income cut-off, which meant that she could not claim the child tax benefit. In her appeal, the taxpayer submitted an affidavit filed by her cohabitant in which he swore that he had 'no relationship with the daughter, emotionally, morally, financially, or anything else,' and she herself insisted that 'he is not, now, nor has he ever been in any way, shape or form responsible financially or other wise, for my child. I am entirely responsible for any and all expenses incurred by or on behalf of my daughter.'

Although the *Poulter* case obviously involved the denial of a benefit on the basis of the taxpayer's deemed marital status – not even her actual marital status – she felt constrained, because of the dimensions of equality discourse, to contend that she was subject to discrimination on the basis of sexual orientation since a lesbian in her situation would not have received the same treatment. Nor could the Court perceive how the taxpayer was disadvantaged by her deemed marital status; it relied on *Bayliss v. M.N.R.*,[100] in which the Tax Court had held that denying a husband the spousal-dependency deduction in 1992 – the year before cohabitants were deemed to be spouses for purposes of the Income Tax Act – did not discriminate against non-married cohabitants because they did not constitute a disadvantaged group.[101] Predictably, the Court dismissed the *Poulter* Charter challenge out of hand, asserting that common-law spouses are not members of a group that has historically been disadvantaged, do not belong to a discrete and insular minority, and therefore cannot raise a claim of 'discrimination' under section 15(1) of the Charter.[102]

It took the litigation in the 'Person's Case' of 1928–9 to establish that women in Canada were entitled to sit in the Senate. Perhaps it will now take nothing less than an 'Individual's Case' to establish that the proper unit of analysis under section 15(1) of the Charter is individual human beings – which includes women – and not the fictional 'marital unit,' 'married couple,' or 'fractured family.' Although corporations are recognized as legal persons and as individuals for purposes of section 15(1), nowhere has legal policy also suggested that the 'marital unit' is a 'person' or an 'individual.'[103]

The fact that the Charter has done little to advance the recognition or protection of women's legal personality particularly affects Aboriginal and low-income women. Aboriginal women have perhaps the strongest moral and legal claims to the recognition of their legal personality and economic autonomy, yet they are still completely unprotected by married women's property legislation, human-rights legislation, provincial matrimonial-property legislation, and the Charter of Rights.[104] Nor are they the only group; women who work in family businesses still run a high risk of having their economic contribution to that business erased on the basis that their 'unity of interest' with their husbands (or deemed husbands) is so complete that they are not entitled to receive social benefits on their own accounts.[105] If even only one group of women still lacks the basic attributes of legal personality that are supposedly guaranteed to all adults in liberal legal culture, then all women's claims to full legal personality and equal economic autonomy will continue to be easily distorted or completely ignored in the name of rationally justifiable income tax policy.

Family Allowance

The provisions of the Income Tax Act that relate to the family allowance, Old Age Security payments, the child care expense deduction, the newly revised child tax credit, the various types of creditable sales taxes, and the northern-resident deduction share one structural feature: each of these provisions, which all relate to social benefits, uses concepts of family or spousal income to measure eligibility. As a result, each has subordinated the legal personality and economic autonomy of women – and, to a certain extent, of children – to the economic status of the family unit as a whole.

Perceived Charter problems with the old family-allowance system, which has now been repealed, partially account for the emergence of the present system of measuring eligibility for social benefits by family or spousal incomes. As soon as the sex-equality guarantees of the Charter of Rights were drafted, the dominant Charter discourse began to take seriously the suggestion that the sex-specific allocation of those payments violated men's sex-equality rights. Women's assertions that the sex-specific allocation of family-allowance payments was necessary to safeguard women's already unequal share of the national income in light of their disproportionate levels of responsibility for care of dependent children did not surface as a significant countervailing consideration in the resulting political debate. Nor did the government appear to consider that its own motives in enacting the initial family-allowance scheme on a sex-specific basis meant that the sex-specific allocation of family-allowance benefits was properly characterized as ameliorative action under section 15(2) of the Charter.[106]

Also during the 1980s, conservative social-benefits discourse shifted away from concepts of universal coverage and began to embrace the suggestion that family-income limits on eligibility would contain the costs of social-benefit programs. The convergence of the equality concerns expressed by men and the movement away from universal coverage resulted in a shift in the structure of several social-benefit and tax-benefit regimes, all of which replaced sex-specific eligibility criteria with facially sex-neutral and income-specific criteria. The family-allowance system was one of the first benefit programs to undergo this restructuring.

Charter challenges to these restructured social-benefit programs have tried to grapple with the fact that low-income individuals – most of whom are women

– no longer receive the full benefit of these programs unless they are single or have husbands who have even lower incomes. Such women are not always the litigants in these cases – their husbands often are the only members of their families who have legal standing. And of course it is difficult to see Charter challenges brought by men as being about the sex equality of women.

Two recent Tax Court of Canada decisions illustrate the barriers to dealing with the impact of family-allowance rules on women as a class. In *Spence v. M.N.R.*,[107] the taxpayer husband appealed his liability for Part I.2 tax. The Part I.2 tax, known as a 'clawback' of social benefits, is payable by either adult in a family whose income exceeds the eligibility cut-offs for family allowance. The clawback can result in the repayment of up to 75 per cent of the allowance.

The husband in the *Spence* case claimed, not that the Part I.2 tax discriminated against him on the basis of his sex or marital status, but that it discriminated against the traditional family. He argued that, if his wife had worked for wages, together they could have earned even more income than he had earned alone without liability for the Part I.2 tax. The Court dismissed the husband's appeal, not because it felt that it should have been framed in terms of sex discrimination, but because, according to its reasoning, the distinctions in Part I.2 of the Income Tax Act revolved around income levels rather than family status. The Court further reasoned that, if the taxpayer and his wife had had equal amounts of income, the taxpayer would still have had to pay the Part I.2 tax.[108] It backed up this reasoning by appealing to the cases which had upheld the Old Age Security clawback rules and by concluding that the distinction in Part I.2 of the Income Tax Act was based on economic grounds, not on a 'personal characteristic.'

The sex discrimination in *Flint v. M.N.R.*,[109] the other appeal that has related to the family-allowance rules, was even more difficult to challenge. When the taxpayer was incarcerated for breaking and entering, the Children's Aid Society had taken physical custody of her children. The minister of national revenue then demanded repayment of $1,135 in child tax credits on the basis that, having lost custody of her children, she was no longer eligible to receive the family allowance and thus was also ineligible to receive the tax credits. The taxpayer challenged this demand on the basis that section 122.2 of the Income Tax Act, which set up regime of the child tax credit, violated her security of the person and equality rights. The Court dismissed the appeal, ruling that the minister was correct in taking the position that the taxpayer no longer met the criteria in section 122.2 of the act because the children were no longer in her custody; that economic benefits such as the child tax credit were not 'fundamental to human life or survival'; and that the taxpayer was no longer maintaining her children.

The structure of the income tax rules at issue in the *Flint* case prevented the taxpayer from bringing the disparate impact of imprisonment of women with children into the presentation of her case. Because the focus was strictly on the Income Tax Act, there was no room for her to object to the loss of custody of her children as the result of imprisonment. Nor was it possible for her to argue that, in the circumstances of her imprisonment, the Children's Aid Society was really acting as agent for her as an otherwise fit mother. In the end, the discrimination against the taxpayer in *Flint* was made up of layers of discrimination against women in Canadian society, which include inappropriate sentencing and prison conditions for women with minor children, the connection between the child tax credit and the family-allowance provisions, and concepts of security of the person and sex equality which do not take serious account of the social and economic realities of women's lives.

Old Age Security Payments

The fragmentation of policy analysis that flaws the way in which cases such as *Spence* and *Flint* have been pleaded and resolved is in part due to the 1980s shift in the use of income levels to measure eligibility for social benefits. The courts so far have accepted that income criteria do not have the same constitutional significance that sex or age criteria might have, and they have not come to terms with the disparate impact of such legislation on groups that receive some social and economic benefits precisely because they are so disadvantaged relative to the rest of the population.

Thus, every Charter challenge that has been brought to the Old Age Security clawback rules has been resolved in the government's favour, and the courts have completely rejected the contention that those rules discriminate on the basis of age. In the leading case, *Lancey v. The Queen*,[110] the Federal Court of Appeal described the taxpayer's Charter challenge as 'unfounded,' stating that the criterion on which the clawback tax was levied was income level, not age, and thus section 15 of the Charter of Rights did not apply. All the other Charter challenges to the OAS clawback have been dealt with in the same way.[111]

Child Tax Benefit

Charter litigation around the provisions of the child tax credits and the newer child tax benefit is fairly limited.[112] To date, taxpayers have challenged two aspects of the new credit as being discriminatory: the failure to allocate the credit between parents, especially in cases of joint custody after divorce or separation, and the extension of eligibility on the basis of family income to common-law spouses. The courts have rejected both types of challenges.

In *Keyes v. M.N.R.*, the taxpayer was a divorced father who claimed a pro rata share of the child tax credits, dependent child exemptions, child care expense deductions, and child sales-tax credits for his children. His former wife had custody of their children, but the taxpayer argued that because the children were with him for 28 per cent of the days in 1986 he was entitled to use 25 per cent of each of those deductions and credits in calculating his income tax liability. He also claimed that the reference to 'female' in the rules governing the child tax credit at that time violated his sex-equality rights, and that his children were qualified relations for purposes of the other provisions because they were dependent upon him for support when they were visiting him.[113]

The *Keyes* ruling is important because the Tax Court of Canada made it clear that, notwithstanding the concerns that had been raised about the use of sex-specific criteria in the allocation of tax benefits, the reference to 'female' in the child tax credit rules did not offend the Charter of Rights. The court reasoned that striking the gender reference from the rules, which was the remedy sought by the taxpayer, would merely eliminate any means of identifying the parent entitled to receive the credit and would not in fact produce the result he sought. The court relied on its ruling in *Keyes* in reaching the same conclusion in *Metz v. M.N.R.*[114]

The courts have dealt with women taxpayer's claims that the 'family income' concept used to means-test their eligibility for the child tax benefit in much the same fashion. Despite the fact that the taxpayer in *Poulter v. M.N.R.*[115] was not married to her cohabitant, received no financial support from him, and parented her daughter as a single mother, she was denied the child tax credit as soon as the expanded definition of 'spouse' in section 253 of the Income Tax Act came into effect.[116]

Other Tax Benefits for Families

Taxpayers have challenged various other tax-credit provisions of the Income Tax Act under the Charter, usually with no success.[117] The one exception is *Mercier v. M.N.R.*,[118] which involved the age-limit provisions in the equivalent-to-married credit. The taxpayer had claimed the credit for her twenty-four-year-old son, and, when the minister disallowed the claim on the basis that the son was over the age limit of eighteen in the provision, she appealed to the Tax Court of Canada on the ground that the provision discriminated on the basis of age. The Court allowed the appeal, severing the age limit from the balance of the provision. Parliament has made no move to respond to this ruling with any legislative changes, undoubtedly because the exemption version of this provision had never contained any age criteria.[119]

Challenges to age limitations in other provisions of the Income Tax Act have not fared as well. In *Tiberio v. M.N.R.*[120] and *Husk v. M.N.R.*,[121] the Tax Court of Canada rejected Charter challenges to the age limits in the dependent child tax credit and the age sixty-five tax credit. In these cases, the Court reasoned that neither age limit was discriminatory within the meaning of section 15 of the Charter because Parliament had rational reasons for imposing them: the sixty-five age limit was based on the fact that persons sixty-five years of age or over generally have small fixed incomes, and the larger deduction with regard to older children took into account the fact that family allowances were not payable in respect of such children. The real distinction between these two decisions and the *Mercier* judgment seems to be that the types of tax benefit at issue in *Tiberio* and *Husk* have always contained age criteria.

The courts have also rejected Charter challenges to the age limitations in the sales tax and GST credit rules. The leading case in this area of tax-benefits eligibility is *Lister v. The Queen.*[122] The taxpayers in this case, who were aged eighteen and thirteen during the taxation years in question, claimed the GST credit on their own account. The minister denied those claims on the basis that the taxpayers did not meet any of the statutory criteria for claiming their own credits – they were living at home with their father, they were his dependants, neither of them were married, and they did not have any children of their own. Both the Tax Court of Canada and the Federal Court of Appeal upheld the minister's position. As the Federal Court of Appeal explained, there was no evidence on the record to suggest that unmarried children under the age of nineteen were members of a group whose claim 'fits within the overall purpose of s. 15 – namely, to remedy or prevent discrimination against groups subject to stereotyping, historical disadvantage and political and social prejudice in Canadian society.'[123] The Federal Court also pointed out that the provision did not 'discriminate' on the basis of age per se, because age was merely being used as a rough indicator of whether taxpayers were likely to be dependent on their parents or not.[124]

Child Care Expense Deduction

The tax treatment of child-care expenses provides an excellent case study on how the deep process of insulating fiscal provisions from Charter challenge has interacted with apparent political preferences for sex-neutral and income-specific benefit legislation. In a litigation context in which most of the Charter challenges have been brought by men, and have been lost by men, two women taxpayers have had limited successes which, if they have achieved nothing else, have helped illuminate fault lines in the legislation along which future challenges might concentrate.

Section 63 of the Income Tax Act initially came into existence specifically to respond to women's concerns, giving it unique status in tax policy as a provision that was, from the outset, designed to promote the equality of women by ameliorating conditions of historical and continuing disadvantage. The first version of this provision, which was enacted in the early 1970s, was deliberately made sex-specific in order to achieve the policy goal of 'adequately caring for children when both parents are working, or when there is only one parent in the family ... and working.' The federal government expected that the child care expense deduction would 'normally' be taken by the child's mother, and, accordingly, placed no limitations on the circumstances in which a woman who incurred child-care expenses could claim the deduction, while claims by men were limited to situations in which it could be expected that men would not be able to rely on their wives to provide child care for the family.

Two reasons for making the provisions sex-specific were given by the government at the time. First, the federal government wanted to limit the revenue cost of this tax benefit, and, given that women's incomes were known to be much lower than men's, restricting the deduction to women would, in most cases, ensure that it would be claimed by the lower-income spouse.[125] Second, the government recognized that women with children faced systemic discrimination in that they were expected to provide their own child care, and that women's decisions to enter the salaried workforce were influenced by the costs of child-care services in a way that men's were not. To put this point another way, fathers were expected to leave their children with their mothers, while mothers were expected to stay home with their children. The child-care deduction reflected the sex-specific assumption that two-parent families would not usually incur child-care expenses unless the mother, who would ordinarily be at home taking care of children, also decided to engage in waged work.[126]

The sex-specificity of the new child care expense deduction by no means precluded men from claiming it. Given the realities of sex roles in Canadian society, Parliament provided equal treatment for male taxpayers who found themselves in the same family situation as women: married men were not expected to provide child care for their wives, and so all married women who wanted to enter the salaried workforce were presumed to need replacement care; married women were expected to provide child care for their husbands, but married men could qualify for the deduction in circumstances in which they could not be expected to care for their children. Single fathers were given the same treatment as single mothers.[127]

Far from discriminating against men, then, the initial limitations on the child care expense deduction were actually designed to ameliorate the effects of discriminatory beliefs about the proper roles for women and men; men were not ordinarily expected to perform child-care work, and women were always expected to be available for child care unless they were dead, severely disabled, or incarcerated. Unlike many ameliorative provisions, however, the child care expense deduction was not reserved exclusively for the benefit of women, simply because the members of the nearly all-male Parliament vigilantly guarded the rights of the few men who might be affected adversely by such a condition.[128]

The subsequent history of the child care expense deduction shows how difficult it is to draft legislation that genuinely meets the needs of women as a class. Despite the fact that the child-care deduction was enacted to ameliorate the effects of systemic discrimination against women, men immediately challenged the sex-specificity of the child care expense deduction under federal human-rights legislation, claiming that it discriminated against them on the basis of sex. Initially, these challenges were all rejected on the ground that the distinctions drawn in section 63 were consistent with valid federal objectives.[129] However, the decision of the federal Human Rights Tribunal in *Bailey v. M.N.R.* radically altered the perception of these rules.[130]

The Tribunal readily agreed that the purpose of section 63 was to combat the systemic effects of discrimination against women and to reduce tax disincentives to women's entry into the salaried workforce: 'In 1973, two out of every five mothers and one out of every three mothers with preschoolers were in the labour force in Ontario. Section 63 is essentially a remedial measure, a tax expenditure by the Government to rectify prior and present discrimination against women in the labour force and to mitigate against the otherwise deterrent effect of the ITA in respect of women joining the labour force.'[131] The Tribunal also found that the section 63 deduction was an indirect government expenditure that amounted to a tax subsidy 'not unlike a statutory provision that provides a conventional direct expenditure by government.'[132] This second finding – that section 63 in effect provided a direct government expenditure – brought the provision within the jurisdiction of the Canadian Human Rights Act on the basis that the deduction constituted a government 'service.'[133]

However, the Tribunal did find that section 63 in fact discriminated against men, a point that the minister did not dispute.[134] It also concluded that the distinction drawn between women and men in the provision was not reasonable,[135] and that it could not be justified as an affirmative-action provision permitting some men to claim the deduction under some circumstances: 'The basic policy premise to section 63 is to further equality of opportunity to a group, women, perceived as being in a disadvantageous economic position. However, the provision is extended to men in limited circumstances, and thus although its thrust is directed primarily in aid of women, the objective is not to differentiate adversely simply on the basis of gender. That is, section 63 cannot be looked upon simply as an "affirmative action" type of approach, because its scope is not limited just to women.'[136] The Tribunal declared that the only thing that prevented it from declaring the sex distinction in section 63 to be inoperative was the fact that the Human Rights Act was a mere statute and did not have constitutional status.[137]

Even though the Tribunal seemed to agree that governments were entitled to 'experiment with different ways to rectify the effects of past discrimination,'[138] it went on to suggest that both of the objectives of the provision could be achieved more effectively and in a less 'discriminatory' fashion by making the entire provision gender-neutral. This could be done, the Tribunal proposed, simply by dropping the limitations on claims by fathers and by requiring the spouse with the lower income to claim the deduction.

The Tribunal issued its decision on 20 November 1980. In 1983 the government announced that it was making these changes to section 63: 'A further change to the child care expense deduction is proposed in response to a ruling by the Canadian Human Rights Tribunal that the measure discriminates in favour of women. The budget proposes to remove this discrimination and will require the spouse with the lower income to claim the deduction. In cases where the lower-income spouse is infirm, in an institution, or registered as a full-time student in a designated educational institution, the higher-income spouse will be permitted to claim a portion of the deduction.'[139]

What is interesting about this change in policy is that the Human Rights Tribunal actually dismissed the male taxpayer's complaint in *Bailey* and did not in fact 'rule' that the measure 'discriminates in favour of women.' The government's statement gave a distorted picture of what actually happened in the *Bailey* case, a distortion that apparently was intended to make it look as if the government had no choice but to make the provisions of section 63 gender-neutral.

The government did not point out that this change in policy meant that it was essentially abandoning its original objective in enacting section 63, which was to counter systemic fiscal barriers to women's participation in the workforce. Notwithstanding that this change in policy was made out of deference to men's perceived needs, however, subsequent Charter challenges to section 63 have predominantly been brought by male taxpayers who still feel that the scope of the deduction is too narrow. It is also disquieting that the few Charter challenges that women have brought against section 63 have all failed, even though this is the one provision that was originally enacted to counter the disparate impact of income tax legislation on women as a class.

Attacks on disparate impact

Once section 63 was redrafted in gender-neutral terms, male taxpayers brought numerous challenges which attempted to complete the transformation of the provision from a measure intended to ameliorate the systemic barriers to women's workforce participation into a tax subsidy that reinforced women's responsibility for non-waged domestic labour. In *Fiset v. M.N.R.*,[140] a male taxpayer convinced the Tax Court of Canada that a sole-support husband who had a dependent wife could claim the child care expense deduction even though his wife did not meet any of the criteria in the revised section 63. The Court reasoned that the higher-income spouse could claim the deduction if the other spouse had no income at all, because an income of nil could not be considered to be a 'lower income' within the meaning of section 63.

The Tax Court's interpretation of section 63 prompted Parliament to enact quickly section 3(f) of the Income Tax Act, effective in the 1990 taxation year.[141] Section 3(f) provides that a taxpayer who has no income for the year is 'deemed to have income for the year in an amount equal to zero.' This ensures that no taxpayer who falls into the *Fiset* scenario can claim any amount under section 63. However, the enactment of section 3(f) has certainly not dissuaded male taxpayers from trying to find other ways to justify the deduction even when their spouse works in the home. For example, the taxpayer in *Copeland v. M.N.R.*[142] claimed that section 63 violated his rights under sections 7, 15, and 28 of the Charter because he could not deduct the cost of his daughter's attendance at a Montessori school while his dependent wife worked in their home.[143] Another male taxpayer raised essentially the same arguments in *Schindeler v. M.N.R.*[144]

The taxpayers in *Boland v. M.N.R.*[145] and *Ross v. M.N.R.*[146] took an even more aggressive position in relation to section 63, claiming child-care deductions for the wages they paid their wives for caring for their children. The taxpayers took the position that the 'lower income' rule in section 63 did not apply to them because it violated their Charter rights and that section 63 discriminated against them on the basis of 'family status.'[147]

In the meantime, many taxpayers who need the child care expense deduction the most – women who are the sole support of their children and whose incomes are much lower, on average, than men's – have been completely denied the benefit of section 63 because it is now gender-neutral but unavailable to taxpayers whose spouses for some reason do not have any income.[148]

The 'reformed' provisions of section 63 harm women's interests in other ways as well. For example, the minister denied the taxpayer in *McCluskie v. M.N.R.*,[149] a teacher who was on maternity leave during the summer months, any deduction for salary paid to a foreign domestic child-care worker who had arrived in Canada in July to work for her. He took the position that the taxpayer was not in fact working during that period of time and thus she had not incurred the child-care expenses in question in order to earn income. The Court was completely unmoved by the taxpayer's explanation that she had to pay the worker's salary from the date of arrival or lose her services and that the period of maternity leave was part of her employment arrangement. It strictly enforced section 63(3)(a)(i)(A) of the act and allowed the taxpayer to deduct just seven days' salary in recognition of the hardship imposed on her.[150] In other litigation the 'earned income' limit in section 63 has been consistently applied by Revenue Canada to exclude alimony and child-support payments received by separated or divorced mothers, which has meant that they have not been able to deduct the full amounts that would otherwise have been permitted to them by section 63.[151]

Attacks on section 63 limits

Charter litigation has also focused on the validity of the arbitrary limits on the amounts that can be deducted for child-care expenses. Ironically, it may well be that, if the taxpayers in *Chyfetz v. M.N.R.*[152] and *Symes v. The Queen*[153] could have switched cases with each other, they both might have won their appeals. As it was, they both lost, and for reasons that appear gender-biased.

The taxpayer in *Chyfetz* deducted the full cost of his child-care expenses, which exceeded the limits in section 63. When the minister disallowed the excess deductions, the taxpayer appealed to the Tax Court of Canada, claiming that the limits in section 63 violated his Charter sex-equality rights because they discriminated against mothers in different situations than contemplated by the legislation. Not surprisingly, the Court rejected this challenge, not the least because the taxpayer himself did not belong to the class of taxpayers he claimed was adversely affected. The Court in *Chyfetz* also ruled that the distinctions in the legislation were not discriminatory because they were not pejorative.

The taxpayer in *Symes* also deducted the full cost of her child-care expenses in excess of the section 63 limits, but she did so not under section 63 but on the basis that they were deductible business expenses. She took this position because, as a partner in a law firm, she earned income from a source that was a business, not income from employment. This strategy meant that the taxpayer did not ask the Courts to apply section 15 of the Charter to invalidate section 63 but instead asked it to use section 15 as an interpretive guide in deciding whether child-care expenses were deductible business expenses. While the trial court allowed the taxpayer's appeal at the first instance, Symes lost at both the Federal Court of Appeal and the Supreme Court of Canada.

The Supreme Court ruled against the taxpayer in Symes on almost every conceivable issue except the government's suggestion that the Income Tax Act should be subject to a lower level of scrutiny than other types of legislation.[154] The Court ruled that Parliament intended section 63 to be a complete code, and thus it treated section 63 – and not the business-deduction provisions – as the focus of the appeal. It held that section 63 did not discriminate against this taxpayer because the provision was gender-neutral, and it rejected the taxpayer's argument that section 63 had a disparate impact on her as a woman because, as the court reasoned, women do bear disproportionate responsibility for child care (although there was no evidence before the court that women disproportionately bear the costs of child care). And the Court stated that, in the absence of evidence of disproportionate costs, it could not impugn section 63.

Fortunately for future litigants, the Supreme Court narrowed its ruling in the Symes appeal on its own initiative. The Court had invited the taxpayer to recast her argument on the basis that, because she was a financially successful woman lawyer, she was really disadvantaged by her family status rather than by her sex. When the taxpayer declined this invitation, the Court suggested that 'in another case, a different subgroup of women with a different evidentiary focus involving s. 63 might well be able to demonstrate the adverse effects required by s. 15(1).' It then commented that an appeal on essentially similar facts by single mothers might succeed where Symes had failed, because single mothers would be in a position to demonstrate that their child-care expenses fell disproportionately on them as women.[156] The Court has virtually invited low-income single mothers disadvantaged by the limits in section 63 to bring forward a challenge under section 15 of the Charter.

Equivalent-to-Married Credit

The litigation and legislative record on the equivalent-to-married credit reveals that Parliament's political deference in the area of income taxation has extended not just to married men in relation to child-care expenses but also to the claims of married taxpayers generally. The equivalent-to-married credit was originally enacted to give single parents the same tax relief for supporting a child that supporting spouses received with respect to the support of dependent spouses. When the Federal Human rights Tribunal suggested that limiting the dependent-spouse exemption in the former section 109 of the Income Tax Act discriminated against non-married cohabitants, Parliament ignored the suggestion that the definition of 'spouse' in the act be expanded to include common-law or deemed spouses.[157]

As soon as the taxpayers in *Schachtschneider v. M.N.R.*[158] and *Landon v. M.N.R.*[159] complained that the equivalent-to-married credit imposed a 'tax on marriage,' however, Parliament rushed to expand the definition of 'spouse' to include non-married cohabitants for purposes of the entire Income Tax Act. The taxpayers had argued that, if they had been unmarried persons, they would have received the full credit for both themselves and one child and that the legislation violated their Charter rights in two respects: it discriminated against them on the basis of marital status, and it infringed their rights to freedom of religion because their religious beliefs prevented them from cohabiting outside marriage. Although these two taxpayers actually lost their court challenges, the resulting changes made by Parliament have deemed non-married cohabitants to be spouses for purposes of the entire Income Tax Act, and the type of differential treatment complained of in *Schachtschneider* and *Landon* can now arise only with respect to lesbian, gay, and non-sexual cohabitants.[160]

The changes generated by this area of fiscal Charter litigation are extensive and fundamental. They also disclose the built-in bias in favour of married heterosexuals and against non-married cohabitants that historically has pervaded income tax legislation. The courts have vigorously resisted the extension of spousal status to common-law cohabitants for decades, despite cogent evidence that this exclusion imposed considerable hardship.[161] So long as the group claiming to be disadvantaged consisted of non-married cohabitants, Parliament also refused to take action[162] and only reluctantly modified some of the rules relating to the taxation of alimony, child support, and matrimonial property to accommodate the extension of provincial family law to such people.[163] The courts supported Parliament in this position, even dismissing Charter challenges to cases brought by non-married cohabitants who had compelling cases.[164]

Nor is Parliament's concern for non-married cohabitants symmetrical with its concern for married taxpayers. The *Poulter* case[165] surely reveals the unfairness of deeming non-married cohabitants to be married in all circumstances: the taxpayer in that case lost all of her child tax benefits because she was living with a man who was in no way related to her daughter and who made no contribution to her support.[166]

Taxation of Divorced/Separated Couples

The income tax rules relating to the taxation of divorced or separated spouses are highly anomalous. Unlike the rules relating to married couples and heterosexual cohabitants, which begin with the proposition that each individual 'owns' their own income, the rules relating to the taxation of alimony and child-support payments deem those payments to be income, not of the person who earned the income out of which the support is paid, but of the recipient.[167] This treatment is anomalous because, despite the growing array of income tax provisions that condition liability or benefits on marital status, 'family' income, and relations of dependency, Canada is still committed, on paper at least, to using the individual as the income tax unit and has resisted quite significant pressure over the last eight decades to move to the marital couple as the basic tax unit. As the one jurisdiction in the Anglo-influenced world that has most consistently adhered to the individual model of taxation, Canada also has the most generous deduction scheme for divorced and separated taxpayers who pay alimony or child support.

Although the Canadian government has contended, in the face of Charter challenges to the validity of the child-support provisions, that these anomalous provisions were enacted for the economic benefit of children in divided families, nothing could be farther from the truth. The origins of what have become the alimony and child-support deductions in section 60 of the Income Tax Act disclose four important facts about the legislative history. First, only the alimony aspect of the current 'deduction/inclusion system' can be traced back to the 1942 legislative debates that are usually cited to explain their alleged 'purpose'; the child-support provisions of the system were not grafted onto these provisions until several years later. Second, the Canadian alimony deduction of 1942 was introduced in complete imitation of the deduction that had been approved by the United States Congress just days before and that was part of a major and radical redefinition of the tax unit in that country.[168] Thirdly, the actual stated purpose of the original alimony deduction in Canada was to offer husbands whose alimony payments had been set in the 1930s, when income tax rates were much lower, some tax relief in the face of sharp increases in tax rates during the Second World War.[169] Finally, because the original alimony deduction enacted in Canada left the bulk of the tax liability for alimony payments in the hands of the husband, it did not deliver a tax subsidy to husbands but merely shifted a modest portion of the overall tax liability associated with that receipt to the wife.[170] In other words, the support provisions as originally discussed in Parliament grew out of a different tax policy context, did not relate in any way to child-support payments, and did not confer any tax benefits on divorced couples.[171]

Both the alimony and child-support provisions continued to be all but ignored on the policy level after the 1940s. All subsequent changes to the legislation merely addressed technical difficulties with the scope of the legislation, or, as family-property law reform unfolded across the provinces, reconciled some of the most important differences between that legislation and the alimony and child-support provisions. Even the Carter Commission, which issued its report in the late 1960s, failed to engage the child-support deduction on a substantive level and, until members of the women's movement articulated the unfairness of the provision to women in the early 1980s, it attracted even less attention than the alimony aspect of the deduction.[172]

When the complete anomaly of the deduction/inclusion system is taken together with the disparate economic impact of the system on men and women, it becomes obvious that rather than being intended as some sort of indirect subsidy to children whose parents divorce or separate, sections 55 and 60 were designed to nullify the tax costs of divorce to men: instead of being able to claim the dependent wife and child credits, divorced and separated men are able instead to claim deductions for support actually paid to their wives and children. In most cases, these provisions mean that a man who divorces – and even remarries – will not experience any change in net after-tax income even if he is ordered to pay alimony or child support to his first wife.[173]

Parliament has steadfastly ignored the criticisms that women have levelled at the child-support provisions and has instead focused on expanding the range of deductions that can be claimed by divorced or separated men.[174] Charter challenges to sections 56 and 60 have reflected the same gender imbalances embedded in the deduction/inclusion system itself. Male taxpayers have invoked the Charter in order to stretch the scope of deductibility that they already enjoy under this system, while women taxpayers have attempted to demonstrate through the language of section 15 of the Charter exactly how this system has discriminated against them and their children since its inception.

Alimony and Support Deductions

Charter challenges brought by men have tested numerous aspects of the section 60 rules. Married men have invoked the Charter equality guarantees in an attempt to expand the scope of deductible payments to include lump-sum payments of maintenance[175] and payments not made pursuant to a written separation agreement or court order.[176] These appeals failed because the Tax Court of Canada concluded that Parliament had a valid federal objective in placing these limitations on the deduction provisions.

Non-married men have invoked the Charter in cases in which they would have been entitled to deductions if they had been married. The leading case is *Bergman v. The Queen*,[177] in which the taxpayer challenged the requirement in section 60(c.1) that payments to non-married persons be made pursuant to a court order. The taxpayer had made child-support payments to his former cohabitant for two years before being reassessed on the basis that he had not met the requirements in section 60(c.1). He then obtained a court decision which deemed those payments to have been maintenance payments. The minister refused to vary the reassessment, and the taxpayer then appealed to the Tax Court of Canada. Both the Tax Court and the Federal Court of Appeal rejected the taxpayer's appeal on the ground that the difference in treatment between married and non-married taxpayers did not violate section 15 of the Charter.[178]

The policy reasons for rejecting these Charter challenges are articulated clearly in *Guilbault v. M.N.R.*,[179] in which the taxpayer argued that Civil Code article 594, which afforded illegitimate children full rights, entitled him to deduct support payments even though they were not made pursuant to a court order. The taxpayer had submitted to the Court that the non-deductibility of these payments frustrated his child's rights because it made it more difficult for him, the father, to provide support for his child. In a refreshingly sensible response to that contention, the Tax Court observed that, if anything, the child's rights were benefited rather than frustrated by the non-deductibility of the payments because they were not taxable in the mother's hands and the child thus had the economic benefit of the full amount of the payments.

Alimony and Support Income

All of the Charter challenges to the inclusion of alimony and child-support payments in women's incomes have been motivated directly by the adverse economic impact that this policy has had on women as a class. And all of them have failed.[180] Of all these challenges, the most important has been *Thibaudeau v. M.N.R.*, in which the taxpayer took the position that the child-support payments she received were, if anything, income to her children and not to her. In one of the most important favourable section 15 decisions on the books, the Federal Court of Appeal upheld her position. Unfortunately, in one of the most narrowly written and poorly reasoned section 15 decisions ever reported, a majority of the Supreme Court of Canada reversed that decision and ruled that assigning child-support payments to the wife for income tax purposes did not constitute discrimination for purposes of section 15 of the Charter.

Despite the fact that the majority in the Federal Court of Appeal had allowed Suzanne Thibaudeau's appeal on the narrow ground that section 56(1)(b) discriminated on the basis of 'family status,' the majority of the Supreme Court ruled that it did not violate section 15 on any grounds. Because there were four written opinions in *Thibaudeau*, each of which took unique approaches to the entire appeal, it is difficult to generalize easily as to what exactly the case did decide, except that at least four justices out of the seven sitting on the appeal agreed with the government.

Justices Corey and Iacobucci, with whom Justice Sopinka agreed, concluded that section 56(1)(b) created a distinction between divorced or separated couples but refused to find that such couples were burdened by this distinction because, when section 56(1)(b) was read together with section 60(b) of the Income Tax Act, it became apparent that the two provisions together operated to confer a tax benefit on the couples to whom they applied.[181] Justice Gonthier, who wrote a separate opinion in which Justice La Forest, concurred, reached the same conclusion but through a narrower reading of section 15(1). He incorporated, virtually the entire section 1 analysis into his analysis of section 15(1), an approach with which the first three justices could not agree.

Justices McLachlin and L'Heureux-Dubé not surprisingly disagreed with the male majority at every step of the analysis. They both concluded that the proper unit of analysis was the individual taxpayer, not the divorced couple, in her capacity as a divorced custodial parent who received child-support payments. They both restricted their analysis of 'discrimination' to the impact that section 56(1)(b) alone had on the taxpayer, instead of reading section 56(1)(b) as part of a larger legislative scheme which encompassed the section 60 child-support rules, other child-related or family-related provisions in the Income Tax Act, or provisions of other statutes such as federal divorce legislation. They both found that, despite facial neutrality, section 56(1)(b) violated section 15(1) of the Charter because it had a disparate and discriminator impact on the taxpayer. And they both rejected the government's justificatory submissions under section 1 of the Charter, preferring instead to give the government twelve months to amend the legislation to bring it into conformity with the requirements of section 15(1).[182]

Conclusions – and More Hopes

When women began to wonder whether and how the Charter might improve their status under the Income Tax Act, one prescient scholar predicted that 'at one extreme, the courts can approach income tax legislation with a judicial deference that will, in effect, render any future attempts at substantive review nugatory.'[183] Against all hopes, the Supreme Court has nearly managed to achieve this extreme in just one short decade.

Does this mean, then, that the *Symes*, *Thibaudeau*, *Lister*, and other decisions have brought the era of fiscal Charter litigation to an end already? I suggest that it has not but that future Charter challenges to the Income Tax Act will have to stretch a large canvas upon which to outline the dimensions of the systemic discrimination that affects women, whether they enter the litigation process as married women, single parents, lesbian partners, daughters supporting older family members, or single women on their own. In one sense, the systemic discrimination that has blocked fiscal Charter challenges involves all of Canadian society – Parliament and judges as well as specific provisions of the Income Tax Act and general federal and provincial laws. To challenge the discrimination against women and other disadvantaged groups that is embedded in the Income Tax Act, litigants will have to show how certain classes of taxpayers are privileged again and again, whether in litigation or legislation, while other classes of taxpayers inevitably end up receiving the burden of taxation with few or no benefits of tax expenditures.

For example, the Supreme Court in the *Symes* case concluded that Parliament has the discretion, even in the face of the Charter equality guarantees, to place severe limits on the amounts that taxpayers can deduct in relation to child-care expenses and to force the spouse with the lower income to claim that deduction. This decision reinforced the initial objective of the child care expense deduction, which was to enable married women to hire child care to make it possible for them to work part-time, clean their houses, or volunteer for charities but not to work full time unless their husbands' incomes were so low that the family really needed that second income.[184] At the present, that Parliamentary discretion translates into the power to cut women off at the level of $2,000 per child. At the same time, the Supreme Court in the *Thibaudeau* case concluded that Parliament has the discretion to give divorced or separated men unlimited deductions for essentially the same kinds of expenditures – child-care expenses – when those payments are made to their former wives for the care of their children. Under section 60 of the Income Tax Act, the sky is the limit on those deductions; any amount of child support, no matter how large, and including amounts that are actually equal to the costs of university room and board, can be deducted by divorced or separated fathers under section 60.

Some people might say that these two provisions are not comparable, that they are like the proverbial 'apples and oranges.' But in the larger systemic context that is called for in fiscal Charter litigation, they are comparable, for they are two of the most clearly sex-linked provisions in the Income Tax Act today. Both sets of provisions have their origins in social expectations and norms of the wartime and the immediate post-war period half a century ago. The alimony deduction that created the pattern into which child-support payments have been cast was designed to respond to the specific fiscal problems raised by men during the Second World War. The child care expense provisions were first devised in response to women's objections to the impact of income tax policy on them as they became mere secondary wage earners again at the end of the war. In the differences between the two sets of provisions lie the differences in the life situations of women and men as taxpayers, but they both relate, in this way, to the same subject matter: responsibility for raising dependent children.

The differences in the levels of tax benefits generated by these two sets of provisions measure the impact of systemic discrimination against women as a class under Canadian income taxation. Unless taxpayers affected by provisions such as these persist in doing the nearly impossible work of bringing fiscal Charter challenges, Canadian income tax policy and equality theory will continue to be driven by the same stereotypes that have driven them in the past.

These concerns are of particular importance for lesbian women and gay men in Canada. If the *Schachtschneider* case is any indication, the next frontier for extending the tax benefits received by married heterosexuals will be to bring lesbians and gays within the net of anti-avoidance provisions while governments continue withholding the most valuable tax benefits on some pretext or other. If lesbian women and gay men are to achieve true equality, and not the punitive kind of 'equality' now given to cohabiting heterosexuals under the Income Tax Act, this will mean continued lobbying, continued efforts to increase political visibility and social presence, and continued engagement with the frustrating doctrines of both income tax and Charter equality law.[185]

Notes

1 Wendy W. Williams, 'Sex Discrimination Under the Charter: Some Problems of Theory,' in *The Study Day Papers* (Toronto: CREF 1985), 6.1–6.47.

2 See, for example, Harry Glasbeek and Michael Mandel, 'The Legalization of Politics in Advanced Capitalism: The Canadian Charter of Rights and Freedoms,' *Socialist Studies*, vol. 2 (1984), 84; Michael Mandel, *The Charter of Rights and the Legalization of Politics in Canada* (Toronto: Wall and Thompson 1989).

3 Gwen Brodsky and Shelagh Day reported that, of the fifty-one Charter challenges that raised sex as a ground of discrimination during the first three years of equality litigation, only nine had been brought by women. Gwen Brodsky and Shelagh Day, *Canadian Charter Equality Rights for Women: One Step Forward or Two Steps Back?* (Ottawa: CACSW 1989), 49, 68.

4 To me, 'critical' scholarship studies the gap between ideals and realities. This method has been described by Horkheimer, an early critical theorist, as 'relating social institutions and activities to the values they themselves set forth as their standards and ideals.' See M. Horkheimer, 'Notes on Institute Activities,' *Studies*

in Philosophy and Social Science, vol. 9, no. 1, 122. As a contemporary critical theorist has put it, 'immanent criticism lives off the gap between what society professes and what it performs.' Joseph McCarney, 'What Makes Critical Theory "Critical"?' *Radical Philosophy*, vol. 42, no. 11, 11, 12.

5 [1989], 56 D.L.R. (4th) 1.

6 For example, the commission concluded that dependent-spouse benefits and the non-deductibility of childcare expenses reinforced both women's and men's preferences for women's non-waged domestic labour. (Ottawa: Information Canada 1970) (Chair Florence Bird), ch. 5.

7 Limited deductions for childcare expenses were provided in the early 1970s in the form of section 63 of the Income Tax Act, and, by 1980, the prohibition on deductions for spousal salaries had been repealed. See S.C. 1980–81–82–83, c. 48, s. 40(1), repealing sections 74(3) and 74(4) of the Income Tax Act effective after the 1979 taxation year.

8 See *Bailey v. M.N.R.* [1981], 1 C.H.R.R. D/193, in which three male taxpayers complained that section 63 of the Income Tax Act discriminated against 'deserted males' because it did not extend the childcare-expense deduction to men in all of the same circumstances as it did to women.

9 Large numbers of traditional women expressed outrage when the federal government floated the suggestion in the 1970s that the dependent-spouse exemption should be repealed in order to reduce the tax incentive for women to remain economically dependent on their husbands. This made it difficult for the government to look at alternative structures for such a provision.

10 CREF recommended that the Income Tax Act be amended to permit the deduction of the full costs of childcare and to restructure the deduction as a fully refundable tax credit, expand credits/exemptions for support of dependent family members, exclude child-support and alimony payments from income, eliminate the tax benefits that accrue to men in relation to women's non-waged domestic labour and the various marital-status benefits, revise RRSP ceilings for low-income taxpayers, and reinstate general-income averaging, with special provisions for low-income, divorced, and separated women. See Charter of Rights Educational Fund, *Report on the Statute Audit Project; Selected Issues Presented to the Equality Sub-Committee* (Toronto: CREF 1985). CREF was the precursor to LEAF, the Women's Legal Education and Action Fund.

11 The committee made only two recommendations in relation to the Income Tax Act: that the term 'spouse' be expanded to include cohabiting heterosexuals who had lived together for at least one year and publicly represented themselves as husband and wife, and that the disability deductions in the act be expanded. See Canada, House of Commons, Report of the Parliamentary Committee on Equality

Rights ('Equality for All'). 1st Sess., 33rd Parl., 1984–5, October 1985, 139, 144, recommendations 15 and 69.

12 The Honourable John Crosbie said that the government had already done enough in relation to disability tax benefits, that Parliament had already taken steps to provide additional financial assistance to disabled persons in the workforce who were not previously considered to be disabled for tax purposes, and that the recommendation to expand the meaning of 'spouse' to include non-married cohabitants was unworkable. See Canada, Department of Justice, *Toward Equality: The Response to the Report of the Parliamentary Committee on Equality Rights*, (Ottawa: Supply and Services Canada 1986), 54–5, 64.

13 The parliamentary committee defined systemic discrimination as 'practices that may not be obviously discriminatory in their formulation or nature but that, in their result, have an adverse impact on those who are protected from discrimination by the Act.' 'Equality for All,' 5, 131, 145, and recommendation 81. John Crosbie took the position that the courts had already recognized that systemic discrimination was prohibited under the Canadian Human Rights Act. See *Toward Equality*, 54–5, 64.

14 *Toward Equality*, 15–16.

15 As of 30 Sept. 1995. Some 196 of those cases involved procedural, evidentiary, or jurisdictional issues such as the constitutionality of searches and seizures, the admissibility of evidence, the jurisdiction of the court, allegations of delay on the part of the government, the constitutional status of penalty provisions in the Income Tax Act, and taxpayers' procedural rights. The other 88 cases have dealt with substantive income tax issues.

16 *Holizki v. M.N.R.*, [1995] F.C.J. No. 1,186 (appeal re application of attribution rules allowed on basis that, by the doctrine of resulting trust, taxpayer's wife had given adequate consideration for assets attributed to husband; Charter issue not reached); *McCluskie v. M.N.R.*, 94 D.T.C. 1,735 (T.C.C.) (appeal re child care expense deduction allowed in part on merits and not on Charter grounds); *Hover v. M.N.R.*, [1992] T.C.J. No. 735 (T.C.C.) (taxpayer won appeal from application of restricted-farm-loss rules; Charter issues not reached); *Binavince v. M.N.R.*, 91 D.T.C. 1,225 (T.C.C.) (taxpayer won appeal against assessment for section 227.1 director's personal liability for unremitted withholding taxes); *Kosowan v. M.N.R.*, 91 D.T.C. 32 (T.C.C.) (director's personal liability; appeal allowed with respect to quantum of liability only); *Kostiuk v. M.N.R.*, [1989] T.C.J. No. 804 (T.C.C.) (taxpayer won appeal from assessment for joint and several liability for unpaid income taxes of transferor of property); *Fleming v. M.N.R.*, 86 D.T.C. 1,628 (T.C.C.) (appeal from application of restricted-farm-loss rules in section 31 granted on merits; court did not address section 7 or section 15 issues); *Overdyk v.*

M.N.R., 83 D.T.C. 307 (T.R.B.) (taxpayer's claim for disability credit allowed on merits; court did not address Charter issue, which predated 1985 in any event).

17 [1994] T.C.J. No. 401 (T.C.C.), following *Thibaudeau v. M.N.R.*, 92 D.T.C. 2,111 (English), 92 D.T.C. 2,098 (French) (T.C.C.), rev'd 94 D.T.C. 6,230 (F.C.A.), before the Federal Court of Appeal was reversed by the Supreme Court in *The Queen v. Thibaudeau*, 95 D.T.C. 5,273 (S.C.C.).

18 92 D.T.C. 1,693 (T.C.C.) (English), 92 D.T.C. 1,681 (A.C.I.) (French).

19 *Krag-Hansen and Krag-Hansen Enterprises Ltd. v. The Queen*, 85 D.T.C. 5,330 (F.C.T.D.) (appeal re associated corporations).

20 *Ontario Public Service Employees Union v. National Citizens' Coalition Inc.*, 87 D.T.C. 5,270 (O.H.C.J.), aff'd 90 D.T.C. 6,326 (O.C.A.).

21 'Bunched income' is income that has accrued over several years but that is included in taxable income all at once – usually in the year of realization – and results in increases in the taxpayer's marginal rate as well as in the quantum of the taxpayer's income. Examples of 'bunched income' include capital gains and deregistered RRSPs.

22 Timing of income, changes in income-averaging annuity-contract legislation, and changes in registered retirement saving plan rules have all been challenged by taxpayers who have been caught with bunched income.

23 See below, 'Taxation of the Family,' for a discussion of these cases.

24 89 D.T.C. 5243 (F.C.T.D.), rev'd [1993] 4 S.C.R. 695, 91 D.T.C. 5,397, discussed in detail under 'Taxation of the Family,' below.

25 92 D.T.C. 2,111 (English), 92 D.T.C. 2,098 (French) (T.C.C.), rev'd 94 D.T.C. 6,230 (F.C.A.), rev'd 95 D.T.C. 5,273 (S.C.C.).

26 The first income tax statute enacted in the United States was declared to be unconstitutional, and the sixteenth amendment to the Bill of Rights was adopted in 1913 specifically to ensure that the next statute would be immune to such challenges. See *Pollock v. Farmers' Loan and Trust Co.*, 157 U.S. 429 (1,895), rehearing 158 U.S. 601 (1,895). The Canadian Income Tax Act has attracted similar litigation, with the difference that no Canadian court has ever held it to be wholly unconstitutional. See, for example, *Mueller v. Canada*, [1993] F.C.J. No. 11 (F.C.T.D.) (constitutional challenge to Income Tax Act and Goods and Services Tax on basis of provincial powers stricken for failure to state reasonable cause of action).

27 87 D.T.C. 26 (T.C.C.).

28 88 D.T.C. 6,207 (F.C.T.C.), 89 D.T.C. 5,503 (F.C.A.), application for leave to appeal dismissed [1990] S.C.C. Bulletin 411, application for reconsideration dismissed 20 Sept. 1990.

29 The Court also stated that section 15 of the Charter did not apply at all in this case.

30 See *Petrini v. The Queen*, 94 D.T.C. 6,657 (F.C.A.), leave to appeal den. [1994] S.C.C.A. No. 504 (23 Feb. 1995); *Hertzog v. M.N.R.*, 91 D.T.C. 720 (T.C.C.); *Woodside v. M.N.R.*, [1993] T.C.J. No. 315 (T.C.C.); *Price-Munn v. M.N.R.*, [1993] T.C.J. No. 907 (T.C.C.).

31 *Woodside v. M.N.R.*, [1993] T.C.J. No. 315 (T.C.C.).

32 In *O'Sullivan v. M.N.R.*, 91 D.T.C. 1,912 (T.C.C.), the Court dismissed the taxpayer's appeal for lack of merit. The taxpayer then appealed, in *O'Sullivan v. The Queen*, 91 D.T.C. 5,374 (F.C.T.D.), to the Federal Court–Trial Division, where the associate senior prothonotary granted the crown's motion to strike the statement of claim as disclosing no cause of action. The taxpayer's subsequent appeal of that dismissal to the Federal Court–Trial Division was also dismissed. See 91 D.T.C. 5,491 (F.C.T.D.).

33 Indian Act, R.S.C. 1985, c. I-5, s. 87; Income Tax Act, S.C. 1970–71–72, c. 63, s. 81.

34 This approach to the liberal interpretation of the exemption can be traced to *Jones v. Meehan*, 175 U.S. 1 (1,899).

35 83 D.T.C. 5,041, [1983] 1 S.C.R. 29.

36 89 D.T.C. 5,032 (F.C.T.D.), 90 D.T.C. 6,399 (F.C.A.), 92 D.T.C. 6,320 (S.C.C.).

37 The taxpayer in this case was a logger who worked off the reserve. The Court found that he was entitled to the benefit of the exemption because the corporation for which he worked had its head office on the reserve, administered the business from the reserve, and paid him by cheque on the reserve. It reasoned that, because the income from the employment which gave rise to the unemployment benefits in question had itself been exempt from taxation, the unemployment benefits that derived from that employment should also be exempt. In a sense, the Court attached the benefits which flowed from the original income stream to that income stream, notwithstanding the change in character that occurred when the income stream indirectly gave rise to economic benefits under the Unemployment Insurance Act.

38 See, for example, *Clarke v. M.N.R.*, 92 D.T.C. 2,267 (T.C.C.), in which the Tax Court of Canada held that the 'connecting factors' test did not extend to income receipts flowing from employment located on or adjacent to a reserve when the minister could find some sort of formal legal distinction between the physical contours of the reserve and the locus of employment – even for Native persons who lived physically on the reserve.

39 92 D.T.C. 2,274 (T.C.C.).

40 The Court refused to see the taxpayer's inability to find employment on the reserve as a reflection of the lack of economic opportunities for Native persons, and described it instead as 'freedom of choice.'

41 [1989] 1 S.C.R. 143.

42 This is the definition of equality found in the much-criticized case of *A.-G. Canada v. Lavell; Isaac v. Bedard*, [1974] S.C.R. 1,349, 38 D.L.R. (3d) 48, in which the Supreme Court of Canada held that the provisions of section 12(1)(b) of the Indian Act, which deprived Native women who married non-status Indians of their own Indian status, did not discriminate on the basis of race because it treated all such women the same.

43 Cambodian-Canadians have the lowest average income of any ethnic group. See Statistics Canada, *Catalogue* 93–154, 93–155, a study of income levels by racial identity for 1985 employment income.

44 See, generally, Ronald Wright, *Stolen Continents: The "New World" Through Indian [sic] Eyes Since 1492* (Toronto: Viking Press 1992) for this history.

45 [1974] S.C.R. 1,349.

46 See Verna Kirkness, 'Emerging Native Woman,' *Canadian Journal of Women and the Law*, vol. 2 (1987–8), 408, for detailed discussion of this history.

47 88 D.T.C. 1,627 (T.C.C.).

48 See *Derrickson v. Derrickson*, [1984] 2 W.W.R. 754 (B.C.C.A.), [1986] 1 S.C.R. 285; *Paul v. Paul*, [1986] 1 S.C.R. 306; *Sampson v. Gosnell Estate*, [1989] B.C.J. No. 426 (B.C.C.A.).

49 87 D.T.C. 5,270 (O.H.C.J.), aff'd 90 D.T.C. 6,326 (O.C.A.).

50 90 D.T.C. 6,597 (F.C.T.D.).

51 91 D.T.C. 5,266 (F.C.T.D.).

52 *Munroe v. M.N.R.*, [1992] T.C.J. No. 281 (T.C.C.) (employee taxpayer denied deductions for living expenses when referred by union to job in another city); *Lyon v. M.N.R.*, [1992] T.C.J. No. 711 (T.C.C.) (employee doctor denied deductions for insurance and professional dues); *Cross v. M.N.R.*, [1991] T.C.J. No. 785 (union member denied deductions for expenses of extensive travel required by the terms of his employment).

53 [1991] T.C.J. No. 352 (T.C.C.).

54 See also *Barrons v. M.N.R.*, 95 D.T.C. 483 (T.C.C.), leave to appeal den. [1995] S.C.C.A. No. 219 (7 Sept. 1995) (refusal to allow taxpayer to rely on $40,000 'basic exemption' in alternative minimum-tax rules in calculating taxable income generally under Division C did not violate sections 7 or 15 or the Charter); *Hokhold v. M.N.R.*, [1993] F.C.J. No. 672 (F.C.T.D.), in which the Court held that the retroactive effect of section 110(1)(f)(iii) of the Income Tax Act, which prevented a dentist from deducting social-assistance payments received for treating patients on social assistance, did not violate the taxpayer's section 7 and 15 rights.

55 [1994] T.C.J. No. 1,038 (T.C.C.).

56 89 D.T.C. 253 (T.C.C.).

57 *Julien v. M.N.R.*, 91 D.T.C. 586 (T.C.C.). See also *Netupsky v. M.N.R.*, 95 D.T.C. 210 (T.C.C.), in which the Court held that the carryback provisions of the alternative-minimum tax (AMT) did not discriminate on the basis of age because the provisions of the AMT credit applied equally to taxpayers of all ages. The taxpayer had argued that the fact that taxpayers over the age of sixty-five almost invariably experienced dramatic reductions in their incomes meant that the AMT carryback provisions had a disparate impact on older taxpayers as a class.

58 90 D.T.C. 1,792 (T.C.C.) (English), 90 D.T.C. 1,785 (A.C.I.) (French), aff'd 94 D.T.C. 6,556 (F.C.T.D.).

59 Both courts in *Huet v. M.N.R.*, in reaching the conclusion that security of the person had not been violated, relied particularly on the fact that the taxpayers had been cautioned about the impending implementation of retroactive legislation when they purchased the IAACs.

60 [1991] T.C.J. No. 1,052 (T.C.C.) (English), [1991] A.C.I. No. 1,052 (A.C.I.) (French).

61 95 D.T.C. 5,224 (F.C.A.).

62 85 D.T.C. 5,561 (O.H.Ct.J.).

63 The RRSP rules also permit contributions to spousal RRSPs from periodic registered-retirement or deferred-profit-sharing-plan income to be deducted. In *Flynn v. M.N.R.*, [1995] T.C.J. No. 523 (T.C.C.), the Tax Court held that section 15 of the Charter did not expand these source rules to include transfers of periodic income between spouses' RRSPs.

64 94 D.T.C. 6,271 (F.C.A.), leave to appeal den. [1994] S.C.C.A. No. 182 (1 Sept. 1994).

65 See also *Rosen v. M.N.R.*, [1992] T.C.J. No. 699 (T.C.C.), in which a disabled older taxpayer was denied deductions for RRSP contributions because super-annuation payments, Old Age Security payments, Canada Pension Plan payments, RRSP income, and interest income did not fall within the statutory definition of 'earned income' in the RRSP rules.

66 The same circularity flawed the reasoning in *Gorman v. M.N.R.*, [1992] T.C.J. No. 798 (T.C.C.), in which the Tax Court of Canada upheld the minister's refusal to include unemployment-insurance benefits in the taxpayer's 'earned income' for purposes of calculating his RRSP contribution limit. This is not to suggest, however, that all taxpayers who are unemployed should be permitted to offset RRSP contributions against income from any source; see, for example, *Androwich v. The Queen*, 90 D.T.C. 6,084 (F.C.T.D.) (unemployed taxpayer denied RRSP deductions against investment income; Charter challenges grounded in sections 7 and 15 rejected); *Fraser v. M.N.R.*, [1993] T.C.J. No. 728 (T.C.C.) (excluding retiring allowance from earned income for purposes of calculating the taxpayer's

RRSP contribution limit did not violate section 15 of the Charter); *Mekuz v. M.N.R.*, [1993] T.C.J. No. 477 (T.C.C.) (proportionate reduction of RRSP room for part-year resident discriminated on the basis not of national origin but of residence); *Smith v. M.N.R.*, 89 D.T.C. 639 ('it is the government's responsibility to ... address the complex social, economic and fiscal problems facing the state'); *Young v. M.N.R.*, 95 D.T.C. 476 (T.C.C.) (exclusion of taxable bursary from earned income did not constitute 'discrimination').

67 [1988] F.C.J. No. 740 (F.C.T.D.), 90 D.T.C. 6,376 (F.C.A.).

68 [1993] T.C.J. No. 316 (T.C.C.).

69 [1993] T.C.J. No. 250 (T.C.C.).

70 This was a particularly weak case in which to bring such a challenge, because the taxpayer had not made any contribution to her RRSP in the taxation year in question.

71 *Viccars v. M.N.R.*, [1991] T.C.J. No. 644 (T.C.C.) has been omitted from this discussion because the taxpayer posed his Charter challenge to the provisions of the Income Tax Act – including the RRSP rules – in such general terms that it does not really have any precedential value and is useful only as a guide to how not to pose a Charter challenge to fiscal legislation.

72 Taxable benefit provisions have an anti-avoidance function to the extent that they prevent taxpayers from receiving in non-taxable form items which would, if received directly in cash, be considered to be taxable income from a source.

73 See generally sections 6 and 7 of the Income Tax Act, as well as the various cross-references in those provisions to other sections of the act.

74 88 D.T.C. 1,392, [1988] T.C.J. No. 433 (T.C.C.).

75 93 D.T.C. 50, [1992] T.C.J. No. 112 (T.C.C.).

76 92 D.T.C. 1069, [1991] T.C.J. No. 1,004 (T.C.C.), [1991] A.C.I. No. 1,004 (A.C.I.).

77 Or that they were creditable under section 118(3) of the act.

78 See also *Witherspoon v. M.N.R.*, 91 D.T.C. 5,550, [1991] F.C.J. No. 367 (F.C.T.D.).

79 *Fleming v. M.N.R.*, 86 D.T.C. 1,628 (T.C.C.) (taxpayer also invoked section 7 of the Charter; Court ruled that section 15 did not apply because the losses were incurred before section 15 became effective); *Wilson v. M.N.R.*, 86 D.T.C. 1,336 (T.C.C.) (taxpayer abandoned his section 15 argument at the hearing of his appeal); *Hover v. M.N.R.*, [1992] T.C.J. No. 735 (T.C.C.).

80 *Hover v. M.N.R.*, [1992] T.C.J. No. 735 (T.C.C.).

81 *Short v. M.N.R.*, 91 D.T.C. 67 (T.C.C.) (appeal dismissed on both merits and Charter grounds); *Binavince v. M.N.R.*, 91 D.T.C. 1225 (T.C.C.) (appeal allowed on tax merits; Charter argument rejected); *Byrt v. M.N.R.*, 91 D.T.C. 923 (T.C.C.) (appeal dismissed on both merits and Charter grounds); *Kosowan v. M.N.R.*, 91

D.T.C. 32 (T.C.C.) (appeal allowed in part on merits; Charter argument rejected); *Edmondson v. M.N.R.*, [1988] T.C.J. No. 708 (T.C.C.) (appeal dismissed on both grounds).

82 91 D.T.C. 923 (T.C.C.).

83 See also *Bennett v. M.N.R.*, [1995] T.C.J. No. 114 (T.C.C.), in which the taxpayer claimed that a section 162(2) penalty relating to his personal liability as a director violated his rights under sections 7 and 11(d) of the Charter; the Court rejected that contention on the basis that section 162(2) did not itself create an offence but was merely a penalty provision which is a matter of private law.

84 85 D.T.C. 5,330 (F.C.T.D.).

85 [1989] T.C.J. No. 804 (T.C.C.).

86 [1995] F.C.J. No. 1,186 (F.C.T.D.).

87 [1980] 2 S.C.R. 834.

88 Indeed, from its inception, United Kingdom income-tax policy aggregated all wives' incomes with their husbands and treated the couple as one person for tax purposes on the basis of the common-law fiction that husbands and wives were one, and that one was the husband.

89 See the Election Act, 1954, S.N. 1954, No. 79, s. 3, which lowered the voting age for women from twenty-five to twenty-one years, the same age as for men.

90 Married women did not accede to full legal capacity until 1969. See An Act Concerning Matrimonial Regimes, S.Q. 1969, c. 77, art. 177. Native women have not yet acceded to full legal capacity. In addition to the effects of section 12(1)(b) of the Indian Act, which have not been fully nullified by Bill C-31, the Indian Act deprives Native women who are status Indians from dealing equally with men in relation to property. See, for example, *A.-G. Canada v. Canard* (1975), 53 D.L.R. (3d) 161, in which the Supreme Court of Canada refused to declare that those sections of the Indian Act that denied an Indian woman the right to act as administrator of her husband's estate were contrary to the Canadian Bill of Rights; see also *Derrickson v. Derrickson*; *Paul v. Paul*; *Sampson v. Gosnell Estate*, [1989] B.C.J. No. 426 (B.C.C.A.), which ruled that Native women who were denied claims to property located on reserves, and which was thus under the jurisdiction of the Indian Act, had no remedies under provincial property law – and thus no remedies at all.

91 At the present time, the Income Tax Act provides seven different tax benefits for taxpayers who support dependent spouses. The married credit in section 118(1)(a) is the only direct credit, but another six tax benefits can be transferred from the dependent spouse to the supporting spouse when the dependent spouse does not have sufficient income to take advantage of them. These transferrable benefits include the age, pension, and disability credits in section 118.8, the dividend tax credits in section 82(3), and the spousal RRSP deduction in section 146. Dozens

of other special provisions relate to other dimensions of family relationship. See
Kathleen A. Lahey, 'The "Tax Unit" Debate: Basic Structural Choices,' written
for the Ontario Fair Tax Commission Working Group on Women and Taxation.

92 For example, women who have no earned incomes may be starting businesses
which have not yet shown a net profit, may be looking for waged work, or may
be developing skills by working in voluntary organizations.

93 Kathleen A. Lahey, *The Taxation of Women in Canada* (Kingston: Queen's
University 1988).

94 95 D.T.C. 5,273 (S.C.C.).

95 95 D.T.C. at 5,275, Sopinka, J. concurring, 95 D.T.C. at 5,274.

96 95 D.T.C. at 5,285, La Forest, J. concurring.

97 95 D.T.C. at 5,294. Arguing that 'Inequality is inequality and discrimination is
discrimination, whatever the legislative source,' Justice L'Heureux-Dubé made
much the same point but drew into the analysis the history of legal policy relating
to married women and the realities of women's economic position within the
family unit. 95 D.T.C. at 5,302–3.

98 [1994] T.C.J. No. 929 (T.C.C.).

99 [1995] T.C.J. No. 228 (T.C.C.).

100 [1995] T.C.J. No. 53 (T.C.C.).

101 In even more twisted logic, the Court in *Bayliss* relied on *Schachtschneider* in
reaching this conclusion, even though the taxpayer in the latter case was a married
woman who claimed that she had been discriminated against because she was not
receiving the same benefit that lesbian or gay couples might receive in relation to
the equivalent-to-married credit. The taxpayer in *Schachtschneider* felt that she
should be entitled to claim the equivalent-to-married credit in relation to one of
her children, even though she was married, did not fall into the class of taxpayers
who were intended as the beneficiaries of that provision, and was more than likely
under a religious duty not only to marry rather than cohabit but to avoid lesbian-
ism.

102 There is some speculation that the Supreme Court ruling in *Miron v. Trudel*,
[1995] 2 S.C.R. 418, may well change the outcome of the cases in which
common-law couples who are deemed to be spouses incur additional tax penalties
as the result of that deemed status, since the majority of the court in *Miron* ruled
that common-law cohabitants are members of historically disadvantaged groups
and thus are entitled to section 15 protection as an analogous group. This is
unlikely to happen, however. *Miron* revolved around the denial of a benefit due to
non-married status; in *Poulter*, the discrimination complained of flowed from
being deemed to have the very status that the plaintiff in *Miron* lacked, which is
the obverse situation. That is why *Poulter* is really an example of denial of equal
benefits to a woman by virtue of marriage, which in this case is deemed marriage.

103 Note that corporations were considered to be legal persons long before women were. See also *Schultz v. M.N.R.*, 93 D.T.C. 953 (T.C.C.) (wife trading on her own account as husband's equal business partner, not as his agent); cf. *Kostiuk v. M.N.R.*, [1989] T.C.J. No. 804 (T.C.C.) (woman's interest in property in section 160 case not affected by provincial matrimonial-property legislation); but see *Holizki v. M.N.R.*, [1995] F.C.J. No. 1,186 (F.C.T.D.) (doctrine of resulting trust used to find wife's ownership interest in shares issued by her husband's business). And see *Giagnocavo v. The Queen*, 93 D.T.C. 5,161 (F.C.T.D.) (held that appellant's husband did not have any 'inherent right' under 'God's law' to represent his wife in tax appeal).

104 Before European contact, Native culture was sex-egalitarian, even matrifocal, in structure. European contact replaced these structures with patriarchal structures at the same time that the romanticization of those structures created a vision of substantive sex equality that has helped fuel the women's movement for over one hundred years and has made the attainment of some property rights possible for some women. See Ronald Wright, *Stolen Continents*. When viewed in this light, the *Gros-Louis*, *Derrickson*, and *Paul* cases make it all too clear that Native women are still caught firmly in the patriarchal property relations that non-Native women have, at least on paper, begun to escape.

105 See, for example, *Thivierge v. M.N.R.*, [1994] T.C.J. No. 876 (T.C.C.), in which the Tax Court held that section 3(2)(c) of the Unemployment Insurance Act, which excludes from insurable employment the employment of a person who is not dealing with the employer at arm's length unless the minister is satisfied that the contract between the parties is commercially reasonable, does not violate section 15(1) of the Charter.

106 As early as 1943, when the Canadian Advisory Committee on Reconstruction, Subcommittee on Post-War Problems of Women, prepared its report, the government had been preparing to push women back into the non-waged sector once the war was over. As the subcommittee said in its final report, the payment of a children's allowance on a non-contributory basis directly to mothers would address the 'new psychological factor in the present situation': 'The addition to the family income from children's allowances paid to the mother and by her spent for the welfare of her children may well be an alleviating factor in the mental attitude which may result from the surrender of the double income.' Canadian Advisory Committee on Reconstruction, Subcommittee on Post-War Problems of Women, *Final Report* (Ottawa: King's Printer 1943), 13. Note, however, that this did not happen in Quebec, where special provisions had to be made to send family-allowance cheques to fathers instead of mothers: married women were still restricted as to their legal capacities in Quebec at that time. See the Family Allowance Act, 8 Geo. VI, c. 40 (1944). Nor was the family allowance really

intended to enhance women's own economic power at all. The subcommittee recommended that 'the administration of these allowances will have to include some supervision in cases where it may be necessary because of the incompetence or unwillingness of the mother to use the allowances for the purposes for which they are given.' See *Final Report*, 30.

107 [1994] T.C.J. No. 259 (T.C.C.).

108 The Court also pointed out that the Part I.2 tax was not, in any event, a tax in the true sense of the term but merely a system for recovering social benefits from high-income recipients.

109 91 D.T.C. 528, [1991] T.C.J. No. 15 (T.C.C.).

110 94 D.T.C. 6,075 (F.C.A.), aff'g [1991] T.C.J. No. 550 (T.C.C.).

111 See *Thomson v. M.N.R.*, [1992] T.C.J. No. 557 (T.C.C.) (Part I.2 differentiated between taxpayers on the basis not of family status but of economic levels); *Triantis v. M.N.R.*, [1992] T.C.J. No. 768 (T.C.C.), [1992] A.C.I. no 557 (A.C.I.).

112 This is partly because the previous version of that credit, which was found in the now-repealed section 122.2 of the Income Tax Act, is no longer in effect, and partly because the revised credit, the child tax benefit found in section 122.6 of the act, did not come into effect until the 1993 taxation year.

113 In 1986 section 122.2(2)(a) of the Income Tax Act incorporated by reference section 7(1) of the Family Allowances Act, R.S.C. 1985, c. F-1, which specified that the family allowance was to be paid to the female parent of a child unless the father had custody of the child.

114 [1995] T.C.J. No. 116 (T.C.C.).

115 [1995] T.C.J. No. 228 (T.C.C.).

116 See below, 'Taxation of the Family,' VI for a discussion of this decision.

117 *Lynn v. M.N.R.*, [1992] T.C.J. Nos. 734, 653 (T.C.C.) (taxpayer with hypothyroid condition not considered to be disabled; Charter rights not violated); *Smith v. M.N.R.*, 89 D.T.C. 639 (T.C.C.) (denial of dependent-relative exemption for sister-in-law after taxpayer divorced wife did not violate taxpayer's Charter rights); *Overdyk v. M.N.R.*, 83 D.T.C. 307 (taxpayer paralyzed from waist down granted disability credit on merits; Charter issues not reached by court).

118 92 D.T.C. 1,693 (English), 92 D.T.C. 1,681 (French), [1992] T.C.J. No. 40 (T.C.C.).

119 See section 109(1)(b) [repealed effective before 1988], which merely referred to a child of the taxpayer.

120 91 D.T.C. 17 (T.C.C.).

121 [1990] T.C.J. No. 930 (T.C.C.).

122 [1992] T.C.J. No. 674 (T.C.C.), [1992] A.C.I. No. 674, aff'd [1994] F.C.J. No. 1,051 (F.C.A.). See also *Von Kaufmann v. M.N.R.* [1990] T.C.J. No. 543 (T.C.C.) (age-eighteen limitation on claims for the federal sales-tax credit did not

so abridge the taxpayer's rights that it outweighed the deference to be shown to the targeting objectives of the credit rules); *McKinnon v. M.N.R.* [1991] T.C.J. No. 509 (T.C.C.) (denial of federal sales-tax credits to prison inmate was a legitimate policy differentiation).

123 *Lister v. M.N.R.*, [1994] F.C.J. No. 1,051, para. 23.

124 [1994] F.C.J. No. 1,051, para. 38, 39. See *Bailey v. M.N.R.* (1981), 1 C.H.R.R. D/ 193, in which the Canadian Human Rights Tribunal found that tax-benefit provisions are functionally the same as direct government expenditures. This reasoning is inconsistent, because the Court applied a lower standard of scrutiny to the tax credit on the basis that it was a fiscal measure and then appealed to the social-benefits nature of the provision to defend its structure. The Court did not address the fact that indirect tax benefits are functionally the same as direct social-benefits legislation. See the discussion of the Bailey case in relation to the child care expense deduction in the next section. Also see *Fenner v. M.N.R.*, [1992] T.C.J. No. 679 (T.C.C.), [1992] A.C.I. No. 679 (A.C.I.) (section 15 challenge to family-income limit on eligibility for northern resident deduction; ITA section 110.7(1), (e) (ii) (B) not considered; taxpayer failed to give proper notice of constitutional question).

125 Canada, House of Commons, Standing Committee on Finance, Trade and Economic Affairs, 1970, 31:14, no. 46 (R.B. Bryce, economic adviser to Prime Minister Pierre Trudeau).

126 Ibid., 31:14 (J.R. Brown, senior tax adviser to the Department of Finance).

127 The legislation established a statutory presumption that the mother would not be able to care for their children when she had been confined for at least fourteen days to bed, wheelchair, hospital, mental hospital, or prison. Summary of 1971 Tax Reform Legislation, June 1971, accompanying introduction of legislation enacted as S.C. 1970–71–72, c. 63, s. 63(1)(a)(i)–(iv). (This tax-reform document was known informally as the 'Raspberry Paper.') The deduction initially had limits of $500 per child and $2,000 per family.

128 For example, the MPP from Edmonton West, Mr Lambert, stated during the debate on section 63: 'I am going to strike out for male liberty in respect of this provision ... The widower is not specifically provided for, nor is the man whose wife decides she wants to play in greener pastures and has left him with children.' Canada, House of Commons, *Debates*, 2nd Session, 24th Parl., 1 Nov. 1971, 9,226–7.

129 See *Martin v. M.N.R.*, 80 D.T.C. 1,011 (T.R.B.) (husband separated from second wife within four months of first divorce denied section 63; held no violation of husband's human rights); *Ayala v. The Queen*, 78 D.T.C. 1,262 (T.R.B.), aff'd 79 D.T.C. 5,083 (F.C.T.D.) (section 63 did not violate sections 1 or 2 of the Canadian Bill of Rights because the establishment of conditions of entitlement

was an integral part of valid federal legislation, there was no discrimination by reason of sex, and there was no inequality before law); *Hurtubise v. M.N.R.*, 78 D.T.C. 1,264 (T.R.B.) (section 63 not violating sex-equality rights of husband when wife attending university; within the powers of Parliament to make distinctions expressed in section 63).

130 *Bailey v. M.N.R.* [1981], 1 C.H.R.R. D/193 (C.H.R.C. Trib.). See also *A.-G. Canada v. Cumming*, 79 D.T.C. 5,303 (F.C.T.D.), in which the Federal Court refused the attorney general's application for a writ of prohibition on the above hearing.

131 *Bailey v. M.N.R.* [1981], 1 C.H.R.R. at D/204 [footnotes omitted].

132 *Bailey v. M.N.R.* [1981], 1 C.H.R.R. at D/205.

133 [1981], 1 C.H.R.R. at D/215.

134 [1981], 1 C.H.R.R. at D/195, D/200, D/203.

135 [1981], 1 C.H.R.R. at D/221.

136 Ibid.

137 [1981], 1 C.H.R.R. at D/222.

138 [1981], 1 C.H.R.R. at D/217.

139 Budget of 19 April 1983 (Marc Lalonde). It is interesting that the move to eliminate 'discrimination' in that provision was considered by some to be a concession to feminists. See, for example, Brian Arnold and Timothy Edgar, *Materials on Canadian Income Tax*, 9th ed. (Toronto: DeBoo 1990), 541.

140 88 D.T.C. 1,226 (T.C.C.).

141 Section 3(f) was added by S.C. 1991, c. 49, s. 1, applicable to 1990 et seq.

142 [1993] T.C.J. No. 3 (T.C.C.).

143 See also *Copeland v. M.N.R.*, [1993] T.C.J. No. 584 (T.C.C.), brought by the same taxpayer on the same issues.

144 [1994] T.C.J. No. 29 (T.C.C.) (taxpayer raised 'cruel and unusual punishment' claim under section 12 of Charter; Court raised section 15 issue).

145 93 D.T.C. 1,558 (T.C.C.).

146 [1993] T.C.J. No. 237 (T.C.C.).

147 See also *James v. M.N.R.*, [1994] T.C.J. No. 1,073, in which the taxpayer tried to argue that the lower-income rule in the child care expense deductions discriminated against him because it forced his wife, whose income was lower than his, to claim the child care expense deduction; he based his claim that section 63 thus discriminated against him on the historical discrimination against women.

148 See, for example, *Andrew v. M.N.R.* [1994] T.C.J. No. 306 (T.C.C.), in which the Tax Court vividly expressed the irrationality of such policy choices.

149 [1994] T.C.J. No. 13 (T.C.C.).

150 Cf. *D'Amours v. M.N.R.*, 90 D.T.C. 1,827 (T.C.C.) (payments during maternity leave deductible when caregiver paid only during part of leave).

151 See, for example, Ellen Zweibel, 'Equality Rights Challenges to the *Income Tax Act:* The Impact of *Andrews v. Law Society of British Columbia*,' *Canadian Current Tax*, vol. 2 (1989), 28: C 137, in which she discusses the statement of claim filed in Federal Court–Trial Division on 25 Jan. 1990 by Joy Stevens challenging the exclusion of support payments from 'earned income.' Ms Stevens was attending university full time, yet was prohibited from taking advantage of the child care expense deduction because of the limitations on the definition of 'earned income' in section 63. Cf. *Keyes v. M.N.R.*, 89 D.T.C. 91, [1989] T.C.J. No. 6 (T.C.C.), in which a divorced non-custodial father sought a pro rata share of the child care expense deduction on the basis that the children spent some of their time visiting him.

152 89 D.T.C. 55 (T.C.C.).

153 89 D.T.C. 5,243 (F.C.T.D.), rev'd 91 D.T.C. 5,397, [1993] 4 S.C.R. 695.

154 On this point, the Court stated that the Income Tax Act 'is certainly not insulated against all forms of Charter review.' [1993] 4 S.C.R. at para. 109. The Court reasoned that the only support for that proposition could be found in cases in which a degree of deference had been exhibited as part of a section 1 analysis. On this point, the Court cited *PSAC v. Canada*, [1987] 1 S.C.R. 424, 442.

155 [1993] 4 S.C.R. at para. 139 per Iacobucci, J.

156 [1993] 4 S.C.R. at para. 139 per Iacobucci, J. Note that this narrow conception of disparate impact will also insulate section 63 from Charter challenges to the requirement that the deduction be claimed by the spouse or deemed spouse with the lower income. See *Collins v. M.N.R.*, [1994] T.C.J. No. 929, in which a woman taxpayer whose income was higher than her husband's was precluded from deducting her child-care expenses because of this rule.

157 *Bailey v. M.N.R.* [1981], 1 C.H.R.R. D/193 is also relevant (C.H.R. Trib.). One of the taxpayers in *Bailey* had challenged the spousal limitations on the dependent-spouse exemption in the pre-1988 Income Tax Act. The Tribunal had agreed with the taxpayer that the exclusion of non-married cohabitants from the scope of the now-repealed section 109 constituted *de facto* discrimination, but it dismissed her complaint on the same grounds as it had in relation to the child care expense deduction.

158 [1991] T.C.J. No. 1,023 (T.C.C.), aff'd 93 D.T.C. 5,298 (F.C.A.), leave to appeal den. [1995] S.C.C.A. No. 335 (1 June 1995).

159 [1991] T.C.J. No. 1,037 (T.C.C.).

160 Parliament added section 252(4) to the Income Tax Act effective after the 1992 taxation year. S.C. 1993, c. 24, s. 140(3). This provision expands the definition of 'spouse' for purposes of the entire act to include taxpayers of the opposite sex who have cohabited in a conjugal relationship for twelve months, or are parents of a child, and deems persons who are spouses under this provision to be married.

Bisexual cohabitants are now deemed to be married under the new definition of spouse in the Income Tax Act. Only those male-female couples in which there is no 'conjugal relationship' will continue to be able to cohabit and qualify for the equivalent-to-married credit.

161 See generally *The Queen v. Scheller*, 75 D.T.C. 5,406 (F.C.T.D.); *McPhee v. M.N.R.*, 80 D.T.C. 1,034 (T.R.B.); *Toutant v. M.N.R.*, 78 D.T.C. 1,499 (T.R.B.).

162 Before the enactment of section 252(4), section 252(3) had drawn the line at including parties to a void or voidable marriage in the category 'spouse.'

163 See, for example, the language of section 60(c), which permits child-support payments to be deducted in calculating taxable income. Before cohabitants were brought into the definition of spouse in 1993, sections 60(c.1) and 60.1(2) had been added to the Income Tax Act to permit taxpayers to claim those deductions for payments made under the support provisions of the Ontario Family Law Reform Act.

164 For example, the Tax Court of Canada had dismissed the appeal in *Christoffersen v. M.N.R.*, [1993] T.C.J. No. 164 (T.C.C.), in which a wife who supported her common-law husband brought a Charter challenge to the minister's denial of the disability credit in relation to her husband.

165 *Poulter v. M.N.R.*, [1995] T.C.J. No. 228 (T.C.C.).

166 See also *Gifford v. M.N.R.*, 91 D.T.C. 953, [1991] T.C.J. No. 503 (T.C.C.).; *Keyes v. M.N.R.*, 89 D.T.C. 91, [1989] T.C.J. No. 6 (T.C.C.) (male taxpayers with shared custody of children denied claims for equivalent-to-married credit).

167 These provisions are found in sections 56 (1) (b), (c), (c.1), 56(1) (c.2), 56(12), 56.1, 60(1) (b), (c), (c.1), 60(1) (c.2), 60.1, and 118(5).

168 The United States alimony deduction was approved on 21 July 1942; the Canadian alimony credit was proposed on 22 July 1942. See Senate *Journal*, 77th Congress, 2d Sess. (21 July 1942), 342; House of Commons *Debates*, vol. 5, 3rd Sess., 19th Parl. (22 July 1942), 4,532. In the United States, the alimony deduction was enacted as part of the process of permitting all married taxpayers to split their incomes for tax purposes. Universal income splitting was introduced in the United States during the 1940s in order to deliver selective tax benefits to single-income married couples, to make good on the post-war promise of immediate tax cuts, and to counter the rush among common-law states to adopt community-property legislation. The alimony deduction extended the principle of universal income splitting to apply to situations of separation or divorce.

169 See Bill No. 115, House of Commons *Journals*, 6 George VI, 22 July 1942, Resolution 26. This was the same justification that had been given in Congress for the alimony deduction in that country. See *Congressional Record* – House, 77th Congress, 2d Sess., vol. 88, Part 5 (18 July 1942), 6,377.

170 The original alimony provision was structured as a tax credit which was calculated at the wife's marginal tax rate. If the wife paid little or no tax on the
   alimony received, the husband could claim little or no credit. See S.C. 1942–3,
   c. 28, sections 7(1), 3(2), 11.

171 For a detailed discussion of the legislative history of these provisions, see
   Kathleen A. Lahey, 'Tax Developments – 1994–95 Term,' *Supreme Court Law
   Review*, vol. 7 (1996).

172 See, for example, Kathleen A. Lahey, 'Income Taxation and the Charter of
   Rights,' in *Report on the Statute Audit Project*, ch. 9.

173 See Lahey, *Taxation of Women in Canada*, 474, table 10–4, for data demonstrating this effect.

174 For example, the legislation was amended several times in succession to ensure
   that non-married cohabitants could qualify for deductions under section 60(c.1),
   that payments to third parties could be deducted, and that interim payments could
   be deducted.

175 *Klement v. The Queen*, 87 D.T.C. 5,284 (F.C.T.D.). The legislation permits the
   deduction only of periodic payments.

176 *Hodson v. M.N.R.*, 85 D.T.C. 615 (T.C.C.). The taxpayer's wife refused to
   recognize their separation in writing or to grant the taxpayer a divorce on
   religious grounds, which meant that he could not meet the requirements of the
   legislation.

177 94 D.T.C. 6,056 (F.C.A.).

178 See also *Boucher v. M.N.R.*, 94 D.T.C. 1,184 (T.C.C.); *Weronski v. M.N.R.*,
   91 D.T.C. 1,105 (T.C.C.).

179 88 D.T.C. 1,682 (T.C.C.).

180 *Thibaudeau v. M.N.R.*, 92 D.T.C. 2,111 (T.C.C.), rev'd 94 D.T.C. 6,230 (F.C.A.),
   rev'd 95 D.T.C. 5,273 (S.C.C.); *Schaff v. M.N.R.*, [1993] T.C.J. No. 389 (T.C.C.),
   leave to appeal den. [1994] S.C.C.A. No. 350 (8 Dec. 1994); *Lazarescu v. M.N.R.*,
   [1994] T.C.J. No. 401 (T.C.C.) (the government never appealed this ruling, which
   granted the taxpayer's appeal, but it has been impliedly overruled by the Supreme
   Court decision in Thibaudeau).

181 95 D.T.C. at 5,275–6, per Corey, J., and Iacobucci, J., Sopinka, J., concurring.

182 See 95 D.T.C. at 5,290–302, per McLachlin, J., and 95 D.T.C. at 5,302–11,
   per L'Heureux-Dubé, J.

183 Faye Woodman, 'The Charter and the Taxation of Women,' *Ottawa Law Review*,
   vol. 22, no. 3, (1980), 625, 660.

184 See 'Does It Really Pay for the Wife to Work?' *U.S. News and World Report*,
   15 March 1957, 154, 156–8, in which the author demonstrated how capping
   childcare deductions for working women ensured that only women with fairly low

incomes would find that their after-tax net income would be high enough to justify working outside the home on anything but a part-time or volunteer basis. To my knowledge, this aspect of the section 63 limits on deductibility has never been addressed either in the tax policy literature or in Charter litigation, but it certainly explains why the section 63 limits particularly discriminate against married women who have moderate or high incomes.

185 *Re Rosenberg* and *A.-G. Canada* (1995), 25 O.R. (3d) 612 (Ont. Gen. Div.), per Charron J. may be the case to watch. Justice Charron ruled that the opposite sex definition of 'spouse' in section 252 (4) of the Income Tax Act does not violate section 15(1) of the Charter because the registered pension provisions of the act are part of the same overall legislative package that was upheld in *Egan*. However, the Ontario Court of Appeal is being asked to reverse that decision on the basis that *Egan* does not apply to surviving-spouse benefits under employer- and employee-funded private pension plans. Argument in *Rosenberg* is scheduled for October 1997.

5

Contemporary Traditional Equality: The Effect of the Charter on First Nations Politics*

JOHN BORROWS

First Nations[1] in Canada have struggled since contact to preserve and exercise their inherent powers of self-government.[2] In the past few years these efforts towards greater self-determination have met with increasing attention and partial success.[3] First Nations now have some protection in the Canadian constitution[4] and a heightened presence and influence in the formal political arena.[5] Yet, despite the gains made by First Nations in the assertion of these freedoms, there is much work left to be done to assure that they and their governments are liberated from the controlling layers of regulation and oppression under which they live and operate.[6] The work to extend self-government must proceed as strongly within First Nations as among groups external to them.[7] First Nations' efforts in both spheres must directly engage the economic, ideological, and social conditions that specifically constrict self-government. As an accompanying strategy,[8] dialogue must be encouraged not only with non-Native people but also within and between the various First Nations. This means that legitimate criticism of government for the oppression that their policies have caused must be augmented with pertinent internal criticism or endorsement of policies that First Nations themselves will adopt.

One of the greatest internal barriers to the enhancement of self-government through the latter procedure is the division the Canadian Charter of Rights and Freedoms[9] has caused within the First Nations community.[10] Discussion concerning the Charter's scope of application to First Nations has provoked severe internal contention which threatens to shatter fragile gains made towards

* The author would like to thank Joel Bakan, Susan Boyd, Christine Boyle, Nitya Iyer, Marlee Kline, and Lynn Smith for their encouragement and helpful comments on earlier drafts of this article. An earlier version of this article appeared in *University of New Brunswick Law Journal*, vol. 43 (1994), 19–48.

self-determination in the last decade. Underlying much of this debate is the appropriateness of invoking the language of 'rights' to achieve progressive social change. Rights are often dismissed as a tool in overcoming subjugation because 'they seem prima facie incompatible with Aboriginal approaches to land, family, social life, personality and spirituality.'[11] For people debating in this corner, the Charter represents 'further encroachment on the cultural identity of the community' of First Nations because it 'use[s] a framework which undermines their objectives.'[12] In the other corner of this controversy, rights are invoked by First Nations because they are deemed an 'aid' in their communal struggle against oppression.[13] These people argue that the Charter contains many precepts that are currently accepted and were traditionally endorsed by a considerable number of First Nation people. It is further contended that these principles must be revived within First Nations to maintain and fortify the inherent authority of Aboriginal self-government as well as to facilitate the exercise of self-government powers.[14]

In order to prevent additional unravelling of the broader consensus surrounding self-government, more attention must be given to reconciling the divergent opinions surrounding the Charter's application of rights to First Nations. This essay explores the profound impact that the Charter and its ideology have had upon First Nations identity and politics since its inception in 1982 and, in the spirit of healing some of the divisions permeating First Nations politics, suggests that its underlying principles can facilitate and enhance self-determination without overpowering Aboriginal society's customs, laws, and traditions. The application of government policy to First Nations throughout the last century has concealed the degree to which many of the precepts underlying the Charter were present in First Nations.[15] The hidden alignment of interests between tradition and equality has caused many Indian people to turn from the Charter's promise of emancipation. Yet intersections in the objectives of the Charter and traditional First Nations practices provide a meeting place for the potential transformation of rights discourse. By creating a conversation between rights and tradition, the Charter presents First Nations with an opportunity to recapture the strength of principles which were often eroded through government interference.

In submitting that the Charter has some role to play in the struggle for First Nations self-government, I am acutely aware of its constraints and limitations.[16] Rights can be applied in a culturally biased way.[17] Also, there is an ideology of formal equality which suggests that everyone should be treated the same regardless of their current disadvantages or differences. Such an ideology is difficult to overcome.[18] The experience in the United States with the application of rights to Native American tribes has not been particularly encouraging[19] and there are economic, social, and political factors that create unequal access to justice.[20] Finally, rights discourse may even absorb and limit First Nations claims and thereby further 'engender regressive and narrow interpretations' of their positions.[21] Yet, despite potential for the language of rights to oppress,[22] this same discourse can also augment political struggle and contribute to emancipation because of its indeterminacy and extensive acceptance.[23] Employing a 'critical pragmatism' which recognizes that the 'acquisition of rights is not the be it and end all' of liberation, rights discourse can be 'added to the range of other activities' First Nations pursue to achieve their political objectives.[24]

This essay will show how the language of rights and the influence of the Charter, in conjunction with other political activities, have helped to liberate partially some First Nations people from discrimination. Perhaps it is too early to claim such victories when the battle still rages all around. In particular, I am quite uncomfortable with the fact that the victories I describe appear to have come at the expense of solidarity within and among First Nations. I am also disappointed that the changes made did not encompass ancillary reforms and occur on a much larger scale.[25] As First Nations we still live with the Indian Act, and that is great cause for sadness. Furthermore, it is entirely conceivable that the benefits conferred by 'rights' displaced more meaningful reform and came in the place of wider liberation. It may be said that we would be celebrating much greater victories if we did not have to filter our proud and distinct traditions through the corruption of rights.

We cannot, however, ignore the world we live in.[26] The parlance of 'rights' has meaning to many people. The non-Native community can partially understand us when we speak this language. It is true that something gets lost in the translation, but what else do we have? In reconstructing our world we can't just do what we want.[27] We require a measure of our oppressors' cooperation to disentangle ourselves from the web of enslavement. While these knots can best be unravelled through the exercise of greater economic and political power by First Nations, the freeing of our people is simultaneously worked out on conversational grounds.[28] Though the forum and process for this discourse belongs to the more powerful party – the Canadian government – words are retranslated and transposed by us to convey our meanings.[29] To some extent this has occurred with First Nations and the Charter. First Nations have engaged in direct social/political activism to challenge the Canadian government while concurrently using the Charter to challenge policies that limit self-government. Thus, despite undeniable grounds for cynicism in much of what continues to happen to, and in, First Nation communities, the vocabulary of the Charter has helped us achieve partial success in our quest for self-determination.

The Political Impact of the Charter

In 1982 Canada's constitution was patriated, and along with it a new Charter of Rights and Freedoms was proclaimed. Three new sections dealing with Aboriginal peoples appeared in the constitution to complement section 91(24), which already had a place in the BNA Act.[30] These new additions were section 25 of the Charter, which was designed to shield Aboriginal and treaty rights from the Charter's influence;[31] and in the Constitution Act itself, section 35, which recognized and affirmed 'existing' Aboriginal and treaty rights,[32] and section 37, which mandated a series of constitutional conferences to discuss Aboriginal rights.[33] Since only section 25 was part of the Charter and did not confer any positive rights on Aboriginal peoples,[34] there were questions early on as to whether the Charter would have any impact on Indian peoples at all. Specifically, some wondered whether the equality provisions of the Charter, sections 15 and 28,[35] would compel the removal of sexual discrimination in the Indian Act.[36]

At the centre of this debate were the sexist rules of the Indian Act[37] that caused Indian women[38] to lose their status when they married non-Native men.[39] These rules resulted in Indian women losing the association and benefits of their communities and the important social and political positions they occupied within them.[40] Prior to the Charter, challenges to this legislation repeatedly surfaced in response to government policy,[41] royal commissions,[42] litigation,[43] and international appeals.[44] Indian women continuously employed a variety of approaches to reconstruct their communities[45] and restore the respect and dignity that their predecessors enjoyed.[46] These efforts, undertaken prior to the Charter's enactment,[47] illustrate that the addition of the Charter served to give greater strength to those already challenging gender discrimination.[48] Use of the Charter was only one among a multiplicity of strategies employed to secure their objectives.[49]

Despite initial doubts about the impact of the Charter on Aboriginal politics and gender issues, its influence is now apparent. The ideas endorsed in the Charter were crucial in securing an amendment guaranteeing sexual equality in section 35, changing provisions of the Indian Act to counter sexual discrimination, and defeating First Nations self-government provisions in the Charlottetown Accord.

The Charter, Constitutional Conferences, and Section 35(4)

Constitutional conferences between the prime minister, the provincial first ministers, and representatives of the Assembly of First Nations (AFN),[50] the Native

Council of Canada (NCC),[51] the Inuit Tapirisat of Canada (ITC),[52] and the Metis National Council (MNC)[53] took place in 1983, 1984, 1985, and 1987. During these conferences the influence of the Charter permeated the various participant's ideologies and made it impolitic to disregard the sexual inequality of First Nations women. Sections 15 and 28 assisted Indian women in securing a guarantee of sexual equality at the conferences because they could draw upon the near-consensus these sections created and persuasively argue that self-government should not be entrenched without confirming this right. Such arguments made Ottawa aware that 'the Indian Act was intimately connected with sexual equality and Aboriginal rights in the Constitution Act [and that] the Canadian Charter dictated a future Indian Act amendment to abolish sex discrimination. Furthermore, since it already appeared at an early stage of Constitutional negotiations that aboriginal self-government would become the most significant subject of constitutional amendment requirements, it was felt necessary to establish principles within aboriginal self-government that guaranteed sexual equality for Aboriginal males and females.'[54] Most who participated in the constitutional conferences recognized this connection between Aboriginal rights of self-government, the Indian Act, and the Charter, and accordingly many agreed that sexual equality had to be placed in the constitution as an Aboriginal right. To ensure that there would be sufficient information to consider sexual equality in the constitutional conferences, each of the four Aboriginal groups represented was given money to study the issue.[55]

The second day of the 1983 conference was entirely dedicated to discussion of sexual equality for Aboriginal women. Deliberations led to section 35(4) being inserted in the constitution to protect Aboriginal gender equality.[56] All governments except the AFN supported the entrenchment of sexual equality as an Aboriginal right.[57] It was the position of the federal and provincial governments that sections 15 and 28 of the Charter gave sexual-equality protections to Aboriginal people,[58] but 'nevertheless the governments were willing to amend the Constitution to make doubly sure of Aboriginal sexual equality.'[59] While ITC, NCC, MNC, and the Native Women's Association of Canada (NWAC)[60] also supported this amendments, the AFN did not wish to entrench sexual equality in the constitution because it felt that sexual-equality protections were already implicit in section 35 as a part of self-government.[61] The AFN stated its position as follows: 'We would like to make it clear that we agree with the women who spoke so forcefully this morning that they have been treated unjustly. The discrimination they suffered was forced upon us through a system imposed upon us by white colonial government through the Indian Act. It was not the result of our traditional laws, and in fact it would not have occurred under our traditional laws. We must make it perfectly clear why we feel so strongly that we must control our citizenship. The AFN maintains that "equality" already does already exist with the traditional "citizenship code" of all First Nations people.'[62] The AFN eventually had to relinquish this opposition to the amendment on sexual equality, and it did so in return for the government's promise not to interfere with Indian citizenship and membership in the future.

The deliberations of the 1983 conference created an environment in which Indian people had to call upon their traditional values to articulate their positions.[63] For example, the Assembly of First Nations, despite its opposition to an amendment, nevertheless regarded traditional Indian 'laws' as upholding an outcome different from the unjust treatment being received under the Indian Act. There was a recognition by all First Nations parties involved that balance and harmony in gender relations was a condition that all wished to return to. The disagreement, at least in the language employed, existed merely over how this was to be achieved. The AFN felt that equality would best be achieved by a partial return to traditional practices through self-definition of citizenship, while NWAC and others believed that an Indian Act amendment was the first step in removing the intolerance towards Indian women found in some communities.

The ideology of the Charter stood as a backdrop in the development of this discourse and subtly helped to strengthen claims for equality. Tradition was brought forward and its concepts were draped around the contemporary language of rights. The dialectical interaction of traditional practices and modern precepts forged a language that bridged two worlds. Rights talk could not overwhelm traditional convictions of symmetry in gender relationships while tradition could not ignore current concerns about equality in these same associations. Each discourse partook of the other and created an exchange of legitimacy. People who were concerned about their traditions could use the language of equality to preserve their interests, and people who sought equality could use tradition to show that it sanctioned and justified the removal of gender discrimination.

This mingling of ideologies constructed an alignment of wider interests because greater individual sovereignty and self-determination for First Nations women could potentially be seen as incorporating these same rights for the First Nations community as a whole. Thus, the use of 'rights' discourse combined the past and the present for First Nations since historical remembrances of gender relations had to take account of current notions of sexual equality. The process of injecting new understandings into customary ancient practices is very much in agreement with the cyclical world-view[64] of many First Nations people and follows the patterns of oral tradition. In communities with oral traditions, time is dynamic and includes both past and present understandings and events. Penny Petrone, a professor emeritus at Lakehead University, describes oral tradition in this way: 'Oral traditions have not been static. Their strength lies in their ability to survive through the power of tribal memory and to renew themselves by incorporating new elements. When contact with the white man is established, a new set of problems arises and requires a logical cultural explanation to restore the world to order. Hence old myths are altered or new ones are generated to explain the process of cultural change.'[65]

The ability of oral tradition to include ancient and modern concepts should convey the lesson that tradition can have great significance in contemporary political and legal discourse within First Nations. At the same time, it must be recognized that understandings of tradition itself change by enveloping new concepts. In the example of the constitutional conferences, the cyclical nature of First Nations concepts of time was revealed and tradition was reinterpreted as rights were invoked to protect traditional practices of respect for gender equality.

The Charter and the Amendment of the Indian Act

Efforts to remove sexual discrimination from the Indian Act were also assisted by the presence of sections 15 and 28 because the federal government believed that the Indian Act's status provisions contravened these parts of the Charter. The political activism of Indian women, the prominence of the *Lovelace* case, and the amendments to section 35 of the Constitution Act were the cornerstone of the campaign to change the existing order. Yet, despite the breadth and directness of these efforts and achievements, there was still little prospect of the discriminatory provisions being eliminated without the equality sections of the Charter. The Charter tipped the balance in support of an amendment because its equality sections compelled the reforms as a legal necessity. As one leading commentator, who worked with and wrote about NWAC throughout this process, has noted 'section 15(1) ... guaranteeing equality between men and women ... [was] perceived as the most important reason to pursue the Indian Act amendment.'[66]

Further evidence of the importance of the Charter in securing an amendment to the Indian Act is that Bill C-31, the legislation that ended much of the discrimination in the act,[67] was passed in conjunction with the coming into force of the Charter's equality rights on 17 April 1985.[68] The federal government felt a great urgency to secure an amendment to the Indian Act before 17 April because it did not want to litigate the act's discriminatory provisions. Its concern to avert a Charter challenge explains why the new provisions of the Indian Act were retroactive to 17 April 1985 while the bill did not actually receive Royal Assent until 28 June of that year. The idea that the Charter's provisions led to amendment is confirmed from a federal perspective in a publication by the government published under the authority of the minister of Indian affairs. This report, entitled *Impacts of the 1985 Amendments to the Indian Act: Summary Report*, stated: 'In June 1985, Parliament passed a series of amendments to the Indian Act known as Bill C-31. The amendments were enacted by all party consent to make the Act compatible with the Canadian Charter of Rights and Freedoms.'[69] Teressa Nahanee, constitutional adviser to NWAC, has also indicated that the Charter had a pivotal impact in making these changes. She writes: 'Stripped of equality by patriarchal laws which created "male privilege" as the norm on reserve lands, Indian women have had a tremendous struggle to regain their social position. It was the Canadian Charter of Rights and Freedoms which turned around our hopeless struggle. It has been argued that the equality provisions of the Charter would not apply to the Indian Act and it would not have resulted in the Supreme Court of Canada overturning the *Lavell* decision. I would argue that the government of Canada believed the Charter did apply to the Indian Act; would have overturned the *Lavell* decision; and this thinking resulted in the passage of Bill C-31.'[70] It is apparent that the people who were involved in changing the discriminatory provisions of the Indian Act viewed the Charter as a vital reason for the passage of Bill C-31.[71]

The objectives of Bill C-31 were to 'remove discrimination on the basis of gender, to restore Indian status and band membership to eligible persons,[72] and to enable bands to assume control over their membership.'[73] The impact that this legislation had on both individuals and communities has been enormous. Individually, the influence of the Charter on the social and political struggles of First Nations caused many Indians to reinterpret their identity and reorient their personal loyalties towards their aboriginal ancestry. This was a significant victory for those using the Charter. A major survey of the effects of Bill C-31 revealed that the primary reasons people applied for registration were personal identity (41 per cent), culture or sense of belonging (21 per cent), correction of injustice (17 per cent), and Aboriginal rights (7 per cent).[74] By June 1990 these aspirations had led over 133,134 people to apply for reinstatement and, as of that date, 75,761 of these people had been approved.[75] Women represented 77 per cent of those to whom status was restored and 58 per cent of all those who were new registrants as a result of the amendments.[76] This development has been at least partially responsible for causing the status-Indian population to grow by one-third in the past seven years.

Ultimately, however, many of these same people recognized that there is a deep and disturbing irony in relying on the Indian Act for their identity. The act is a government-imposed system which dictates who is entitled to be an

Indian, and, as such, it rests on a strategy of divide and conquer.[77] Many people know that the preferred course for reform would have been to pursue definitions of Indian identity without reference to the Indian Act. Yet, since this was not possible in 1985, First Nations chose obtainable, interim innovations. Some natives now refuse to distinguish on the basis of prior status or recent registration.[78] The process of cultural reawakening, influenced by the Charter, helped to mobilize this significant body of people aspiring for greater cultural control. Others, however, still maintain that the amendments to the Indian Act have negatively affected the communities.

These ancillary influences of the Charter have had a powerful impact on Indian politics and resulted in no end of concern over lack of resources and communal personality.[79] For example, great adjustments are being made in the areas of health care and post-secondary education benefits,[80] economic development,[81] political participation,[82] and the administration of membership. Ugly divisions have sometimes ensued as a result,[83] and the battle over rights and the Charter is still being fought in many First Nations.[84] Some people within First Nations communities resented returning members as competitors for scarce resources[85] rather than focusing on the need for expanded resources to support the implementation of Bill C-31.[86] Respondents to the survey assessing the feelings of long-time band members about Bill C-31 found that it had created a great deal of disharmony.[87] Statements from a variety of people portray this turmoil: 'It has become harder for people in the community to get to know each other.' 'Bill C-31 has effectively disrupted community life because it creates rifts amongst family members and amongst community members.' 'There has been an inordinate amount of energy, time, and money spent with little regard for the social, emotional, and psychological impact; consequently, there is bigotry and fighting because of misunderstanding.' Bill C-31 'has segregated and labelled people: those who were living here before against those returning.'[88]

The àttitude underlying such statements had led to name-calling of children from mixed families, people being shunned in the community and prevented from accessing services available to band members, registrants feeling unwelcome and isolated, and people not being allowed on their reserve.[89] The continued discrimination against the predominantly women registrants is greatly discouraging to say the least.[90] It illustrates the limits of rights discourse in being able to redirect community structures away from discriminatory practices.

Litigation is currently being pursued to address inequality in both the definition of Indian status[91] and the exclusion of community people from membership.[92] This is bound to raise new dilemmas for communities. Many people who used the Charter to argue for reinstatement continue to look to its equality provisions to remove the Indian Act's remaining discriminatory elements and to compel recalcitrant communities to accept their newly registered relations. Some are insisting that the Charter be used to define membership codes within communities.[93] Other new registrants who live off reserve claim services equal to those which Indians can access on reserves. Again, they do so by using the Charter. As one newly registered applicant puts it: 'We strongly believe that we should also benefit from all aboriginal rights throughout Canada, and we have the right to choose where we want to live. It is unfair for the government to reinstate us and only provide services and benefits to on reserve natives. We are requesting equality in the services that could be provided to on reserve natives. In the Charter of Rights, the equality clause guarantees equal rights to everyone. Therefore, we ask the minister and his government to apply this Charter to all native people on and off reserves.'[94] Thus, despite all the limitations that Indian Act classifications produced, people are nevertheless pursuing their rights to status because it is also a source of positive identity.[95] Such short-term reliance on Indian Act status is symbolic of the distinctive culture and self-government (though the act encumbered its exercise) of Native society.

While these remaining problems demonstrate that Indian peoples must escape from the narrow confines of the Indian Act,[96] the number of those recapturing their identity and reviving their community through its provisions illustrates that at least some First Nations peoples have been partially unfettered as a result of the act's new classifications. Yet, despite all that has been accomplished, people must be careful not to think that the Charter and status under the Indian Act is the 'answer' for full liberation. Restructuring the balance of power between Canada and First Nations must continue to lie at the heart of Aboriginal self-determination. However, using the language of rights to assist in this restructuring has not proved as fatal as some predicted because, while many have suffered because of the contradictions built into the Indian Act's amendments, many others have greatly benefited from the reinvigoration of traditional extended-family relationships. Many have come home. There is hope that the reuniting of families will help to recapture much of what was lost through the exclusionary and sexually discriminatory provisions of the Indian Act. Though the path to decolonization will be hard because of external and internalized oppression, negotiations between tradition and rights in the midst of the economic, political, and social struggles of First Nations can have some influence on the evolving debates about status and citizenship within Indian communities.

The Charter and the Charlottetown Accord

The Charlottetown Accord of 1992 included potential amendments to the Canadian constitution that, among other things, explicitly entrenched an Aboriginal right of self-government. The accord's provisions in this regard sparked debate about the position and protection of First Nations women in Aboriginal self-government.[97] Some feared that the entrenchment of self-government would place greater control in the hands of men to the detriment of women. To address concerns that First Nations women would be disadvantaged by self-government, the framers of the accord proposed a series of amendments to the constitution that dealt with gender equality. For example, section 35.7 stated: 'Notwithstanding any other provision of this Act, the rights of the Aboriginal peoples of Canada referred to in this part are guaranteed equally to male and female persons.' Yet, despite such provisions, doubt was cast on the acceptability of these sections because some First Nations women felt that they were being marginalized by their male counterparts in the framing of the accord's definition of self-government.[98] NWAC stated its concerns as follows:

What we want to get across to Canadians is our right as women to have a voice in deciding upon the definition of Aboriginal government powers ... Aboriginal women have sexual equality rights. We want those rights respected. Governments simply cannot choose to recognize the patriarchal forms of government which now exist in our communities. The band councils and Chiefs who preside over our lives are not our traditional forms of government. The Chiefs have taken it upon themselves to decide that they will be the final rectifiers of the Aboriginal package of rights. We are telling you, we have a right, as women, to be part of that decision. Recognizing the inherent right to self-government does not mean recognizing or blessing the patriarchy created by a foreign government.[99]

NWAC backed up its conviction that women were not being granted equal rights of participation in defining self-government by initiating litigation against the four Aboriginal organizations that were participating in constitutional discussions[100] and the federal government.

Two cases were brought to restrain governmental groups from further discussion until NWAC was granted a greater role in defining self-government in the constitution. In one, NWAC asked for an order prohibiting the government of Canada from making further payments to the four organizations until equal funding was granted to NWAC and until it was granted an equal right of participation in the constitutional-review process.[101] Justice Mahoney of the Federal Court of Appeal granted NWAC something of a victory since he held that the federal government's failure to provide NWAC with funding and rights of participation in the constitutional-review process was a violation of Aboriginal women's rights to freedom of expression as set out in sections 2(b) and 28 of the Charter.[102] He also implicitly accepted NWAC's contention that the interests of aboriginal women in the constitutional discussions were threatened by male-dominated native organizations. His decision stated:

The interests of aboriginal women, measured by the only standard this court can recognize in the absence of contrary evidence, that of Canadian society at large, are not represented in this respect by AFN, which advocate a contrary result, nor by the ambivalence of NCC and ITC.

...

In my opinion, by inviting and funding the participation of organizations in the current constitutional process and excluding equal participation of NWAC, the Canadian government has accorded the advocates of male dominated aboriginal self-governments a preferred position in the exercise of expressive activity ... in a manner offensive to ss. 2(b) and 28 of the Charter.[103]

Though the Court of Appeal's holding was eventually overturned by the Supreme Court of Canada,[104] the case nonetheless provides an important example of the impact of the Charter on First Nations politics.

In the other case, NWAC again sought to prevent further constitutional discussions among the different groups and it also asked for an injunction to stop the national referendum on the Charlottetown Accord.[105] The Federal Trial Court was not as generous in this instance; it refused to block either constitutional discussions or the referendum. Its reasoning was constructed around the idea that it could not interfere with a legislative process aimed at producing a constitutional amendment. It also held that the question concerning with whom the governments ought to meet with to arrive at an amendment was not justiciable. In short, NWAC's claim was struck down because it disclosed no reasonable cause of action. The decision was appealed, but by the time the case came before the Court of Appeal the referendum had already been held. The court thus ruled: 'That it is common ground that the Charlottetown Accord and the related Accords are now a dead letter ... In these circumstances, we decline to exercise our discretion and would dismiss the appeal.' The case was then taken to the Supreme Court of Canada for a final determination of whether the Aboriginal organizations or the federal governments had violated the Charter by not including NWAC in the constitutional process. Despite losing at the Supreme Court, NWAC nonetheless accomplished some of its purposes since its challenge received national media attention.[106]

These cases are quite difficult for me on many levels because of the tensions that they harbour. I am quite uncomfortable with a judge assessing First Nations society from 'the only standard the court can recognize in the absence of contrary evidence, that of Canadian society at large.' Anyone familiar with case law involving First Nations knows that such an approach has been at the root of many of injustices.[107] I am also apprehensive about using litigation to resolve intergroup conflict among First Nations. Adversarialism seems inimical to First Nations professions of consensus, harmony, and respect.

At the same time, I have a great deal of sympathy with the frustrations of those who have been excluded from constitutional discussions. It does seem to me that NWAC's concerns were not being taken seriously enough and that litigation was the only way of forcing the other Aboriginal organizations to listen to these concerns. The four national Aboriginal organizations were under considerable pressure to keep constitutional discussion focused on self-government to avoid the attenuation of their interests, but this should not have caused them to disregard a group that was raising significant challenges to their position. After all, the same Aboriginal organizations have levelled similar complaints of exclusion against the federal government for many years. It would be perverse if NWAC could not invoke the very privileges other First Nations organizations employed just because in this instance they were being used to these organizations' disadvantage.

While I am aware that NWAC was not representative of all Aboriginal women, and that their tactics threatened the consensus and public support needed to facilitate self-government,[108] I nonetheless appreciate that a discrete and specific group of people were suffering[109] and that their leaders were being ignored by those with greater access to power and resources. Ideally, rights discourse should have engaged the parties in a shared political conversation, as had happened in the framing of the Constitution Act of 1982 and in the amending of the Indian Act. Still, I do not dispute NWAC's decision to litigate. That decision was no different from what other First Nations have done in combatting crown failures to protect their lands and culture. Why should this group of First Nations women have been prevented from exercising the same liberties that other First Nations organizations regularly utilize?

The Notwithstanding Clause

Besides worrying about proper representation in the constitutional process, some other First Nations women were also concerned that the Charter would not apply to the Aboriginal governments recognized by the Charlottetown Accord. This was of great concern because, as we have seen, many First Nations women viewed the Charter as a vehicle to regain a social position that had been lost to them through the application of racist and sexist laws. NWAC wrote:

The Native Women's Association of Canada supports individual rights. These rights are so fundamental that, once removed, you no longer have a human being. Aboriginal Women are human beings and we have rights which cannot be denied or removed at the whim of any government. These views are in conflict with many Aboriginal leaders and legal theoreticians who advocate for recognition by Canada of sovereignty, self-government and collective rights. It is their unwavering view of the Aboriginal male leadership that the 'collective' comes first, and that it will decide the rights of individuals.

                    ...

[NWAC] recognizes that there is a clash between collective rights of sovereign Aboriginal governments and individual rights of women. Stripped of equality by patriarchal laws which created 'male privilege' as the norm on reserve lands, Aboriginal women have a tremendous struggle to regain their social position. We want the Canadian Charter of Rights and Freedoms to apply to Aboriginal governments.[110]

Considerations such as these prompted negotiators of the Charlottetown Accord to ensure that the Charter would apply to Aboriginal governments.[111] It was hoped that this would confirm, among other things,[112] that women would have the protection of the Charter against abusive individual or collective actions on the part of First Nations men.

    Some First Nations women were concerned, however, that protection of the Charter could not be guaranteed because Aboriginal governments were granted the right to use the some provision for opting out of the Charter that was available to other governments. This section, 33.1, read: 'Section 33 applies to legislative bodies of the Aboriginal peoples of Canada with such modifications, consistent with the purposes of the requirements of that section, as are appropriate to the circumstances of Aboriginal people concerned.' Through this section, it was feared, First Nations governments could conceivably override women's equality rights if such action was collectively considered appropriate to the circumstances of Aboriginal people. The potential application of section 33 to Aboriginal governments prompted NWAC to state: 'If the Government agrees that the Charter does apply to Aboriginal governments, and if the Government agrees that Aboriginal governments may use section 33, the following rights of Aboriginal citizens could be suspended: freedom of conscience and religion, freedom of thought, belief and opinion and expression, including freedom of the press and other media of communication; freedom of peaceful assembly; and freedom of association. Aboriginal governments could also suspend legal and equality rights guaranteed under the Charter ... The powers of suspension under section 33 should not be allowed to federal and provincial governments, let alone to Aboriginal governments.'[113] This statement demonstrates the tremendous lack of confidence that some First Nations women had in Aboriginal governments.[114] They felt that such governments would not be sensitive to their interests and would dispossess them of their rights. As a result, NWAC put greater trust in the Charter and common law courts to protect their rights than they did in their own people, because they worried that these rights were being threatened by the process and substance of the Charlottetown Accord. As Sharon McIvor put it, 'this Constitutional deal wipes out the 20 year struggle by native women for sexual equality rights in Canada.'

NWAC's rebuke of Aboriginal bands and governments contains powerful words – 'no longer a human being,' 'male privilege,' 'clash of rights,' and 'rights of Aboriginal people could be suspended.' These are words I take seriously. First Nations women have too often been excluded from the circle of decision making, and their exclusion has led to male bias and perpetuated the disintegration of harmony between male and female in Aboriginal societies. Such conduct is unconscionable.[115] While colonialism is at the root of our learned disrespect for women, we cannot blame colonialism for our informed actions today. First Nations men must take some measure of responsibility for their conduct and attitudes. It is no longer enough to say 'the Indian Act made us do it.' Positive acceptance of responsibility is an important step in healing the divisions that have occurred.

Having accepted the need to renounce and abandon practices that maintain colonialist-inspired sexual discrimination, we should also recognize the danger in such acknowledgments. Concern for Aboriginal women may be 'piously invoked by closet opponents of aboriginal sovereignty' and these people will 'use a new-found solidarity with women as an expedient and politically correct justification for their resistance.'[116] This problem can best be avoided by First Nations women continuing to assert their aspirations for self-government[117] (which includes gender equality and respect). People who express support for First Nations women but who harbour hostility towards self-government could then no longer honestly claim to be endorsing these women.

A second peril that follows the acknowledgment of sexual discrimination in our communities is that it could paint all First Nations men with the same brush. It can be discouraging working for and with your people and then being accused of actions you do not sanction. There are many Aboriginal men who work with great dedication for a return to tradition and for the fostering of self-government in a way that honours, respects, supports, and includes women. Much has been accomplished to help our people through their efforts, and these efforts may be made more difficult if they have to overcome insinuations of sexism every time they speak. A 'belief in an inherent or irremediable chauvinism of Aboriginal men, worse than the chauvinism of non-Aboriginal men, must be shown for what it is: false, pernicious and racist.'[118]

A posture that recognizes, supports, and promotes positive contributions from First Nations men does not excuse those who exercise oppressive authority, but it does require that people avoid making exaggerated statements merely to sustain their position. There is a great temptation to make such statements because they seem to make the point of sexism stand out in greater relief. But I would argue that this is dishonest and serves only to separate the speaker from the community and individuals in the community from each other. There is room in both law and politics for interpretations of rights that avoid these consequences. Equality rights do not have to mean sameness;[119] individual and collective rights do not have to be dichotomized.[120] Many First Nations men can be strongly and legitimately censured, but such criticism need not encourage adversarialism between First Nations men and women. My grandmothers and grandfathers lived and taught that the circle of life, encompassing the four directions, encourages honesty, sharing, strength, and kindness.[121] These directions were encompassed by a vision that connected the whole of First Nations. It is my hope that people will reinterpret the language of rights with vision and esteem, to honour and revere the lessons that tradition teach us in the application of this discourse. The continued return to these principles will enlarge our existing and inherent right to self-government. Indeed, such an approach has already achieved some success in bringing about self-determination and liberation for First Nations women.

Conclusion

The Charter, in employing the language of rights, has helped to liberate some First Nations people from the oppression they encounter in Canada by facilitating the exercise of self-government. This has been accomplished through the contemporary discourse of equality rights building upon traditional understandings of gender symmetry and harmony. The result has been an amendment to the Canadian constitution recognizing equality rights and an amendment of the Indian Act to remove most gender discrimination.

The effect of the Charter on Aboriginal politics illustrates the complications that are involved in working with rights discourse. While there are many constraints in the employment of rights, such rights possess the potential to remove impediments to greater individual and collective self-determination for Aboriginal peoples. Those invoking the language of rights should have no illusions or misconceptions that summoning rights will always produce the desired results. Indeed, using rights discourse can lead to the loss of the very thing being claimed. This danger is compounded when rights are used by peoples from a different cultural tradition with less access to economic, political, and legal resources. Yet, despite these dangers, rights can work to assist, though not replace, the struggle for progressive social change. The fact that the Charter's role in progressive social struggle has been interpreted favourably at the political level and outside the courts[122] demonstrates that there is still room to use rights discourse to realize the community aspirations of First Nations.[123]

Notes

1 The First Nations consist of the peoples who trace their ancestry to the original inhabitants of North America, namely North American Indians, Metis, and Inuit. I prefer the term First Nations because it denotes the diversity of their composition and their existence as organized societies before European colonization.

2 For an overview of First Nations' understanding of contemporary self-government, see *Aboriginal Self-Determination*, ed. Frank Cassidy (Lantzville, BC: Oolichan Books 1991) and *Nation to Nation: Aboriginal Sovereignty and the Future of Canada*, eds. Diane Engelstad and John Bird (Concord, Ont.: Anansi 1992).

3 For a description of the recent history of self-government see, *DrumBeat: Anger and Renewal in Indian Country*, ed. Boyce Richardson (Toronto: Summerhill Press 1989); Michael Asch, *Home and Native Land: Aboriginal Rights and the Canadian Constitution* (Toronto: Methuen 1984); Kathy Brock, 'The Politics of Aboriginal Self-Government: A Canadian Paradox,' *Canadian Public Administration*, vol. 34 (1991), 272; Paul Tennant, 'Aboriginal Governments and the Penner Report on Indian Self-Government,' in *The Quest for Justice: Aboriginal Peoples and Aboriginal Rights*, eds. Menno Boldt, John Long, and Leroy Little Bear (Toronto: University of Toronto Press 1985), 383; J.E. Chamberlain, 'Aboriginal Rights and the Meech Lake Accord,' in *Competing Constitutional Visions: The Meech Lake Accord*, eds. Katherine Swinton and Carol Rogerson (Toronto: Carswell 1988), 11.

4 See sections 25 and 35 of the Constitution Act, 1982, being schedule B of the Canada Act 1982 (U.K.), 1982, c. 11. For an example of how these sections can potentially be used to protect First Nations, see Patrick Macklem, 'Aboriginal Peoples, Criminal Justice Initiatives and the Constitution,' *U.B.C. Law Review* (1992; special edition on aboriginal justice), 280.

5 See Bryan Schwartz, *First Principles; Constitutional Reform with Respect to the Aboriginal People of Canada* (Kingston: Institute of Intergovernmental Relations 1985).

6 See comments of Ovide Mercredi, grand chief of the Assembly of First Nations, in *First Peoples and the Constitution: Conference Report of March 13–15 1992* (Ottawa: Supply and Services 1992), 34.
7 I recognize that increasingly visible internal debate over different policy option may cause the non-native public to become more sceptical about First Nations' ability to govern themselves. However, I would argue that non-Natives should not hold Aboriginal people to higher standards of political unity than that of the general polity. As is the case with other individuals and groups, First Nations are entitled to display and assert their diversity. In order for self-government to be truly meaningful, First Nations must be able to test ideas in the public forum and then have rigorous debate about them. In this vein, I would submit that further debate about the Charter in First Nations communities needs to continue. Others may worry that internal debate allows Canadian governments to escape the pressure they have been under recently to address the devastation that their policies have caused First Nations. But I do not view internal debate as precluding continued governmental lobbying; in fact, I think that internal dialogue has the potential to reinforce such lobbying.
8 In using rights discourse, First Nations do not abandon associated efforts to change their economic and social conditions. A discussion of the importance of maintaining a 'wider social context' in working for progressive social change is found in Joel Bakan and Michael Smith, 'Rights, Nationalism, and Social Movements in Canadian Constitutional Politics,' in this volume.
9 Part I of the Constitution Act, 1982, being schedule B to the Constitution Act, 1982 (U.K.), 1982, c. 11 [hereinafter Charter].
10 For a sample of the divisions over the Charter, see Rudy Platiel, 'Aboriginal women divide on constitutional protection,' *Globe and Mail*, 20 Jan. 1992; Susan Delacourt, 'Natives divided over Charter,' *Globe and Mail*, 14 March 1992; André Picard, 'Native women cling to the charter,' *Globe and Mail*, 29 May 1992; Canadian Press, 'Inuit negotiators say deal will protect native women,' *Globe and Mail*, 24 Sept. 1992; Sheile D. Genaille, 'Metis women endorse agreement,' *Globe and Mail*, 30 Sept. 1992.
11 Mary Ellen Turpel, 'Aboriginal Peoples and the Charter: Interpretive Monopolies, Cultural Differences,' *Canadian Human Rights Yearbook* (1989), vol. 6 37. See also Mary Ellen Turpel, 'Patriarchy and Paternalism: The Legacy of the Canadian State for First Nations Women,' *Canadian Journal of Women and the Law*, vol. 6 (1993), 174.
12 Turpel, 'Aboriginal People and the Charter,' 40 and 10.
13 Teressa Nahanee, 'Dancing With a Gorilla: Aboriginal Women, Justice and the Charter,' in *Aboriginal Peoples and the Justice System* (Ottawa: Supply and Services 1993), 364.

14 One organization has written of the potential compatibility between the Charter and First Nations traditions: 'The matriarchal/equalitarian system can operate within the Canadian Constitution and the Charter and shape a future together in partnership with Canada. The matriarchal/equalitarian system has the principles and requirements of equality and fairness, consultation and peaceful dialogue, accommodation, tolerance, and respect for diversity, compassion, generosity, respect for Canada's natural beauty.' See, Native Women's Association of Canada, *Matriarchy and the Canadian Charter: A Discussion Paper* (Ottawa: Native Women's Association of Canada, n.d.).

15 Respect for the beliefs, values, and practices of all people was a hallmark of Aboriginal society throughout the millennia before contact. The close-knit interdependence of individuals within First Nations necessitated behaviour that gave a wide latitude of personal freedom to balance the stresses of living in a small community. While there were variations and exceptions, First Nations demonstrated a widespread acceptance of individual autonomy and an equally widespread desire to protect it. At the heart of this outlook were the ethics of non-interference, non-competitiveness, respect, and restraint. For a discussion of these ethics within First Nations, see Clare Brant, 'Native Ethics and Rules of Behavior,' *Canadian Journal of Psychiatry*, vol. 5 (1990), 534, and James Dumont, 'Justice and Aboriginal People,' in *Aboriginal Peoples and the Justice System*, 42.

16 See Didi Herman, 'Beyond the Rights Debate,' *Social and Legal Studies*, vol. 2 (1993), 25, for a thoughtful discussion about the opportunities and limits of 'rights' in the politics of progressive social change.

17 Douglas Lee Donoho, 'Relativism versus Universalism in Human Rights: The Search for Meaningful Standards,' *Stanford Journal of International Law*, vol. 27 (1991), 350.

18 Joel Bakan, 'Constitutional Interpretation and Social Change: You Can't Always Get What You Want (Nor What You Need),' *Canadian Bar Review*, vol. 70 (1991), 307.

19 For information about the dismal U.S. experience in the application of rights to native Americans, see John R. Wunder, *Retained by the People: A History of American Indians and the Bill of Rights* (New York: Oxford University Press 1994); Donald L. Burnett Jr., 'An Historical Analysis of the 1968 Indian Civil Rights Act,' *Harvard Journal of Legislation*, vol. 9 (1972), 557; *Martinez v. Santa Clara Pueblo* (1978) 436 U.S. 49; Catherine McKinnon, 'Whose Culture? A Case Note on Martinez v. Santa Clara Peublo,' in *Feminism Unmodified: Discourses on Life and Law* (Cambridge: Harvard University Press 1987); Alvin J. Ziontz, 'After Martinez; Civil Rights under Tribal Government,' *University of California, Davis Law Review*, vol. 12 (1979), 1; Gregory Schultz, 'The Federal Due Process and Equal Protection Rights of Non-Indian Civil Litigants in Tribal Courts after Santa

Clara,' *Denver University Law Review*, vol. 62 (1985), 761; David C. Williams, 'The Borders of the Equal Protection Clause: Indians as Peoples,' *UCLA Law Review*, vol. 38 (1991), 759; Carla Christofferson, 'Tribal Courts' Failure to Protect Native American Women,' *Yale Law Journal*, vol. 101 (1991), 169.

20 For a description of these difficulties more generally, see Mary Jane Mossman, 'The Charter and Access to Justice in Canada,' in this volume. For a discussion of the social factors that contribute to the defeat of First Nations' rights, see Susan Zimmerman, 'The Revolving Door of Despair: Aboriginal Involvement in the Criminal Justice System,' *U.B.C. Law Review*, 1992 special edition, 367; Robin Ridington, 'Fieldwork in Courtroom 53: A Witness to Delgamuukw,' in *Aboriginal Title in B.C.: Delgamuukw v. The Queen*, ed. Frank Cassidy (Montreal: Institute for Research on Public Policy 1992), 206. Political obstacles are described in Mary Ellen Turpel, 'On the Question of Adapting the Canadian Criminal Justice System for Aboriginal Peoples: Don't Fence Me In,' in *Aboriginal Peoples and the Justice System*, 161. Economic factors are surveyed in John Goddard, *Last Stand of the Lubicon Cree* (Toronto: Douglas and McIntyre 1991), particularly 100–15.

21 Bakan and Smith, 'Rights, Nationalism, and Social Movements.'

22 Allan C. Hutchinson, *Waiting for Coraf: A Critique of Law and Rights* (Toronto: University of Toronto Press 1995).

23 For a discussion of this point, see Alan Hunt, 'Rights and Social Movements: Counter-Hegemonic Strategies,' *Journal of Law and Society*, vol. 17 (1990), 309. And for a discussion of this point as applied to First Nations, see Patrick Macklem, 'First Nations Self-Government and the Borders of the Canadian Legal Imagination,' *McGill Law Journal*, vol. 36 (1991), 382.

24 Didi Herman, 'The Good, the Bad, and the Smugly: Sexual Orientation and Perspectives on the Charter,' in this volume.

25 In particular I would have favoured the explicit recognition and affirmation of First Nations self-government simultaneously with the reinstatement of many First Nations women to their communities. Furthermore, I would have also preferred, and still am in favour of, rights discourse being translated solely by First Nations through an Aboriginal charter.

26 'What needs to be stressed is all struggles begin on old ground': Hunt, 'Rights and Social Movements,' 324.

27 Bakan, 'Constitutional Interpretation.'

28 See Jennifer Nedelsky and Craig Scott, 'Constitutional Dialogue,' in *Social Justice and the Constitution: Perspectives on a Social Union for Canada* eds. Joel Bakan and David Schneiderman (Ottawa: Carleton University Press 1992), 63–4, 69–70.

29 First Nations people should be familiar with the ability to transform and subvert ideas and events, for the trickster is a cultural hero who teaches us about such things. We need reawakening of the trickster in First Nations intellectual discourse. See John Borrows, 'Constitutional Law from a First Nation Perspective: Self-Government and the Royal Proclamation,' *U.B.C. Law Review*, vol. 28 (1994), 1; John Borrows, 'With or Without You: First Nations' Law (in Canada)' *McGill Law Journal*, vol. 41 (1996), 629–65. For a successful attempt to reinterpret equality as applied to First Nations sovereignty, see Patrick Macklem, 'Distributing Sovereignty: Indian Nations and Equality of Peoples,' *Stanford Law Review*, vol. 45 (1993), 1311.

30 Section 91(24) reads: ' ... the exclusive Legislative Authority of the Parliament of Canada extends to all matters coming within the Classes of Subjects next hereinafter enumerated; that is to say, (24) Indians, and Lands reserved for the Indians.' See Constitution Act, 1867, R.S.C. 1985, app. II, no. 5.

31 Section 25 reads: 'The guarantee in this Charter of certain rights and freedoms shall not be construed so as to abrogate or derogate from any Aboriginal, treaty, or other rights or freedoms that pertain to the Aboriginal peoples of Canada including: (a) any rights that have been recognized by the Royal Proclamation of October 7, 1763; and (b) any rights or freedoms that now exist by way of land claims agreements or may be so acquired.'

32 Section 35(1) reads: 'The existing Aboriginal and Treaty Rights of the Aboriginal Peoples of Canada are hereby recognized and affirmed.'

33 Section 37 states: '(1) A Constitutional conference composed of the Prime Minister of Canada and the first ministers of the provinces shall be convened by the Prime Minister of Canada within one year after this Part comes into force: (2) The conference convened under subsection (1) shall have included in its agenda an item respecting constitutional matters which affect the aboriginal peoples of Canada, including the identification and definition of the rights of those peoples to be included in the Constitution of Canada, and the Prime Minister of Canada shall invite representatives of those peoples to participate in the discussions on that item.

34 Section 25 appeared in the Charter, though it did not confer any positive rights on Aboriginal people, and sections 35 and 37 were in part II of the constitution and were therefore not part of the rights and freedoms delineated.

35 Section 25 was viewed by some as possibly preventing the application of charter sections 15(1) and 28, which dealt with equality. Section 15(1) reads: 'Every individual is equal before and under the law and has the right to equal protection and equal benefit of the law without discrimination and, in particular, without discrimination based on race, national or ethnic origin, colour, religion, sex, age

or mental or physical ability.' Section 28 is as follows: 'Notwithstanding anything in this Charter, the rights and freedoms referred to in it are guaranteed equally to male and female persons.'

36 For differing viewpoints on whether the equality provisions of the Charter would compel the removal of sexual discrimination from the Indian Act, see Mary Eberts, 'Sex and Equality Rights,' in *Equality Rights and the Canadian Charter of Rights and Freedoms*, eds. Anne Bayefsky and Mary Eberts (Carswell: Toronto 1987), 217–18, and Douglas Sanders, 'The Renewal of Special Status,' ibid., 554.

37 During the greater part of the Indian Act's existence, sex discrimination was largely concealed from the general public because it was the explicit policy of the act eventually to compel all Indians, male and female alike, to relinquish their status: see J.R. Miller, *Skyscrapers Hide the Heavens: A History of Indian-White Relations in Canada* (Toronto: University of Toronto Press 1989), 207; John Leslie and Ron Maguire, *The Historical Development of the Indian Act* (Ottawa: Treaties and Historical Research Branch, Department of Indian and Northern Affairs, 1979); and John Tobias, 'Protection, Civilization, Assimilation: An Outline History of Canada's Indian Policy,' in *As Long as the Sun Shines and the Water Flows: A Reader in Canadian Native Studies*, eds. Ian Getty and Antoine Lussier (Vancouver, University of British Columbia Press 1983), 29. This policy was officially promoted as recently as 1969, when the government of Pierre Trudeau proposed to eliminate all special Indian status in its 'White Paper.' That document stated: '[For Indians] different status [is] a road which has led to a blind alley of deprivation and frustration. This road, because it is a separate road, cannot lead to full participation, to equality in practice as well as in theory ... The Government has ... another road for Indians, a road that would lead gradually away from different status to full social, economic and political participation in Canadian life.' See 'Statement of the Government of Canada on Indian Policy: White Paper' [1969].

38 The Charter's impact on First Nations politics can best be illustrated through examining its place in status Indian communities. Its effects among Metis and Inuit peoples have been important as well, but that subject requires a separate essay.

39 Section 12(1)(b) of the Indian Act R.S.C. 1970, C. I-6 states: The following persons are not entitled to be registered, namely ... a person who married a person who is not an Indian.'

40 For a discussion of how sexual discrimination was introduced through the Indian Act, see 'Aboriginal Women,' in A.C. Hamilton and C.M. Sinclair, *The Justice System and Aboriginal People: Report of the Aboriginal Justice Inquiry of Manitoba*, vol. 1 (Winnipeg: Queen's Printer 1991), 476–7.

41 While the principles underlying the Charter had their greatest impact in Indian gender politics, and highlighted the sexual inequality that exists in Indian

communities, debate about this subject prevailed long before the Charter was implemented. Indian criticism of the provisions of the Indian Act which caused women to lose their status have been present since at least 1872. See Kathleen Jameson, *Indian Women and the Law in Canada: A Citizens Minus* (Ottawa: Supply and Services 1978), 30.

42   As Indian desires to maintain their status became more widely known in the late 1960s, the inequality Indian women faced in losing their status became a more conspicuous issue. Mary Two-Axe Early's presentation to the Royal Commission on the Status of Women about the sexual discrimination she faced as a non-status Mohawk woman is the prime example. See *Report of the Royal Commission on the Status of Women in Canada* (Ottawa: Supply and Services 1970). Early told of how she had been requested to leave her reserve because she was married to a non-Native man, and she spoke of how she had organized a group called 'Indian Rights for Indian Women' to protest the Indian Act provisions that decreed her eviction. Other Indian women also came before the commission to make the same point. When the commission made its recommendations it suggested that status be restored to Indian women and that Indian women should have the same civil rights as other Canadians with respect to marriage and property (ibid., 238). For a critique of the commission's effects on First Nations Women, see Turpel, 'Patriarchy and Paternalism.'

43   In the early 1970s sexual inequality in Indian communities once again gained public attention when the issue was argued before the Supreme Court of Canada. The case of *Lavell and Bedard v. The Attorney General of Canada*, (1973) 38 D.L.R. (3d) 481 was brought by Jeanette Corbiere and Yvonne Bedard, Ojibway and Iroquois non-status Indians respectively who had lost their status when they 'married out.' The Supreme Court found that 'equality before the law as employed in the Canadian Bill of Rights referred only to the application or enforcement of law.' As such, since the rule of law treated all Indian women the same (that is, it discriminated against all Indian women equally!), it was held that the Indian Act did not breach the equality provisions of the Bill of Rights.

44   *Lovelace v. Canada*, 36 U.N. GOAR Supp. (No. 40) Annex XVIII. Doc. A/36/40 [1981] was the last incident before the advent of the Charter to highlight sexual discrimination in the Indian Act. Sandra Lovelace was a Maliseet women from the Tobique Indian Reserve in New Brunswick who lost her status when she married a non-Native man. She and the women of her reserve struggled for many years for her right to status and membership in her community. Eventually, Lovelace took her claim of discrimination before the United Nations Human Rights Committee, which found that the Canadian government breached section 27 of the International Covenant on Civil and Political Rights by denying her band membership and the concomitant access to her culture. The committee did not rule on whether

Canada had discriminated on the basis of sex because Lovelace had already lost her status before Canada ratified the covenant in 1976. Nevertheless, the Lovelace decision caused Canada considerable international embarrassment and was regarded by many Indian women as a significant step towards regaining full status in their communities.

45 There is a need for community reconstruction because of the Indian Act's effect on internal community gender relations, described by the United Nations in its Lovelace decision as follows: 'Unfortunately, Aboriginal men, over the centuries, have adopted the same attitude towards women as the Europeans. As a result, the cultural and social degradation of Aboriginal Women has been devastating' (481).

46 The search for a return to equality for Aboriginal women has been explained by Verna Kirkness: 'Native women are emerging in search of the equality once enjoyed by women within Indian society. Traditional Native societies are examples of democracies in which all people were accorded equal rights. Further discourse will enable members of the dominant society to gain new understanding. The potential exists for the structure of traditional Native communities to act as a model for gender equality.' Verna Kirkness, 'Emerging Native Women,' *Canadian Journal of Women and the Law*, vol. 2 (1987–8), 415.

47 As Mary Two-Axe Early, Jeanette Corbiere, Yvonne Bedard, and other women in similar circumstances brought forward their dilemma for resolution, it became apparent that they were not strongly supported by the national Indian organizations. Organizations such as the National Indian Brotherhood (NIB) and the Native Council of Canada (NCC) wanted to use the sexual-equality provisions of the Indian Act to negotiate wholesale changes to the act. (This was in response to the federal government's desire to change its Indian policy; see Sally Weaver, *Making Canadian Indian Policy: The Hidden Agenda, 1968–1970* [Toronto: University of Toronto Press, 1981]). While these organizations viewed sexual discrimination as wrong, they wanted Indian women to subordinate their objectives to other goals; see C. Cheda, 'Indian Women: An Historical Example and Contemporary View,' in *Women in Canada*, ed. M. Stephenson (Don Mills: General Publishing 1977), 195–208. Furthermore, Indian people within reserve communities often accepted the colonial structures of the Indian Act and thus did not provide active support to the women who were attempting to secure their status. This meant that Indian women had to organize themselves to press their concerns and to provide a network of support for those who were victims of the act's discrimination. One prominent group that formed at the time of the *Lavell* case to fulfil these goals of advocacy and support was the Native Women's Association of Canada. NWAC would henceforth play a major role in pressing for sexual equality for Indian women.

48 See Mary Eberts, 'Memorandum of Law to NWAC, 19 December 1991:3':
    Teressa Nahanee, 'Dancing With a Gorilla: Aboriginal Women, Justice and the
    Charter,' in *Aboriginal Peoples and the Justice System*, 367.
49 Indian people have long asserted that, rather than wanting to be absorbed by the
    general population, they are determined to preserve their culture, traditions,
    treaties, lands, and powers of self-government. In the 1960s natives began to
    attract greater attention to their opposition to assimilation by insisting on the
    maintenance of their separate status. Two representative examples of the expand-
    ing literature in this era on Indian desires to maintain special status are Harold
    Cardinal, *The Unjust Society: The Tragedy of Canada's Indians* (Edmonton:
    Hurtig 1969) and H.B. Hawthorne, *A Survey of the Contemporary Indians of
    Canada*, 2 vols. (Ottawa: Indian Affairs 1966–7).
50 The AFN was the successor to the NIB and is the organization that represents
    status Indians.
51 NCC represents non-status and off-reserve Aboriginal people.
52 ITC represents the Inuit people of Canada.
53 The MNC represents descendants of the historic Metis nation that originated in
    Manitoba.
54 Lillianne Ernestine Krosenbrink-Gelissen, *Sexual Equality as an Aboriginal
    Right: The Native Women's Association of Canada and the Constitutional Process
    on Aboriginal Matters, 1982–1987* (Saarbrucken: Verlag breithenbach 1991), 148.
55 Ibid.
56 Section 35(4) states: 'Notwithstanding any other provision of this Act, the
    aboriginal and treaty rights referred to in subsection (1) are guaranteed equally
    to male and female persons.'
57 Despite widespread acceptance of including sexual equality for First Nations in
    the constitution, there was a considerable range of opinions as to the appropriate
    wording to accomplish this objective and as to whether this guarantee should be
    placed in section 25 or 35. See Sanders, 'Renewal of Special Status,' 557.
58 *Proceedings of the Standing Committee on Legal and Constitutional Affairs*,
    32nd. Parliament, 1st session, issue no. 69: 46.
59 See Richard Dalon, 'An Alberta Perspective on Aboriginal Peoples and the
    Constitution,' in *The Quest for Justice: Aboriginal Peoples and Aboriginal Rights*,
    eds. M. Boldt and J.A. Long (Toronto: University of Toronto Press 1985), 95.
60 Throughout the constitutional conference process the federal government did not
    allow NWAC to participate because it was considered not sufficiently representa-
    tive of Aboriginal people. See Krosenbrink-Gelissen, *Sexual Equality*, 115. The
    AFN also opposed NWAC's direct participation in the constitutional conferences
    (ibid., 148). However, despite being denied formal participation, NWAC was able

to communicate its position at the conferences by making written submissions through a subgroup called the National Committee on Aboriginal Rights, by working through the Native Council of Canada (NCC) and AFN at various stages of the process, and even by speaking through provincial representatives. In pursuing their objectives Indian women were faced with a dilemma because they had to decide whether pre-eminence should be given to their gender rights or to their Aboriginal rights. For a description of this challenge, see generally Nitya Iyer, 'Categorical Denials: Equality Rights and the Shaping of Social Identity,' *Queen's Law Journal*, vol. 19 (1993), and Nitya Duclos, 'Disappearing Women: Racial Minority Women in Human Rights Cases,' *Canadian Journal of Women and the Law*, vol. 10 (1993), 25.

61 This was consistent with the AFN's position that section 35 contained a 'full box' of Aboriginal rights and therefore only their definition, and not their creation, was required. See Bryan Schwartz, 'Unstated Business: Two Approaches to Defining s. 35 – What's in the Box and What Kind of Box?' in Schwartz, *First Principles, Second Thoughts* (Montreal: Institute for Research and Public Policy 1986), ch. 24.

62 'Statement on Equality at First Ministers Conference,' in Krosenbrink-Gelissen, *Sexual Equality*, 154.

63 Ibid., chapter 5, 'Traditional Indian Motherhood: A Strategy.'

64 'Native people think in terms of cyclicity. Time is not a straight line. It is a circle. Every day is not a new day, but the same day repeating itself ... A characteristic of cyclical thinking is that it is holistic, in the same way that a circle is whole. A cyclical philosophy does not lend itself readily to dichotomies or categorizations, nor to fragmentations and polarizations.' Leroy Little Bear, 'Aboriginal Rights and the Canadian Grundnorm,' in *Arduous Journey: Canadian Indians and Decolonization*, ed. J.R. Ponting (Toronto: McClelland and Stewart 1988), 245.

65 Penny Petrone, *Native Literature in Canada: From the Oral Tradition to the Present* (Toronto: Oxford University Press 1990), 17.

66 Krosenbrink-Gelissen, *Sexual Equality*, 160.

67 The sections of the Indian Act that discriminated on the basis of sex, 12(1)(b), were removed when Bill C-31 was introduced in Parliament and section 6 was inserted in the act; see R.S.C. 1985, C. I-5.

68 Bill C-31 was introduced in the House of Commons on 28 Feb. 1985 while a constitutional conferences took place on 2 and 3 April of that same year. Hearings on the bill were taking place while the conference was proceeding.

69 *The Impacts of the 1985 Amendments to the Indian Act (Bill C-31): Summary Report* (Ottawa: Supply and Services 1990), i.

70 Nahanee, 'Dancing with a Gorilla,' 372.

71 Despite the amendments, there is residual discrimination in the Indian Act in the area of citizenship and reserve residency. The question of determining who is an

Indian is a problem because a 'second generation cutoff clause' in the new legislation serves to create a new class of Indian people and conceal sexual discrimination. The problem results from section 6(2) of the Indian Act, which entitles a person to registration if only one parent has a right to be registered under section 6. The provisions in section 6(2) do not allow status to be passed on to succeeding generations if the registrant's partner/spouse does not have status. This has led to the unequal treatment of male and female siblings since women who lost status prior to 1985 cannot pass status along through successive generations while their brothers who married non-Indian women prior to 1985 can do so. A second potential difficulty lies in the area of who will be entitled to live on a reserve. Bands were given the power to take control over their membership lists when the new registration provisions were enacted. Problems could arise if communities decide to discriminate in an arbitrary manner when membership decisions are made. While reserves were obliged to place reinstated people on their band lists, newly registered people who never possessed status before do not enjoy this same privilege. Since 232 of 615 bands now control their own membership lists, it is possible that many newly registered people who never before possessed status will be denied access to their community or culture. If this happens a new class of Indian citizens will be created.

72 A person was eligible to receive or have their status restored if they lost their status under former sections 12(1)(b) or 109(1) of the Indian Act, or if one or both of a person's parents was a status Indian or was eligible for status under the 1985 changes. These people included women who lost status through marriage to a non-status person, individuals who lost status through enfranchisement, and children of people in these categories. See *Changes to the Indian Act: Important Changes to Canada's Indian Act Resulting from the Passage of Bill C-31* (Ottawa: Indian and Northern Affairs 1986), 3.

73 Ibid.

74 *The Impacts of the 1985 Amendments to the Indian Act (Bill C-31): 2) Survey of Registrants* (Ottawa: Indian and Northern Affairs, Supply and Services 1990), 15–20.

75 *Summary Report*, ii.

76 Ibid. Most Bill C-31 registrants are female (58 per cent); educated (43 per cent graduated from high school, 25 per cent from post-secondary education); employed (59 per cent); with household incomes over $25,000 (41 per cent); live off reserve (90 per cent); and own their own homes (55 per cent). The on-reserve registrant is more likely to be male, unemployed, and to live in a household that contains children under eighteen years of age.

77 *Survey of Registrants*, 5.

78 Ibid., 17.

79 As a result of the amendments the average band size increased by 19 per cent. *The Impacts of the 1985 Amendments to the Indian Act (Bill C-31): 3) Bands and Communities Studies* (Ottawa: Indian and Northern Affairs, Supply and Services, 1990), 12.

80 A foreshadowing of the future tests Indian communities will have to meet as more newly registered people move to the reserve is found in the following quote regarding health care and education: 'Socially, C-31 registrants moving to the band have made a difference to the fabric of the community. Many have never been on a reserve before. Some want to affect change and expectations are very high. In many cases, they have not been able to articulate their demands very well, but band staff feel that they have a demanding attitude just the same. Some C-31's were petitioning to have the health services and education coordinators removed from their jobs. But people on the reserve would not sign the petition.' *Bands and Communities Studies*, 21n82.

81 Reinstatement will bring many challenges in community economic development. Bill C-31 registrants were seen as a threat to the few jobs available on the reserve: 'They will take jobs away from reserve members'; '[long-time] band members should get jobs first, before outsiders.' Other respondents voiced the fear that Bill C-31 registrants moving to the reserve could mean changes to the traditional economy and standard of living or could affect the reserve land base. Ibid., 24.

82 Future political difficulties arising from reinstatement are evident in this quote: 'Some regular[?!] band members feel threatened by the numbers and vocalism of the C-31 registrants returning to the band. They are returning in sufficient numbers that they could influence the political process, but ... they lack an understanding of the band's history and way of life.' Ibid., 22.

83 The wedge that has been driven into some bands is exemplified by one community's experience: 'All women reinstated under Bill C-31 from the Cold Lake First Nations (Alberta) reserve have been refused treaty monies ... We are being denied our right to practice our cultural heritage on the reserve level and are being treated like second class citizens by our own people, and now we are nomads in our own land because we chose to marry who we wanted to.' Comment of Celina Minoose-Ritter (Edmonton), *The Impacts of the 1985 Amendments to the Indian Act (Bill C-31): Aboriginal Inquiry* (Ottawa: Supply and Services 1990), 59.

84 To can gain a sense of the impact of these amendments on the author's own community, the Chippewa of the Nawash in southern Ontario, see John Borrows, 'Contemporary Traditional Equality: The Effect of the Charter on First Nations,' *University of New Brunswick Law Journal*, vol. 43 (1994), 36 –8. For a short history of this band and its resistance to colonial control, see John Borrows, 'A Genealogy of Law: Inherent Sovereignty and First Nations Self-Government,' *Osgoode Hall Law Journal*, vol. 30 (1992), 291.

85 There is no doubt that the registration of hundreds of new people initially caused political strife. Many band councils refused to accept certain funding that was available for newly registered people as they returned to the reserve. The housing program in particular illustrates the resistance to newly registered people becoming part of the community again. As one chief expressed the concern: 'Housing, in itself, has caused special political problems. Lifelong band members are entitled to housing under either the standard DIAND subsidy program of the band CMHC program. Reinstated C-31 members, on the other hand, are entitled to participate in the special C-31 housing program and this program is limited exclusively to Bill C-31. The special C-31 housing program has created a degree of animosity between lifelong band members and reinstated band members. Lifelong band members have to put in their application for housing and wait as long as eight years for their name to reach a level in priority listing ... C-31 members on the other hand, can jump to the head of the lineup as a result of the special C-31 housing program.' Chief Harry Coo, Lac La Ronge Band, Saskatchewan, *Aboriginal Inquiry*, 39.

86 Ibid., 28.

87 Furthermore, the full impact of Indian community growth has yet to be felt: *Summary Report*, 33. As of June 1990 the number of people who had moved back to my reserve since reinstatement was only .03 per cent. Though the numbers are uneven across bands, the number of Bill C-31 people living on reserves is closer to 10 per cent; while 80 per cent of bands have fewer than 15 newly registered people living on reserve; see *The Impacts of the 1985 Amendments to the Indian Act (Bill C-31): 4) Government Programs* (Ottawa: Indian and Northern Affairs, Supply and Services, 1990), app. 2: 25, and ibid., 25–37, for a broader description of demographic trends. Statistics indicate that eventually over 50 per cent of all reinstated people will want to move to their reserves; see *Survey of Registrants*, 34. When this happens there will further adjustments in the life of the community as resources to meet their needs will be stretched and opinions on how to meet their requirements will be diverse.

88 *Bands and Community Study*, 20.

89 Ibid.

90 For an account of the direct impact of this discrimination, see Cindy Sparvier (Saskatoon), *Aboriginal Inquiry*, 30. Despite calls for looking beyond the categories created by the government when defining membership, many still have difficulties accepting their newly registered 'cousins' among them.

91 A case is being brought by Sharon McIvor to challenge the 'second generation cut-off clause.'

92 See *Twinn v. Canada* (1986) 6 F.T.R. 138, [1987] 2 F.C. 450; *Courtois v. Canada* [1991] 1 C.N.L.R. 40 (Canadian Human Rights Tribunal); *Mantel v. Omeasco* (1992), 58 F.T.R. 231 (F.C.T.D.).

93 'The Quebec Native Women's Association argues that membership rules developed by bands ought to be consistent with section 15 of the Canadian Charter of Rights and Freedoms ... The QNWA maintains that any government, whether it be a band government or the federal government, must protect the right of the individual.' See *Aboriginal Inquiry*, 26.

94 Rheal Boudrais (Quebec), in ibid., 34.

95 Liz Pointe of the United Native Nations made this statement: about Indian peoples realizing positive identity through Bill C-31: 'It is no great surprise to me that, increasingly, these people who are legally adopted or fostered and are requesting our assistance in applying for status under Bill C-31 are doing so with the hope of determining where they come from and thereby determining who they are. For the most part, obtaining status means that, for the first time, they will be connected to family and family necessarily connects them to a distinct aboriginal group of people, perhaps to a sense of community they have never known and a culture they do not know how to begin to define.' Ibid., 12–13.

96 Mary Ellen Turpel, 'Discrimination and the 1985 Amendments to the Indian Act: Full of Snares for Women,' *Rights and Freedoms* (September 1987), 6.

97 See Thomas Issac and Mary Sue Maloughney, 'Dually Disadvantaged and Historically Forgotten?: Aboriginal Women and the Inherent Right of Self-Government,' *Manitoba Law Journal*, vol. 21 (1992), 453, and Joyce Green, 'Constitutionalising the Patriarchy: Aboriginal Women and Aboriginal Government,' *Constitutional Forum*, vol. 4 (1993), 110.

98 Teressa Nahanee, 'What we are dealing with in this constitutional process is the silencing of Native women,' *Kahtou News*, 15 Oct. 1992, 5.

99 Native Women's Association of Canada, 'Statement on the Canada Package' (Ottawa: NWAC 1992), 7.

100 These organizations were the Assembly of First Nations, the Native Council of Canada, the Metis National Council, and the Inuit Tapirisat of Canada.

101 *Native Women's Association of Canada v. Canada* (1992) 95 D.L.R. (4th) 106 (F.C.A.), (1992) 90 D.L.R. (4th) 394 (F.C.T.D.).

102 Sections 2(b) the Charter states that: 'Everyone has the right' to 'freedom of thought, belief, opinion and expression.' Section 28 reads: 'Notwithstanding anything in this Charter, the rights and freedoms referred to in it are guaranteed equally to male and female persons.'

103 *NWAC v. Canada*, 120–1.

104 [1994] 3 S.C.R. 627 (S.C.C.). For commentary on this case, see Leon Trackman, 'The Demise of Positive Liberty? Native Women's Association of Canada v. Canada,' *Constitutional Forum*, vol. 6 (1995), 71.

105 *Native Women's Association of Canada v. Canada* (1992) 97 D.L.R. (4th) 537 (F.C. T.D.), (1992) 97 D.L.R. (4th) 548 (F.C.A.).

106 Sean Fine, 'Native Women Aim to Block National Referendum in Court,' *Globe and Mail*, 13 Oct. 1992.

107 See Louise Mandell, 'Native Culture on Trial,' in *Equality and Judicial Neutrality*, eds. Sheilah Martin and Kathleen E. Mahoney, (Toronto: Carswell 1987), 358.

108 Bakan and Smith, 'Rights, Nationalism and Social Movements.'

109 'A decision that does not speak to them, one that is not grounded in an appreciation of their moral identity, is a decision that sacrifices real people to abstractions,' Nitya Duclos, 'Lessons of Difference: Feminist Theory on Cultural Diversity,' *Buffalo Law Review*, vol. 38 (1990), 377.

110 NWAC, 'Statement on the Canada Package,' 9–11.

111 See Geoffrey York, 'Native women's fears led to text change,' *Globe and Mail*, 7 Oct. 1992.

112 Some felt that the best protection of individual rights for First Nations peoples would be an Aboriginal charter. While others were not adverse to this idea, they were cynical about its implementation. See Gail Stacey-Moore, leader of NWAC, as quoted in Susan Delacourt, 'Natives divided over the charter,' *Globe and Mail*, 14 March 1992.

113 NWAC, 'Statement on the Canada Package,' 11–12.

114 As one leader said: 'Native women and children need a safeguard against the abuse of power by male leaders and, until an acceptable alternative is put in place, we insist on having the safeguard of the Charter.' Gail Stacey-Moore, quoted in André Picard, 'Native women cling to the charter.'

115 *Aboriginal Justice Inquiry of Manitoba*, 485.

116 Donna Greshner, 'Aboriginal Women, The Constitution and Criminal Justice,' *U.B.C. Law Review*, 1992 special edition, 339.

117 For a stance that criticizes sexual discrimination yet supports self-government, see Bernice Hammersmith, 'Aboriginal Women and Self-Government,' in *Nation to Nation: Aboriginal Sovereignty and the Future of Canada*, eds. D. Engelstad and J. Bird (Toronto: Anansi 1992), 53.

118 Greshner, 'Aboriginal Women,' 339.

119 Ibid., 350–3.

120 Wendy Moss, 'Indigenous Self-Government in Canada under the Indian Act: Resolving Conflicts Between Collective and Individual Rights,' *Queen's Law Journal*, vol. 15 (1990), 279.

121 For a description of these teachings, see Dumont, 'Justice and Aboriginal People,' 54.

122 John Brigham, 'Rights, Rage and Remedy: Forms of Law in Political Discourse,' *Studies in American Political Developments* (1987) 303.

123 For discussion about the impact of the Charter in other social arenas, see 'Impact of the Charter on the Public Policy Process: A Symposium,' *Osgoode Hall Law Journal*, vol. 30 (1992), 501.

6

The Good, the Bad, and the Smugly: Sexual Orientation and Perspectives on the Charter*

DIDI HERMAN

Within the Canadian academic community, the Charter has its advocates, its enthusiasts, its sceptics, and its denouncers. It is, for some, the crowning glory in the firmament of liberalism. Other commentators represent the Charter as a most dangerous form of capitalist class rule while writers occupying a different point on the political spectrum have characterized it as a powerful weapon in the hands of self-seeking 'special interest groups.' Some people, less committed to macro-ideologies, take a pragmatic approach to the Charter – 'it's here, it's a tool, let's use it as best we can.' Neither its magnificence nor its menace are much discussed.

Most Charter litigants would likely fall into this last group. Many activists, fed up with political manoeuvrings and the slow pace of parliamentary reform, have turned to the Charter as another forum (one with particular promise) in which to make their case. Some, however, have been more successful than others. In early litigation, for example, rights to strike and secondary picketing were found, by judges, not to exist as Charter guarantees.[1] At the same time, corporations brought successful Charter cases by arguing that they were defending 'freedom of expression,' 'religion,' and so on.[2] In the eyes of some critics, these decisions confirmed their view that the Charter was inherently facilitative of the economic status quo and hence not capable of promoting progressive social transformation;[3] activities that were directed against the accumulation of capital, such as the above examples of worker protest, would clearly not receive the stamp of Charter legitimacy.

* This essay was written in 1993 specifically for the volume and appeared in *Oxford Journal of Legal Studies*, vol. 14 (1994), 589–604. For comments on an earlier draft, thanks to: Joel Bakan, Davina Cooper, Marlee Kline, Bruce Ryder, and Carl Stychin. Thanks to Susanna Tam for research assistance and the Centre for Constitutional Studies for financial support.

During this same period, women's groups, many of which had welcomed the Charter's arrival after they had fought for and won changes to the document that recognized the principle of gender equality,[4] became alarmed as men began to claim section 15 equality rights *against* the interests of women. Gradually, however, it became clear that the courts would not easily entertain these sorts of challenges and that the paradigmatic section 15 group was one demonstrating a history of 'disadvantage.'[5] While the ensuing development of womens' rights through Charter challenges was uneven and debatable, there have been some notable successes and the Charter is perceived by many to *be at least capable of* promoting women's equality in Canada.[6]

Indeed, so-called 'social movement successes' such as this have precipitated a right-wing backlash; the Charter, some now argue, has been manipulated by liberal 'social engineers' in order to alter the course of Canadian society.[7] Echoing many of the criticisms made by left-wing critics, the new reactionaries decry the undemocratic nature of 'Charter change.'[8] However, in stark contrast to the left-wing critics who argue that the Charter is, at its heart, an instrument of *class* rule with provisions that simply reinforce the status quo, the right-wing critics insist that, on the contrary, the Charter has become an instrument of *'interest group'* rule and that Canadian society is, implicitly, in the process of substantive social transformation.

And, yet, it is incontrovertible that several 'social groups' have been nearly invisible within Charter discourse and have had little effect upon evolving jurisprudence. For example, since the early cases, labour unions have had a decreasing presence in Charter litigation. And, if we examine the diverse grounds for discrimination cited in section 15, it becomes clear that the 'race' and 'disability' grounds, among others, have almost never been the subject of a Charter challenge.

Rather than making overarching pronouncements on the Charter's effects, perhaps it would be more useful to ask whether some groups have made more out of the Charter than others, and, if so, why. Instrumentalist critics could suggest that the answers are obvious: those with power get what they want. The labour movement has been crushed while women's groups have been publicly funded. Sociologists could note that the anti-racist movement does not have the formal, national bureaucratic structures that appear to have facilitated Charter-challenges for the group 'women.' The disability movement is perhaps similarly amorphous (and underfunded). Certainly, the explanations are far more complex than this, but I do not propose to address these disparities in outcome directly.

Instead, I am concerned with one social movement, which is perceived (and perhaps perceives itself) to have achieved a certain measure of success in the

Charter era – the lesbian and gay rights movement.[9] This theme is pursued through an examination of several existing 'Charter perspectives' – those, for lack of better phrases, I term 'debunker,' 'promoter,' 'reactionary,' and 'pragmatist.' There is an unavoidable element of generalization in my discussion. Still, while I hope that I am not creating 'straw people,' I do set out these positions quite starkly, and, in the process, understate the variation within each of the views explored. My excuse is that the contrasts provided as a result of this approach are useful foundations on which to build further analysis.

My questions, then, are how well, if at all, do these approaches explain the inclusion of 'sexual orientation' within section 15? If they fail to provide sufficient explanation, what alternatives may there be? And what implications does all of this have for understanding the relationship between constitutional rights and social change?

Background: 'We Are an Analogous Ground'

Though not having quite the same ring as 'we are family,'[10] lesbian and gay demands for inclusion under section 15 were rather similar. Yet, in this case, the plea was not that lesbians and gay men formed 'normal' family units identical to those of heterosexuals. Instead, lesbian and gay rights activists sought the official recognition of a status 'different from' the 'norm' – one requiring special protections. 'Sexual orientation' was not, however, an enumerated ground under the Charter's equality section. Experience had also shown that judges were far from willing to extend existing grounds (such as 'sex') to cover lesbian and gay claims. For example, while it was theoretically possible for lesbian and gay litigants to allege discrimination under the 'sex' ground in section 15, this had been tried several times under human-rights legislation with no success.[11] Rather than pursue what was perceived as a lost cause, the lesbian and gay rights movement deemed as necessary the inclusion of 'sexual orientation' as a protected ground in section 15 (a similar strategy had been adopted around the statutory codes).[12] Fortunately for the activists, it had been established that section 15 was open-ended – the enumerated grounds did not comprise a final list. Other grounds of discrimination could be argued for providing they were proved to be 'analogous' to those already there.

The legal 'test' for determining whether a particular ground of discrimination was worthy of inclusion in section 15 had been set up by the Supreme Court of Canada in *Andrews* and then refined in subsequent cases.[13] Simply put, it was necessary that a non-enumerated ground of discrimination be the basis to identify a group with a shared experience of disadvantage based on 'irrelevant' characteristics. In fighting for Charter protection, then, the establishment of sexual orientation as a 'non-enumerated but analogous ground' was the first significant hurdle for lesbians and gay men.

It was anticipated that this initial obstacle would be difficult to surmount. Activists and academics expected government respondents to argue strongly that sexual orientation was not analogous to the enumerated grounds and that lesbians and gay men were not a legitimate 'target group' for Charter protection. Several articles were thus published in law journals outlining the appropriate argument for lesbian and gay litigants to make.[14]

When the question came to court, however, it was a non-issue. In one of the first cases, a federal trial judge found that 'sexual orientation' was analogous to the enumerated grounds.[15] *Veysey* is the only decision where the issue was discussed at length; Madame Justice L'Heureux Dubé found that sexual orientation was probably immutable and that 'those who deviated from sexual norms' were stigmatized.[16] Citing provincial human-rights legislation where sexual orientation had been recognized, L'Heureux Dubé went on to find that it was clearly an analogous ground. There is no indication, from the reported case, that the government respondent attempted to introduce any evidence to the contrary. The Federal Court of Appeal, upholding the decision on other grounds, made a point of noting that the inclusion of sexual orientation in section 15 was not contested by the government on appeal.[17]

In subsequent cases, the status of sexual orientation as an analogous ground was confirmed and, with few exceptions, governments, including conservative ones, did not object. For example, in *Brown* the trial judge, noting that 'counsel for the defendants concedes that sexual orientation is akin to the enumerated grounds in the section,' stated that 'discrimination based on sexual orientation contravenes the equality provisions of the Charter.'[18] In *Knodel*, the Social Credit government of British Columbia again conceded the point, and the judge was happy to concur.[19] In *Haig*, the Ontario Court of Appeal noted that the federal government had once more chosen to accept the inclusion and, the Court stated, 'the concession is right.'[20] By the time of *Egan*, the Federal Court of Appeal was able to remark that it was 'settled law that sexual orientation can be invoked as an analogous ground of discrimination under subsection 15(1).'[21] The right of lesbians and gay men to claim inclusion under section 15 now seems indisputable. Yet *Veysey* appears to remain the sole case where the question was even summarily mooted.

It is, in my view, interesting that this first hurdle, one anticipated to be a formidable one, was overcome with such ease, and with so little comment. Why was this so? Why, particularly, would a Conservative federal government have chosen not to contest lesbian and gay claims for official protection as a minority?

Possible Explanations

There are several analytic approaches that offer explanatory assistance. Rights debunkers, for example, who tend to employ an economistic critique, argue that the Charter is an example of capitalist legal form. It is an abstraction promising far more than it can deliver, and one diverting people from pursuing more effective means of struggle. The Charter, in this view, is all about form and little about the substantive redressing of inequality; as Harry Glasbeek has put it, 'better manners at the dining table do not necessarily mean better food on it.'[22]

This type of Charter analysis suggests that the recognition of new 'rights-deserving' groups is nothing more than an example of the ways in which the capitalist state contains any 'real' challenge to its authority. The state, by exploiting 'historical lines of fragmentation' such as hierarchies of gender and race, deflects the experience of class inequality onto these other areas through the enactment of 'rights documents' that encourage further estrangement from class identification.[23] In an ultimately meaningless gesture, legal rights are attached to these non-class-based identities; the energies and efforts of social groups are then diverted into making 'rights claims' rather than in fighting for economic transformation 'at the site of production.'[24] To quote Glasbeek:

This argument is that if people feel bruised or disadvantaged, there is a political-legal route to take, one which does not depend on numbers (the one respect in which the property-less have an advantage in political terms over property owners) but which relies on rational, objective reasons, which will be listened to, and adjudicated upon, by unbiased tribunals. The idea is to reinforce the notion that the problems of the property-less are caused by an unresponsive and oppressive state which must be curtailed ... If this deflection of politics can be achieved, it will be functional from the point of view of the few, the property owners, as their position will not be subjected as much to the vicissitudes of direct and indirect political struggles in the electoral sphere. Further, the courts can be counted on to treat the claims of the disadvantaged against the state in such a way as to bolster the rights of the wealth-owners. It is in the nature of the judiciary as an institution to do this.[25]

The Charter, in this view, is undemocratic, untransformative, and, ultimately, an obstacle to fundamental social change.[26]

Those subscribing to this debunker perspective could suggest that the inclusion of 'sexual orientation' in section 15 simply facilitates fragmentation, obfuscation, and, in the end, the reproduction of capitalism. It is not surprising, then, that the Conservative government of the day, in cases such as *Veysey* or

Egan, chose not to contest the 'analogous grounds' argument and that the courts accepted it with so little comment. According to the debunker approach, the inclusion of sexual orientation in section 15 was no more important (analytically speaking) than its exclusion would have been.

For rights promoters,[27] the recognition of lesbians and gay men as a minority deserving of official protection may also have been inevitable, although for different reasons. Here, minority rights are viewed as a key feature of a truly liberal society; a failure to extend these rights to those who need and deserve them is a failure of the philosophy and practice of liberalism. According to Richard Mohr, an American liberal philosopher, 'liberalism makes moral sense of gay issues; gay issues make moral sense of liberalism.'[28]

In Canada, rights promoters emphasize the Charter's positive potential as a facilitator of justice. For example, Kathleen Mahoney claims that 'the Supreme Court of Canada, to quite a remarkable degree, has recognized the egalitarian challenge the Charter presents. In the past few years, it has launched a promising new era for equality jurisprudence quite unique in the western world. The equality theory it has developed goes far beyond that which underlies constitutional law of other western societies including Europe and the United States. It has fashioned principles which give disadvantaged groups a better chance than ever before to alleviate the inequities they experience in laws, policies, and practices of governments and government officials.'[29]

While not all rights promoters share Mahoney's enthusiasm, the view that the Charter could potentially offer such justice is echoed by others.[30] Lorenne Clark, for instance, argues that liberalism is not a bar to substantive social change; on the contrary, liberal theory, properly understood, 'does contain principles which allow for a wider rather than a narrower, a substantive, rather than a merely formal, interpretation of equality, and recognizes that the promotion of greater substantive equality is a legitimate social goal.'[31] Though the Charter could be read narrowly, thus preventing this expansion of liberalism, writers such as Clark see such a possibility as almost 'unnatural.' 'Liberalism is quite capable of supporting that large and liberal reading which is necessary to enable the Charter to fulfil its mandate within the context of Canada's evolving social democracy ... the Charter can, and will, be significant in ridding us of the dusty relics of the past.'[32]

The rights promoters' analysis stands, then, in stark contrast to that of the rights debunkers who deny the Charter these kinds of effects. Yet debunkers and promoters tend to share a construction of lesbians and gay men as largely irrelevant to the process of social change. In the former's analysis, lesbians, gay men, and other members of 'new social movements' are either 'acted upon' by economic processes, no threat to 'capital' (the most important enemy), or simply of little interest. In the words of Meiksins Wood, 'unless class politics becomes the unifying force that binds together all emancipatory struggles, the "new social movements" will remain on the margins of the existing social order, at best able to generate periodic and momentary displays of popular support but destined to leave the capitalist order intact, together with all its defences against human emancipation and the realization of "universal human goods."'[33]

For rights promoters, on the other hand, their political philosophy itself is the agent of change rather than those who become included within its terms. 'Minority groups' do play a role in making their 'disadvantage' known; once having done so, however, legal liberalism moves forward to meet, recognize, and resolve it. For example, during the struggle in 1986 to amend Ontario's Human Rights Code to include sexual orientation as a ground of discrimination, politicians and media argued in support on the basis that the amendment must pass if liberalism was to 'be true to itself.' At the same time, these actors insisted that the passage of the amendment would not cause any serious social change.[34] Some promoters' view of the 'analogous ground' development might be somewhat similar – it was simultaneously important and harmless.

There are also those who hold what may be called a pragmatic view of the Charter when it comes to lesbian and gay rights. This approach, often espoused by activists and lawyers, suggests that the Charter is a tool or resource to take advantage of if possible – Charter jurisprudence will affect all Canadians and so one should attempt some input into its making.[35] Some operate on the basis that it will be used by 'them' (political opponents) and therefore 'we' ought not to be left out in the cold, while others argue that Charter litigation provides a highly visible forum where political points can be made that resonate far beyond the courtroom.[36]

In explaining the inclusion of sexual orientation in section 15, pragmatists, in contrast to both debunkers and promoters, could insist that this development was both significant and hardly inevitable. In other words, the court's taking 'judicial notice' of lesbian and gay oppression was the result of several decades of struggle and conflict. Far from embracing lesbians and gay men with open arms, capitalist liberal democracies fought these rights movements every step of the way and, to a large extent, still do. Neither liberalism nor capitalism requires the extension of sexual-orientation rights.

While some pragmatic activists may believe that the acquisition of rights is not the 'be it and end all' of liberation, most would likely view the inclusion of lesbians and gay men within existing rights regimes as necessary first steps. Some may agree, with the debunkers, that these rights are not going to resolve class antagonisms, but few would discount their importance in terms of the regulation of sexuality. Finally, most pragmatists would not see lesbian and gay rights as simply facilitating the maintenance of the economic status quo, or, being committed to that status quo, would approve of such effects.

There is still at least one more perspective – that of social (and legal) reactionaries who deplore what they perceive to be the fragmentation of social life resulting from the pursuit of individual self-interest. A 'rights-seeking' society epitomizes, for them, increasing cultural decay. For these 'new reactionaries,' public institutions, including governments and courts, have fallen into the hands of radical groups intent on reshaping society in their own image.

Lesbians and gay men, according to many of these writers, have become, together with 'women,' one of the most powerful interest groups in social life.[37] According to James Dobson and Gary Bauer, two activists of the American Christian Right, 'today there are few political and social movements as aggressive, powerful, or successful as "gay rights" advocates.'[38] Similarly, Rainer Knopff and F.L. Morton, in their analysis of the Charter's effects in Canada, have written that 'more than any other interest group, Canadian feminists have done their homework and are poised to advance their policy objectives.'[39] In this view, governments have become 'emasculated'[40] and policy-making power has shifted to undemocratic institutions, with disastrous consequences.

In Canada the Charter is viewed as a chief culprit in this process – encouraging minority rule rather than representative democracy. Knopff and Morton, for example, argue that the Charter has encouraged 'interest groups' to pursue their own, anti-majoritarian ends and that the courts have been, unfortunately in their view, responsive. Many of those who oppose women's and gay rights agree. Knopff and Morton's thesis is that a 'court party' has evolved – a new undemocratic mechanism for furthering substantive, liberal social reforms: 'Historically the "court party" rallied around the "court" of the king (the executive branch) in opposition to the power of democratic legislatures. Today the new court party's undemocratic vehicle is the judiciary. The modern court party includes not only ... "citizen" interest groups ... but also important elements within state bureaucracies, law schools, the broader intellectual community, and the media.'[41]

Some reactionaries attempt to reclaim the liberal ground by arguing that 'true' liberalism requires parliamentary process, not substantive social change through government apathy and judicial fiat. Morton suggests that the Charter has encouraged the 'moral tyranny' of minorities; this, he argues, is the antithesis of liberalism.

When groups claim their cause is the 'moral equivalent of war,' democracy and the rule of law are in for trouble. The 'moral majority' is usually singled out as the culprit of this kind of self-righteous intolerance. But what about the 'moral minority'? Does the fact that moral views are strongly held by a minority (rather than a majority) give them any more right to impose their preferred policies on the rest of society in the name of 'rights'?

Moral zealotry is not a monopoly of majorities or minorities, of the right or the left. In whatever form, it is the enemy of liberal democracy. Liberal democracy was born in the eighteenth century largely to combat moral zealotry of a religious nature. Religious zealots still exist, but the ideological carnage of the twentieth century suggests that we have far more to fear from zealots devoted to secular causes.[42]

While Morton notes that 'the Charter hardly threatens us with such calamities,' he does blame it for fostering an environment in which government rules by 'edict and coercion rather than by conversation and persuasion.'[43] These remarks sit uncomfortably with the notion, expressed by Knopff and Morton in *Charter Politics*, that governments have abdicated all responsibility to the courts; nevertheless, according to their viewpoint, the uncontested inclusion of sexual orientation in section 15 could be seen as yet another proof that the Canadian state had lost its direction, its will, and its understanding of its own heritage.

The reactionaries, like the pragmatic activists, regard lesbians and gay men as powerful agents of substantive change. For the rights activists, successful developments followed years of demoralizing defeat: movements and organizations were built and nurtured, and alliances were painfully constructed and carefully sustained, with lives literally lost in the process. Reactionaries, no doubt, would agree with some of this. Indeed, aside from disputing that lesbians and gay men were 'oppressed,' which is a different issue, the reactionaries would depart from the above description only in measuring levels of 'power.' For many lesbians and gay men, much work still remains – the 'victories' are fragile and often momentary, opponents are active, and 'the state,' far from being a passive servant to lesbian and gay desires, remains a formidable obstacle to further extension and implementation of rights. But, according to the reactionaries, this is far from the truth. For them, lesbians, gay men, and also feminists are *the* most powerful groups in society at the present time. They have fought, and they have won, or, in the words of one Christian activist, 'they are driving for final victory.'[44] Liberal philosophy has been perverted, and democratic values subverted, by the new 'cultural elite.'

To summarize, it would seem that debunkers and reactionaries share the view that the Charter is a fundamentally anti-democratic and fragmenting force. However, their reasons for this conclusion differ wildly. According to the debunkers, legal form and institutions are creatures of capital – not only will no positive change come from the pursuit of constitutional rights but such endeavours actually inhibit struggle where it could count. The reactionaries, on the other hand, insist that the Charter *is* being used as an instrument of social change by powerful interest groups.

The theme of fragmentation runs deep within both the debunker and reactionary approaches. However, they have starkly different ideas as to content and process. According to many debunkers, capital proffers rights documents which fragment working-class solidarity; the reactionaries, on the other hand, find that a Devlinesque 'seamless web' is fragmented by interest-group rights-seeking. These positions are paradoxically similar, yet irreconcilable.

Rights promoters agree, with the reactionaries, that the Charter's potential is enormous. This potential, however, must be realized in allowing the Charter to take its natural course – making a substantive difference in the lives of 'disadvantaged people.' This, they suggest, would fulfil the promise of liberalism and be profoundly democratic. The reactionaries, of course, warn that the Charter's potential is something quite different – the facilitation of fragmentation, isolation, and national anomie.

Pragmatic activists stand somewhere off to the side of these debates. Fed up with the slow pace and unfulfilled promise of 'democratic process,' they view the Charter as a potential short cut to achieving the goals of social movements. Many are critical of the strategies of rights activists, yet their view is that the Charter is not going away, it will be used, gains are possible, and mistakes will be learned from. Most would find both the debunkers' pessimism and the promoters' optimism too extreme, but in the case of lesbian and gay rights activists, they would tend to concur more with the optimists. Many rights activists, in conformity with the reactionaries' caricature of them, do perceive themselves to have achieved a great deal in 'Charterland.'

Assessing the Effects of Inclusion

In responding to elements of the debunker critique, I will address two separate points.[45] Are social movements putting all their eggs in the Charter basket? And do Charter challenges pose a threat to more substantive social struggles generally, particularly those directed at the distribution of wealth?

With regard to the first of these questions, there is little indication that social movements are turning to Charter litigation at the expense of other strategies. When I began my research on lesbian and gay movements, I was nearly convinced that 'rights' were being uncritically pursued to the exclusion of everything else. Quickly, however, it became clear that this was not the case.

In Canada 'rights' were fought for by lesbian and gay organizations from the early 1960s.[46] A 'rights movement' thus existed alongside and interwoven among other strands of lesbian and gay politics – community-building, cultural activities, left and feminist activism, service provision, and a host of other things. The Charter has not changed any of this; constitutional litigation has simply been added to the range of activities pursued by different sectors of diverse and vibrant lesbian and gay movements. In questioning an uncritical approach to social-movement activity, Glasbeek has written that while 'movement can be forward, it can also be lateral, circular or backward.'[47] On one level, Glasbeek is correct; only rarely is 'movement' merely one of these things at any one time. In other words, the activities of social movements, including ones based on economic class, can have unpredictable, contradictory, and, ultimately, chaotic effects in the long term – particularly when different sectors are engaged in different sorts of struggles.

The matter of whether rights strategies actually facilitate the entrenchment of ruling class power is a different question. I am not sure if or how this is measurable. A key point made by the debunkers is that the Charter, because it does not directly constrain the activities of private actors but can only be used to challenge legislation, encourages people to identify the 'state' as the enemy. Private, corporate power is left untouched; indeed, business is actually able to claim rights under the Charter while not being subject to its provisions. This entrenchment of the public/private divide is viewed, particularly by economistic critics, as a fundamental obstacle to any transformative potential the Charter might otherwise have had.

Yet, in the case of lesbian and gay rights, how valid is this critique? First, it has become clear that private actors are bound indirectly by the equality provisions in the Charter – not least through constitutional challenges to human-rights legislation. The *Leshner* case, in which an Ontario tribunal found that the definition of 'spouse' in the Human Rights Code contravened the Charter, is an example. Although the defendant in the case was the Ontario government, the tribunal's decision theoretically also affects private business, which is subject to the Code's provisions.[48] Furthermore, the constitutional recognition of sexual orientation as a legitimate ground filters through society symbolically, possibly encouraging private actors to 'come on board.' And, as I have argued elsewhere, lesbian and gay legal challenges also have the potential to reveal the inauthenticity of the nuclear family ideal; in this way, Charter cases can be used to challenge one of society's most prized 'private' possessions.[49]

The power of the debunker perspective lies not, I think, in those elements of its critique which scoff at those who advocate rights, nor in its assertion that 'shop floor struggles' are being subverted by the strategies they pursue. Rather, the perspective is important for two reasons. First, it insists that economic *transformation* is the key to economic *justice* for the vast majority of people.

All too often, rights-seeking strategies are divorced from socialist values and the redistributive principles they imply. The economistic critics remind people, and many of us unfortunately need reminding, not so much that the pursuit of constitutional rights must not be a substitute for other forms of struggle (we know this already), but that an analysis of capital and class is as relevant as it ever was.

Second, debunkers are among the few to offer a sustained and vigorous analysis of why one should not look to courts and judges for social justice. In other words, the rights debunkers explain, persuasively I think, that courts are not 'neutral arbiters'; on the contrary, they exist within a state structure and operate under all of the constraints appropriate to their role – namely, facilitating the reproduction, rather than the subversion, of the status quo.[50] Though the debunkers overstate their case, their intervention is nevertheless an important one.

Useful points are also made by the liberal-rights promoters. Lorenne Clark argues that liberalism 'contains within itself principles which give it the ability to transcend some of its more objectionable presuppositions and to find new and different contexts for valid principles whose past instantiations have not only outlived their usefulness but have become real impediments to both liberty and equality.'[51] In this view, liberalism has something to offer – its fluid capacity to expand and reconstitute itself into new forms that recognize 'new' realities. There seems to be some historical evidence for thinking so, and while some may say that this is a particularly insidious feature of liberalism, one could in contrast view it as a strength. Consequently, I have some sympathy with Clark's view, particularly in the face of an economistic critique which often seems unable to display similar openness.

Yet, in discussing the Charter's potential, the rights promoters clearly pay insufficient attention to the constraints within which Charter adjudication takes place. Here, the materialist debunker critique provides a necessary dose of realism. Further, it is worth noting another problem with liberal politics. Liberals are particularly interested in maintaining the perceived fairness and neutrality of liberalism itself. When formal exclusions become obvious and unsupportable within liberal discourse (this takes time and struggle), they must be remedied. It is when faced with the potential *effects* of adding new grounds to lists that they may retreat.

For example, it is one thing to say that you support 'equal rights for lesbians and gays'; it is quite another to champion lesbians' and gay mens' right to foster and adopt children. The backlash over so-called 'political correctness' is a case in point; while the outcry neatly dovetails with conservative political agendas, many of the outraged are actually liberals pushed beyond their limits.[52] Lesbian and gay claims under the Charter to 'spousal' benefits, as well as the right to become 'spouses,' may be 'one bridge too far' even for those sympathetic to the extension of formal guarantees.

But does *any* legal recognition of lesbian and gay rights imply the disintegration of gender and, as a necessary corollary, 'the family'? This is the claim made by the new reactionaries – particularly conservative, evangelical Christian activists.[53] For them, substantive shifts in social values are currently taking place in North American society and 'homosexual activists' are leading the way. Charter reactionaries, such as Knopff and Morton, ultimately make the same argument, although in less apocalyptic language. The 'court party' that they identify bears a striking resemblance to right-wing Christian constructions of the 'secular humanist conspiracy.'

Are the effects of including sexual orientation under section 15 worthy of these descriptions? Yes and no. Reactionaries are correct in thinking that lesbian and gay movements have had a significant impact on the development of social policy in the last decades of the twentieth century. These movements (including HIV/AIDS activism), together with women's movements, have been both at the forefront of social struggle and, as a result, key recipients of new extensions of rights. As a consequence of many years of struggle for recognition, lesbians and gay men were able to persuade decision makers that they have historically suffered discrimination which must now be redressed. But their 'success' is still in its infancy – in Canada, with one exception (Quebec), lesbian and gay statutory and constitutional rights did not exist until the late 1980s. To suggest, as some reactionaries do, that lesbians and gay men have 'taken over' public bodies seems fatuous; it does appear, however, that change in this area is now happening at an exponential, rather than incremental, rate – although, recently, it has provoked an increasing backlash.[54]

Governments and courts, when presented with the rights demands of lesbians and gay men, can no longer, at least publicly, deride and dismiss them. Legal liberalism, which once sought to criminalize and punish homosexuality out of existence, now holds itself up (albeit precariously) as a protector of lesbian and gay rights. The quiet acceptance of sexual orientation as an analogous ground was partly a result of this conjunction between the 'new power' of lesbian and gay movements and the relative responsiveness of the liberal paradigm to new demands.

But there was, no doubt, more to it than this. Other factors surely played a role, including: the 'pro-family' lobby not having, at that time, sufficiently turned its energies towards fighting lesbians and gay men in the courts;[55] the Department of Justice being to some extent, influenced by its more liberal members; and the government itself having given, at that time, little thought to the long-term implications of including sexual orientation under section 15. Disputing the claims of lesbians and gay men to be a 'disadvantaged group' was simply not seen as a significant issue, partly because it was unclear what the implications of inclusion might be. In other words, liberals themselves may have trusted too much that liberal law reforms were relatively meaningless gestures.[56]

Conclusion

My own view is that the Charter's potential depends on who is claiming what and why. Clearly, the economistic critics are correct to argue that the Charter cannot be deployed to undermine corporate power. Similarly, there is little evidence that any dents have been made in institutional racism in the wake of the Charter's advent. Yet there is some indication that the Charter can be used to challenge or at least highlight other forms of power, including, perhaps, that which exists between women and men. What is needed is a comparative analysis – one that examines what different groups have achieved, or not, and why. Contrasting the struggles of these groups with those of similar movements in countries which lack constitutional rights would also be helpful.

From my own research on lesbian and gay rights I would suggest an approach to the Charter *in this area* that I term 'critical pragmatism.' The Charter is here to stay and social actors do have some power to shape its effects; yet those considering using the Charter as a 'tool for change' must consider questions beyond those of how best to win immediate rights. Some ways of conducting Charter challenges are 'better' or 'more progressive' than others, and all forms of social struggle need to be self-reflexive.[57]

And so the Charter may offer different strokes to different folks. For example, the constraints of class interest may not determine how courts respond to some demands in the field of sexuality, while liberal possibilities may be sharply diminished when claims impinge upon economic ordering. But to say that the economic order may not be fundamentally challenged by Charter litigation is *not* to say that Charter litigation is therefore 'bad.'

Understanding the interaction between constitutional rights and social change is not an easy task; the effects of rights documents are complex, contradictory, and, in many respects, unpredictable. The Charter perspectives that I have discussed all pose important questions. And each, like pieces of an analytic jigsaw, contributes a partial and necessary explanatory element. At the same time, no one approach by itself completes the picture.

Notes

1 See, for example, *Re Public Service Employees Relations Act*, [1987] 1 S.C.R. 313; *PSAC v. R.*, [1987] 1 S.C.R. 424; *R.W.D.S.U. v. Sask.*, [1987] 1 S.C.R. 460.
2 For instance: *Hunter v. Southam* [1984], 11 D.L.R. (4th) 641; *Edwards v. R.* [1986], 30 C.C.C. (3d) 385.
3 See, for example, Joel Bakan, 'Constitutional Interpretation and Social Change: You Can't Always Get What You Want (Nor What You Need),' *Canadian Bar Review*, vol. 70 (1991), 307, and 'Strange Expectations: A Review of Two Theories of Judicial Review,' *McGill Law Journal*, vol. 35 (1990), 439; Judy Fudge and Harry Glasbeek, 'The Politics of Rights: A Politics With Little Class,' *Social and Legal Studies*, vol. 1 (1991), 45; Harry Glasbeek, 'A No-Frills Look at the Charter of Rights and Freedoms or How Politicians and Lawyers Hide Reality,' *Windsor Yearbook of Access to Justice*, vol. 9 (1989), 293, and 'From Constitutional Rights to "Real" Rights – "R-i-g-hts Fo-or-wa-ard Ho"!?,' ibid., vol. 10 (1990), 468; Harry Glasbeek and Michael Mandel, 'The Legalization of Politics in Advanced Capitalism: The Canadian Charter of Rights and Freedoms,' *Socialist Studies/ Etudes Socialistes*, vol. 2 (1984), 84; Michael Mandel, *The Charter of Rights and the Legalization of Politics in Canada* (Toronto: Wall and Thompson 1989).
4 For different accounts, see Penny Kome, *The Taking of Twenty-Eight* (Toronto: Women's Press 1983); Judy Fudge, 'The Effect of Entrenching a Bill of Rights upon Political Discourse: Feminist Demands and Sexual Violence in Canada,' *International Journal of Sociology of Law*, vol. 17 (1989), 445.
5 See *Andrews v. Law Society*, [1989] 1 S.C.R. 143; *R v. Turpin*, [1989] 1 S.C.R. 1296.
6 See Gwen Brodsky and Shelagh Day, *Canadian Charter Equality Rights For Women: One Step Forward or Two Steps Back?* (Ottawa: Canadian Advisory Council on the Status of Women 1989); Lorenne M.G. Clark, 'Liberalism and the Living-Tree: Women, Equality, and the Charter,' *Alberta Law Review*, vol. 28 (1990), 384; Kathleen E. Mahoney, 'The Constitutional Law of Equality in Canada,' *New York University Journal of Law and Politics*, vol. 24 (1992), 759; N. Colleen Sheppard, 'Recognition of the Disadvantaging of Women: The Promise of *Andrews v. Law Society of British Columbia*,' *McGill Law Journal*, vol. 35 (1989), 207.
7 Rainer Knopff and F.L. Morton, *Charter Politics* (Scarborough: Nelson Canada 1992); F.L. Morton, *Morgentaler v. Borowski: Abortion, the Charter and the Courts* (Toronto: McClelland and Stewart 1992). See also Rainer Knopff, *Human Rights and Social Technology: The New War on Discrimination* (Ottawa: Carleton University Press 1989); and *Constitutionalism, Citizenship and Society in Canada*,

eds. Alan Cairns and Cynthia Williams (Toronto: University of Toronto Press 1985).

8 See also T.C. Pocklington, 'Some Drawbacks of the Politics of Constitutional Rights,' *Constitutional Forum*, vol. 2 (1991), 43; Peter Russell, 'On Standing Up for Notwithstanding,' in *Contemporary Political Issues*, eds. Mark Charlton and Paul Barker (Scarborough: Nelson Canada 1991).

9 In *Rights of Passage: Struggles for Lesbian and Gay Legal Equality* (Toronto: University of Toronto Press 1994) I explore the relationship between legal struggle and the lesbian and gay rights movement at a more general level. Here, I extend that analysis to focus upon the Charter specifically.

10 This was the theme of one early Charter case, *Andrews v. Ont. (Min. of Health)* [1988], 49 D.L.R. (4th) 584. I discuss this further in 'Are We Family?: Lesbian Rights and Women's Liberation,' *Osgoode Hall Law Journal*, vol. 28 (1990), 789.

11 *Bd. of Gov. v. Sask. Hum. Rts. Comm.*, [1976] 3 W.W.R. 385; *Vogel v. Manitoba* [1983], 4 C.H.R.R. D/1654.

12 For a review of this history, see my *Rights of Passage*, ch. 2.

13 *Andrews v. Law Society*.

14 Arnold Bruner, 'Sexual Orientation and Equality Rights,' in *Equality Rights and the Canadian Charter of Rights and Freedoms*, eds. Anne Bayefsky and Mary Eberts (Toronto: Carswell 1985), 457; Philip Girard, 'Sexual Orientation As a Human Rights Issue in Canada, 1969–1985,' *Dalhousie Law Journal*, vol. 10 (1986), 267; James Jefferson, 'Gay Rights and the Charter,' *University of Toronto Faculty Review*, vol. 43 (1985), 70; Margaret Leopold and Wendy King, 'Compulsory Heterosexuality, Lesbians, and the Law: The Case For Constitutional Protection,' *Canadian Journal of Women and the Law*, vol. 1 (1985), 163; Bruce Ryder, 'Equality Rights and Sexual Orientation: Confronting Heterosexual Family Privilege,' *Canadian Journal of Family Law*, vol. 9 (1990), 39 (written subsequent to the first section 15 cases).

15 *Veysey v. Corr. Serv. of Cda* [1989], 29 F.T.R. 74.

16 Ibid.

17 *Veysey v. Canada*, [1990] 109 N.R. 300.

18 *Brown v. B.C. (Min. of Health)* [1990], 42 B.C.L.R. (2d) 294.

19 *Knodel v. B.C. (Med. Serv. Comm.)* [1991], 58 B.C.L.R. (2d) 356.

20 *Haig v. Canada* [1992], 9 O.R. 495 at 501.

21 *Egan v. Canada* [1993] [unreported].

22 Glasbeek, 'From Constitutional Rights,' 473.

23 See Fudge and Glasbeek, 'The Politics of Rights.' See also Ellen Meiksins Wood, *The Retreat from Class: A New 'True' Socialism* (London: Verso 1986).

24 Glasbeek, 'From Constitutional Rights,' 487.

25 Glasbeek, 'No frills,' 341.
26 In 'Beyond the Rights Debate,' *Social and Legal Studies*, vol. 2 (1993), 25, I offered several arguments against this view that I only touch upon later in this essay.
27 I do not consider in this essay the views of those who advocate rights from a left-wing perspective. I have done this elsewhere: see 'Beyond the Rights Debate' and *Rights of Passage*, ch. 4. Here, I explore the approaches of those who identify themselves as 'liberal.'
28 Richard Mohr, *Gays/Justice: A Study of Ethics, Society, and Law* (New York: Columbia University Press 1988), 5. See also Evelyn Kallen, *Label Me Human: Minority Rights of Stigmatized Canadians* (Toronto: University of Toronto Press 1989).
29 Mahoney, 'Constitutional Law of Equality,' 761; however, for a less enthusiastic evaluation of similar cases, see Diana Majury, 'Equality and Discrimination According to the Supreme Court of Canada,' *Canadian Journal of Women and Law*, vol. 4 (1990–1), 407.
30 See, for example, David Beatty, *Talking Heads and the Supremes: The Canadian Production of Constitutional Review* (Toronto: Carswell 1990) and 'A Conservative's Court: The Politicization of Law,' *University of Toronto Law Journal*, vol. 41 (1991), 147; Patrick Monahan, 'Judicial Review and Democracy: A Theory of Judicial Review,' *University of British Columbia Law Journal*, vol. 21 (1987), 87.
31 Clark, 'Liberalism and the Living-Tree,' 389–90.
32 Ibid., 395; see also Beatty, *Talking Heads*.
33 Wood, *Retreat from Class*, 199.
34 See my *Rights of Passage*, ch. 3.
35 See, for example, Gwen Brodsky's comments in my 'Beyond the Rights Debate.'
36 See comments by Brian Mossop and Ken Popert in my *Rights of Passage*, ch. 4.
37 The fury over 'political correctness' also ties neatly into these understandings.
38 James Dobson and Gary Bauer, *Children at Risk: The Battle for the Hearts and Minds of Our Kids* (Dallas: Word Publishing 1990), 107. For a much fuller discussion of the Canadian Christian right, see my *Rights of Passage*, chs. 5 and 6. See also my *The Antigay Agenda: Orthodox Vision and the Christian Right* (Chicago: University of Chicago Press 1997).
39 Knopff and Morton, *Charter Politics*, 29.
40 I use this word quite deliberately.
41 Knopff and Morton, *Charter Politics*, 79.
42 Morton, *Morgentaler v. Borowski*, 320.
43 Ibid.
44 Dobson and Bauer, *Children at Risk*, 109.

45 In 'Beyond the Rights Debate,' I considered others.

46 For a brief review of this history, see my *Rights of Passage*, ch. 2.

47 Glasbeek, 'From Constitutional Rights,' 492.

48 The 'private sector' in Ontario was well aware of *Leshner*'s potential. See, for example, the briefing paper 'Ontario Human Rights Board of Inquiry Decision on Extension of Pension Benefits to Same-Sex Spouses,' prepared by the Toronto law firm Osler, Hoskin and Harcourt, 1992; L. Hurst, 'Fighting the Gay Fight: Will Ruling on Gay Spouses Open Door to Widespread Changes in Family Law?' Toronto *Star,* 13 Sept. 1992.

49 See my *Rights of Passage*, afterword.

50 See Bakan, 'Strange Expectations.'

51 Clark, 'Liberalism and the Living-Tree,' 387.

52 Unfortunately, too many Marxists have also jumped on the backlash bandwagon, thereby also confirming *their* disinterest in and indeed hostility to what they define as non-class-based, anti-discriminatory measures.

53 See my *Rights of Passage*, ch. 5.

54 Witness recent attempts to repeal pro-gay-rights legislation in several American states.

55 This has changed. See my *Rights of Passage*, ch. 6.

56 The federal government has subsequently been more careful. In introducing a sexual-orientation amendment to the Canadian Human Rights Act in 1992, the justice minister simultaneously made a concession to Tory backbenchers by adding a new restrictive 'marital status' definition to the act. Clearly, the Tory right mobilized more effectively in this instance than at the time of the section 15 inclusion. For a discussion of right-wing factionalism and the development of anti-gay legislation in Britain, see Davina Cooper and Didi Herman, 'Getting the Family "Right": Legislating Heterosexuality in Britain, 1986–1990,' *Canadian Journal of Family Law*, vol. 10 (1991), 45.

57 I develop this point further in 'The Politics of Law Reform: Lesbian and Gay Rights Struggles into the 1990s,' in *Activating Theory*, eds. J. Bristow and A. Wilson (London: Lawrence and Wishart 1993).

7

Rights, Nationalism, and Social Movements in Canadian Constitutional Politics*

JOEL BAKAN and MICHAEL SMITH

The Charlottetown Accord was defeated in a national referendum on 26 October 1992, an event that marked the end of a constitutional-amendment process designed in part to address some of the contradictions of Canadian nationhood.[1] The idea of a Canadian nation, founded as it is on seldom acknowledged histories of conquest and colonialism, has long been vulnerable to competing claims of nationhood from First Nations and Quebec. Historically, Quebec nationalism was minimally accommodated through the creation in 1867 of a federal system that provided Quebec, along with the other provinces, some measure of political autonomy; First Nations nationalism, on the other hand, was constitutionally denied and brutally repressed. Today, Quebec and First Nations nationalism are substantial factors in Canadian politics. The Charlottetown Accord attempted to accommodate them in the Canadian constitution by modifying Canada's federal political system, which currently recognizes two basic socio-political units: federal and provincial.[2] The accord would have gone some way towards adding a third unit, First Nations, and thus used the federal structure as a vehicle for constitutionalizing First Nations self-government. It would have also affected the regime under which political authority is currently distributed among existing units, breaching the underlying principle of formal equality among the provinces by recognizing Quebec as a 'distinct society.' Overall the accord would have adapted Canadian federalism to recognize (albeit in limited terms) First Nations and Quebec as collective entities

* The authors wish to thank the following people for commenting upon earlier drafts: John Borrows, Susan Boyd, Davina Cooper, Robin Elliot, Avigail Eisenberg, Didi Herman, Nitya Iyer, Marlee Kline, Patrick Macklem, Wes Pue, David Schneiderman, and Lynn Smith. This work was supported by a Humanities and Social Sciences Grant (UBC) and by the Centre for Constitutional Studies at the University of Alberta. A version of this piece appears in *Social and Legal Studies.*

defined in terms of histories, languages, and cultures different from those of the majority of people in Canada.

Earlier constitutional changes in 1982 provide an important background for understanding those proposed by the Charlottetown Accord in 1992. In 1982 a regime of individual rights and freedoms, the Canadian Charter of Rights and Freedoms,[3] became part of the 'supreme law of Canada.'[4] It recognized universal equality rights, fundamental freedoms (such as expression and association), and rights to life, liberty, and security of the person; and it explicitly imposed obligations upon federal and provincial governments and legislatures (including the National Assembly and government of Quebec) to act consistently with those rights. Quebec opposed the Charter from the start as a general limitation on the collective power of the Quebec 'nation' and, more specifically, as an attempt by the federal government to deepen the protection of anglophone language rights in Quebec.[5] The then sovereigntist government of Quebec refused to assent to the Charter's entrenchment in the Canadian constitution,[6] but this did not stop the Liberal federal government of Pierre Trudeau from proceeding with entrenchment. The Charter was thus imposed on the province of Quebec, a source of continuing resentment among Quebec nationalists. The difficulties raised by the Charter for Quebec nationalists apply with equal, if not greater, force in relation to First Nations. Both Quebec and First Nations nationalists resent the Charter's imposition of *Canadian* national standards that potentially constrain the political autonomy of their respective 'nations.' For First Nations this is exacerbated by the cultural specificity of the Charter's liberal concepts, ones firmly rooted in European political traditions often incompatible with those of First Nations.[7] Many people within the First Nations self-government movement argued on these bases during recent constitutional debates that the Charter should not apply to First Nations governments. The Charlottetown Accord responded to Quebec and First Nations concerns about the Charter by including provisions that would have imposed restrictions on the Charter's application to policies of Quebec or First Nations governments designed to preserve and promote those societies' languages, cultures, and traditions.

Though the reasons for the failure of the accord in the referendum are complex, the outcome was hailed in dominant media narratives as a watershed for Canadian democracy – an historical moment when the vast majority of 'ordinary Canadians' abandoned their habitual political quiescence to deliver a resounding 'No' to Canada's 'elites,' despite the latters' apocalyptic forecasts of the consequences of rejecting the accord. The people had prevailed over their governments and a new era of Canadian politics had begun: politicians now had to earn, rather than take for granted, the trust of the electorate. A central part of this story involved the provisions in the accord relating to the Charter's application to Quebec and First Nations governments. Throughout the campaign leading up to the referendum one of the most often-heard arguments on the 'No' side was that the accord threatened to undermine Charter rights and freedoms. This concern came to shape the very terms of debate about the accord, and its final defeat was widely hailed as a victory for people's rights.

This essay will examine the events surrounding the Charlottetown Accord in light of current debates about the politics of rights.[8] More specifically, we will focus on the constructions within dominant rights ideology of the rights strategies of two organizations, the Native Women's Association of Canada (NWAC) and the National Action Committee on the Status of Women (NAC), during the political commotion that preceded the referendum. Both NWAC and NAC made rights issues important parts of their strategies to defeat the accord. They argued that the accord, if entrenched in the constitution, would override the Charter's equality rights, and they succeeded (at least outside Quebec) in generating opposition to the accord on this basis. Importantly, however, in their support of Charter rights, neither NWAC nor NAC adopted the classical liberal discourses of dominant rights ideology. Each organization's rights claims contained elements different from, and often oppositional to, those of classical liberalism. Yet – and this is the point around which the present discussion is built – those claims were almost invariably presented by the media and punditry as supporting a developing 'consensus' against the accord that drew upon elements of classical liberalism: individualism, suspicion of governmental and collective power, and formal equality. In describing that process in the second section of this essay (after a general discussion of the 'rights debate' in the first section) we do not mean to suggest that NAC and NWAC were under any illusions regarding the practical mutability of prevailing constructions of rights claims, nor that they failed to derive any positive benefits from their use of rights discourse. Rather, our purpose in focusing on NAC and NWAC is only to illustrate through concrete examples how rights claims are sometimes translated into dominant ideological terms. The essay's third section discusses potential implications of this translation effect for the internal politics of social movements, and the fourth section analyses some of the ideological processes that sustain the dominance of liberal-rights discourse.

The Rights Debate

The 'rights debate' has been an important feature of social and political theory in the last two decades. With the emergence of critical legal studies in the

United States in the 1970s, and the earlier revitalization of Marxian analyses of law and rights in other countries, there was a renewal of efforts to evaluate the potential of law, and specifically legal rights, to achieve progressive political aims. More recently, critics of rights have themselves been criticized by progressive people for their denigration of rights strategies. Many activists and scholars draw upon the campaign for civil rights and the experience of other progressive organizing to argue that rights discourse, especially when analysed beyond the narrow frame of litigation, has had important and positive effects for social movements. Such responses to the 'rights critique' arguably mark a shift in the discursive terrain on which debates about rights are conducted. Analysts of rights now often focus less on the capacity of litigation to advance specific political goals and more on the role of rights discourse in influencing the terrain, tactics, and balance of forces in the political field itself.[9] In their work, the equation of rights strategies with litigation tactics has been displaced by a more complex understanding: rights are not just inert tools that can be used by social movements to advance their causes through litigation; rather, they actively structure the very nature of political struggle.[10] Moreover, rights discourse is understood as an important, and unique, political language because of its universal form and presumptive validity in liberal-democratic societies. It is 'hegemonic' in two senses: first, it elevates particular claims to the 'plane of the universal,'[11] and second, it is a dominant form, perhaps *the* dominant form, of political discourse in western capitalist states such as Canada.[12] Rights discourse is also 'indeterminate,' its elements unstable and thus open to reinterpretation. The combination of hegemony and indeterminacy, rights advocates claim, gives rights discourse a unique capacity to mobilize social movements, affirm marginalized identities, and attract support for progressive goals in the wider community.

We agree with rights advocates that expressing social-movement positions in rights language may have these kinds of effects. However, we think it is important to examine the *nature* of these processes – *what* is actually symbolized, mobilized, or affirmed when rights strategies are used in specific contexts?[13] This is the general question we will address in the following analysis of the politics surrounding the Charlottetown Accord. Central to our argument is the idea that in any time and place reinterpretive work with rights discourse occurs within a context of dominant ideological discourses of rights (hereinafter 'dominant rights ideology').[14] Chief among the elements of dominant rights ideology in Canada (and other western capitalist societies) today are the liberal discourses of anti-collectivism and formal equality. The first of these, anti-collectivism, is apparent in the representation of rights as protecting individuals (sometimes groups) from interference by the 'collective' (primarily the state and its institutions) in their private affairs. Following from this, state regulation, not the oppressive and exploitative social relations and institutions of the so-called 'private' sector, is viewed as the primary threat to human liberty and equality. Formal equality, a second and related element of dominant rights ideology, represents social actors as abstract equals, thus erasing structural forms of domination and subordination – between men and women, capital and labour, heterosexuals and lesbians and gays, whites and people of colour. Anti-collectivism and formal equality, it should be emphasized, are not essential to rights discourse. Their status as dominant rights ideology depends upon the history and geography in which they are embedded (a point we will return to below), not some 'truth' about what a right is or should be.

Rights discourse, being wider in scope than dominant rights ideology, is open to progressive interpretations that reject anti-collectivism and formal equality. This point lies at the heart of arguments for the use of rights strategies by progressive social movements. Such arguments correctly point out that rights discourse can accommodate collective rights,[15] communal rights,[16] rights as sites of dialogue,[17] and social rights,[18] and that it can be opened up to include historically subordinated identities and groups. There remains, however, the difficulty that the rights claims of social movements, despite their progressive, even radical, intentions and interpretations, may be absorbed into and limited by dominant rights ideology. Didi Herman illustrates this point with her account of the public debate in Ontario around Bill 7, an amendment to human-rights legislation concerning sexual orientation, in which the construction of gay and lesbian identities through rights discourse yielded a formal equality construction of sexual identity and excluded other perspectives.[19] The effect, according to Herman, was to reinforce the assumption that gays and lesbians are abnormal members of an immutable sexual minority.[20] In similar terms, Kim Crenshaw has demonstrated how the use of rights strategies by African-Americans, while working to their benefit in attacking formal inequality, has served to 'absorb, redefine and limit the[ir] language of protest.'[21] More particularly, it has helped legitimate the material subordination of African-Americans by creating 'an ideological framework that makes the present conditions facing underclass blacks appear fair and reasonable.'[22]

Herman and Crenshaw concur with those who suggest that rights strategies mobilize social actors and affirm marginalized identities. Yet they remain ambivalent about rights, largely because their work also reveals how the effects of these processes – *what* is actually mobilized and affirmed – can sometimes be politically problematic. In their analyses the reinterpretation process appears as a two-way street: alongside the potential gains to social movements of progressive rights strategies exists the difficulty that the channelling effects of dominant rights ideology may engender regressive and narrow interpretations of social-movement politics and positions. This is what happened, we argue, to the rights claims of NWAC and NAC during the period leading up to the referendum on the Charlottetown Accord.

Two points are in order before we proceed with our argument. First, the relationship between dominant rights ideology and the other discourses, ideologies, and political cleavages that constellated around the accord is a complicated one. We will suggest that dominant rights ideology produced certain effects in the political struggle over the accord, but we do not mean to imply that it determined, on its own, the course of events. Rather, it operated through complicated interactions with ideologies inherent in unequal social relations of race, gender, class, and so on; and, to that extent, our analysis of rights discourse explains only one aspect – albeit an important one – of the political anatomy of Charlottetown.[23] Secondly, throughout the following discussion we will rely upon an account of 'common sense' ideas about certain features of the accord that developed outside First Nations and Quebec. That account is based upon our experience of events as they unfolded as well as subsequent analysis of the print-media coverage. We are aware that any attempt to identify a coherent 'common sense' involves selection and interpretation and hence is bound to eliminate some of the complexity of multifaceted political phenomena. Nevertheless, we are reasonably confident that we have captured how the public debate about the accord was shaped by the elements of dominant rights ideology.

Social Movements, Rights Ideology, and the Charlottetown Accord

The fate of the accord is referrable to the tension between federalism, with its collectivist orientation, and dominant rights ideology's suspicion of collective power and blindness to social inequality. As the referendum campaign progressed, the perceived clash between the Charter's individual rights and the (arguably quite minimal) collective powers gained by Quebec and First Nations in the accord became a – if not *the* – central point of contention. Most interesting for our purposes is the way the concerns of the 'No' side were regularly expressed through the discursive elements of dominant rights ideology. These elements were soon firmly entrenched, intransigent, and effective in popular discourse, serving not only to foreclose inconsistent discursive alternatives within the debate but also to articulate the claims and identities of various oppositional movements in their terms. Most notable was the manner in which the relationship among individual rights (women's equality rights being the most discussed example), nationalisms (those of First Nations and

Quebec), and state power was constructed within the traditional liberal framework of dominant rights ideology – individualism, anti-statism, formal equality – in 'common sense' accounts of the accord. The dominant message conveyed by the media (and we will be focusing mainly on print-media accounts) was simple and unequivocal: there is a fundamental contradiction between collective power (especially when harnessed to nationalist politics) and women's equality; and the only way to ensure women's equality, in light of the threat posed to it by collective power, is through the protection of the Charter's individual rights.

The media was persistent, and largely unquestioning, in reporting the 'fact' that the accord threatened individual rights and formal equality by granting collective powers to Quebec and First Nations. 'When collective rights take precedence over individual liberties,' noted former Liberal prime minister Pierre Trudeau in a strategically timed and reverentially reported intervention, 'we see what can happen to people who pretend to live freely in these societies. When the citizen is not equal to all other citizens in the state, we're in the presence of a dictatorship which sets the citizens in a hierarchy based on their beliefs.' Trudeau continued by arguing that the accord would create 'an unacceptable hierarchy of classes of citizens ... threatening the survival of official language minorities and depriving women and racial, ethnic and religious minorities of true equality before the law.'[24] The point was picked up by other liberals, such as Sharon Carstairs (formerly leader of the Manitoba Liberal Party), who decried the 'group-based shopping list we find in the new Canada Clause [which] risks turning the Charter into a hierarchy of claims for rival interests,'[25] and William Johnson, columnist for the Montreal *Gazette*, who was concerned that the accord 'create[d] a hierarchy of rights as a basis of discrimination.'[26]

Such statements usefully illustrate how the various elements of dominant rights ideology were effective in criticizing the accord. Taken on their own, they do not offer much of interest – given the liberal proclivities of their authors, they were predictable. What *is* interesting, however, is that the positions elaborated by Trudeau *et al.* largely reflected the developing 'common sense' about the accord, at least outside Quebec and First Nations communities. Media accounts in particular tended to place strong emphasis on classical liberal themes when describing and analysing the positions of various groups on the accord. Right-wing positions were cast in terms of the potential impact of the self-government proposals and the distinct society clause on individual rights, and the threat posed to formal equality by the so-called 'special status' granted to First Nations and Quebec in the accord.[27] Not dissimilarly, feminist concerns about the impact of 'government rights' (of First Nations and other governments) on the individual equality rights of women, particularly First Nations women, were a primary focus of media attention. To this extent, groups with contradictory political positions were forged – at least within media constructions – into a *de facto* coalition (the 'No side') that opposed the accord because (among other reasons) its conferral of collective powers, whether on First Nations or Quebec, threatened the Charter's rights and freedoms. This construction served to override concerns about the historically unequal power relations, rooted in histories of conquest and colonization, among First Nations, Quebec, and the rest of Canada, and it created a substantial obstacle for those promoting the constitutional recognition of collective powers as necessary for redressing social injustice. Especially significant is the way in which NWAC's and NAC's arguments about rights and the Charter tended to be swept into and represented as part of the liberal 'common sense' despite the fact that these organizations' actual positions often contradicted its central tenets.

Among media and academic pundits, and in political and legal circles more generally, the issue of First Nation women's equality rights quickly became a focal point for opposition to the accord. The accord extended already existing limits on the Charter's application[28] to include the protection of First Nations language, cultures, and traditions, and it granted First Nations governments the power that provincial legislatures and the federal Parliament currently have to enact laws 'notwithstanding' certain provisions of the Charter.[29] NWAC opposed these proposals on the ground that they subordinated the Charter's equality rights to the collectively defined powers of First Nations. It received strong support (and assistance) from non-First Nations pundits and lawyers for this stand. Conspicuously absent from media and other accounts of NWAC's pro-Charter position, however, was any discussion of NWAC's location of the causes of gender inequality in First Nations communities in the colonial policies of the Canadian state. The need for Charter protection of First Nations women in the first place, according to NWAC's position paper, arose because 'the *Indian Act* ha[d] imposed upon [First Nations] a patriarchal system and patriarchal laws which favour men:'[30] 'By 1971, this patriarchal system was so ingrained without [*sic*] our communities, that 'patriarchy' was seen as a 'traditional trait.' In other words, even the memory of our matriarchal forms of government, and our matrilineal forms of descent were forgotten or unacknowledged.'[31] From this perspective, then, First Nations communities are inherently *non*-patriarchal but have been restructured in patriarchal terms through colonization, thus necessitating application of the Charter's equality provisions.

Consistent with this analysis, NWAC's statement supported the constitutional recognition of an inherent right to self-government so long as the Charter applied to First Nations governments.[32]

NWAC's position, with its understanding of patriarchy as a product of colonialism and its support of First Nations self-government, tended to be reduced in mainstream media to the much simpler elements of classical liberal ideology: a clash between the *collective* powers of First Nations polities, construed as intrinsically patriarchal, and the *individual's* right to gender equality – with the only tenable solution lying in the application of the Charter to limit the scope of First Nations self-government. Within this framework, the accord's limitations on the Charter's application to First Nations governments were easily portrayed as dangerous steps towards authoritarianism. Their effect, according to columnist Michelle Lansberg,[33] was to 'cast native women out into the cold,' and the accord thereby represented the 'greatest crisis in civil liberties in Canada since the internment of the Japanese.'[34] In similar spirit, William Johnson noted that, should the accord pass, 'the aboriginal citizens [among them women] will be left relatively powerless before the swollen power of the aboriginal state, sanctioned by the Constitution of Canada.'[35] Such comments indicate a profound distrust of First Nations governments, a sense that, free of Charter constraints, they would wield their collective power against women with impunity. While NWAC's actual position on the accord undoubtedly included elements of such distrust, the mainstream media's obsession with the issue, along with its failure to discuss NWAC's support of self-government and its analysis of patriarchy, seemed to imply what Donna Greschner has referred to as 'the bias of aboriginal patriarchy' – the '[false, pernicious, and racist but nonetheless pervasive] belief in an inherent or irremediable chauvinism of aboriginal men worse than the chauvinism of non-aboriginal men.'[36]

Equally disturbing is the related implication, found throughout media and pundit portrayals of the NWAC challenge, that gender equality and self-government are irreconcilable without the protection of liberal rights. For example, in a widely circulated and reported memorandum a group of Canadian law professors expressed their concern that, in the absence of the Charter, clashes between First Nations traditions and women's equality would be resolved in favour of the former, thus implying that the two are inherently contradictory (a notion belied by NWAC's recognition that the tension between the two is a symptom of colonialism, not something inherent in First Nations).[37] This position, along with the above noted 'bias of aboriginal patriarchy,' not only distorts history but also draws upon and reinforces racist stereotypes of First Nations as lacking a requisite degree of 'civilization' to restore and develop their own conceptions and practices of gender equality. Compounding these tendencies was the view expressed by some pundits that the rejection of rights and the Charter by First Nations organizations was itself a sign of backwardness. Again, according to Weinrib *et al.*: 'The Charter reflects ideas of individual dignity now accepted by a large variety of countries, many of which are neither western or white'[38] – the implication being that First Nations are outside the steady march of progress in the international community. Such views are unfortunate but not surprising. Rights, and liberal notions of law more generally, have often been taken by western observers as indicators of civilization, their absence in a society confirming its status as uncivilized 'other.'[39]

Behind such criticisms of the accord's limitations on the Charter's application to First Nations governments was the further problematic presumption that the Charter is necessary, and even sufficient, for protecting and advancing women's equality. Limitations on the Charter's application were presented in the media as restrictions on women's equality itself, the implication being that the Charter automatically translates into actual equality for women. As one columnist noted in discussing NWAC's position: 'Canadians' equality is protected by the Charter. Anyone who believes they [*sic*] are being discriminated against can go to court, claiming a violation of their [*sic*] Charter rights.'[40] This statement, however naive and unquestioning of liberal ideology, succinctly expresses the common assumption in media accounts that the Charter's application to First Nations governments would have ensured gender equality for First Nations women: and this despite the fact the society in which the Charter *does* apply is fraught with inequality, the causes and effects of which are largely beyond the Charter's judicially determined reach.[41] There is some irony, indeed hypocrisy, in a patriarchal society such as non-First Nations Canada imposing its values (the Charter) on other societies in the name of gender equality – especially when its colonial policies are implicated in creating and perpetuating the inequalities that exist in those societies.[42]

Moving from the First Nations context to more general issues concerning Charter equality rights, we again find the media emphasizing traditional liberal themes. The National Action Committee on the Status of Women had condemned the accord's 'Canada Clause,' an interpretive provision whose enumeration of 'fundamental characteristics' of Canada was designed to guide the application of the accord, the Charter, and other parts of the constitution. Included as 'fundamental characteristics' in the Canada Clause were First Nations self-government, Quebec's distinctiveness as a society, democratic government, official language minorities, equality (for provinces, men, and women and racial and ethnic groups), and respect for individual and collective rights. NAC argued forcefully that the clause would unduly circumscribe judicial interpretations of the Charter's rights and thus undermine its guarantees of equality. Shelagh Day, vice-president of NAC, stated that it would 'claw back rights that were won in 1982,' ones that were still 'new and fragile.'[43] The clause articulated mainly 'government rights' (those relating to First Nations and Quebec governments and the parliamentary system), according to NAC, and failed to affirm as fundamental the individual and group equality rights of the Charter. Moreover, its statements of gender and race equality were weaker than those in the Charter and excluded altogether grounds of discrimination such as religion, age, disability, sexual orientation, and poverty.

The clause therefore created, according to NAC, a 'hierarchy of rights,' placing 'government rights' at the top and equality rights at the bottom: it wrongly conferred rights on governments and obligations on individuals when exactly the opposite was needed. Hence this comment from Day: 'The fundamental characteristic of this country that needs endorsement is not the commitment of residents [private actors], but the commitment of governments to the rights and freedoms in the Charter and to a high standard of protection and promotion of rights.' On its face, NAC's position appears consistent with the liberal suspicion of collective power found in dominant rights ideology, and this is exactly how it most often appeared in the media. NAC, however, is not an adherent of classical liberal ideology. To the contrary, it supports an activist state and the collective empowerment of Quebec and First Nations. Consistent with this, NAC's support of the Charter is premised on a distinctively *non-classical* liberal conception of constitutional rights in which equality provisions should and do impose *positive* obligations on government, ones to take action against poverty and other social disparities, for the benefit of subordinated groups.[44] Understood in this light, NAC's concern about the Canada Clause overriding Charter rights, far from expressing a liberal anxiety about the overbearing state, was clearly motivated by a fear that the clause would in fact *reduce* governmental obligations to support social equality.

Perhaps not surprisingly, these subtleties in NAC's understanding of equality rights did not make their way into most media accounts. NAC's position was instead presented as indistinguishable from and supportive of the developing classical liberal 'consensus' that the accord unduly bolstered the power of government to trample individual rights. Jeffrey Simpson,[45] for example, an influential columnist with the *Globe and Mail* (Canada's self-styled newspaper of record), suggested that Shelagh Day's position on the Canada Clause was no different than that of Pierre Trudeau; it placed her among 'les enfants de Trudeau.' More generally, media reports tended to treat NAC's concerns about women's equality as wrapped up primarily in the Charter issue, separate from its concerns about social equality and programs.[46] At the same time, however,

NAC was probably at least partly responsible for the way its position was portrayed. Its strategists must have known that, by condemning the expansion of collective powers as an illegitimate conferral of 'government rights' and using the phrase 'hierarchy of rights,' NAC risked being misunderstood as endorsing traditional liberal positions. That risk, however, may have been considered worth taking given the power of anti-government themes to attract publicity and media attention.[47]

What conclusions can be drawn from this (admittedly incomplete) discussion of the representation of NAC's and NWAC's rights strategies in relation to the Charlottetown Accord? We began this section by suggesting that certain developments in debates around the accord illustrate how progressive political positions may be absorbed into the dominant ideology of rights and framed in terms which are inconsistent with a social movement's wider political aspirations and positions. Our more general point is that rights strategies do not easily escape the pull of dominant rights ideology. The discourses of dominant rights ideology are powerful exactly because they are embedded in social structures and relations, as are the dominant knowledge-producing institutions, particularly the media, that perpetuate them. In this context, it was perhaps not surprising during the Charlottetown debates to see the issue of women's equality rights constructed in classical liberal terms. The problem is that these terms served, implicitly and sometimes explicitly, to occlude the social and historical determinants of gender inequality, as recognized by NAC and NWAC, and to undermine implicitly the wider political goals of those organizations – such as state activism and self-government.

Dominant Rights Ideology and the Internal Politics of Social Movements

To this point we have focused on the question of how the use of rights by a social movement organization may affect the public, or external, perception of its politics. We want now to take our argument a step farther. Once it is recognized that rights strategies can give a social movement's 'public face' a liberal complexion, questions are raised about the effect this may have on on-going political struggles *within* the movement – particularly those between liberals, whose positions will be consistent with and affirmed by the discourses of dominant rights ideology, and those, such as socialists or nationalists, for whom collectivist values are central. Such concerns about rights strategies are only raised, of course, if political divisions within social movements are acknowledged to exist. There is a tendency in some contemporary writing on social movements to ignore or downplay this possibility. In what follows we will begin by describing this tendency and then, again relying on examples drawn from the Charlottetown Accord debates, link it to some of the difficulties raised by social movements' use of rights strategies.

According to E. Laclau and C. Mouffe, new social movements represent a fundamental break from the politics of the past, with 'new' identities, like race and gender, having emerged out of the ashes of deconstructed 'old' ones, like class. The pursuit of progressive aims, they argue, requires recognition that '[social struggle does] not have a necessary class character'[48] – nor, for that matter, any necessary character. Political community and citizenship are defined not through the universalization of *an* identity but through commitment to equality and liberty for all identities, a 'chain of equivalence' being forged among them. To the extent that this project questions analytical and political tendencies which view class as the *exclusive* focus of legitimate critical inquiry and action, it is part of a laudable movement in critical social theory and political practice. However, Laclau and Mouffe, and others in the 'left pluralist' school,[49] go beyond this in rejecting a *necessary* place for class politics in struggles for progressive social change. This aspect of their position has attracted considerable and justified criticism. We share the critics' concerns and are convinced of the continuing importance (now more than ever) of class to critical theory and practice. At the same time, however, we are concerned that, paradoxically, some of those critics appear sometimes to share Laclau's and Mouffe's presumption that 'new social movements' and class-based movements are mutually exclusive. R. Miliband, for example, argues that new social movements reject and ignore class as an essential structure of exploitation and domination.[50] Thus, in his view, they do not seek *fundamental* social change but only narrowly and sectorally defined interests; class is universal while all other social positions and political identities are particular.[51]

One difficulty with these 'classless' conceptions of new social movements is that they leave little room for socialists within, for example, the feminist, environmentalist, or lesbian and gay movements. They imply that political struggles around class simply do not occur within new social movements. This, in turn, can be related to the characteristic presumption of new social-movement theory that 'old' political affiliations – classical liberalism and nationalism as well as socialism – do not play a role in new social-movement politics. We rather doubt that such a sharp break between 'old' and 'new' politics exists in the actual claims, operation, struggles, and politics of and within particular social movements.[52] Miliband acknowledges this point, though without any apparent recognition that in doing so he contradicts his own definition of social movements as lacking class politics. Social movements, according to him, are politically divided among liberals, socialists, and radicals.

Liberals seek reform in particular areas but eschew analyses and strategies that locate the roots of oppression in the nature of the social order itself; radicals 'are moved by a search for entirely new ways of life' and include nationalist movements; and finally, socialists believe that oppression is rooted in class relations.[53] We agree with Miliband, and others who have made this point, that these (and other) different and conflicting positions can be found within most contemporary social movements – the women's movement,[54] lesbians and gay men,[55] environmental and peace movements,[56] and anti-racism.[57] Their presence militates against any easy inference that social movements are politically homogeneous or that they represent a decisive break with older political identities and cleavages.

The political diversity of social movements is a matter that must be considered in analysing rights strategies. If a group *within* a social movement has a political orientation consistent with the tenets of dominant rights ideology (that is, a liberal one), then rights strategies may serve to advance the political goals of that group at the expense of groups representing conflicting positions within the movement, such as socialists and nationalists. Herman argues that this kind of dynamic was one of the 'unintended implications, and under-considered effects' of the use of rights strategies by the Coalition for Gay Rights in Ontario: 'CGRO's choice to be a voice of lesbian and gay liberalism, implicitly meant that the organisation was not speaking for feminists, socialist and other progressive lesbians and gay men. Thus, whilst some apolitical people may have been gathered into the process, others, such as myself at the time, became increasingly marginalised from the 'public face' of the lesbian and gay movement.'[58] Once it is acknowledged that social movements are internally divided among political tendencies, it becomes difficult to speak, in the abstract, of rights strategies being appropriate and useful for a social movement.

The public debate about the Charlottetown Accord once again illustrates the point. During that debate opposition to women's oppression came to be synonymous, at least within the media, with support of the Charter (which itself was reduced to support of liberal ideology, as noted above). This construction was built upon the pro-Charter positions of NWAC and NAC. It implied that those, including women, who did not support the Charter, and rights more generally, were not part of the struggle to end women's oppression. The effect was not only to simplify the issue of women's oppression but also to discredit and exclude from the 'women's movement' those whose struggle against unequal gender relations involved politics and strategies that could not be fit into the liberal contours of the debate. We will now look at this dynamic in relation to First Nations and Quebec nationalist women and socialist feminists.

Many First Nations women in the self-government movement, including those in NWAC, consider colonialism to be at the root of gender inequality in First Nations communities. According to them, equality for First Nations women requires a break with colonialism, and the First Nations 'women's movement' is therefore inseparable from the struggle for self-government. It follows for some – and this is where women in the Assembly of First Nations (AFN) disagreed fundamentally with NWAC's position on the accord – that the Charter, as an instrument of the colonial (Canadian) state, is part of the gender inequality problem for First Nations, not its solution. Moreover, the Charter's Eurocentric valorization of individual rights and freedoms is viewed as alien, and potentially harmful, to First Nations cultures and traditions. 'Divisions between First Nations people based upon the non-native fascination with extreme individualism,' according to a statement by the Musqueam band in British Columbia, 'simply support the assimilation of our people into non-native culture.'[59] The AFN's opposition to the Charter was part of its wider project of breaking with colonialist power and ideology; and because colonialism was considered to be a root cause of patriarchy in First Nations communities, such opposition was viewed as necessary for achieving sexual equality. On this basis many women within the self-government movement supported the accord's limitations on the application of the Charter.

The idea that *opposition* to the Charter might be part of a strategy to promote women's equality, at least for First Nations women, was too easily dismissed – when considered at all – in debates around the accord. Not surprisingly, it made little sense in a dominant framework that equated women's equality issues with liberal rights and the Charter. L. Weinrib, for example, condemned the accord's limitations on the Charter's application to First Nations, arguing that rights are a universally valid concept and agreeing with the Federal Court of Appeal that 'the norms of Canadian society dictate that the Charter should apply to aboriginal governments' – the latter point demonstrating a startling disregard for the fact that an important aim of First Nations self-government is precisely to avoid the imposition of Canadian norms and institutions. Moreover, in countering the position of some First Nations organizations that the Charter imposes alien norms on their people, Weinrib made the statement quoted earlier: 'The Charter reflects ideas of individual dignity now accepted by a large variety of countries, many of which are neither western nor white.'[60] Here she ignores not only that liberal-rights regimes were often forcibly imposed on these countries but also that they were essential components of colonial strategy in Canada and elsewhere. This denial of history is less than innocent: it perpetuates the myth that rights are one of the 'gifts *we* gave *them*'[61] and implies a dangerous colonialist ambition.[62] More to the point, perhaps, liberal rights are neither the only nor the best mode of governance and political action; and to argue that they are is Eurocentric, analytically suspect, and ignorant of the intimate connection between neo-liberal doctrine and *current* (as well as past) forms of Western imperialism.[63] The position of First Nations nationalist women demonstrates that in a colonial context, such as Canada, the struggle against women's oppression may involve collective resistance to rights rather than embracement of them.

The kind of connection between gender and nationalism that we have reviewed in the context of First Nations nationalist women has a parallel in the other major nationalist struggle in Canada, that of Quebec. For many Quebec feminists, gender equality issues are indissolubly bound up with Quebec's pursuit of greater political autonomy (either within Canadian federalism or as a sovereign state), a sentiment captured by the slogan 'no women's liberation without Quebec liberation. No Quebec liberation without women's liberation.'[64] The Charter, being a pan-Canadian document, is often viewed from this perspective as an unwarranted extension of Canadian federal power over the Quebec 'nation' – a point underlined by Quebec's refusal to accept the Charter in the first place. Moreover, some Quebec feminists question the necessity of the Charter on the grounds that, first, there is already a Quebec Charter of Rights; and, second, women's equality receives greater protection under Quebec's social and human rights policies than it does in other provinces or at the federal level. Like First Nations women in the self-government movement, then, nationalist feminists in Quebec do not necessarily accept the 'Charter must be paramount' view so strong elsewhere in Canada (though the issue of their acceptance of non-Charter rights may be another matter).[65]

Quebec nationalism has posed some difficulties for NAC, a national organization that is insistently pan-Canadian, supports the Charter, and advocates a strong federal presence in social programs. In the debates surrounding the Meech Lake Accord (a predecessor of the Charlottetown Accord defeated in June 1990), for example, NAC was critical of the distinct society clause, fearing that it could be used to undermine the Charter equality rights of women in Quebec. Nationalist feminists in Quebec, on the other hand, saw in the same clause a minimal, though welcome, recognition of Quebec's unique status in Canadian federalism.[66] Tension developed between NAC (and other women's groups) and nationalist feminists in Quebec, which was exacerbated by the media's portrayal of NAC as anti-Quebec. In the Charlottetown debate, NAC endorsed the distinct society clause, and perhaps more important, the central argument of nationalist feminists. According to Judy Rebick: 'We understand in the women's movement ... that equality doesn't mean treating everyone the same way. Equality often means special measures – that terrible word – to correct historical inequalities ... We also need special powers ... for Quebec ... to recognize the fact that they have a disadvantage in being the only French-speaking nation or province in the whole of North America. They need those powers and they want those powers to protect their language, their culture and their institutions.'[67] Presumably it was on the basis of similar reasoning that NAC supported the idea of First Nations self-government. However, as we have seen, it did not go so far as to endorse restrictions on the Charter's application to First Nations governments. Instead, it vigorously supported NWAC and implicitly adopted NWAC's analysis of the relationship between self-government and gender, rather than that of First Nations women in the AFN.

Quebec and First Nations nationalist women are not the only groups opposing women's oppression whose politics were effectively overridden by the liberal 'public face' given to women's struggles during the Charlottetown Accord debates. Jill Vickers has noted that women's movements throughout Canada have tended to be sceptical of equality-rights strategies because such strategies risk abstracting issues out of their socio-political and economic context.[68] This is especially true of socialist feminism, which considers women's equality politically and analytically inseparable from class structure. Socialist feminists have argued that the anti-statist form of dominant rights ideology, and the Charter more specifically, obscures the structural gender/class inequalities of 'private' social relations, like those of work and family, and restricts the state from playing a positive role in transforming the loci of women's subordination.[69] This does not deny a recognition among socialist feminists that in some contexts rights strategies can have tactical utility;[70] however, socialist feminism, like nationalist feminism, relies upon analyses and strategies that emphasize the need for collective mobilization to change social structures. Its central tenets are often contradicted by the liberal orthodoxy of dominant rights ideology, and so the classical-liberal spin put on feminist politics during the Charlottetown Accord debates potentially had damaging implications for socialist (and even social-democratic) groups within the women's movement.

The Production of Rights

Perhaps our analysis so far demonstrates only that oppositional rights strategies and all other political strategies share the risk of co-option. The fact NWAC's and NAC's rights strategies were equated with liberal rights ideology arguably illustrates merely that these organizations used the wrong kinds or amounts of reinterpretive work in their particular strategies[71] or that they made strategic choices to risk such representation of their position so as to secure the accord's defeat. Our analysis would not be inconsistent, then, with the central argument of Laclau and Mouffe, Hunt, and other rights advocates: namely, that rights strategies are effective tools for social change when they involve social movements in the production of counter-hegemonic rights discourses that challenge elements of dominant ideological discourses of rights. Two difficult questions are raised by this argument, however, neither of which is sufficiently addressed by its proponents: first, why do some discourses of rights become part of the dominant ideology of rights while others do not; and second, how are dominant ideological discourses of rights produced and reproduced? These questions, we argue, require consideration of factors outside rights discourse that operate both to ensure the power and centrality of dominant ideological rights discourses and to block the entrance of alternatives. The production of rights discourse occurs within material and ideological constraints that, at least in western capitalist states, tend to favour traditional liberal articulations over radical ones.

Left pluralism often conceives of politics as largely about the struggle over language, discourse, and other modes of cultural representation. Both in terms of its analyses and strategies, it focuses on the symbolic aspects of politics, with less (if any) emphasis on other dimensions of existing social and political institutions and economic relations. Political struggle is understood and engaged in primarily at the representational level, with different discursive elements combined and re-combined to create radical and progressive articulations. Such 'semio-activism,' as T. Ebert[72] describes it, often remains theoretically unconnected to constraints imposed by extra-discursive elements, a point acknowledged by Laclau and Mouffe, who write that 'discursive practice ... does not have a plane of constitution prior to, or outside, the dispersion of the articulated elements.'[73] Though Laclau and Mouffe recognize 'structural constraints' on the articulation process of liberal-democratic discourses, their theoretical framework does not consider the effects of such constraints.[74] Davina Cooper's observations about Mouffe's discussion of discourses of citizenship are equally applicable, we think, to the left-pluralist account of rights: 'Mouffe's focus is on the process of rearticulation ... But where and how do we rearticulate? What kinds of struggles are appropriate for what kinds of terrains? How do we deal with discursive and material limitations and constraints? And how do we decide which articulations are the right ones? Mouffe's work is perhaps not intended to deal with such "practical" considerations. However, if radical democracy is to be empowering beyond the level of theoretical struggle, texts with greater specificity are required.'[75] In similar spirit, Stuart Hall has said of left-pluralist work that it views society as a 'totally open discursive field' where 'there is no reason why anything isn't potentially articulable with anything.'[76]

Too little weight is attached by left pluralists to the wider social context in which rights discourse is produced, a context that creates differential power relations, narrows the scope of conflict, and favours some positions over others. There is no clear sense of 'how [rights] discourses are constituted and reproduced, nor how some [rights] discourses come to be more powerful and privileged than others.'[77] Rights discourse may offer endless possibilities for symbolic rearticulation, but that process inevitably comes up 'against the grain of historical formations,'[78] an 'accumulated historical weight which serves as a check on the[ir] potential "moveability."'[79] In other words, rights discourse is not some free-floating set of signifiers: it is connected at the root to historical and social forces and the existing social structures and institutions they have produced. Though rights discourse may not be conceptually fixed, it is historically and geographically anchored. This is at least part of the reason why the rights positions of NWAC and NAC, despite their progressive potential, were ultimately appropriated to support an undifferentiated liberal-rights hegemony that developed around the Charlottetown Accord.

Questions still remain, however, about the *specific* links that may exist between rights and constraints outside rights discourse that affect its articulation. Here we will suggest several different lines of connection. First, particular social practices and relations, rooted in history and geography, support and are supported by the various discourses of dominant rights ideology. The language of rights, and liberal ideology more generally, did not develop spontaneously but originated within a particular historico-geographic formation – the rise of European capitalism and the corresponding break up of feudal estates, guilds, and other forms of enforced association, including state religion. Its individualism, suspicion of collective power (including that of the state), formal egalitarianism, and construction of 'coercive' public and 'free' private spheres made intelligible, and were made intelligible through, among other things, the emergence of market economies.[80] Second, the material interests of powerful actors within existing social institutions – property owners, men, dominant racial groups – have a stake in the continuation of those institutions, and, therefore, in opposing attempts to reinterpret the discourses that serve to legitimate them.[81] The elements of dominant rights ideology have assisted, for example, in the portrayal of capitalist, colonialist, and patriarchal societies as bastions of individual freedom and equality, despite the oppression and inequality that constitute their social relations. It has also played a major role, more recently, in the backlash against feminism and other progressive movements.[82] Those who have power and whose interests are legitimated, universalized, or otherwise reinforced through dominant rights ideology will surely use their resources in specific instances to attack oppositional reinterpretations of rights put forward by social-movement actors.

This brings us to the third and related issue of knowledge-producing institutions. The production of rights discourse for public consumption largely takes place within an ideological infrastructure – media, schools, political institutions, courts, and so on. These institutions play a substantial, though not wholly determinative, role in constructing and disseminating dominant ideological discourses of rights, a point that can be made without endorsing some of the more simplistic analyses of their nature and influence.[83] The final issue is how communicated rights discourses are received by audiences (the other side of concerns about their production).[84] Laclau and Mouffe, Hunt, and other rights advocates depend upon the notion that counter-hegemonic rights discourses will have certain effects, in relation to social-movement activists, potential members, and the public in general, yet they tend not to consider how the varying social conditions of these peoples' lives may shape their responses to such discourses. It is arguable, for example, that conditions of economic fear and insecurity, like that fomented by capital's current 'restructuring,' may dampen people's receptivity to radical egalitarian ideas,[85] as the contemporary rise of egoism and xenophobia within liberal democracies suggests. More generally, the institutions, practices, and ideologies of everyday life constitute a context that helps determine the relative degree of credibility and value attached to alternative rights discourses by those who receive them.

There are, then, important constraints, material and ideological, affecting the articulation process of rights discourse. At a general level, this means that rights are more than a discursive problem. The power of dominant rights ideology and its role in absorbing and distorting the rights claims of NAC and NWAC was likely the result of a combination of all the factors we have been discussing. Knowledge about the precise dimensions of this process requires an analysis much broader and deeper than what we have attempted here. Yet this does not prevent us from concluding that social movements which use rights strategies risk having their positions and internal politics distorted by rights ideology, a risk that is not necessarily avoided through careful construction of arguments and interpretations within rights discourse. Rights are rooted in material and ideological conditions. These conditions, in addition to interpretive questions about rights discourse, must be at the core of analyses and strategies involving rights. Failure to consider them may not only result in wasted efforts and resources but also entails the real possibility that rights strategies will backfire.

Conclusion

We have argued that dominant rights ideology may construct the values and identities of social-movement actors in ways that distort their positions and implicitly delegitimate and suppress non- or anti-liberal political tendencies within a movement. The rights-defined positions of NWAC and NAC in the Charlottetown debates were each represented within mainstream media so as to reflect the classical-liberal anxiety about collective power and a corresponding celebration of individual rights, thus attributing political commitments to these organizations that contradicted their actual positions. This was due at least in part to the channelling effects of dominant rights ideology. The media's liberal construction of the 'women's movement' tended to marginalize, and implicitly delegitimate, the alternative view that women's struggle is inseparable from nationalist or class struggle. We should emphasize, however, that our argument offers little more than a basis for speculation regarding the impact of dominant rights ideology on the post-Charlottetown political dynamics of women's movements in First Nations, Quebec, and Canada. Finally, we argued that the potentially distorting and narrowing effects of dominant rights ideology cannot be avoided by reinterpretation alone because its elements are anchored in wider material and ideological structures.

In conclusion, our central point is that strategies involving rights discourse are necessarily shaped by dominant rights ideology. The effect of this process is not only to limit the utility of such strategies in advancing progressive goals but also to create the risk of negative political consequences. We do not want to suggest that rights strategies are unique in being problematic – any political strategy may fail or backfire. It is probably impossible to say in the abstract that rights strategies are necessarily worse than other strategies. We do believe, however, that it is possible to identify some of the particular difficulties raised by the use of rights strategies, and that is what we have tried to do. Such an analysis does not lead to the conclusion that rights strategies should be abandoned. It only underlines that rights strategies, like all other political strategies, have a constitutive effect on social-movement politics that is not always positive. This is an important point, not least because it tends to be discounted, even ignored, in some of the more sanguine academic writing on rights as vehicles for progressive social change. The analysis of such change must assess not only the possible advantages of rights strategies but also the full range of potential drawbacks and constraints.

Notes

1 *Charlottetown Accord Draft Legal Text* (Ottawa: Queen's Printer, 9 Oct. 1992) was an agreement to amend the Canadian constitution reached by federal, provincial, (including Quebec), and First Nations leaders at Charlottetown in August 1992. It

was the culmination of a two-year process of public consultations and intensive negotiations that followed the failure of an earlier package of constitutional amendments, the Meech Lake Accord of 1990 (see *A Renewed Canada: The Report of the Special Joint Committee of the Senate and House of Commons* [Ottawa: Queen's Printer, 28 Feb. 1992] and *Shaping Canada's Future Together* [Ottawa: Minister of Supply and Services 1991]. Amending the Canadian constitution requires either substantial or unanimous agreement by the provinces, depending on the issue. The holding of a referendum in relation to the Charlottetown Accord was viewed as a political necessity (the Meech Lake Accord process had been criticized for its elitism), but it was not legally required. For more general discussions of the events leading to the referendum, see J. Bakan and D. Schneiderman, 'Introduction,' in *Social Justice and the Constitution: Perspectives on a Social Union for Canada*, eds. Bakan and Schneiderman (Ottawa: Carleton University Press 1992), 1; and J. Bakan and D. Pinard, 'Getting to the Bottom of Meech Lake,' *Ottawa Law Review*, vol. 21 (1989), 247–61.

2 Federalism as a political structure is primarily concerned with the relationship among social collectivities that usually, but not necessarily, have a territorial base. It raises questions about what kinds of collectivities – which socio-political units – should have the status of coordinate (as opposed to subordinate) levels of government and thus exclusive political authority within their constitutionally defined jurisdictions. In Canada there are currently two kinds of political units so recognized: federal and provincial.

3 Part I of the Constitution Act, 1982, being schedule B to the Canada Act, 1982 (U.K.), 1982, c. 11 [hereinafter the Charter].

4 Ibid, section 52.

5 Ibid, sections 16–23.

6 Other provinces, too, had concerns about the Charter. The social-democratic (NDP) government of Saskatchewan was concerned about potential constraints on progressive state activism, while the Conservative government in Manitoba condemned the Charter on the basis of right-wing concerns about liberal rights.

7 See M.E. Turpel, 'Aboriginal Peoples and the Canadian Charter: Interpretive Monopolies, Cultural Differences,' *Canadian Perspectives on Legal Theory*, ed. R. Devlin (Toronto: Emond Montgomery 1991), 503.

8 See Janet Hiebert, 'Rights and Public Debate: The Limitation of a "Rights Must Be Paramount" Perspective,' *International Journal of Canadian Studies*, vol. 7 (1993), 117, for a similar analysis.

9 See J. Fudge and H. Glasbeek, 'The Politics of Rights: A Politics with Little Class,' *Social and Legal Studies* (1992), 1; S. Scheingold, 'Constitutional Rights and Social Change: Civil Rights in Perspective,' in *Judging the Constitution*, eds. M. McCann and G. Houseman (Boston: Little Brown 1989), 73. It is, however,

questionable whether rights strategies can ever be fully separated from law and litigation, especially where, as in Canada, abstract rights are part of the constitution and justiciable. In the case of the Charlottetown Accord, rights claims were made primarily in forums other than courts and did not centre around a particular litigation (though NWAC did, at one point, challenge the constitutional-amendment process in court). Yet, at the same time, the claims were deeply legal in the sense they were about the potential *legal* effects of entrenching the accord in the constitution.

10 See E.M. Schneider, 'The Dialectic of Rights and Politics: Perspectives from the Women's Movement,' *New York University Law Review*, vol. 61 (1986), 589–652; P. Williams, 'Alchemical Notes: Reconstructing Ideals from Deconstructed Rights,' *Harvard Civil Rights – Civil Liberties Review*, vol. 22 (1987), 401.

11 See A. Hunt, 'Rights and Social Movements: Counter-Hegemonic Strategies,' *Journal of Law and Society*, vol. 17 (1990), 320.

12 See J. Nedelsky and C. Scott, 'Constitutional Dialogue,' in *Social Justice and the Constitution*, 59.

13 See J. Bakan, 'What's Wrong with Social Rights,' in ibid., 85.

14 See M. Smith, 'Language, Law and Social Power: *Seaboyer*; *Gayme v. R* and a Critical Theory of Ideology,' *University of Toronto Faculty of Law Review*, 51 (1993), 118–55. By 'dominant rights ideology' we mean the set of rights discourses that constitutes the prevailing and generally unquestioned 'common sense' about what rights are; helps sustain the dominant order of social relations by allowing that order to be presented as natural and legitimate, masking social facts that reveal its nastier sides and universalizing the interests of dominant groups; and that embodies elements sufficiently attractive and plausible to command popular support. Dominant rights ideology, then, is a particular set of rights discourses. Its elements, identified by the above-noted characteristics, are drawn from a much wider range of discursive possibilities and are variable across history and geography. However, because these elements constitute the 'common sense' understanding of what rights are in a particular society, such contingency is concealed.

15 Schneider, 'Dialectic of Rights.'

16 S. Lynd, 'Communal Rights,' *Texas Law Review*, vol. 62 (1984), 1417–41.

17 See n.12.

18 See G. Brodsky, 'Social Charter Issues,' in *Social Justice and the Constitution*, 43.

19 See D. Herman, 'Are We Family?: Lesbian Rights and Women's Liberation,' *Osgoode Hall Law Journal*, 789.

20 Ibid.

21 See K. Crenshaw, 'Race, Reform and Retrenchment: Transformation and Legitimation in Anti-Discrimination Law,' *Harvard Law Review*, vol. 101 (1988), 1331–87.

22 Ibid.

23 The political mix was further complicated by the fact the accord dealt with a whole range of issues in addition to recognizing Quebec as a distinct society and creating a structure for First Nations self-government. Among these were a social-rights regime (Bakan and Schneiderman, 'Introduction,' in *Social Justice and the Constitution*), proposals to promote free trade among the provinces, restrictions on the power of the federal government to spend money in areas outside its legislative jurisdiction, explicit recognition of provincial jurisdiction in certain areas, and creation of an elected Senate. (See *Charlottetown Accord.*) In the referendum, voters had to say yes or no to the whole package.

24 'Trudeau says scare scenario a "lie,"' *Globe and Mail*, 2 Oct. 1992, A4.

25 See S. Carstairs, 'Some good reasons for voting no,' *Winnipeg Free Press*, 27 Sept. 1992, A7.

26 W. Johnston, 'Accord fatally flawed when it comes to protecting rights,' Montreal Gazette, 24 Oct. 1992, B5.

27 The Reform Party, for example, a right-wing political party representing the Canadian version of what Stuart Hall has called authoritarian populism (*The Hard Road to Renewal: Thatcherism and the Crisis of the Left* [London: Verso 1988]), encapsulated its opposition to the accord in the slogan 'equal rights for all, special rights for none.' See also 'Reform attacks native self-rule,' *Globe and Mail*, 5 Oct. 1992, A1; 'An uprising against the Charlottetown native deal,' *Western Report*, 19 Oct. 1992, 14; M. Smith, 'What the deal means for the West,' *Western Report*, 5 Oct. 1992.

28 Charter, section 25.

29 Charter, section 33.

30 See Native Women's Association of Canada (author: Gail Stacey-Moore, speaker), 'Statement on the Canada Package,' (Ottawa: NWAC 1992), 4.

31 Ibid., 5.

32 Ibid., 7–8.

33 Quoting in part L. Weinrib, 'Legal Analysis of Draft Legal Text of October 12, 1992' (University of Toronto: 21 October) (unpublished document on file with the authors). The following indicated their agreement with Weinrib's legal analysis by signing it: P.E. Benson, R.J. Cook, R.J. Daniels, B.M. Dickens, R.E. Fritz, J.P. Humphrey, H.N. Janisch, R. St. J. MacDonald, W.H. McConnell, A.N. Stone, C. Valcke, E.J. Weinrib, G. Triantis.

34 See 'Unity deal will rob Native women of key rights,' Toronto *Sun*, 22 Sept. 1992, B1.

35 Johnston, 'Accord fatally flawed.'

36 See D. Greschner, 'Aboriginal Women, the Constitution and Criminal Justice,' *U.B.C. Law Review*, 1992 special edition, 339.

37 Weinrib, 'Legal Analysis'; NWAC, 'Statement.'

38 Weinrib, 'Legal Analysis.'

39 See P. Fitzpatrick, *The Mythology of Modern Law* (London: Routledge 1992);
    M. Kline, 'The Colour of Law: Ideological Representations of First Nations in
    Legal Discourse,' *Social and Legal Studies*, vol. 3 (1994), 451–76.

40 See P. Graham, 'Native women sidelined,' Vancouver Sun, 22 Oct. 1992, A15.

41 See J. Fudge, 'The Public/Private Distinction: The Possibilities and Limits to the
    Use of Charter Litigation to Further Feminist Struggle,' *Osgoode Hall Law
    Journal*, vol. 25 (1987), 485–554.

42 See NWAC, 'Statement,' 4; Musqueam band, 'Charter Equality Rights and
    Self-Government,' 1992, unpublished document on file with the authors.

43 See S. Day, 'What's Wrong With the Canada Clause,' *Canadian Forum*,
    21 Oct. 1992, 22.

44 Ibid.; Brodsky, 'Social Charter Issues.'

45 'Les enfants de Trudeau,' *Le Devoir*, 19 Oct. 1992.

46 'Women's group says No,' *Globe and Mail*, 14 Sept. 1992, A1.

47 See D. Herman, 'Beyond the Rights Debate,' *Social and Legal Studies*, vol. 2
    (1993), 25–43.

48 See E. Laclau and C. Mouffe, *Hegemony and Socialist Strategy: Towards a
    Radical Democratic Politics* (London: Verso 1985), 58.

49 See K. McClure, 'On the Subject of Rights: Pluralism, Plurality and Political
    Identity,' in *Dimensions of Radical Democracy: Pluralism, Citizenship and
    Community*, ed. C. Mouffe (London: Verso 1992), 108.

50 See R. Miliband, *Divided Societies: Class Struggle in Contemporary Capitalism*
    (Oxford: Oxford University Press 1991).

51 The latter point is picked up as well in liberal and conservative political theory,
    where social movements are often portrayed as representing particular and
    narrowly defined interests in contrast to 'universal' ones, such as, for example, the
    constitutional order (see A.C. Cairns, 'Constitutional Minoritarianism in Canada,'
    in *Canada: The State of the Federation 1990*, ed. R.L. Watts [Kingston: Institute
    of International Government Relations 1990], 71), quasi-national communities
    (see C. Taylor, *Reconciling the Solitudes: Essays on Canadian Federalism and
    Nationalism* [Montreal: McGill-Queen's University Press 1993]), or the conserva-
    tive consensus of society's silent majority (see F.L. Morton and R. Knopff, 'The
    Supreme Court as the Vanguard of the Intelligentsia: The Charter as Post-material
    politics,' occasional paper, research study 8.1 [Research Unit for Socio-Legal
    Studies, Faculty of Social Sciences, University of Calgary 1992]).

52 See L. Weir, 'Limitations of New Social Movement Analysis,' *Studies in Political
    Economy*, vol. 40 (1993), 73–102; Herman, 'Are We Family.'

53 See n. 56.

54 Weir, 'Limitations.'
55 See L. Duggan, 'Making it Perfectly Queer,' *Socialist Review*, vol. 22 (1992), 11–31; D. Herman, 'Reforming Rights: Lesbian and Gay Struggle for Legal Equality in Canada,' (PhD Dissertation, University of Warwick, U.K., 1992).
56 Miliband, *Divided Societies*.
57 See M. Tushnet, *The NAACP's Legal Strategy Against Segregated Education: 1925–1950* (Chapel Hill: University of North Carolina Press 1987).
58 Herman, 'Reforming Rights,' 120–1.
59 Musqueam band, 'Charter Equality Rights.'
60 See n.38.
61 See P. Fitzpatrick, 'Racism and the Innocence of Law,' *British Journal of Law and Society*, vol. 14 (1987), 130.
62 See B. Parekh, 'The Cultural Particularity of Liberal Democracy,' in *Prospects for Democracy*, ed. D. Held (Stanford: Stanford University Press 1993), 167–8.
63 See N. Lazarus, 'Imperialism, Cultural Theory, and Radical Intellectualism Today: A Critical Assessment,' *Rethinking Marxism*, vol. 3 (1990), 157.
64 See J. Vickers, 'The Canadian Women's Movement and a Changing Constitutional Order,' *International Journal of Canadian Studies*, vol. 7 (1993), 267.
65 Ibid.; Hiebert, 'Rights and Public Debate.'
66 See N. Duclos, 'Lessons of Difference: Feminist Theory on Cultural Diversity,' *Buffalo Law Review*, vol. 38 (1990).
67 As cited in Hiebert, 'Rights and Public Debate,' 127.
68 Vickers, 'Canadian Women's Movement.'
69 Fudge, 'Public/Private Distinction'; D.H. Currie and M. Kline, 'Challenging Privilege: Women, Knowledge and Feminist Struggles,' *Journal of Human Justice*, vol. 2 (1991), 7.
70 Herman, 'Are We Family.'
71 Hunt, 'Rights and Social Movements'; A. Hunt and A. Bartholomew, 'What's Wrong with Rights?' *Journal of Law and Inequality*, vol. 9 (1990), 1–58.
72 See T. Ebert, 'Ludic Feminism – The Body, Performance and Labour: Bringing Materialism Back into Feminist Cultural Studies,' *Cultural Critique*, vol. 24 (1993), 5–50.
73 Laclau and Mouffe, *Hegemony*, 109.
74 See B. Smarden, 'Liberalism, Marxism and the Class Character of Radical Democratic Challenge,' *Studies in Political Economy*, vol. 37 (1992), 129–46.
75 D. Cooper, 'The Citizen's Charter and Radical Democracy: Empowerment and Exclusion within Citizenship Discourse,' *Social and Legal Studies*, vol. 2 (1993), 164.
76 See S. Hall, 'On Postmodernism and Articulation,' *Journal of Communication Inquiry*, vol. 10 (1986), 56.

77 Susan B. Boyd, 'Some Postmodernist Challenges to Feminist Analyses of law, family and State: Ideology and Discourse in Child Custody Law' *Canadian Journal of Family Law*, vol. 10 (1991), 79–113, 97.

78 Hall, 'Postmodernism,' 54.

79 See T. Bennet, *Outside Literature* (London: Routledge 1990), 263.

80 See R. Weitzer, 'Law and Legal Ideology: Contributions to the Genesis and Reproduction of Capitalism,' *Berkeley Journal of Sociology*, vol. 24 (1980); J. Bakan, 'Constitutional Interpretation and Social Change: You Can't Always Get What You Want (Nor What You Need),' *Canadian Bar Review*, vol. 70 (1991), 307–28.

81 Hall, 'Postmodernism,' 53–4.

82 Rights discourse has, for example, been instrumental in the backlash against feminism, with men portraying themselves as victims of rights denials at the hands of institutions, including the courts, that have allegedly been taken over by feminists; the same is true of anti-'political correctness' discourses which invariably draw upon free-speech ideology.

83 See Y. Zhao, 'The "End of Ideology" Again? The Concept of Ideology in the Era of Post-Marxian Theory,' *Canadian Journal of Sociology*, vol. 18 (1993), 78–80; J.B. Thompson, *Ideology and Modern Culture: Critical Social Theory in the Era of New Communication* (Stanford: Stanford University Press 1990), 136, 137–57; D. Kellner, *Television and the Crisis of Democracy* (Boulder: Westview Press 1990).

84 See J. Lewis, *The Ideological Octopus: An Exploration of Television and Its Audience* (London: Routledge 1991).

85 Smarden, 'Liberalism,' 134.

8

The New Equality Paradigm: The Impact of Charter Equality Principles on Private Law Decisions*

KATE SUTHERLAND

From the Charter's inception, there was considerable speculation as to the scope of its application. Would its ambit be restricted to review of government action, or would it subject all manner of private interactions to the scrutiny of the courts? While some Charter guarantees are clearly connected solely with government activity, others might plausibly be of general application, for example, the section 15 guarantee of equality. The Supreme Court of Canada seemingly put this debate to rest when it pronounced in the Dolphin Delivery case[1] that the Charter does not apply to private litigation.

In this essay, I suggest that subsequent developments leave the above conclusion open to question. While the Supreme Court made clear in *Dolphin Delivery* that the Charter has no direct application to private litigation, it did allow room for Charter influence on private law by suggesting that courts should apply and develop the principles of the common law in a manner consistent with Charter values. This opening expanded further with the Court's interpretation of the section 15 equality guarantee in *Andrews*.[2] The tenuous division between public and private that the Court sought to maintain in *Dolphin Delivery* is rendered still more fragile by an embrace of substantive rather than formal equality. I will illustrate this point by examining the ways in which Charter equality principles, at least with respect to gender equality, have been insinuated into the recent development of tort-law doctrines relating to consent, limitation periods, and the quantification of damages. The conclusion to be drawn is that the development of the common law in a manner consistent with

* The author wishes to thank Lisa Fishbayn for her comments on an earlier version of this paper, and the Social Sciences and Humanities Research Council of Canada, the Frank Knox Memorial Foundation, and the Centre for Constitutional Studies at the University of Alberta for research funding.

substantive equality has become a much more significant process than the Supreme Court perhaps originally imagined.

It would be overly simplistic to assume that the sensitivity to historic and contemporary inequalities which is becoming increasingly evident in tort decisions is related solely to the Charter. Other factors must also be considered. For example, the recent influence of feminist and other critical legal scholars on the theoretical underpinnings of tort law could be said to parallel the influences that gave rise to the contextual approach to Charter interpretation in the *Andrews* decision. There is thus no necessary cause and effect relationship. Further, changes in the make-up of the judiciary as well as innovations in judicial education surely play a role. The same social forces that led legislators to adopt the Charter must also operate on judges and lawyers. Nevertheless, there is evidence of a ripple effect whereby Charter values exert an influence beyond constitutional litigation, and this effect ought not to be overlooked by equality seekers in evaluating the utility of such litigation for promoting social change.

The Charter and Private Law

In *Dolphin Delivery*, the Supreme Court of Canada addressed the question of whether the Charter applies to the common law and private litigation. Mr Justice McIntyre began with the following proposition: 'The Charter was set up to regulate the relationship between the individual and the government. It was intended to restrain government action and to protect the individual. It was not intended in the absence of some governmental action to be applied in private litigation.'[3] With respect to the common law, then, Justice McIntyre concluded that the Charter does apply but 'only in so far as the common law is the basis of some governmental action which, it is alleged, infringes a guaranteed right or freedom.'[4] In the case before him, the respondent business had sought and acquired an injunction against picketing which the appellant union alleged infringed its freedom of expression. Thus, while founded in common law, this action was generated by a private party, not by the government.

Justice McIntyre was not persuaded by the argument that the court's role in granting and enforcing the injunction constituted an element of governmental intervention sufficient to invoke the Charter. He stated:

While in political science terms it is probably acceptable to treat the courts as one of the three fundamental branches of government, that is, legislative, executive, and judicial, I cannot equate for the purposes of Charter application the order of a court with an element of governmental action. This is not to say that the courts are not bound by the Charter. The courts are, of course, bound by the Charter as they are bound by all law. It is their duty to apply the law, but in doing so they act as neutral arbiters, not as contending parties involved in a dispute ... A more direct and a more precisely defined connection between the element of government action and the claim advanced must be present before the Charter applies.[5]

He concluded that, in the absence of such a direct connection with government action, the Charter does not apply to private litigation.

Justice McIntyre, however, did state that courts should nonetheless 'apply and develop the principles of the common law in a manner consistent with the fundamental values enshrined in the Constitution.'[6] The precise implications of this statement are open to debate.

Allan Hutchinson and Andrew Petter contend that, in deciding *Dolphin Delivery* as it did, the Supreme Court insulated the primary source of inequality in our society from Charter scrutiny: 'the maldistribution of property entitlements among individuals.'[7] They continue: 'When confronted with questions of Charter justice, the courts, like Lord Nelson, turn a blind eye to underlying disparities in wealth and power.'[8] By styling itself a neutral arbiter, the court overlooks pre-existing inequalities between the parties, behaving as though each party appears before the court on an equal footing.

What, then, does it mean for courts to apply and develop common-law principles in a manner consistent with the Charter guarantee of equality? Does it simply mean that courts ought not to create overtly discriminatory precedent? Or could it nevertheless mean that courts have an obligation when making contentious decisions to come down on the side of the issue which best promotes substantive equality interests?[9] I contend that the latter is the more plausible approach, particularly in light of recent pronouncements of the Supreme Court of Canada. For example, in *R. v. Salituro*, Mr Justice Iacobucci, speaking for the Court, stated: 'Where the principles underlying a common law rule are out of step with the values enshrined in the Charter, the courts should scrutinize the rule closely. If it is possible to change the rule so as to make it consistent with Charter values, without upsetting the proper balance between judicial and legislative action ... then the rule ought to be changed.'[10] In this instance, the Court deemed the common-law rule with respect to spousal incompetency to testify in a criminal trial incompatible with 'the importance now given to sexual equality,' at least in situations of irreconcilable separation.[11]

I attribute this apparent shift in, or at least expansion of, the Court's approach to the Charter's application to the common law, and therefore to private law, to the meaning assigned to the Charter guarantee of equality in *Andrews v. Law Society of B.C.*,[12] a case subsequent to *Dolphin Delivery*. Prior to the *Andrews* elucidation of the section 15 equality guarantee, several commentators expressed concern that this right would be defined as purely formal, not substantive, thereby posing no challenge to the public/private split and leaving women and other equality-seeking groups no farther ahead than they were before the inception of the Charter. Echoing the concerns of Hutchinson and Petter, Judy Fudge stated: 'The public/private distinction may be used in the first instance to explicitly deny the Charter's application, and in the second, it may be used to foster a concept of formal equality which by denying the relevance of the history of women's subordinate status perpetuates it. Consequently, it is crucial that the public/private split be overcome (or at least eroded) if Charter litigation is to be used to further feminist struggles.'[13] This analysis builds on Hester Lessard's insight that, 'in order to give substantive content to equality rights, the private – in the sense of legally irrelevant – world of the victim's actual experience of oppression must be given credence.'[14] But while the public/private split was indeed reinforced by the determinations made in *Dolphin Delivery* with respect to the Charter's application, the fear that the scope of Charter equality rights would be similarly narrowed was not realized.

The Development of Charter Equality Principles

The judiciary has traditionally operated behind a screen of neutrality. But Justice McIntyre's characterization of courts as neutral arbiters in *Dolphin Delivery* aside, judges in Charter cases have been forced to come out from behind that screen and confront the fundamentally political nature of constitutional interpretation. Madam Justice McLachlin has stated that 'there is no way to interpret the Charter without making judgments involving social and moral questions of profound importance and difficulty.'[15] I contend that the Charter has provided the impetus for a process of 'contextualization' of Canadian law.[16]

Of course, no judicial decision is without context. But that context has often been hidden or extremely narrow. In cases where judges purport to apply neutral rules objectively, there is no lack of context but rather the very narrow context of that judge's subjective perspective. We cannot expect anyone to leave their subjective context behind, but we can seek to have them broaden it by taking into account other subjectivities in their decision-making process, and this is just what the Charter has forced, or at least encouraged, courts to do. Ruth Colker states: 'In order to understand an issue, one must try to grasp its specific meanings for a wide variety of people, by listening closely to how they describe the issue's impact on their lives. When we try to speak at too great a level of generality, we often fail to account for the multiple perspectives that exist on a particular issue by falsely assuming that our particular perspective is reflective of everyone's experience.'[17] In Charter adjudication, Canadian judges have been compelled to take other subjectivities into account as well. They must make decisions against the backdrop of 'the values of a free and democratic society,'[18] thereby stepping beyond their own.

Colker's caution against false universals does not preclude the use of broad principles to guide choices between subjectivities. It is my contention that the Charter guarantees themselves provide decision makers with just such guiding principles. In suggesting how judges may transcend their personal beliefs and values in Charter adjudication, Madam Justice McLachlin states:

The best solution, it seems to me, lies in seeking the dominant views being expressed in society at large on the question in issue. What has been written and said on the point in question? What values are inherent in what has been written and said? Often conflicting views are presented. The judge must then examine the values on which the conflict arises and decide which is most in keeping with the purposes of the Charter guarantee in question. The reference to external values will ensure that the judge does not decide on the basis of his or her prejudices, while the emphasis on the purposes of the Charter ensures that the judge will not stray too far from the essence of the guarantee in question. The result will be an objective, responsible approach to constitutional decision-making.[19]

This process of contextualization has manifested itself in a number of ways. First, a purposive approach has been taken to the interpretation of Charter guarantees generally.[20] Second, Charter guarantees have had their focus defined in the context of each other.[21] Finally, Charter guarantees, in particular equality, have begun to infuse private law decisions.

The first layer of contextualization is perhaps nowhere better exemplified than in the purposive approach taken to equality in the *Andrews* decision. That decision endorsed a substantive conception of equality which invokes the all-important context of disparities in power and of histories of discrimination. In *R. v. Turpin*, Madam Justice Wilson summarized the Court's position in *Andrews* as follows:

It is only by examining the larger context that a court can determine whether differential treatment results in inequality or whether, contrariwise, it would be identical treatment which would, in the particular context, result in inequality or foster disadvantage. A finding that there is discrimination will, I think, in most but perhaps not all cases, necessarily entail a search for disadvantage that exists apart from and independent of the particular legal distinction being challenged ... [As] I suggested in my reasons in *Andrews* ... the determination of whether a group falls into an analogous category to those specifically enumerated in s. 15 is 'not to be made only in the context of the law which is subject to challenge but rather in the context of the place of the group in the entire social, political and legal fabric of our society.' If the larger context is not examined, the s. 15 analysis may become a mechanical and sterile categorization process conducted entirely within the four corners of the impugned legislation.[22]

This approach is tailored to advancing the purposes of section 15, which are described by Justice Wilson as 'remedying or preventing discrimination in our society.'[23]

Further, Justice McIntyre made clear in his majority judgment in *Andrews* that this conception of equality focuses not just on discriminatory intent but on discriminatory impact: 'The main consideration must be the impact of the law on the individual or the group concerned.'[24] He stated: 'The promotion of equality entails the promotion of a society in which all are secure in the knowledge that they are recognized at law as human beings equally deserving of concern, respect and consideration. It has a large remedial component.'[25] A primary purpose of the Charter guarantee is, then, the amelioration of the effects of discrimination.

This contextual interpretation of the section 15 equality guarantee clearly builds on feminist approaches to law generally and to constitutional interpretation in particular. Feminists have argued against a sameness approach to equality, making clear that applying facially neutral rules without regard to historical and existing power relations perpetuates rather than remedying inequality.[26] As Diana Majury states: 'The concept of equality is meaningful only in the context of an understanding and response to inequality.'[27] We can progress towards equality only 'through responding to and remedying the inequalities experienced by so many members of our society.'[28] Majury stresses the importance of assessing discrimination claims against both a general and a specific context.[29] The general context includes the relevant group's history of oppression and the social, economic, and legal inequalities it currently faces. The specific context includes the same factors but as they relate to the particular person bringing forward the complaint. The *Andrews* decision opens the door to such an analysis and thereby to a positive remedial approach.[30]

Justice McIntyre did state explicitly that section 15 does not create a 'general guarantee of equality': 'It does not provide for equality between individuals or groups within society in a general or abstract sense, nor does it impose on individuals or groups an obligation to accord equal treatment to others. It is concerned with the application of the law.'[31] Thus, the focus remains on state action, as dictated by *Dolphin Delivery*. Yet the broad interpretation given to section 15 in *Andrews* necessarily chips away at the public/private distinction which the court tried so valiantly to retain in *Dolphin Delivery*. Richard Moon states: 'It is difficult to see how the right to equality under subsection 15(1) does not amount to a "general guarantee of equality." In some sense, all inequality (whatever may be regarded as a condition of inequality) is the result of a particular law or, more often, a combination of laws or the entire legal order – for example, the laws which create and protect private property and the market system.'[32] The move towards substantive equality blurs the public/private split, indicating that perhaps the *Dolphin Delivery* distinction cannot hold fast.

Colleen Sheppard comments on the potential of *Andrews* to deconstruct the public/private split and the impact of such a deconstruction as follows: 'Recognizing the disparate effects of laws and government policies would appear to extend the reach of what is considered "public" to areas formerly defined as "private." A positive remedy to redress such effects-based discrimination makes clear that the socially constructed line between the public and the private sphere has shifted. For women, the public/private dichotomy has been used to deny redress for abuses of "private" power. Legal developments which promote recognition of the ways in which government affects, through action and inaction, the scope and nature of "private" power, are helpful for women.'[33]

The Impact of Charter Equality Principles

I stated above that the increasing contextualization of law under the Charter extends beyond the first layer of a purposive approach to each of the Charter guarantees. The next layer is made manifest in those decisions where certain Charter guarantees are interpreted in the context of other Charter guarantees. The equality principles articulated in *Andrews* have, explicitly and implicitly, been used to form an important backdrop for the interpretation of other rights. This has occurred not in the initial interpretation of the scope of those rights but rather within the section 1 analysis, which states that the 'Canadian Charter of Rights and Freedoms guarantees the rights and freedoms set out in it subject only to such reasonable limits proscribed by law as can be demonstrably justified in a free and democratic society.' In articulating the values and principles that are essential to a free and democratic society and consequently ought to guide courts in making determinations under section 1, courts have turned back to the very values embodied in the Charter as a whole. In *Oakes*, Chief Justice Dickson listed the following values as central to the Charter: 'respect for the inherent dignity of the human person, commitment to social justice and equality, accommodation of a wide variety of beliefs, respect for cultural and group identity, and faith in social and political institutions which enhance the participation of individuals and groups in society.'[34] He explained: 'The underlying values of a free and democratic society are the genesis of the rights and freedoms guaranteed by the Charter and the ultimate standard against which a limit on a right or freedom must be shown, despite its effect, to be reasonable and demonstrably justified.'[35]

A prominent example of this second kind of contextualization is the way equality principles have been used to bolster section 1 limits on the right to freedom of expression. In *R. v. Keegstra*,[36] the section of the Criminal Code prohibiting the wilful promotion of hatred was challenged by an accused on the ground that it violated his Charter guarantee of freedom of expression. The accused, James Keegstra, was a high school teacher in Eckville, Alberta. In this role, for approximately ten years, he communicated anti-Semitic statements to his students, ultimately requiring that these statements be reproduced in class and on exams. He was convicted of wilful promotion of hatred and thereby gained standing to challenge the constitutionality of this offence. The Supreme Court held that the section did violate freedom of expression but that the prohibition could stand nonetheless as a reasonable limit on that right in a free and democratic society as per section 1.

In its reasons, the Court expressly declined to use section 15 to narrow the scope of the section 2(b) right to freedom of expression. The argument in favour of such an approach was described in the judgment as follows:

It has been argued in support of excluding hate propaganda from the coverage of s. 2(b) that the use of ss. 15 and 27 of the Charter – dealing respectively with equality and multiculturalism – and Canada's acceptance of international agreements requiring the prohibition of racist statements make s. 319(2) incompatible with even a large and liberal definition of the freedom ... The general tenor of this argument is that these interpretive aids inextricably infuse each constitutional guarantee with values supporting equal societal participation and the security and dignity of all persons. Consequently, it is said that s. 2(b) must be curtailed so as not to extend to communications which seriously undermine the equality, security and dignity of others.[37]

Chief Justice Dickson, speaking for the majority, declined to follow this approach, citing the danger of 'balancing competing values without the benefit of a context.' He did not dismiss the possibility of injecting the appropriate contextual concerns into a section 2(b) analysis, but he concluded that 'section 1 of the Charter is particularly well-suited to the task of balancing' and that, therefore, 'the preferable course is to weigh the various contextual values and factors in section 1.'[38]

Equality principles thus found their way into the section 1 analysis, bolstering the 'pressing and substantial' nature of the objective of the prohibition against the promotion of hatred. Chief Justice Dickson expressly stated that other sections of the Charter provide important indicia of the importance of the objective behind impugned legislative provisions.[39] With respect to section 15, he stated that 'promoting equality is an undertaking essential to any free and democratic society ... The principles underlying s. 15 of the Charter are thus integral to the s. 1 analysis.'[40] In arriving at this conclusion he cited with approval the following passage from the intervening factum presented by LEAF (Women's Legal Education and Action Fund): 'Governmental sponsored hatred on group grounds would violate section 15 of the Charter. Parliament promotes equality and moves against inequality when it prohibits the wilful public promotion of group hatred on these grounds. It follows that government action against group hate, because it promotes social equality as guaranteed by the Charter, deserves special constitutional consideration.'[41] Section 15 equality principles thus became integrally entwined with the section 1 analysis.

This approach was again sanctioned in the case of *R. v. Butler* in which the Supreme Court upheld the constitutionality of the criminalization of obscenity under section 1 of the Charter.[42] Once more the Criminal Code provision at issue was held to violate the section 2(b) guarantee of freedom of expression but here, too, the objective behind the provision was deemed to be sufficiently important to justify imposing limits on the guarantee. That important objective was again articulated as the promotion of equality, this time between women and men. Justice Sopinka stated that, while the imposition of certain standards of public and sexual morality is no longer a defensible objective in the suppression of obscenity, the avoidance of harm is a different matter.[43] He explained: 'If true equality between male and female persons is to be achieved, we cannot ignore the threat to equality resulting from exposure to audiences of certain types of violent and degrading material. Materials portraying women as a class as objects for sexual exploitation and abuse have a negative impact on "the individual's sense of self-worth and acceptance."'[44]

Equality Principles and Tort Law

The third layer of contextualization is the injection of Charter values, particularly the equality principles, into private law decisions that have no overt constitutional dimension. Despite the Supreme Court's pronouncement in *Dolphin Delivery* that the Charter does not apply to private litigation, courts appear to be bringing to their resolution of private disputes an understanding of the backdrop of power imbalances against which such disputes arise. In doing so they may be said to have heeded Justice McIntyre's call that they apply and articulate 'the principles of the common law in a manner consistent with the fundamental values enshrined in the Constitution.'

To illustrate this point, I will explore a number of recent tort decisions. Tort law is, of course, not the only area of private law that seems increasingly to be affected by Charter values, but it provides a convenient example.[45] The influence of the *Andrews* articulation of the principle of equality on the development of tort law is apparent in a number of recent cases relating to the defense of consent, the operation limitation periods and the quantification of damages.

Consent

In *Norberg v. Wynrib*,[46] Laura Norberg sued Morris Wynrib, a doctor who exploited her addiction to the drug Fiorinal by providing her with the drug in exchange for sex. The plaintiff put forward several potential causes of action upon which her claim could be decided, but ultimately the majority in the Supreme Court decided it on the basis of her action in tort. They held that the sexual assault alleged constituted battery and that the plaintiff's entitlement to relief depended upon whether or not the defence of consent had been established. In analysing the issue of consent, Mr Justice La Forest, for the majority, stated: 'The concept of consent as it operates in tort law is based on a presumption of individual autonomy and free will. It is presumed that the individual has freedom to consent or not to consent. This presumption, however, is untenable in certain circumstances. A position of relative weakness can, in some circumstances, interfere with the freedom of a person's will. Our notion of consent must, therefore, be modified to appreciate the power relationship between the parties.'[47] Justice La Forest noted that a doctor-patient relationship is frequently an unequal one and, as such, bears close scrutiny; further, a doctor-addict relationship is a markedly unequal one. The judge held that 'the unequal power between the parties and the exploitive nature of the relationship removed the possibility of the [plaintiff's] providing meaningful consent to the sexual contact.'[48]

Justice La Forest, admittedly, mentioned gender only in passing as one of the variables in the inequality of power between the parties, emphasizing instead the defendant's professional status and the plaintiff's addiction. Nonetheless, the description of the dynamics of sexual exploitation put forward seems to be infused with an understanding of gender inequality.

No such understanding with respect to the impact of race was present. Patricia Peppin has stated: 'As Mary Eberts, one of the "founding mothers" of LEAF, has pointed out, the case proceeded on a "race neutral basis"; nowhere in the judgment is it evident that Laura Norberg is an Aboriginal woman, a further and intersecting condition of disadvantage.'[49] It is unclear at what stage of the litigation Norberg's racial identity was effectively edited out. Regardless, the result was the segmentation of Norberg's identity and the oversimplification of the analysis of the power dynamics that were operating in her case.[50] The need to be vigilant in presenting complex cases in a manner true to plaintiffs' experience of them, and to fight against the disposition of courts to privilege artificially some facets of plaintiffs' identity over others, is clear.[51]

Limitation Periods

In *K.M. v. H.M.*,[52] the Supreme Court undertook a contextual analysis of the limitation period that applies to the tort of battery when the latter is invoked to sue for damages arising from incest. In that case LEAF, as an intervenor, explicitly argued that 'the Limitations Act should be interpreted in a manner consistent with the Charter in effecting a liberal application of the limitations provisions as they affect incest victims.'[53] Mr Justice La Forest, writing for the majority, stated that it was unnecessary for him to consider the constitutional argument, given the result he reached. But his judgment appears to exemplify the kind of interpretation of the legislation that LEAF argued was mandated by Charter equality provisions. He held that, in the context of incest, the reasonable discoverability principle operates and so the limitation period does not begin to run until the plaintiff has 'a substantial awareness of the harm and its likely cause,' most often not until she has entered therapy.[54] In reaching this conclusion, he considered the power dynamic of incest which enables the perpetrator to render the victim 'entirely dependent on [him] for whatever reality is assigned to the experience.'[55]

Damages

Equality principles have explicitly and implicitly entered into the process of quantifying damages in a number of appellate cases regarding loss of future earning capacity of female plaintiffs. Such principles have come to the fore in two categories of cases. The first category involves cases in which female children are injured so severely that their future earning capacity is reduced to nil; the second involves cases in which adult women who have devoted themselves to homemaking are injured to such an extent that they are no longer able to perform this work. In both categories, the concern is the way in which these losses are evaluated and the consequent size of the damage awards based on such evaluations.

With respect to infant plaintiffs, the debate has revolved largely around the actuarial tables which have been used to predict future earnings and the disparity therein between projected earnings for males and females. As such tables are based on statistics regarding past and current earning levels of men and women, they reflect biases that have operated and continue to operate against women in the labour force. Using these tables to project earnings as much as sixty years into the future is to presume women's involvement in the paid labour force will remain static and ensures perpetuation of existing inequities despite changing market trends.[56] Further, as Elaine Gibson has pointed out, the statistics upon which these tables are based relate primarily to married women and, as such, rest 'on a traditional family model in which the wife subordinates at least a portion of her earning potential for the sake of invest-ment of time and energy in caring for her family.'[57] Gibson concludes: 'As the family dynamic alters, the inaccuracy of the actuarial statistics intensifies.'[58]

Two approaches have been suggested for rectifying the inaccuracy and in-justice of calculating future income loss of female infant plaintiffs in this way, both of which have been considered in recent appellate court judgments. The first involves altering the tables relating to women's earning capacity to take into account current trends in the labour market towards increased equality. The second involves using the tables relating to men's earning capacity to calculate the loss of future earnings for women as well as men.

In his dissenting judgment in *Tucker v. Ayleson*,[59] Chief Justice McEachern of the British Columbia Supreme Court embraced the first approach. He stated:

It is not difficult to predict a continuing trend in society towards equality in both opportunity and economic rewards for women and men. Such is the policy of all levels of government, institutions and professions, as well as most segments of the private sector. Greater equality is not just a Charter value: it is also a realistic goal. Over the expected working life of the plaintiff, starting at about age 20, and extending for about 45 years thereafter, it may safely be assumed that the present spread between income for men and women will be greatly narrowed if not eliminated. Legislation requiring equal pay for work of equal value may be enacted during her time. It is to be hoped that equality may be achieved within the plaintiff's pre-employment years.[60]

Despite this optimistic statement, however, Chief Justice McEachern was not willing simply to substitute male-earning tables for purposes of calculation. He stated that, in fairness to defendants, actual differences in earning power given the current state of the market must be taken into account: 'While we may strive for social justice, as it is perceived from time to time, the courts must deal with the parties who are before them, plaintiffs and defendants, on the basis of realistic predictions about the future, and not just in accordance with understandable wishes that society, in some of its aspects, were different from what it really is.' At the present time, as the average statistics clearly show, women earn far less than men. Deplorable as that is, it would be unfair to defendants in this and other cases, some of whom are under-insured women, to ignore that reality. The most the courts can do is to ensure, so far as may be possible, that proper weight is given to identifiable societal trends so that the assessment of the plaintiff's future losses will reflect relevant future circumstances.[61]

Susan Griffin, co-counsel for the plaintiff in Tucker, has, however, made a persuasive argument for the alternate approach of using male-earnings tables to calculate future losses of female infant plaintiffs. She contends that the emphasis ought not to be on probable future earnings but on earning capacity, arguing: 'It cannot be contended in this day and age that women have an inferior capacity to men. That would be just as abhorrent as saying that certain races are of an inherently inferior capacity.'[62] The Supreme Court had an opportunity to rule on this point in *Toneguzzo-Norvell v. Burnaby Hospital*[63] but declined to do so given the lack of a proper evidentiary foundation upon which to base any conclusions. Justice McLachlin did, however, leave the argument open for future consideration.[64]

With respect to adult female plaintiffs, a major issue has been the devaluation of homemaking in the quantification of damage awards. Historically, damages for the loss of homemaking capacity were not awarded to women at all but to their husbands or families. This has changed in recent decades, but even so, because homemaking is unpaid labour, judges have continued to discount its worth regardless of which party is being compensated for its loss. In *Fobel v. Dean*,[65] the Saskatchewan Court of Appeal was faced squarely with the issue of how damages for the loss of homemaking capacity ought to be quantified. The primary question was whether damages should be restricted to the replacement cost of domestic labour or whether they should also include the 'care and management of a household.' Justice Vancise recognized that, with respect to the latter, 'awards tend to minimize the importance of such contributions and work by homemakers.'[66] Ultimately, he concluded that awards should include both components, direct labour and management. He described direct labour as including 'food preparation, cleaning, clothing and linen care, maintenance, gardening, and physical child care,' and management as including 'marketing (in the broadest sense including shopping for all items required for the efficient organization and operation of a home), food planning (including the determination of menus and quality and amount of food), tutorial child care, activity coordination and organization, health care and counselling.'[67] Justice Vancise concluded that these lists, while not exhaustive, would go some way towards an accurate evaluation of the value of homemaking and therefore towards fair and just compensation. Leave to appeal to the Supreme Court was sought in the case but denied.[68]

In the cases discussed above, the Charter is mentioned only obliquely, if at all. Yet each appears to integrate an *Andrews*-type equality analysis into tort-law development. In *Norberg v. Wynrib* and in *K.M. v. H.M.*, the Supreme Court did not treat plaintiffs and defendants as though they came into court on an equal footing. The power dynamics central to doctor-patient relationships and to incest situations were taken into account in the application of tort rules relating to consent and limitation periods. In the quantification of damages cases involving female infant plaintiffs and adult homemakers, historic disadvantage and inequality were acknowledged.

Feminism, Equality, and Tort Theory

It would, of course, be overly simplistic to treat the development of constitutional equality principles and the enhanced sensitivity to equality issues in tort-law decisions as if there is a straightforward cause-effect relation between them. In many respects, there has been a parallel development in constitutional and tort theory. The impact of feminist and other critical scholarship on both merits consideration here.

While feminist constitutional theorists like Colleen Sheppard have been suggesting that equality analyses be infused with 'caring,' feminist tort theorists like Leslie Bender have been asserting that tort-law concepts such as care ought to be formulated with equality in mind. Both these strands of theory emphasize the centrality of a consideration of human relationships, particularly as they are structured by an 'ethic of care,'[69] to progressive law reform.[70]

Sheppard first suggests that we seek to understand problems of inequality by 'examin[ing] the nature of the human relationships within which they arise' and to remedy it through a restructuring of those relationships.[71] Stressing the need not simply to assess unequal relationships against equal ones but also to distinguish between types of inequality, she turns to psychologist Jean Miller's distinction between temporary and permanent relations of inequality. Temporary relations of inequality tend to involve the more powerful serving the less powerful with a view to eventual empowerment of the latter, for example, parent-child relationships, while permanent relations of inequality reverse and entrench this dynamic.[72] Caring is central to temporary, but not to permanent, relations of inequality. The concept of caring can thus provide a tool by which to determine what relationships require restructuring and consequently should be taken seriously as a source of political and legal insight. Sheppard states that 'in relations of equality, I would expect a fluid shifting of taking care of and being cared for between individuals and/or groups.'[73]

The contextual analysis described earlier is a precondition to a caring approach to equality since, in order to be responsive to the needs of other individuals and groups, there must be some basis for understanding of, or at least empathy towards, them. Sheppard proposes that this be achieved by 'adopting the standpoint of the "concrete other,"' that is, in the words of Seyla Benhabib, by viewing 'each and every rational being as an individual with a concrete history, identity and affective-emotional constitution.'[74] Sheppard concludes: 'In elaborating a legal approach to equality, the concept of caring may be helpful at two stages. First, it may contribute to the process of identifying inequality or discrimination. Second, it may provide insights into the structuring of legal remedies.'[75]

A substantial body of feminist tort theory has been building in recent years which on its face would appear to be the corollary of the above.[76] Feminist tort theorists contend, not that equality needs to be infused with care, but that care needs to be infused with equality. The sources of the contention and the ends for which it is put forward are, however, strikingly similar.

While this body of theory is diverse, a common starting point is the tort standard of reasonable care. Scholars such as Leslie Bender and Lucinda Finley have argued that application of the facially neutral standard of reasonable care may operate to the detriment of women and minority groups much as application of formal equality does.[77] They suggest that a standard of reasonable care would be more equitable if the emphasis were taken off the reasonable component (a gendered concept which operates more favourably for men) and placed on the care component (a concept which has the potential to bring values more commonly held by women to the fore). Such a shift could rectify current inequalities in tort law relating to the standards by which female defendants are judged and to the evaluation of the harm female plaintiffs suffer.

Many torts scholars decry the possibility of tort law acting as a potential avenue of progressive change in the way outlined above, contending that tort is too firmly embedded in an individualistic liberal philosophy, a philosophy founded on formal rather than substantive equality.[78] Others, however, find promise in some of the underlying principles of tort law and in two trends in modern tort law – shifting conceptions of autonomy and the 'etherialization' of tort law.[79] These factors point to a central influence for substantive equality principles in the development of tort law.

Martin Kotler tracks the development in American tort law of a shift away from the primacy of property concerns, which compels tort law in a more egalitarian direction. He asserts that American tort law is currently 'between paradigms,' but that autonomy has been and remains its primary goal. The change that has occurred has been in the way that autonomy is conceived: 'Although at one time protection of autonomy was understood primarily in terms of protection of private property rights, now the societal and legal perception of autonomy focuses on the protection of one's bodily integrity.'[80] In support of his thesis, Kotler points to the fact that preventative remedies are now available to protect individuals from bodily invasion in advance, for example, in the context of domestic violence, whereas before-the-fact remedies are no longer as readily available to protect private property from damage.[81] Putting bodily integrity at the core of autonomy in place of property interests necessarily gives tort law a more egalitarian character. At the very least, it affords tort protection to a broader range of people.

Nancy Levit describes a process of the progressive 'etherialization' of tort law which marks a further evolution in conceptions of autonomy beyond bodily integrity to emotional integrity. She points to the recent trend towards successful claims for intangible and emotional injuries, claims to which courts have not traditionally been receptive because of social and legal devaluation of the injuries that give rise to them.[82] Martha Chamallas and Linda Kerber persuasively argue that, most often, the privileging of tangible over intangible injuries has meant devaluation of harms suffered disproportionately by women.[83] The continuing etherialization of tort law could amount to further reconceiving autonomy in a way that better protects the interests of women.[84] Again, the trend is towards substantive equality.

In two recent essays, Ken Cooper-Stephenson stresses that Anglo-Canadian 'tort law locates itself in, and is throughout influenced by, a socio-legal context which includes important norms of substantive equality.'[85] He suggests that tort law not only can and should integrate concepts of substantive equality that have developed in human rights law, but that it already has.[86] He asserts that tort law frequently 'serves to redistribute collective wealth for the benefit of the underprivileged and disadvantaged at the expense of the privileged and the advantaged' through the way threshold questions of duty and tort obligation are constructed and answered.[87] This is evident in determinations of what counts as a loss for purposes of tort law, the choice of fault requirements for different relationships, and, finally, in the types of relationships that tort law recognizes as significant in the imposition of duties.[88] Though conceding that at one time tort law concerned itself primarily with protecting the advantaged, by virtue of their status as property owners, he asserts that tort law's distributive sympathies have changed gradually to address the interests of the underprivileged and powerless.[89] He concludes: 'In short, a tort remedy is corrective at its core but is set in a distributive egalitarian context which drives its content.'[90]

Ted DeCoste suggests that tort law can act in furtherance of substantive equality if it is viewed as a site of progressive practice. Women can attempt to inscribe their authentic subjectivities into tort law 'by secreting into law's subject ... the lived realities of women's lives.'[91]

It would seem, then, that equality principles have been gradually insinuated into the development of tort law through the influence of feminist and other critical scholarship, as well as shifting societal values, without benefit of a constitutional equality guarantee. Perhaps rather than resulting from the influence of the Charter, the awareness of societal power imbalances evident in recent Canadian tort decisions is a development parallel to the constitutional theory and Charter jurisprudence which gave rise to the Supreme Court's embrace of substantive equality in *Andrews*.

Nevertheless, DeCoste's program for continuing progressive change in tort law points to, if not a cause-effect relationship between Charter guarantees and a tort law grounded in substantive equality, at least a productive partnership between them. The contextual approach to equality embraced in *Andrews* provides an opportunity for bringing the subjectivities of litigants to the fore in tort cases. And the constitutional origin of that opportunity is bound to have some effect on the scope of its application given the convictions judges hold about their roles as arbiters of private disputes. Judges who may not previously have thought it appropriate to look closely at the subjective realities of the parties before them may be emboldened to do so by a constitutional provision which can be regarded as validating such an approach.

Judicial Attitudes

Joel Bakan cautions that 'an adequate account of the role of the Charter in progressive social struggles requires going beyond prescriptive analysis to consider what courts are likely to do with the Charter given their historical and political context. Analysis of judicial review must take account of constraints and pressures imposed by the particular order of social and economic relations in which the Charter and judiciary are situated.'[92] This statement relates specifically to constitutional adjudication but clearly it is also relevant to the subject of this essay, the influence of constitutional values on private adjudication. Bakan's caution is intended to curb artificial optimism about the Charter's progressive potential. I would argue, however, that in taking the historical and political context of courts into account to produce a realistic picture of the potential of litigation strategies, it is important to consider positive factors as well as negative ones.

In exploring constraints on judicial review, Bakan highlights prevailing judicial ideologies which lead judges to an affinity with 'the interests of litigants who represent the social and economic elite.'[93] This stems in part from the personal identities of judges: 'We hear, time and again, that judges see the world through dominant ideological lenses because of their elite backgrounds and social positions. We hear this a lot because it is true. Judges are for the most part white, male, wealthy, and they are always lawyers.'[94] Robin West adds the 'jurisprudential identity' of judges to the equation, suggesting that their 'conservative' readings of legal texts may 'be rooted in the Court's and courts' institutional identity as interpreters of law. The vast majority of legal actors understand law as jurisprudentially requiring, by definition, the identification of rights, wrongs and remedies, applied in a way that restores the pre-injury, or pre-wrong status quo.'[95] Thus, even judges who do not suppose themselves to be neutral arbiters of the law, devoid of a social context, may nonetheless believe that their judicial role compels them to attempt to apply the law in a neutral and objective fashion.[96]

In looking for explanations for the insinuation of Charter equality principles into private law decisions against this backdrop, a number of social forces must be considered. First, the personal identities of the judiciary are becoming more diverse, albeit slowly. More women and members of minority groups are being appointed to the bench and these individuals may well be adjudicating disputes with different concerns in mind than those traditionally brought to bear on the decision-making process.[97] Second, all judges are exposed to, and potentially affected by, not just the changing social values that led legislators to propose a Charter of Rights in the first place, but also education programs specifically aimed at sensitizing them to equality issues.[98]

While these factors may be regarded as alternate explanations for recent trends in private law decisions, I think it important to view them in conjunction with the influence of the Charter. For example, judicial-education programs are in some cases probably inspired by the Charter in the sense that they are perhaps regarded as necessary because of the kind of decisions judges are expected to make under it. Their effect can nonetheless expand beyond Charter cases. More important, the Charter may act to lift some of the constraints judges have previously felt bound by, giving them some official sanction for bringing equality concerns to bear on whatever case is before them. Chief Justice Bayda of the Saskatchewan Court of Appeal has written that, while the law-making opportunities afforded by the common-law system have 'always allowed the Canadian judge a discretion to draw upon community values and public morality in the formulation of his or her judgments, it is only after the enactment of the Charter that the judge acquired what may be described as a true freedom in that regard.'[99] This freedom may extend beyond constitutional adjudication to the kinds of private law decisions discussed above.

Conclusion

Although many factors have contributed to the increasing emphasis on equality issues in private law, it is clear that the constitutional enshrinement of an equality guarantee has been central to this development. Clearly then, the section 15 equality guarantee has promise beyond constitutional litigation.

In stressing that promise, I am not suggesting that the Charter is an unequivocally positive force for women or other equality-seeking groups. The Charter has been the source of some serious setbacks for Canadian women, for example, the invalidation of the rape-shield provisions in the Criminal Code.[100] As well, many of the decisions that have been regarded as victories for women and minority groups did not involve the positive application of the Charter but rather the saving of legislation under section 1 which would not have been in jeopardy in the first place were it not for the Charter, as in *Keegstra* and *Butler*. Further, decisions regarded as victories by some are not embraced as such by all. The *Butler* decision, touted by some as a victory for women, has been heavily criticized by others as having provided leeway to customs officials to harass gay and lesbian artists and writers.[101] Finally, as other contributors to this volume have illustrated, some disadvantaged groups have had more success than others under the Charter, generally those that are already closest to privilege.[102]

What I do wish to emphasize, however, is the breadth of the influence of the Charter's equality guarantees and, in that light, their value, not instead of but in conjunction with other forms of social action.[103] Colleen Sheppard states: 'I do not think use of the Charter should be limited to litigation, despite the importance of this function. We also need to use the Charter as a tool for legislative reform, to encourage positive government action needed to secure greater social, economic, familial and political equality, and to demand such action even in the absence of litigation.'[104] I would add that, even within the arena of litigation, use of the Charter need not be limited to straightforward constitutional litigation.

Catherine Dauvergne has argued recently that, in assessing the utility of engaging in rights discourse in a given situation, careful attention must be given to context.[105] She notes that the criminal context, where much constitutional litigation takes place, is the one where rights discourse is least effective for women, because there women's equality claims are set against the rights of accused persons. And the latter, despite occasional protests to the contrary, are part of a different order of rights. Dauvergne concludes that other types of cases, for example, *Janzen* in the human-rights arena and *Norberg* in the tort arena, 'must be included in order to present a complete picture of how the Charter has influenced the protection of women from sexual violence and victimization.'[106]

In the broader pursuit of equality, therefore, the private-law context must not be overlooked as an arena where rights discourse and litigation strategies may be used successfully. It is of central importance, in order to evaluate accurately the potential of the Charter for effecting social change, to gain an appreciation of the full extent of the influence of Charter equality guarantees beyond constitutional litigation, namely on private law decisions as well as on the attitudes of the judges and other legal professionals who forge such decisions.

Notes

1 *S.D.G.M.R. v. Dolphin Delivery Ltd.* [1986], 33 D.L.R. (4th) 174 (S.C.C.).
2 *Andrews v. Law Society of B.C.* [1989], 56 D.L.R. (4th) 1 (S.C.C.).
3 *Dolphin Delivery* at 191.
4 Ibid., at 195.
5 Ibid., at 196.
6 Ibid., at 198.
7 Allan C. Hutchinson and Andrew Petter, 'Private Rights/Public Wrongs: The Liberal Lie of the Charter,' *University of Toronto Law Journal*, vol. 38 (1988), 292.
8 Ibid.
9 Sheilah Martin, 'Some Constitutional Considerations on Sexual Violence Against Women,' *Alberta Law Review*, vol. 32 (1994), 5. See also Joel Bakan's discussion and critique of this idea in 'Constitutional Interpretation and Social Change: You Can't Always Get What You Want (Nor What You Need),' in *Canadian Perspectives on Legal Theory*, ed. R. Devlin (Toronto: Emond Montgomery 1991), 453.
10 *R. v. Salituro* [1991], 68 C.C.C. (3d) 289 (S.C.C.) at 305.
11 Ibid., at 301. In *Dagenais v. Canadian Broadcasting Corp.* [1995], 120 D.L.R. (4th) 12 (S.C.C.), Chief Justice Lamer, in the majority judgment, used similar reasoning in deeming it 'necessary to reformulate the common-law rule governing the issuance of publication bans in a manner that reflects the principles of the Charter' (at 37). There the original rule did reflect the Charter value of ensuring a fair trial, but it did so by privileging that value absolutely over the Charter value of freedom of expression. The Court found this unacceptable and reformulated the rule to achieve a better balance.

12 See n.2.
13 Judy Fudge, 'The Public/Private Distinction: The Possibilities of and the Limits to the Use of Charter Litigation to Further Feminist Struggles,' *Osgoode Hall Law Review*, vol. 25 (1987), 489.
14 Hester Lessard, 'The Idea of the "Private": A Discussion of State Action Doctrine and Separate Sphere Ideology,' in *Charterwatch: Reflections on Equality*, eds. C. Boyle *et al.* (Toronto: Carswell 1986), 127.
15 Madam Justice Beverly McLachlin, 'The Charter: A New Role for the Judiciary,' *Alberta Law Review*, vol. 29 (1991), 543.
16 For a discussion of contextualization of judicial decision making, see Martha Minow and Elizabeth V. Spelman, 'In Context,' *Southern California Law Review*, vol. 63 (1990), 1,597; and Ruth Colker, 'Section 1, Contextualization, and the Antidisadvantage Principle,' *University of Toronto Law Journal*, vol. 42 (1992), 77.
17 Colker, ibid., 79.
18 Canadian Charter of Rights and Freedoms, Part I of the Constitution Act, 1982, being Schedule B of the Canada Act, 1982 (U.K.), 1982, c. 11, s 1.
19 McLachlin, 'The Charter,' 547.
20 *R. v. Big M Drug Mart* [1985], 18 D.L.R. (4th) 321 (S.C.C.).
21 See *R. v. Keegstra*, [1990] 3 S.C.R. 697 (hate speech) and *R. v. Butler*, [1992] 1 S.C.R. 460 (pornography). In these cases, limitations on the exercise of freedom of expression were approved on the grounds that they fostered equality.
22 *R. v. Turpin*, [1989] 1 S.C.R. 1296, 1,331–2.
23 Ibid., 1,333.
24 *Andrews*, at 165.
25 Ibid.
26 See, for example, Catherine MacKinnon, 'Difference and Dominance: On Sex Discrimination,' in *Feminism Unmodified* (Cambridge, Mass.: Harvard University Press 1987); Ruth Colker, 'Anti-Subordination Above All: Sex, Race, and Equal Protection,' *New York University Law Review*, vol. 61, (1986), 1,003; Mary Joe Frug, 'Sexual Equality and Sexual Difference in American Law,' *New England Law Review*, vol. 26 (1992), 665; Donna Greschner, 'Judicial Approaches to Equality and Critical Legal Studies,' in *Equality and Judicial Neutrality*, eds. K. Mahoney and S. Martin (Toronto: Carswell 1987), 59; and Kathleen Lahey, 'Feminist Theories of (In)Equality,' ibid., at 71.
27 Diana Majury, 'Equality and Discrimination According to the Supreme Court of Canada,' *Canadian Journal of Women and the Law*, vol. 4 (1990–1), 419.
28 Ibid.
29 Ibid., 417.
30 Kathleen Mahoney, 'The Constitutional Law of Equality in Canada,' *Maine Law Review*, vol. 44 (1992), 247.

31 *Andrews* at 163–4.
32 Richard Moon, 'A Discrete and Insular Right to Equality: Comment on *Andrews v. Law Society of British Columbia*,' *Ottawa Law Review*, vol. 21 (1989), 572.
33 Colleen Sheppard, 'Recognition of the Disadvantaging of Women: The Promise of *Andrews* v. Law Society of British Columbia,' *McGill Law Journal*, vol. 35 (1989), 217.
34 *R. v. Oakes*, [1986] 1 S.C.R. 103 at 136.
35 Ibid.
36 McLachlin, 'The Charter.'
37 Ibid., 733.
38 Ibid., 734.
39 Ibid., 755.
40 Ibid., 756.
41 Ibid.
42 See n.21.
43 *Keegstra*, at 492–3.
44 Ibid., at 497.
45 See, for example, Alison Diduck and Helena Orton, 'Equality and Support for Spouses,' *Modern Law Review*, vol. 57 (1994), 681, where *Andrews* is cited as a necessary backdrop to the way family law with respect to spousal support was interpreted in the Supreme Court's decision in the *Moge* case. Further, this phenomenon is not confined to private law. Sheilah Martin has undertaken a similar analysis of the impact of Charter values on non-constitutional criminal cases. Of the divergence in *R. v. McCraw*, [1991] 3 S.C.R. 72 between the Ontario Court of Appeal's assessment of a letter containing rape threats and that of the Supreme Court, Martin states: 'The primary difference is that the Supreme Court used the Charter rights of women as the prism through which they analyzed the prohibition in issue and the acts in question. Even though women's equality rights and their equal right to life, liberty and security of the person constituted no formal part of the Court's reasons and were not expressly cited in the judgment, an understanding of the social context of women's inequality and women's constitutional entitlements infused the judgment. The spotlight was not directly on women's Charter interests, but they clearly illuminated the entire decision' ('Some Constitutional Considerations,' 18).
46 *Norberg v. Wynrib*, [1992] 2 S.C.R. 224.
47 Ibid., at 247.
48 Ibid., at 261.
49 Patricia Peppin, 'Power and Disadvantage in Medical Relationships,' *Texas Journal of Women and the Law*, vol. 3 (1994), 260.

50 This is consistent with the results of Nitya Iyer's analysis of the treatment of race and sex in human-rights cases. In 'Disappearing Women: Racial Minority Women in Human Rights Cases,' *Canadian Journal of Women and the Law*, vol. 6 (1993), 25, Iyer states: 'There is virtually no consideration of the complex interactions of race, sex and the various other grounds of discrimination that are so much a part of the lived experience (as opposed to the legal analysis) of discrimination,' (40).

51 For a parallel, see *State v. Wanrow* (1977), 88 Wn. 2d 221, where the U.S. Supreme Court concluded that to hold Yvonne Wanrow to a male standard of reasonableness in her claim of self defence in the killing of a male assailant constituted sex discrimination. Yet the Court refused simultaneously to take account of the impact of Wanrow's 'Indian culture upon her perceptions and actions' (at 241). For a fuller account of the case, see 'Yvonne Wanrow: The Logic of Cultural Narrative,' in Janice Schuetz, *The Logic of Women on Trial: Case Studies of Popular American Trials* (Carbondale, Ill.: Southern Illinois University Press 1994).

52 *K.M. v. H.M.* [1993], 96 D.L.R. (4th) 289 (S.C.C.).

53 Ibid., at 298.

54 Ibid., at 314.

55 Ibid., at 300.

56 Elaine Gibson, 'Loss of Capacity for the Female Tort Victim: Comment on *Toneguzzo-Norvell (Guardian ad litem of) v. Burnaby Hospital*,' 17 CCLT (2d) 78 at 83.

57 Ibid., 83–4.

58 Ibid., 84.

59 [1993], 102 D.L.R. (4th) 518 (B.C.C.A.).

60 Ibid., at 536.

61 Ibid., at 533–4.

62 Susan A. Griffin, 'The Value of Women – Avoiding the Prejudices of the Past,' *The Advocate*, vol. 51 (1993), 546.

63 [1994] 110 D.L.R. (4th) 289 (S.C.C.).

64 Ibid., at 295.

65 [1991], 93 Sask. R. 103 (C.A.).

66 Ibid., at 115.

67 Ibid., at 116.

68 *Fobel v. Dean* [1992], 97 Sask. R. 240 (S.C.C.).

69 For the genesis of the concept of an ethic of care, see Carol Gilligan, *In a Different Voice: Psychological Theory and Women's Development* (Cambridge, Mass.: Harvard University Press 1982); and for evaluation of its application to law and politics, see Joan Tronto, *Moral Boundaries: A Political Argument for*

and *Ethic of Care* (New York: Routledge 1993), and *An Ethic of Care: Feminist and Interdisciplinary Perspectives*, ed. Mary Jeanne Larrabee (New York: Routledge 1993).

70 Other feminist scholars who conceptualize rights as founded not in individuals but in the relationships between them include Jennifer Nedelsky, 'Reconceiving Rights as Relationship,' *Review of Constitutional Studies*, vol. 1 (1993), 1; and Sherene Razack, 'Collective Rights and Women: "The Cold Game of Equality Staring."' *Journal of Human Justice*, vol. 4 (1992), 1.

71 Colleen Sheppard, 'Caring in Human Relations and Legal Approaches to Equality,' *National Journal of Constitutional Law*, vol. 2 (1993), 307, 310.

72 Ibid., 311.

73 Ibid., 321.

74 Ibid., 326–7.

75 Ibid., 333.

76 For a survey of feminist tort scholarship, see Leslie Bender 'An Overview of Feminist Torts Scholarship,' *Cornell Law Review*, vol. 78 (1993), 575.

77 See Leslie Bender, 'A Lawyer's Primer in Feminist Theory and Tort,' *Journal of Legal Education*, vol. 38 (1988), 3; idem., 'Changing the Values in Tort Law,' *Tulsa Law Journal*, vol. 25 (1990), 759; and Lucinda Finley, 'A Break in the Silence: Including Women's Issues in a Torts Course,' *Yale Journal of Law and Feminism*, vol. 1 (1989), 41.

78 See, for example, Richard L. Abel, 'A Critique of Torts,' *UCLA Law Review*, vol. 37 (1990), 785; Joanne Conaghan and Wade Mansell, 'Tort Law,' in *The Critical Lawyers Handbook*, eds. Ian Grigg-Spall and Paddy Ireland (London: Pluto Press 1992); Bruce Feldthusen, 'If This is Torts, Negligence Must Be Dead,' in *Tort Theory*, eds. Ken Cooper-Stephenson and Elaine Gibson (North York, Ont.: Captus Press 1993); Allan C. Hutchinson and Derek Morgan, 'The Canengusian Connection: The Kaleidoscope of Tort Theory,' *Osgoode Hall Law Journal*, vol. 22 (1994), 69; and Allan C. Hutchinson, 'Beyond No-Fault,' *California Law Review*, vol. 73 (1985), 755.

79 See Martin A Kotler, 'Competing Conceptions of Autonomy: A Reappraisal of the Basis of Tort Law,' *Tulane Law Review*, vol. 67 (1992), 347; Ken Cooper-Stephenson, 'Corrective Justice, Substantive Equality and Tort Law,' in Cooper-Stephenson and Gibson, *Tort Theory*, 48.; idem., 'Economic Analysis, Substantive Equality an Tort Law,' ibid., 131; Lucie Legere, 'The Culture of the Common Law in the 21st Century: Tort Law's Response to the Needs of a Pluralist Society,' ibid., 162; Ted DeCoste, 'Taking Torts Progressively,' ibid., 240; and Nancy Levit, 'Ethereal Torts,' *George Washington Law Review*, vol. 61 (1992), 136.

80 Kotler, 'Competing Conceptions,' 351.

81 Ibid., 370–4.
82 Levit, 'Ethereal Torts,' 172–4.
83 Martha Chamallas and Linda K. Kerber, 'Women, Mothers and the Law of Fright: A History,' *Michigan Law Review*, vol. 88 (1990), 814.
84 See Jennifer Nedelsky, 'Reconceiving Autonomy: Sources, Thoughts and Possibilities,' *Yale Journal of Law and Feminism*, vol. 1 (1989), 7, where she lists some of the necessary elements in a feminist conception of autonomy: 'comprehension, confidence, dignity, efficacy, respect, and some degree of peace and security from oppressive power' (11).
85 Cooper-Stephenson, 'Corrective Justice,' 49.
86 Ibid., 48.
87 Ibid., 53.
88 Ibid.
89 Ibid., 55–6. He cites, as an example, the explicit policy analysis that has become part of the duty of care analysis in Canadian law.
90 Ibid., 57.
91 'Taking Torts Progressively,' 274.
92 'Constitutional Interpretation,' 445.
93 Ibid., 450.
94 Ibid.
95 Robin West, 'The Meaning of Equality and the Interpretive Turn,' *Chicago-Kent Law Review*, vol. 66 (1990), 469.
96 For one judge's account of the constraints in decision-making stemming from the nature of the judicial role, see Chief Justice E.D. Bayda, 'Moral Values in Judicial Decision-Making: Do Judges Really Need to Think?' in *Legal Theory Meets Legal Practice*, ed. Anne Bayefsky (Edmonton: Academic Printing 1988), 109.
97 See, for example, Madam Justice Bertha Wilson, 'Will Women Judges Really Make a Difference?' *Osgoode Hall Law Journal*, vol. 28 (1990), 507; and Susan Moloney Smith, 'Diversifying the Judiciary: The Influence of Gender and Race on Judging,' *University of Richmond Law Review*, vol. 28 (1994), 179.
98 Mr Justice Melvin L. Rothman, 'Prospects for Change in Canada: Education for Judges an Lawyers,' in Mahoney and Martin, *Equality and Judicial Neutrality*, 421. See also Mary Jane Mossman, 'The Charter and Access to Justice in Canada,' in this volume.
99 'Moral Values,' 113.
100 *R. v. Seaboyer and Gayme* [1991], 128 N.R. 81 (S.C.C.). However, see Catherine Dauvergne, 'A Reassessment of the Effects of a Constitutional Charter of Rights on the Discourse of Sexual Violence in Canada,' *International Journal of the Sociology of Law*, vol. 22 (1994), 291, where she considers *Seaboyer's* effect in mobilizing women to seek legislative changes in the law of consent, as well as its

effect on public discourse about sexual violence. Thus, though the decision was a
setback, its consequences may be regarded as a step forward.

101 See, for example, Persimmon Blackbridge, 'Against the Law: Sex Versus the
    Queen,' in *Kiss & Tell, Her Tongue on My Theory* (Vancouver: Press Gang
    Publishers 1994). Blackbridge states: 'When the *Butler* decision was being
    argued, many lesbians and gay men spoke out against it. It wasn't a case of us
    wanting "special rights" for out sexual images. It was a case of knowing our
    history. We knew that anti-porn laws are applied unequally, against gays and
    lesbians. We knew that, no matter what LEAF's intentions, there was a good
    chance of *Butler* being used against us by the courts and the cops – people with a
    proven track record of homophobia. And we were right, as a look at some recent
    applications of *Butler* show,' (85). For other analyses of the impact of *Butler* on
    gay and lesbian communities, see Karen Busby, 'LEAF and Pornography:
    Litigating on Equality and Sexual Representations,' *Canadian Journal of Law and
    Society*, vol. 9 (1994), 165; Christopher N. Kendall, ' "Real Dominant, Real
    Fun!": Gay Male Pornography and the Pursuit of Masculinity,' *Sask. Law Review*,
    vol. 57 (1993), 21; and Ann Scales, 'Avoiding Constitutional Depression: Bad
    Attitudes and the Fate of *Butler*,' *Canadian Journal of Women and the Law*, vol.
    7 (1994), 349.

102 See, in particular, the essays of Mary Jane Mossman, Didi Herman, John
    Borrows, and Joel Bakan and Michael Smith in this volume.

103 I am alert to the concerns that have been raised in this volume and elsewhere
    by Didi Herman, John Borrows, and Joel Bakan and Michael Smith about the
    potentially negative consequences which can stem from reliance on rights
    discourse and litigation strategies in social struggles.

104 Colleen Sheppard, 'Equality in Context: Judicial Approaches in Canada and the
    United States,' *University of New Brunswick Law Journal*, vol. 39 (1990), 125.

105 Dauvergne, 'Reassessment.'

106 Ibid., 301.

9

The Charter and Access to Justice in Canada*

MARY JANE MOSSMAN

One assumption access reformers may make is that the legislative creation of a right implies a societal commitment to its full enforcement. The political reality is much more complicated ... New rights may represent [merely] political symbols enacted by those who wish to mollify dissent without effecting any serious change.[1]

This bleak assessment of the limited impact of new legislative rights was written in 1981, the very time when Canadian law reformers were endeavouring to repatriate the constitution and entrench constitutional guarantees in the Canadian Charter of Rights and Freedoms. Although they probably did not have these Canadian developments in mind, the authors' assertion offers a serious challenge to access reformers in the context of the Charter.[2] For those who perceive the Charter as a means of achieving greater access to justice, the pessimistic view that legal measures are not generally useful in accomplishing lasting or fundamental change to the status quo must be addressed.

It is also important to note the authors' warning in the above quotation that political reality is often 'much more complicated' in relation to access reforms. Indeed, the complexity of the context means that reforms may accomplish diverse results and that it may be difficult to assess their impact with any degree of precision. In thinking about the Charter and access reforms, therefore, it is critical at the outset to decide what questions are appropriate to such an assessment. What kinds of measures are helpful in determining whether substantive change has occurred, and, if it has, in whose interests? Even if we can agree that change has occurred since the Charter took effect in 1982, how do we know that such change is the result of the influence of the Charter? And

* The author wishes to thank Hazel Pollack for excellent word-processing assistance.

how do we assess the impact of the Charter in preventing certain kinds of developments, as well as in fostering those that (arguably) have occurred? Has the Charter been a significant factor in achieving concrete objectives concerning access to justice, or has it operated only in a more symbolic way by creating a climate in which claims for substantive justice are encouraged? And to what extent has the existence of legal remedies in the Charter deterred or deflected other, especially political, interventions relating to access to justice claims?

These are difficult and important questions, and this paper does not attempt to answer all of them. Indeed, some of them may be unanswerable. However, we should consider the significance of framing our questions in this way, that is, in terms of the impact of Charter guarantees on access to justice in Canada. For those who see the law as instrumental and malleable to diverse political ends, Charter guarantees appear to offer useful tools for accomplishing specific and identifiable goals.[3] By contrast, others have been more sceptical about the usefulness of law in making social and political change; for them, the law 'is more likely to be in the rearguard, rather than the vanguard, of social change'[4] and in fact legal guarantees have often seemed to mask the law's intransigence towards meaningful social change.[5] In this context, therefore, it is essential to decide how to ask the right questions about the Charter and access to justice goals so as to assess their relationship during the past decade.

In my view, this task needs to be approached by acknowledging the tension between differing points of view about the law's usefulness as a means of accomplishing change. In part, the differing points of view may be explained as the result of different objectives: for example, those who emphasize the law's usefulness may focus on its impact on formal or procedural changes, while those who challenge this view take more seriously the law's failure to accomplish substantive changes. In the context of Charter challenges, however, such an explanation is not sufficient because some Charter claims have accomplished substantive changes in legal principles and applications, not just formal or procedural changes.[6] Yet, at the same time, the adoption of new legal principles by courts may not concretely improve the lives of ordinary citizens. As suggested elsewhere, for instance, nothing in the decisions of the Supreme Court of Canada about sexual harassment or wife battering 'has concretely enhanced the resources of human rights commissions across Canada to ensure access to remedies for sexual harassment or prevented [governmental] cutbacks in funding for battered women's shelters.'[7] Thus, from the perspective of substantive changes in people's lives and circumstances, the law may not be helpful. Indeed, it may impede change by foreclosing or discouraging other kinds of action to accomplish social change.[8]

By acknowledging the tensions between differing perspectives on the law and social change, it is possible to see the ways in which such perspectives influence the kinds of questions we ask about the law's role.[9] Such an approach can also show how the law and social change influence each other in diverse, and frequently unplanned, ways.[10] In relation to access rights, for example, it is just as important to investigate the impact of two decades of political organizing about access to justice reforms on the creation of Charter guarantees as it is to examine the impact of the Charter on access to justice issues after 1982. Finally, by recognizing these tensions, we can also begin to move away from the stark simplicity of an 'either/or' formulation about the law's effect (or lack thereof) on change and instead see the relationship between the law and social change as a more complex – and mutually interactive – process that occurs within a social context. In doing so, we can explore the ways in which the law 'both facilitates change and is also an obstacle to change.'[11] Such an understanding of the law's paradoxical role allows us to affirm the success of some Charter litigation concerning access issues but without foreclosing equally important questions about its real impact on the lives of Canadians, especially those who are most disadvantaged.

From such a perspective, which assesses the impact of the Charter in terms of *concrete* achievements for those who are *most* disadvantaged in Canadian society, I conclude that access to significant justice reforms has not yet been achieved. At the same time, Charter jurisprudence has affected many Canadians' expectations about their legal equality rights, thereby encouraging disadvantaged individuals to use the Charter to challenge long-standing practices of discrimination. In this way, the Charter has provided a symbolic catalyst for social justice goals,[12] in some cases encouraging (and perhaps in other cases discouraging) political and social debate about the need for change on a range of legal issues. Thus, although the Charter may have had all too little impact on the concrete reality of the most disadvantaged Canadians, it may nonetheless have had an influence, one that is perhaps both unquantifiable and contested, as a 'touchstone for change.'[13] And although it is incumbent on all of us to avoid confusing symbolism with concrete reality, we also need to acknowledge the complexity of relationships between the law and social change as well as the sometimes incremental ways in which change happens. Only by doing so can we ask the right questions and thus design workable solutions to concrete problems.

This essay addresses essential issues concerning the role of Charter guarantees in access to justice. Specifically, it reflects on the relationship between the Charter's guarantees and two interconnected aspects of access to justice: the delivery of legal aid services in the context of the Charter, particularly its equality guarantees; and the impact of these guarantees on the demography and processes of the legal profession. By focusing both on legal services provided to the most disadvantaged Canadians and on changes among 'service provid-ers' in the justice system, it is possible to test the influence of the Charter in contrasting situations affecting access to justice. Generally, the essay suggests that Charter guarantees have had a greater impact on the make-up of the legal profession than on access to legal aid services.

Access to Justice: The Charter and Legal Aid Services

The 'access to justice' movement after the Second World War fostered the creation of legal rights and processes in western societies that were generally 'aimed at the challenging problem of making rights effective' in welfare states of the late twentieth century.[14] The pattern of access-to-justice initiatives in Canada conformed to similar developments in other western societies, both in the creation of substantive rights for disadvantaged groups and in relation to procedural reforms, including access to representation in courts and tribunals. At the same time, some of the Canadian developments reveal unique aspects of our particular legal and political culture.

In early-twentieth-century Canada, as in other western countries at that time, legislation was used relatively infrequently as a means of accomplishing general societal goals, although the lack of such legal intervention for many Canadians contrasted sharply with the more substantial intrusion routinely ex-perienced by others: for Native peoples pursuant to the *Indian Act*, for mothers in receipt of welfare assistance, and for people with mental disabilities, for example, legal regulation was often extensive. After the Second World War, however, the use of legislative action to accomplish defined governmental purposes increased significantly. In terms of access-to-justice goals, post-war legislation was characterized by a focus on the needs of groups previously disadvantaged by law or unprotected by it: 'The rights at the center of access-improving reforms are those typical of welfare state efforts to bolster the position of the weak – especially individuals in such capacities as consumers, tenants, or employees – against relatively powerful organizations. The welfare state has been characterized increasingly by the proliferation of such rights – rights that are designed to promote social change on behalf of the "have-nots." '[15]

In addition to an increased use of legislation to accomplish societal goals, other developments in Canada in the 1960s and 1970s affirmed the positive role of law in the accomplishment of social change. For example, the establish-ment of law reform commissions by the federal government and the provinces in the 1970s demonstrated the importance attached to the process of reform through the legal system as well as the need for specialized institutions to design reform proposals.[16] Law reform commissions initiated reviews in a number of different areas, sometimes in relation to issues affecting ordinary citizens, such as family law,[17] reinforcing ideas about the possibilities of using law effectively to achieve social change. Federal and provincial human-rights agencies and tribunals were also established in the post-war decades, their mandate being to interpret legislatively defined standards of non-discriminatory conduct.[18] Indeed, from the perspective of the 1990s, it is arguable that human-rights jurisprudence prior to the Charter contributed significantly to a judicial climate increasingly receptive to generous interpretations of the 1982 Charter guarantees.[19]

These kinds of developments signalled the generally positive expectations for legal reform activities during the 1960s and 1970s, a period in which access reformers also renewed their efforts to reform legal aid services.[20] As Dieter Hoehne has shown, the Canadian Bar Association had called for governmental funding for the provision of legal counsel as early as the 1920s and 1930s, but legal aid services had nonetheless remained charitable and ad hoc in nature.[21] By the late 1960s, however, governmental support for legal aid programs had increased significantly: as Canada's minister of justice stated in 1969, one of his three main objectives was 'to move as far as we can towards equality of access and equality of treatment before the law for rich and poor alike.'[22]

This commitment to access-to-justice goals was reflected in different ways in the legislative schemes for legal aid services enacted by provincial governments. The first provincial legislation enacted in Ontario in 1966 created a legal aid program based closely on the experiences of the judicare program earlier established in the United Kingdom[23]: lawyers who provided legal services to paying clients were reimbursed by government for the provision of the same kinds of services to non-paying legal aid clients. Conceptually, such a program did not distinguish between the needs of paying clients and legally aided ones, either in terms of substantive legal problems or in relation to clients' problems of accessibility to legal services.[24]

By contrast, other provinces' legal aid schemes were more influenced in their formative years by developments in the United States, where government-funded legal aid programs were initiated by the Office of Economic Opportunity as part of the federal 'War on Poverty.' Because the objective of these legal aid services was the elimination of poverty, the American programs defined available legal aid services in terms of the special needs of poor clients and utilized employed staff lawyers who offered 'expert' poverty-law services only to legal aid clients.[25] These programs were more broadly political in both their objectives and their structures, often involving poor people's groups in the determination of goals and strategies for using law to achieve changes within poor communities.

Legal aid programs adopted initially in Quebec and in some of the western provinces in Canada in the early 1970s reflected this different approach. As the Carter Commission stated in Saskatchewan, for example, 'a legal aid scheme should be capable of acting, on proper occasions, as a vehicle for social change.'[26] Even in Ontario, the American approach was later evident in the work of community legal clinics, initially established outside the provincial legal aid scheme but incorporated as part of the province's 'mixed delivery system' from 1978.[27] Thus, by contrast with judicare programs, which offered legal advice and representation within the (often inadequate) existing legal system,[28] this alternative model focused directly on using law to achieve substantive societal change, although it generally ignored the fundamental ways in which law is itself embedded in existing social arrangements. As Hoehne has argued so persuasively in relation to legal aid services generally, such an approach may strengthen clients' 'position within the adversary system of justice' but it also 'subjects them ... to a legal system whose logic militates against their interests.'[29]

The tension between these conceptual goals for legal aid schemes was also reflected in the structures that evolved for funding legal aid services. Because of the constitutional division of powers in Canada, the federal government financially supported legal aid services in criminal (and later Young Offender) matters, but it did not contribute directly to legal aid services in civil law matters.[30] Because the provinces needed financial contributions to operate legal aid schemes, the federal-provincial legal aid cost-sharing agreements systematically influenced the disproportionate funding of criminal legal aid services and diminished the availability of legal aid for civil law matters, especially when legal aid budgets began to shrink in the 1980s in the face of governmental cutbacks.[31] This focus on criminal law (and the need for services for accused persons) necessarily tended to emphasize legal aid services as primarily responsive to individual legal problems, simultaneously discouraging the idea of legal services for more systemic (group-based) legal issues such as inadequate housing or unemployment. In this way, the federal-provincial cost-sharing agreements contributed to reducing the usefulness of legal aid services as a means of accomplishing systemic social change.

At the same time, however, increased availability of legal representation for indigent persons across Canada reflected widespread community agreement with the Ontario legislative committee which recommended the adoption of a legal aid program in 1965: 'Legal aid is no longer a charity but a right' and 'the responsibility of the whole community.'[32] Two decades later, the Canadian Bar Association's report on legal aid services re-emphasized the need for legal aid services in terms of political values in Canada: 'Legal aid services are essential because they help to ensure equality before the law. Together, representative government and equality before the law form the base of our democratic system. The first requires the right to vote and the second requires equal access to the judicial system.'[33] Thus, as has been suggested elsewhere, even though debate continues about objectives and levels of funding, there is general consensus about the need both for legal aid services as an accepted feature of the administration of justice in Canada and for the existence of some degree of governmental obligation to provide such services.[34]

From the perspective of legal aid and similar developments before 1982, access-to-justice initiatives arguably contributed to a political and legal consensus receptive to the idea of entrenched legal and equality rights in Canada. In this way, the Charter's guarantees may have resulted from the contributions of the access-to-justice movement prior to 1982 at least as much as (or perhaps more than) the Charter has positively affected access to justice since then. Particularly in provinces that adopted legal aid programs modelled on the U.S. approach (using law to make change on behalf of the poor and disadvantaged), community involvement in legal aid clinics meant that people other than lawyers became involved in issues about the administration of justice. Moreover, because these legal aid programs encouraged the use of group actions to address poverty issues, they also fostered the creation of legal-interest groups among disadvantaged people: tenants, the unemployed, welfare recipients, and those with mental or physical disabilities.[35]

At the same time, however, broad consensus about access-to-justice issues prior to the Charter's enactment did not result in judicial acceptance of principles of entitlement to legal aid services. In *Re White and the Queen*[36] in 1976, for example, Justice McDonald considered the extent of an Alberta court's inherent power to appoint legal counsel for an indigent accused and concluded that the power was discretionary only.[37] In addition to this limited interpretation of a court's inherent power to appoint counsel, a majority of the British Columbia Court of Appeal in *Re Ewing and Kearney and the Queen* held that the wording of section 2(c)(ii) of the Canadian Bill of Rights did not create a right to legal counsel at public expense.[38] The two dissenting judges in *Ewing* relied on the need for counsel to ensure a fair trial, citing both American jurisprudence[39] and Canadian cases in which the absence of legal representation had called into question the fairness of trial processes.[40] Yet, overall, the courts denied the existence of a guaranteed right to counsel in criminal or other matters.

Thus, at the time of Charter negotiations in 1982, there was no established right to legal aid services in Canada, although legal aid programs, administered on a discretionary basis within statutory or other guidelines, were accepted throughout the country as an important feature of the administration of justice. By 1982 as well, governmental funding problems had resulted in reductions in the availability of some services (especially for civil cases) and the dismantling of some structures for ensuring community involvement in legal clinics.[41] For these reasons, the enactment of Charter guarantees, perhaps understandably, tended to generate renewed expectations among access-to-justice reformers about the law's potential for benefiting the poor and disadvantaged in Canadian society.

In terms of access to legal aid services, such expectations have not generally been fulfilled by the Charter. In the first place, Charter guarantees expressly referring to legal processes focused on the traditional values of the adversary system, thereby reinforcing a narrow focus on individual representation rather than on broader systemic legal action. For example, both section 10(b) relating to the right to counsel and section 11(d) guaranteeing a fair trial expressly protect important elements of criminal-trial processes for individuals,[42] but they cannot easily be adapted to guaranteed legal services for group actions involving political organization and lobbying as well as court action. Moreover, from the beginning, drafters of the Charter denied that section 10(b) conferred a 'right' to legal aid services even for those accused of criminal offences, thereby narrowing even further its potential for achieving access-to-justice goals.[43]

These views were reflected subsequently in the decision of the Alberta Court of Appeal in *R. v. Robinson*[44] in 1990. The Court decided that neither section 10(b) nor section 7 required legal aid assistance in relation to representation for a criminal appeal and for the provision of funds for preparing appeal books. On the basis that the provincial legal aid program had determined that the applicant's appeal was without merit, the Court held that there was no denial of fundamental justice according to section 7 and that there was no absolute right to legal aid guaranteed by section 10(b) to indigent accused. For access-to-justice reformers, such a decision represents 'a cautionary tale about the Charter's unfulfilled promise to the indigent criminally convicted.'[45] Interestingly, by contrast with a right to legal counsel, the Supreme Court of Canada decided in 1990 that section 10(b) required police officers to provide to persons who are arrested or detained information about the availability of legal aid services, arguably a much more limited right. Decisions about section 11(d) have similarly confined its interpretation so as to preclude a right-to-counsel guarantee.[46]

Some decisions pursuant to section 7 have revealed more expansive approaches to the interpretation of Charter guarantees. In *R. v. Rowbotham*,[47] for example, the Ontario Court of Appeal decided to overrule a decision to deny legal aid funding in a criminal case. Although the legal aid administrator had decided that the accused had earnings sufficient to enable her to retain a lawyer, the Court of Appeal concluded that she could not afford a lawyer for a twelve-month hearing in a complex drug case, relying on both sections 11(d) and 7. In *Re Glen Howard*, the Federal Court of Appeal also held that section 7 required the provision of counsel for penitentiary inmates in disciplinary proceedings.[48] The Supreme Court of Canada has also generally interpreted section 7 more purposefully, suggesting a need to override administrative convenience where other issues are at stake[49] and recognizing the complex and adverse consequences of the adversary process for accused persons.[50] Yet courts have also defined limits to section 7[51] and have tended to prefer to base a decision to appoint counsel on the inherent power of the court rather than on section 7 or other Charter guarantees.[52]

In addition to these Charter provisions, the focus on 'disadvantage' in the interpretation of section 15 of the Charter in the Supreme Court of Canada's decision in *Andrews v. Law Society of British Columbia*[53] offered the possibility of extending legal aid services pursuant to the equality guarantee. Even though 'poverty' was not an enumerated ground in section 15, the Court's analysis in *Andrews* and subsequently in *R. v. Turpin*[54] confirmed that the guarantee of equality before the law 'is designed to advance the value that all persons be subject to the equal demands and burdens of the law and not suffer any great disability in the substance and application of the law.'[55] According to this view, the provision of legal counsel in both criminal and civil matters could arguably enhance the guarantee of equality before the law. Moreover, those who are poor and needing legal aid services are more frequently among the enumerated groups identified in section 15: groups discriminated against because of sex, race, and disability, in particular.[56]

In *R. v. Robinson*, however, the Court concluded that section 15 was not infringed by the denial of legal aid services to convicted appellants in criminal cases. Commenting that the right of appeal from conviction in Canada is a 'sharply qualified, often merely permissive, right,' the Court held that it was impossible to find 'an unqualified right to state-funded counsel': 'The refusal does not flow from some irrelevant personal characteristic of the convicted accused. The indigent with meritorious appeals will be funded. The indigent without meritorious appeals will not ... Indigency does not decide; trial guilt that is not reasonably disputable, in fact or law does ... If indigency can fell legislation under the Charter, the Charter should say so ... Legislation that allows a court or judge to declare that public funding should be refused where an appeal is undeserving does not pose a violation of established Canadian values either.'[57] As suggested by David Schneiderman and Charalee Graydon, the Court's conclusion in *Robinson* 'failed to recognize the frailties of the criminal justice system,'[58] a matter of special concern in the context of recent inquiries into miscarriages of justice such as those involving Donald Marshall, Helen Betty Osborne, and Guy Paul Morin.

The issue about section 15 and legal aid services raises two problems for courts. One is that the right to equality before the law may arguably confer an economic benefit, not just the participatory or political rights traditionally recognized as fundamental civil rights. As the Nova Scotia decision in *Hebb v. the Queen* recognized, poor people have less ability to pay a fine – with the consequence of imprisonment for non-payment – by contrast with non-poor members of society.[59] Thus, an extension of legal aid services pursuant to section 15 transforms a formal right into a more effective one. At the same time, it also augments the need for financial resources for provincial legal aid programs, an increasingly pressing challenge.

The second and related problem is that judicial recognition of a right to legal aid pursuant to section 15 requires the court to define the scope of the right granted and may require the court to extend legislative provisions to remedy an infringement of the equality guarantee.[60] As is evident from decided cases about section 15 and legal aid services in criminal cases, courts have been generally reluctant to rule that legal representation is mandated by Charter guarantees when it has not been provided by statutory legal aid schemes. This reluctance to use the Charter to enhance representation in criminal cases suggests that courts would be even more loath to recognize broader rights for litigants in civil cases and to create rights for group rather than individual representation. In this sense, the Charter's guarantees appear to offer little help to the access-to-justice movement in its broadly defined challenges on behalf of society's 'have-nots.'

Indeed, the use of Charter equality guarantees to challenge arrangements for providing legal aid services requires a fundamental reassessment of the justice system in terms of broad societal values and objectives. As the evaluators of the legal aid program in Saskatchewan noted in 1988, the substantial costs of the current justice system necessitate a reconsideration of the appropriateness of existing arrangements: 'Is the trend to greater amounts of litigation serving the cause of justice or is it self-serving to those who work in the justice system? If trying minor cases abuses the justice system, should rich and poor have equal opportunity to do so? Since the rich are rarely even charged with minor offences, can the poor be denied even access to counsel? Is the achievement of perfectly equal access to justice worth the social and economic costs, and do those costs in turn deny justice to the greater public?'[61]

In this context, there is also a need to re-examine access to justice *among* claimants to legal aid services. As I have suggested elsewhere, legal aid programs in Canada tend to respond more favourably to claimants charged with criminal offences than to those in other cases, a situation that disproportionately favours men who are poor.[62] In those provinces where government cutbacks have diminished the availability of legal aid services, in particular, such a trend may mean that poor men charged with offences relating to family violence may be entitled to legal aid services while their wives, equally poor, may be denied legal aid services to pursue divorce or other family law claims. As Deborah Rhode has argued, substantive equality for women in the justice system must go beyond the provision of legal representation to confront the underlying equality of the law and its processes[63]: 'The law's approach to rape, sexual harassment, and domestic violence must reach beyond the relatively rare circumstances in which an individual plaintiff comes forward with conclusive proof of injury' and 'focus more critically on the cultural conditions that foster sexual abuse and on the law-enforcement practices that discourage redress.'[64] Such recommendations transcend concerns about providing legal aid services to men and women equally within current arrangements, and instead define a need to reconceptualize fundamentally access-to-justice goals.[65] Moreover, this analysis demonstrates the limited impact of Charter guarantees, not only for narrowly defined rights to legal representation in criminal cases but also with respect to broader issues about access to justice.

Access to Justice: The Charter and the Legal Profession

The 1993 report of the Canadian Bar Association's Task Force on Gender Equality in the Legal Profession began its exploration of the issues with an analysis of Charter equality guarantees. As its report stated: 'The starting point for a discussion on the need for change must be the recognition that gender equality is a fundamental norm. The Charter, human rights legislation, and Canada's adoption of various international conventions, involve a commitment to eradicating discrimination against women and achieving gender equality. The law in Canada now demands adherence to the equality principle. The legal profession should show leadership by adopting equality norms as its own. The failure to rise to this challenge raises serious questions about the ability of the legal profession to regulate itself according to law.'[66]

The use of equality guarantees as the starting point for the task force's analysis clearly signals the increasing importance of ideas about Charter equality in framing issues about change in the legal profession. The CBA report is one of numerous recent reports in different parts of Canada, all focusing on equality norms in relation to the legal profession and the judiciary.[67] Similar inquiries have also been undertaken in the academic legal context.[68] In this way, Charter equality guarantees appear to have had a more significant influence on the legal profession than on legal aid services. Yet, just as in relation to legal aid services, it is important to test this conclusion by assessing the extent to which equality recommendations have been implemented, beyond these reports and recommendations, by and within the legal profession.

In the past two decades, law schools and law practices have experienced profound demographic change in Canada and other western nations. Beginning in the early 1970s, the rate of entry of women to law schools in Canada increased significantly,[69] an increase characterized by an American sociologist as 'nothing short of revolutionary.'[70] In Quebec, women constituted over 50 per cent of the total number of enrolling students from 1979 at l'Université Laval and from 1981 at l'Université de Montréal. Among common law schools, the *Globe and Mail* reported in 1986 that women constituted just over 50 per cent of the first-year class at the University of Windsor, while entrance rates for women at other common law schools then ranged from 35 to 45 per cent.[71] During the 1970s women were hired in university faculties of law and in law firms and government and some women were appointed as judges; it was not until 1982, however, that a woman was appointed to the Supreme Court of Canada.[72]

Overall, the period of the 1970s was one of expansion within law schools and the legal profession, with unprecedented growth in the numbers of entrants and generally favourable economic conditions. Curricular offerings in law schools expanded along with the trend to lawyers' specialization and law schools adopted new teaching methods, including clinical-education programs which were often connected to delivering legal aid services.[73] During the 1970s also, a number of law schools designed more appropriate admission programs for 'mature' students,[74] and, with respect to Aboriginal People, some law schools developed admission processes to encourage First Nations students in conjunction with the Native law program at the University of Saskatchewan. Finally, it was in this period as well that the law schools and the Federation of Law Societies established the Joint Committee on Foreign Accreditation, conferring on it authority to define educational requirements for admission to the Canadian legal profession for applicants with degrees and/or practice experience outside Canada.[75]

Yet none of these initiatives fully addressed the continuing inequality of access to legal education and the profession on the part of 'minority' students, male and female. For women minority students especially, access to legal education has been relatively recent: the first black woman lawyer in Ontario was admitted to practice only in 1960 and the first woman from a First Nations graduated only in 1976.[76] More recently, a 1990 study by Brian Mazer and Samantha Peeris revealed that 2.8 per cent of lawyers in Canada were members of a visible minority (according to 1986 census data), whereas visible-minority adults constituted 5.9 per cent of the total population; and that .8 per cent of lawyers were aboriginal people, even though they constituted 2.3 per cent of the adult population.[77] Available data for 1986 suggested that disabled people were similarly underrepresented in the legal profession.[78] Thus, as the 1991 report of the Canadian Association of Law Teachers concluded: 'Visible minorities, aboriginal people and disabled persons are seriously underrepresented in the legal profession and in the professoriate.'[79]

The entrenchment of the Charter's equality guarantees has encouraged some efforts to redress inequality in the legal profession. As early as 1986, for example, a national judicial conference on 'The Socialization of Judges to Equality Issues' emphasized 'the importance of the social processes by which judges develop their attitudes, expectations and values [and which] are crucial to the developing concept of equality.'[80] Although many of the conference papers expressed serious concerns about potential problems in the interpretation of equality guarantees, particularly relating to sex discrimination,[81] they also reflected the influence of gender-bias training programs developed for judges in the United States.[82] Indeed, while the papers revealed the impact of Charter equality guarantees, American research on gender bias appears to have been equally important in shaping ideas at the conference.[83]

In subsequent years, several provincial law societies conducted studies on gender bias in the legal profession. In 1991 the Law Society of Upper Canada released its report, 'Transitions in the Ontario Legal Profession,' which focused on differing experiences of male and female lawyers in relation to their work as lawyers and in the difficulties of balancing work and family life.[84] In the same year, the Law Society of British Columbia issued a report, 'Women in the Legal Profession,' which concluded that many women lawyers in British Columbia found that the practice of law did not accommodate their family responsibilities and also denied them equal access to the rewards of the profession.[85] In 1992 the Law Society of Alberta released its report, 'Identifying the Issues,' and its findings were similar to those reported in Ontario and British Columbia.[86] Gender-bias studies have also been undertaken in Saskatchewan and in Nova Scotia[87]; and an early study of 900 members of the Association du Jeune Barreau de Montréal about work and childcare responsibilities[88] resulted in the Quebec bar's creation of a committee on women in the legal profession.

In addition to these initiatives on the part of law societies, there have been three reports by the Manitoba Association of Women and the Law[89] and several governmental initiatives concerning women in the workforce[90] and women and the justice system (including women lawyers and judges).[91] Many of these studies reached conclusions similar to those of gender-bias task forces established in the United States[92] and made similar recommendations to address inequality in the legal profession.[93]

However, most of these studies did not expressly take account of differences *among* women lawyers in terms of race, class, disability, or sexual orientation, even though their focus on women's exclusion from equal opportunities as lawyers[94] arguably created a climate within the legal profession more receptive to rethinking the profession's traditions of exclusivity.[95] Thus, when participants at the 1992 CBA conference sponsored by the Task Force on Gender Equality in the Legal Profession voiced concerns about the absence of Aboriginal women and other 'minority' women from the task force, two additional members were appointed. Significantly, several recommendations of the final report identified different experiences among minority and Aboriginal women lawyers,[96] leading members of the task force to alter their initial interpretation of their mandate:

At the outset, [we] had a tendency to see women as a monolithic group of individuals. The picture was one of white, middle class, able-bodied, heterosexual women. Over the course of the project, both the Task Force and the Association came to realize that it is essential to look at women in the legal profession as a diversity. To do otherwise would be a sterile and formalistic exercise which would exclude Women of Colour, Aboriginal women, lesbians, and women with disabilities. You cannot separate people from their fundamental characteristics. They must be seen and appreciated as whole persons. *This is not a broadening of the Task Force's mandate but a realistic interpretation of it* [emphasis added].[97]

The Task Force's approach, 'realistically interpreting' equality issues for the legal profession, has also been evident in recent developments in law schools. In 1992, for example, First Nations law students in Ontario organized a conference and issued a report, 'Broadening the Law School Perspective,' which recommended[98] curricular changes (especially) in the first year of the LLB program to reflect the experience of native peoples with criminal law, property law, constitutional law, and family law.[99] In a number of law schools, there have been efforts to encourage the admission of students from 'previously excluded groups in Canadian society.'[100] Perhaps the most ambitious was the program for Indigenous Blacks and Micmacs at Dalhousie Law School, established in part as a response to the Donald Marshall inquiry.[101] The program included outreach efforts to attract students, a pre-law summer program, in-house tutorials and counselling services (for all three years of the LLB program), a somewhat reduced course load in first year (followed by an intensive short course the next summer), and course development to increase the relevance of existing courses (and the curriculum as a whole) for minority students.[102]

Changing demography at Canadian law schools also motivated the 1991 study conducted by the Canadian Association of Law Teachers (CALT). Starting from the norms created by the Charter's equality guarantees and Canadian human-rights legislation,[103] the report noted the continuing under-representation of minority groups in law schools and among practising lawyers, suggesting that it represented a 'systemic' problem for those in the 'mainstream' of the legal profession: 'The problems of inequality belong to all, not just to those who feel the pain of racism, disability phobia, sexism, homophobia, heterosexist bias, religious bias and other forms of systemic discrimination and/or hatred most acutely.'[104] The report also identified principles for addressing the exclusionary practices of legal education, including 'the recognition of equality as central to legal education'[105] and 'the need for institutional processes capable of addressing the systemic nature of the problems.'[106] The report recommended rethinking the concepts of 'merit'[107] and 'knowledge'[108] as well as efforts to create a more cooperative and humane climate among members of the legal profession. It also made more immediate recommendations, including changes to hiring and admissions policies, increased financial and other support for students, curricular reforms,[109] and training in anti-discrimination for both faculty and students.

Beyond law schools and the education process, provincial law societies have also addressed equality issues. Both Ontario and British Columbia, for example, have issued policies on sexual harassment, and an Ontario lawyer has been disciplined in accordance with the policy.[110] The Law Society of Upper Canada produced a report on equity in legal education and practice, addressing the need for positive actions by law schools and the profession to ensure greater equity within the legal profession.[111] Provincial law societies have also recognized the need to redefine standards of professional conduct in terms of equality and non-discrimination. The Law Society of British Columbia amended its rules of conduct in 1992 to include explicitly a duty of non-discrimination (including sexual harassment),[112] and the CBA Task Force on Gender Equality in the Legal Profession reported that other law societies are considering such a rule. The task force report also affirmed the need for self-regulating professions to adopt such rules, notwithstanding the existence of human-rights legislation, because law societies are in many cases 'better able to ensure that legal requirements are met by their membership' and because they have 'a well-defined interest in ensuring that [their] members are treated fairly.'[113] The report recommended as well the adoption of non-discrimination rules for members of the Canadian Bar Association, along with other practices to foster more equality in the legal profession.[114]

This brief overview of the work of law schools, provincial law societies, the Canadian Bar Association, and others thus demonstrates a significant level of professional attention to issues of equality and non-discrimination in the years since the enactment of Charter equality guarantees. Moreover, both the CBA report and the CALT report explicitly acknowledged lawyers' responsibilities to foster greater equality in the profession and the law schools as a result of the Charter's equality guarantees. On this basis, it is arguable that Charter equality has had a significant impact on the legal profession and legal practice, as well as legal education. Such a conclusion may also suggest that Charter equality guarantees have been more effective in achieving change within the legal profession than in relation to legal aid clients. Yet, while it is important to acknowledge these developments in the legal profession, it may be premature to suggest that the Charter has accomplished substantial (or substantive) change for lawyers. Indeed, it may be that the Charter's promise remains elusive for lawyers – as well as for their legal aid clients.

This more pessimistic conclusion is the result of two problems. One is that much of the work to date, on the part of law schools and professional legal organizations, has been directed to documenting inequality in the legal profession, not eliminating it. While studies may be necessary first steps, the process of implementing recommendations is often more difficult and more time-consuming. As a result, it may be harder to gauge the long-term impact of the CBA report or to assess the future implications of more egalitarian admissions standards in law schools. Moreover, the process of change itself is not without hidden costs: as the CBA task force report noted, for example, there may be some 'backlash' to recommendations for change, such as the reaction that occurred when the Law Society of British Columbia introduced its sexual harassment policy: 'The week following the [Law Society's] enactment of its new rule on the duty of non-discrimination (which includes a definition of sexual harassment) was reported to the Task Force as the "worst week for women lawyers ever." Women were subjected to relentless teasing about what does or does not constitute sexual harassment.'[115]

Similarly, discussion about the proposed non-discrimination rule in Ontario has revealed misconceptions about the nature of systemic discrimination and resistance to rethinking the extent to which women and men as lawyers are able to exercise effective 'choices' about the practice of law.[116] Judges have routinely resisted the creation of *mandatory* gender-bias training sessions, citing the need to preserve their judicial independence; and some academics have resisted requests for inclusion of race or gender materials on the basis of academic freedom.[117] Accordingly, one can conclude that Charter equality guarantees have made these issues visible while recognizing that lengthy and difficult discussions may still be necessary for all those involved. In any event, it is difficult to argue that Charter equality guarantees have accomplished substantive change in the legal profession to date, although their influence may be evident in issues and in discussions.

The second reason for a more pessimistic assessment of the Charter's impact on the legal profession is its failure to change the profession's culture of resistance to challenges to the status quo. As Bruce Feldthusen has noted, even 'the Supreme Court of Canada becomes invisible to many male [lawyers] when it rules on gender discrimination.'[118] More significantly, as has been suggested elsewhere,[119] the legal profession's lack of an internal culture of dissent reinforces both its resistance to change and its power to silence critics, especially those who are marginalized within the profession. The relative absence of formal complaints to law societies *by lawyers* about discriminatory conduct in articling interviews, hiring and partnership decisions, and sexual harassment, by contrast with graphic and detailed anecdotal information within the profession (much of it substantiated by the CBA task force's report), suggests that there are costs to making such complaints, costs that are far too substantial for any individual lawyer to bear. Has anything changed in the two decades since Marguerite Ritchie cautioned a researcher about the perils of relying on information formally collected about discrimination against women in the legal profession? Ritchie had then noted: 'You may discover that some replies indicate an apparent lack of discrimination; in many cases I have found that women are unwilling to admit discrimination, either because they are trying to conceal the fact from themselves or because they must play the role of "Uncle Tom" and that *their chances of promotion depend absolutely upon their conformity to and acceptance of the existing patterns*' [emphasis added].[120]

Thus, although the contexts of legal aid services and the legal profession differ, and although it may appear that constitutional guarantees of equality have been more effective in accomplishing change for lawyers than for their legal aid clients, the reality is that equality remains an elusive but pressing goal both for reformers of the legal profession and for those involved in the delivery of legal aid services. This conclusion means that we need to look again at the question of legal and social change and the role of equality guarantees – their potential as well as their limits – in achieving substantive change in access to justice.

Access to Justice: The Charter and Substantive Change

Legal historians tend to concentrate on change and innovation. They wish to explain why an innovation occurred when it did. But to understand law and society one must also explain why a legal change did not occur when society changed, or when perceptions about the quality of the law changed.[121]

Alan Watson's comments suggest a relationship between law and social change which is discordant, one that challenges the assertion that 'law reflects the needs and desires of society.'[122] Although his comments were not directed at analysis of the impact of Charter equality guarantees, they usefully remind us that the relationship between law and social change is not linear and may be extremely complex. In such a context, any effort to connect changes in the law to changes in legal aid services or in professional practices (or even, perhaps, the lack of such changes) seems fraught with impossible difficulties. As Watson has suggested, any theory of law and social change 'will have to be complex and take into account, for instance, inertia and transplanting – all the causes of divergence in fact – as well as issues of power and will.'[123]

Such a conclusion does not preclude an assessment of the role of Charter equality guarantees in reforming legal aid services and the legal profession. Even just as symbols for needed change in legal aid services and the legal profession, Charter equality guarantees may ground arguments for reform and provide a catalyst for new ideas. They may also be useful as the basis for legal challenges to status-quo arrangements and, in combination with other factors, contribute to the acceptance of new ideas about those arrangements. But the process of legal change must also be understood as one that does not move inexorably forward; as one analysis of Charter equality demonstrates, it may more often be 'one step forward [and] two steps back.'[124]

In the realm of legal aid services, the traditional focus on individual representation, challenged briefly in the 1970s and early 1980s, has created a barrier to using Charter equality guarantees to extend the availability (as a right) of legal aid services beyond accused persons. Even in the context of accused persons, moreover, judicial unwillingness to characterize poverty as an analogous ground[125] has generally prevented the use of Charter guarantees to extend the availability of legal aid services beyond the limits defined by provincial legal aid schemes. Within the legal profession, by contrast, Charter equality guarantees have often been used as the starting point for recommendations for changes in legal education and in professional practices. Yet, while there have been some changes reflective of equality goals, those most disadvantaged in law schools and in the legal profession remain unconvinced that substantive change has occurred. As the CBA task force report concluded, 'many women who have "made it" in the legal profession have done so by conforming to the male model, by not reacting to sexist comments and attitudes, by not reporting sexually harassing behaviour, and by forcing themselves to develop interests that match those of their male colleagues.'[126] The report acknowledged that the cost of these compromises was unacceptable within the profession.[127]

Thus, suggesting that Charter equality guarantees have had no impact at all on access to justice in Canada is just as untenable as asserting defined and measurable gains because of the Charter's guarantees. Particularly if we assess the Charter's impact in terms of concrete benefits for the most disadvantaged Canadians, Charter equality guarantees appear to have been ineffective in accomplishing better access to justice. At the same time, the Charter's promise has grounded demands for change, particularly in relation to access to legal education and the profession, and these demands may increase access to justice for the future. Such an outcome seems especially likely if the 'new' brand of lawyers bring new perspectives to law and legal processes.

In understanding the role of Charter equality guarantees, the idea of paradigmatic change may help us to focus on the process of change itself and thereby avoid the sense of pessimism that comes from expecting substantive changes to occur quickly, profoundly, and irrevocably. Significantly, both the CBA task force report and the CALT report focused on processes of change. The CBA report identified six barriers to change and concluded that a 'multifaceted strategy for achieving change' should be devised.[128] In making these recommendations, moreover, the report again identified the symbolic importance of equality goals: 'The basics of equality rights jurisprudence are woven throughout this Report. These messages should be repeated until they form the basis of a common understanding of our legal duties to our colleagues in the profession and beyond.'[129]

The CALT report's conclusions about the necessity for change in the legal profession (and the justice system) are quite similar, although it is less sanguine about the likelihood of accomplishing needed changes quickly or easily. Perhaps because of law schools' greater experiences to date with concrete problems of 'diversity,' the CALT report focused more explicitly on the need to understand different 'world views,' including the views of those who accept the philosophy of liberal individualism (which holds that accomplishments derive from 'personal effort and ability and professional commitment') and, by contrast, of those who 'see the world as a series of systemic advantages and disadvantages, where sex, race, culture, physical and mental ability, sexual orientation, religion, mother tongue and social class' determine one's accomplishments.[130] According to the CALT report, 'the challenge is to bring these two world views together,' a challenge that presents a clear choice for all of us concerned about access to justice: 'Those who know disadvantage have the power to educate, or they have the power to denounce. Those who do not know disadvantage have the power to learn and to teach and to experiment, all the while maintaining a high degree of security and self-esteem, or they have the power to deny and retrench. We all share one choice: to make common cause in the interest of professionalism and justice and education, or to fight and turn our institutions and our lives into battle camps.'

The choice, concluded the CALT report, 'ought to be self-evident.'[131]

Notes

1 Mauro Cappelletti and Bryant Garth, 'Access to Justice as a Focus for Research' *Windsor Yearbook of Access to Justice*, vol. 1 (1981), xvii–xviii.
2 The authors asserted that legislators always make clear assumptions about the level of enforcement of new substantive rights, assumptions that 'impose a more or less predictable burden' on those against whom they are to be enforced. Ibid.
3 The commitment of feminist lawyers to the process of drafting and negotiating the language of sections 15 and 28, for example, demonstrated their concern to shape Charter guarantees carefully for their future use. See Penney Kome, *The Taking of Twenty-Eight* (Toronto: Women's Educational Press 1983); and Sherene Razack, *Canadian Feminism and the Law* (Toronto: Second Story Press 1991).
4 Margaret Thornton, 'Feminism and the Contradictions of Law Reform,' *International Journal of the Sociology of Law*, vol. 19 (1991), 467–8.
5 Judy Fudge, 'The Effect of Entrenching a Bill of Rights upon Political Discourse: Feminist Demands in Sexual Violence in Canada,' *International Journal of the Sociology of Law*, vol. 17 (1989), 445.
6 In the context of Charter equality analysis, for example, the Supreme Court of Canada's decision in *Andrews v. The Law Society of British Columbia*, [1989], 56 D.L.R. (4th) 1, adopted new principles for defining an infringement of the equality guarantee, apparently departing from the 'similarly situated' test. As well, the Court has recognized important principles in the context of sex equality concerning matters such as systemic discrimination (*Action Travail des Femmes v. C.N.R.* [1987], 76 N.R. 161); sexual harassment (*Janzen v. Platy Enterprises Ltd.* [1989], 59 D.L.R. (4th) 352); and family violence (*R. v. Lavallee* [1990], 108 N.R. 321).
7 Mary Jane Mossman, '"Shoulder to Shoulder": Gender and Access to Justice,' *Windsor Yearbook of Access to Justice*, vol. 10 (1990), 356–7.

8 Judy Fudge, 'The Public/Private Distinction: The Possibilities of and Limitations to the Use of Charter Litigation to Further Feminist Struggles,' *Osgoode Hall Law Journal*, vol. 25 (1987), 485.

9 See Martha Minow, 'Breaking the Law: Lawyers and Clients in Struggles for Social Change,' *University of Pittsburgh Law Review*, vol. 52 (1991), 723.

10 Roger Cotterrell, *The Sociology of Law* (London: Butterworths 1984), 69.

11 Carol Smart, 'Feminism and Law: Some Problems of Analysis and Strategy,' *International Journal of the Sociology of Law*, vol. 14 (1986), 117.

12 John Claydon, 'International Human Rights Law and the Interpretation of the Canadian Charter of Rights and Freedoms,' *Supreme Court Review*, vol. 4 (1982), 287; Roy Romanow, John Whyte, and Howard Leeson, *Canada ... Notwithstanding* (Toronto: Carswell 1984); and Erika Abner, 'The Merits of the Use of Constitutional Litigation to Unravel the Fabric of the Feminization of Poverty in Canada,' (LLM thesis, Osgoode Hall Law School, 1989).

13 See Task Force on Gender Equality in the Legal Profession, 'Touchstones for Change: Equality, Diversity and Accountability' (Ottawa: Canadian Bar Association 1993).

14 Cappelletti and Garth, 'Access to Justice,' xvi–xvii.

15 Ibid.

16 The enthusiasm for law reform commissions is reflected in the expressed expectations of those involved in their creation and operation. See Leslie Scarman, *Law Reform: The New Pattern* (London: Routledge and Kegan Paul 1968); Allen Linden, 'Some Thoughts about the Future Research of the Law Reform Commission of Canada,' in *Taking Law Reform Seriously* (Ottawa: Law Reform Commission of Canada 1989); and Michael Kirby, 'Change and Decay or Change and Renewal,' in *Reform the Law!*, ed. Kirby (Oxford, U.K.: Oxford University Press 1983).

17 For a different view, see Mary Jane Mossman, '"Running Hard to Stand Still": The Paradox of Family Law Reform,' *Dalhousie Law Journal*, vol. 17 (1994), 1.

18 See Walter Tarnopolsky, *Discrimination and the Law in Canada* (Toronto: De Boo 1982); and Judith Keene, *Human Rights in Ontario* (Toronto: Carswell 1992).

19 Some human-rights decisions that reached the Supreme Court of Canada in the 1980s were critical to the formation of subsequent Charter jurisprudence. See Lynn Smith, 'Adding a Third Dimension: The Canadian Approach to Constitutional Equality Guarantees,' *Law and Contemporary Problems*, vol. 55 (1992), 211.

20 See, for example, Mauro Cappelletti, James Gordley and Earl Johnson, Jr, *Toward Equal Justice: A Comparative Study of Legal Aid in Modern Societies*

(Dobbs Ferry, N.Y.: Ocean 1975); *Research and the Delivery of Legal Services*, ed. Peter Cashman (Sydney, Australia: Law Foundation of New South Wales 1981); Michael Cass and John Western, *Legal Aid and Legal Need* (Canberra, Australia: Commonwealth Legal Aid Commission 1980); Michael Zander, *Legal Services for the Community* (London: Temple Smith 1978); Jeremy Cooper, *Public Legal Services* (London: Sweet and Maxwell 1983); Legal Action Group, *A Strategy for Justice* (Legal Action Group 1992); *The Legal Services Corporation and the Activities of its Grantees: A Fact Book* (Washington, D.C.: U.S. Legal Services Corporation 1979); Carrie Menkel-Meadow, 'Legal Aid in the United States: The Professionalization and Politicization of Legal Services in the 1980s,' *Osgoode Hall Law Journal*, vol. 22 (1984), 29; *Legal Aid Services in Canada* (Ottawa: National Legal Aid Research Centre 1981); *Perspectives on Legal Aid*, ed. Frederick Zemans (Westport, Conn.: Greenwood Press 1979); and Groupe de Travail sur L'Accessibilité à la Justice, 'Jalons pour une plus grande Accessibilité à la Justice' (Quebec City: Le Ministre de la Justice et Procureur Général du Québec 1991).

21 Dieter Hoehne, *Legal Aid in Canada* (Queenston, Ont.: Edwin Mellen Press 1989), 11 ff. In spite of the CBA recommendations, legal aid services remained primarily a matter of charity offered by individual members of the legal profession until the Second World War. During the war, modest efforts were made by CBA committees in each province to organize free legal services to those in active war service and their families, but these committee structures were disbanded after 1945.

22 John Turner (House of Commons, 7 Nov. 1969), as cited by Hoehne, *Legal Aid*, 99.

23 *Report of the Joint Committee on Legal Aid* (Toronto: Ministry of the Attorney-General 1965).

24 Hoehne, in *Legal Aid*, notes that judicare programs did not fundamentally challenge the traditional service roles of lawyers; only the source of funding was altered. For further analysis, see *Report of the Task Force on Legal Aid* (Toronto: Ministry of the Attorney-General 1974; also known as the Osler Report); and *Report of the Commission on Clinical Funding* (Toronto: Ministry of the Attorney-General 1978; also known as the Grange Report); Mary Jane Mossman and E. Lightman, 'Towards Equality Through Legal Aid in Canada,' *Journal of Canadian Studies*, vol. 21 (1986), 96; and E. Lightman and Mary Jane Mossman, 'Salary or Fee-for-Service in Delivering Legal Aid Services: Theory and Practice in Canada,' *Queen's Law Journal*, vol. 10 (1984), 109.

25 See Carrie Menkel-Meadow, 'Legal Aid in the United States'; and Douglas Besharov, 'Legal Services for the Poor: Time for Reform' (Conference on Access to Justice in the 1990s, New Orleans: 1989).

26 The Carter Commission recommended the creation of a legal aid program in Saskatchewan and the broad outlines of its organization and mandate. For further details see DPA Group Inc., 'Evaluation of Saskatchewan Legal Aid' (Ottawa: Department of Justice 1988), 149. See also Jennie Abell, 'Ideology and the Emergence of Legal Aid in Saskatchewan,' *Dalhousie Law Journal*, vol. 16 (1993), 125.

27 See *Report of the Commission on Clinical Funding* and *Report of the Task Force on Legal Aid.*

28 See Mary Jane Mossman, 'Community Legal Clinics in Ontario,' *Windsor Yearbook of Access to Justice*, vol. 3 (1983), 375.

29 Hoehne, *Legal Aid*, 310.

30 See Peter Hogg, *Constitutional Law of Canada*, 3rd ed. (Toronto: Carswell 1992); Andrew Petter, 'Federalism and the Myth of the Federal Spending Power,' *Canadian Bar Review*, vol. 68 (1989), 448; and Petter 'Meech Ado about Nothing? Federalism, Democracy and the Spending Power,' in *Competing Constitutional Visions*, eds. Katherine Swinton and Carol Rogerson (Toronto: Carswell 1988).

31 See, for example, Avrim Lazar, 'Legal Aid in the Age of Restraint' (Canadian Institute for the Administration of Justice Conference on the Cost of Justice: 1979).

32 *Report of the Joint Committee on Legal Aid*, 97 and 51 (citing the brief submitted by the Ontario Federation of Labour).

33 National Legal Aid Liaison Committee, *The Provision of Public Legal Aid Services in Canada: Report to the National Council* (Ottawa: Canadian Bar Association 1985), 2. See also R.H. Tawney, *Equality* (London: Allen and Unwin 1964).

34 See Mary Jane Mossman, 'Toward a Comprehensive Legal Aid Program in Canada: Exploring the Issues,' *Windsor Review of Legal and Social Issues*, vol. 1 (1993), 1.

35 See Minister of Supply and Services Canada, *The Justice System – Improved Program Delivery: A Study Team Report to the Neilson Task Force on Program Review* (Ottawa: 1986); and, for a contrasting view, Richard Abel, 'Law Without Politics: Legal Aid under Advanced Capitalism,' *UCLA Law Review*, vol. 32 (1985), 474.

36 [1976], 1 Alberta Law Review 292 (Alberta S.C.).

37 He listed six criteria for consideration in the exercise of such discretion, including the accused's financial circumstances, his or her educational level, the availability of legal aid services, difficulties with evidence, the likelihood of imprisonment on conviction, and the complexity of the case ('in the sense of raising any question of

fact or of law as to which an accused is likely to be at a significant disadvantage if he is unrepresented by counsel'). *Re White and the Queen* (see n. 36) at 306.

38 [1974], 49 D.L.R. (3d) 619 (B.C.C.A.). See also *R. v. Burnshine* [1974], 15 C.C.C. (2d) 505.

39 *Powell v. Alabama*, 287 U.S. 45 [1932] and *Gideon v. Wainwright*, 372 U.S. 335 [1963]. See also *Argersinger v. Hamlin*, 407 U.S. 25 [1972].

40 See *R. v. Johnson* [1973], 11 C.C.C. (2d) 101; *R. v. Butler* [1973], 11 C.C.C. (2d) 381; and *Vescio v. The King*, [1949] 92 C.C.C. 161.

41 See Mary Jane Mossman, 'Legal Aid in Canada' (7th International Congress on Procedural Law, Wurzburg: 1983).

42 See Mary Jane Mossman, 'The Charter and the Right to Legal Aid,' *Journal of Law and Social Policy*, vol. 1 (1985), 30. As suggested there, it is possible that section 10(b) may extend legal aid services to persons charged with summary-conviction offences, some of whom are now routinely denied legal aid services. Section 10(b) has been used most frequently in relation to cases involving prompt notice of an accused's right to counsel in relation to breathalyzer testing. For a more recent analysis, see Patricia Hughes 'Domestic Legal Aid: A Claim to Equality,' *Review of Constitutional Studies*, vol. 2 (1995), 203.

43 Jean Chrétien, then minister of justice, stated to the joint committee hearings on the Charter in 1981: 'How to retain and compensate the counsel is to be decided by the person involved and his lawyer and there are some programs that are shared costs where, for certain categories of citizens, because he cannot afford it, he receives legal aid from the provincial administration ... [The] legal adviser is not a matter of right. It is a question of a private citizen dealing with society with his own problem. Legal aid is a social measure that exists in Canada and is available under the criteria that are established by the Attorney-Generals of the provinces.' *Minutes of Proceedings and Evidence of the Special Joint Committee of the Senate and of the House of Commons on the Constitution of Canada (1980-1)*, 46: 125 (27 Jan. 1981). See also Peter Hogg, *Canada Act, 1982 Annotated* (Toronto: Carswell 1982).

44 [1990], 63 D.L.R. (4th) 289.

45 David Schneiderman and Charalee Graydon, 'An Appeal to Justice: Publicly Funded Appeals and *R. v. Robinson*; *R. v. Dolejs*,' *Alberta Law Review*, vol. 28 (1990), 874. *R. v. Robinson* confirmed the Alberta court's approach in 1983 in *R. v. Stiopu*; *Re MacKay and Legal Aid Society of Alberta* [1983], 8 C.R.R. 216 (affirmed without reasons by the Alberta Court of Appeal at 8 C.R.R. 217). See also Andrew Petter, 'Immaculate Deception: The Charter's Hidden Agenda,' *The Advocate*, vol. 45 (1987), 857; and Lorenne Clark, 'Liberalism and the Living Tree: Women, Equality and the Charter,' *Alberta Law Review*, vol. 28 (1990), 384.

46 See *R. v. Brydges*, [1990] 1 S.C.R. 190; and *Deutsch v. Law Society of Upper Canada Legal Aid Fund, Lawson and Legge* [1985], 48 C.R. (3d) 166, where Justice Craig noted that there might be rare cases where the right to a fair trial would be impossible to achieve in the absence of counsel. He concluded, however, that any decision to order state-funded legal aid on the part of a court was grounded in the right available at common law, thus precluding the need to resort to the guarantee in section 11(d) of the Charter.

47 [1988], 25 O.A.C. 321.

48 [1985], 14 W.C.B. 131; [1985], 14 W.C.B. 250; a further appeal to the Supreme Court of Canada was quashed because it had become moot; see [1987] 2 S.C.R. 687.

49 *Singh v. Minister of Employment and Immigration*, [1985] 1 S.C.R. 177.

50 See Chief Justice Dickson in *R. v. Morgentaler*, [1988] 1 S.C.R. 30, quoting from *Mills v. The Queen*, [1986] 1 S.C.R. 863.

51 See *Bernard v. Dartmouth Housing Authority* [1989], 88 N.S.R. (2d) 190, where the Nova Scotia Court of Appeal held that security of tenure of a public-housing tenant was an economic interest and therefore not protected within section 7. For a contrasting view, see John Whyte, 'Fundamental Justice: The Scope and Application of Section 7 of the Charter,' *Manitoba Law Journal*, vol. 13 (1983), 455.

52 For example, see *R. v. Powell and Powell* [1984], 4 C.R.D. 800–1, where Justice Litsky ordered counsel to represent accused parents charged with truancy in relation to their children. See also *Gonzalez-Davi v. Legal Services Society* [1990], 18 A.C.W.S. (3d) 973, a decision overturning a denial of legal aid to a refugee claimant on the part of the Legal Services Society of British Columbia, focusing on the statutory requirements of the B.C. legislation.

53 [1989] 2 S.C.R. 143.

54 [1989], 69 C.R. (3d) 97.

55 *R. v. Turpin* (see n. 54) at 123.

56 See Schneiderman and Graydon, 'Appeal to Justice,' 892; William Black and Lynn Smith, 'The Equality Rights,' in *The Canadian Charter of Rights and Freedoms*, eds. G.A. Beaudoin and E. Ratushny (Toronto: Carswell 1989); and Wade MacLauchlan, 'Of Fundamental Justice, Equality and Society's Outcasts,' *McGill Law Journal*, vol. 32 (1986), 213.

57 *R. v. Robinson* (see n. 44) at 321.

58 Schneiderman and Graydon, 'Appeal to Justice,' 894.

59 [1989], 89 N.S.R. (2d) 137. As Justice Kelly noted, poor persons do not, as a result of their poverty, have the same choices as others in our society.

60 In some early cases, courts remedied inequality by eliminating benefits to groups singled out by statute: see *Reference re Family Benefits Act (N.S.) section 5* [1987], 75 N.S.R. (2d) 338; and *Silano v. the Queen in Right of British Columbia*

[1987], 42 D.L.R. (4th) 406. See also *Treteault-Gadoury v. Canada Employment and Immigration Commission* [1988], 88 N.R. 6 and *Schachter v. Canada* [1992], 93 D.L.R. (4th) 1 involving the court's remedial powers; and Brian Morgan, 'Charter Remedies: The Civil Side after the First Five Years' in *Charter Issues in Civil Cases*, eds. N. Finkelstein and B. Rogers (Toronto: Carswell 1988).

61 DPA Group Inc., *Evaluation of Saskatchewan Legal Aid*, 172. The evaluators did not try to answer these questions because of 'the complexity of the issues.'

62 See Mary Jane Mossman, 'Gender Equality and Legal Aid Services,' *Sydney Law Review*, vol. 15 (1993), 47: 'Gender bias research needs to take account of the impact of the law's traditional dichotomy between the public and private spheres. Thus, to the extent that legal aid may be generally more available in criminal matters (the "public" realm) than in family law matters (the "private" realm), for example, the preference accorded to criminal law in legal aid schemes may correspond to the ways in which the public/private distinction in law has traditionally excluded and disadvantaged women. In this context, it is important to reassess the philosophical rationales for the priority accorded to legal aid services in criminal matters.'

63 Deborah Rhode, *Justice and Gender: Sex Discrimination and the Law* (Cambridge, Mass.: Harvard University Press 1989).

64 Ibid., 320. See also Mary Jane Mossman (with Heather Ritchie), 'Access to Civil Justice: A Review of Canadian Legal Academic Scholarship,' in *Access to Civil Justice*, ed. Alan Hutchinson (Toronto: Carswell 1990), 53.

65 See also Peter Hanks, *Social Indicators and the Delivery of Legal Services* (Canberra, Australia: Australian Government Publishing Service 1987); Elizabeth Wolgast, *The Grammar of Justice* (Ithaca, N.Y.: Cornell University Press 1987); and Iris Marion Young, *Justice and the Politics of Difference* (Princeton, N.J.: Princeton University Press 1990).

66 CBA task force report (see n.13), 17 and especially chapter 1, 'Equality in the Legal Profession: A Framework for Change.'

67 For an overview, see Law Society of British Columbia, *Gender Equality in the Justice System* (Vancouver: Law Society of British Columbia Gender Bias Committee 1992), 2–1 ff.

68 See Advisory Committee to the Canadian Association of Law Teachers, 'Equality in Legal Education ... : Sharing a Vision ... ; Creating the Pathways ... ' (Kingston: Canadian Association of Law Teachers 1991; also published as Special Advisory Committee to CALT, 'Equality in Legal Education,' *Queen's Law Journal*, vol. 17 [1992], 174). The report is also available in French and on disk (in French and English) and cassette.

69 See Richard Abel, 'Comparative Sociology of Legal Professions: An Exploratory Essay,' *American Bar Foundation Research Journal*, vol. 1 (1985), 5.

70 See Richard Abel, 'The Contradictions of Professionalism,' in *Lawyers in Society*, eds. R. Abel and P. Lewis (Berkeley, C.A.: University of California Press 1988), 202–3.

71 Mary Jane Mossman, '"Invisible" Constraints on Lawyering and Leadership: The Case of Women Lawyers,' *Ottawa Law Review*, vol. 20 (1988), 584.

72 When Helen Kinnear was appointed a judge of a county court in Ontario in 1943, she was the first woman to serve on a court at this level in the British commonwealth. A woman was not appointed to a superior court in Canada until 1969, when Rejanne Laberge-Colas was made a judge of the Quebec Superior Court. Six years later, Bertha Wilson became the first woman appointed to a provincial appellate court in Canada, and then, in 1982, the first woman appointed to the Supreme Court of Canada. See Linda Silver Dranoff, *Women in Canadian Life: Law* (Toronto: Fitzhenry and Whiteside 1977). See also Beverley Baines, 'Do Women Law Professors and Law Students Count?' in *Femmes et Droit*, ed. Helene Dumont (Montreal: Les Éditions Thémis, Université de Montréal 1991), 171; and John Hagan and Susan Zimmerman, 'Multiple Discrimination: Issues of Gender and Multiple Discrimination in Canadian Law School Settings' (Ottawa: CBA Task Force on Gender Equality in the Legal Profession, appendix 9: 1993).

73 See Mossman, 'Community Legal Clinics.'

74 See Report of the Special Committee on Legal Education (Toronto: Law Society of Upper Canada 1972), especially recommendations 4 and 5.

75 See Joint Committee on Accreditation, 'Evaluation of Legal Credentials for Accreditation: General Information' (Ottawa: Federation of Law Societies of Canada and Committee of Canadian Law Deans 1993). Nothing in the joint-committee process, however, guaranteed applicants admission to law schools in Canada, a situation that created barriers for those unable to obtain one of the limited number of spaces available for such students.

76 Constance Backhouse, *Petticoats and Prejudice: Women and Law in Nineteenth-Century Canada* (Toronto: Osgoode Society/Women's Press 1991).

77 Brian Mazer and Samantha Peeris, *Access to Legal Education in Canada, Databook 1990* (Windsor, Ont.: 1990), 80 and 74. See also, for a discussion of these figures, 'Equality in Legal Education,' 5.

78 See 'Equality in Legal Education,' 5. The report cited Employment and Immigration Canada's study *1986 Employment Equity Availability Data Report* and data from Statistics Canada for 1986 which indicated that nearly 2 million Canadians of working age were disabled, and it concluded that the proportion of disabled persons within the legal profession was clearly too low. See also David Lepofsky, 'Disabled Persons and Canadian Law Schools,' *McGill Law Journal*, vol. 36 (1991), 636.

79 'Equality in Legal Education,' 5. See also Brian Mazer, 'Access to Legal Education and the Profession in Canada,' in *Access to Legal Education and the Legal Profession*, eds. Rajeev Dhavan *et al.* (Toronto: Butterworths 1989), 114.

80 *Equality and Judicial Neutrality*, eds. Sheilah Martin and Kathleen Mahoney (Toronto: Carswell 1987).

81 Ibid. See also in that volume: Mary Eberts, 'Risks of Equality Litigation,' 89; Anne Bayefsky, 'Defining Equality Rights under the Charter,' 106; and Dale Gibson, 'Canadian Equality Jurisprudence: Year One,' 128.

82 *Equality and Judicial Neutrality*, eds. Martin and Mahoney. See Norma Wikler, 'Identifying and Correcting Gender Bias,' 12; Margrit Eichler, 'Foundations of Bias: Sexist Language and Sexist Thought,' 22; Lynn Hecht Schafran, 'The Success of the American Program,' 411; and Melvin L. Rothman, 'Prospects for Change in Canada: Education for Judges and Lawyers,' 421.

83 Although the conference mainly emphasized issues about judicial bias in relation to gender, there were some papers about judicial insensitivity to First Nations cultures as well. See in Martin and Mahoney, *Equality*: Joan Ryan and Bernard Ominayak, 'The Cultural Effects of Judicial Bias,' 346; and Louise Mandell, 'Native Culture on Trial,' 358.

84 See Mary Jane Mossman, 'Work and Family in the Legal Profession' (Toronto: CBA Task Force on Gender Equality National Conference 1992).

85 See also Joan Brockman 'Identifying the Barriers: A Survey of Members of the Law Society of British Columbia,' (Vancouver: Law Society of British Columbia Subcommittee on Women in the Legal Profession 1991).

86 See also Deborah L. Rhode, 'Perspectives on Professional Women,' *Stanford Law Review*, vol. 40 (1988), 1,163.

87 The Saskatchewan study was undertaken in 1990 by a joint committee of the Law Society, the Canadian Bar Association, and the College of Law, University of Saskatchewan. In Nova Scotia, a gender equality committee was established by the Nova Scotia Barristers' Society in 1991 and included questionnaires for members of the legal profession and the judiciary.

88 See S. Barron, 'Balancing Act' (CBA, *The National* 1989), 15.

89 Manitoba Association of Women and the Law, *Gender Equality in the Courts* (Winnipeg: 1988); *Gender Equality in the Courts: Criminal Law* (Ottawa: 1991); and *Fairness in Family Law* (Winnipeg: 1994).

90 Government of Canada, 'Integration of Work and Family Responsibilities: Report on Strategies' (Ottawa: Annual Conference of First Ministers 1989).

91 In June 1991 the federal Department of Justice sponsored a national symposium entitled 'Women, the Law, and the Administration of Justice.' In the same year, the federal government established a task force to investigate family violence.

In June 1990 a federal-provincial/territorial working group was established to review gender bias in the justice system. For other initiatives, see 'Measuring the Dimensions of Equality,' *Perspectives*, fall/winter 1992.

92 See Elizabeth Schneider, 'Task Force Report on Women in the Courts: The Challenge for Legal Education,' *Journal of Legal Education*, vol. 38 (1988), 87; Lynn Hecht Schafran, 'Lawyers' Lives, Clients' Lives: Can Women Liberate the Profession?' *Villanova Law Review*, vol. 34 (1989), 1,105; Hecht Schafran 'Gender Bias in the Courts: Time is Not the Cure,' *Creighton Law Review*, vol. 22 (1989), 413; and Hecht Schafran, 'Women in the Courts Today: How Much has Changed,' *Law and Inequality*, vol. 6 (1988), 27.

93 'Summary of Hearings, ABA Commission on Women in the Profession' (February 1988). See also the special report 'Women in Law: The Glass Ceiling,' in American Bar Association *Journal* (June 1988), 49.

94 See Sheilah Martin, 'Women in the Legal Profession: The Dynamics of Exclusion' (Toronto: CBA National Task Force on Gender Equality Conference 1992); and Marie-France Bich, 'De L'Art de passer à travers les Mailles du Filet: Prolégomènes et Polémique' (Toronto: CBA National Task Force on Gender Equality Conference 1992).

95 See Diana Majury, 'Collective Action on a Systemic Problem' (Ottawa: Federation of Social Sciences, *Proceedings* 1991).

96 For example, the CBA task force report (85) addressed the 'general pattern' in large law firms of women's 'early entry in equal numbers followed by more rapid attrition' by comparison with male lawyers. For some groups of women lawyers (including Women of Colour, Aboriginal women, women with disabilities, and lesbians), such a pattern did not exist because these groups are not well represented in large law firms. According to the report this indicates discriminatory practices in a number of areas including hiring. The report also identified problems for aboriginal women in large law firms (87): 'Aboriginal women face bias which works in two opposite ways. On the one hand, they are expected to work on native law files regardless of individual expertise or interest and, on the other, they are barred from Aboriginal law sections within some large law firms because of perceptions that they cannot perform this work in an unbiased manner.' As well, the report addressed problems for Asian women (87): 'The stereotypical view of Asian-Canadian women may prevent them from acquiring litigation positions. These women are perceived as being soft-spoken, demure and non-confrontational and therefore not having the temperament that would allow them to succeed as litigators.'

97 CBA task force report, 268. See also appendix 10: 'Women of Colour in the Legal Profession'; appendix 11: 'Aboriginal Women in the Legal Profession';

appendix 9: 'Issues of Gender and Multiple Discrimination in Law School Settings'; and appendix 14: 'Annotated Bibliography on Gender Equality in the Legal Profession.'

98 See First Nations Law Students, 'Broadening the Law School Perspective' (Toronto: Curriculum Conference Report 1992), 11, with detailed recommendations.

99 For example, in relation to property law, the report stated (25): 'The position of Aboriginal peoples in Canadian society is based on their relationship with the land. This special relationship is not considered in most property law courses in Ontario law schools. The Aboriginal law students felt that Aboriginal land rights and land claims should be examined in the core property law courses. Also, materials on the *Indian Act* property provisions and the effect of this legislation on reserve lands are other topics the property curriculum presently lacks. Information on the system for possession of reserve land by the certificate of possession or of occupation, on the descent of property and on the surrender of land should be included in the discussion on the *Indian Act* among other issues. In addition, the Aboriginal law students felt that the special case of Métis land claims should also be covered in property law classes.'

100 For example, the 'access admission' policy of Osgoode Hall Law School as set out in the law school calendar (1992–3), 64.

101 'A Proposal to Enhance Minority Participation at Dalhousie Law School' (Halifax: Dalhousie University 1989).

102 Ibid.

103 'Equality in Legal Education,' 1.

104 Ibid., 4. See also the presentations at the Conference on Access to Legal Education (Canadian Association of Law Deans: 8 Nov. 1990).

105 This principle most clearly reflected the influence of equality discourse. As the report stated (11): 'Teaching about equality, about legal responses to inequality, and about professional attentiveness to difference ought to lie at the core of legal education.'

106 See 'Equality in Legal Education,' 11.

107 The report reviewed some data released by the Law School Admission Council, for example, showing that law students are generally from more privileged backgrounds in terms of income than Canadians overall. See 'Equality in Legal Education,' 15 and n.10.

108 See ibid., 19 ff., citing (in part) Robert Wilkins, 'The Politics of the Law School Experience,' *University of Toronto Faculty of Law Review*, 1987, 98; Christine Boyle, 'Teaching Law As if Women Really Mattered, or, What About the Washrooms?' *Canadian Journal of Women and the Law*, vol. 2 (1986), 96; and Mary O'Brien and Sheila McIntyre, 'Patriarchal Hegemony and Legal Education' *Canadian Journal of Women and the Law*, vol. 2 (1986), 69.

109 See 'Equality in Legal Education,' 35.

110 In Ontario, see 'A Recommended Personnel Policy Regarding Employment-Related Sexual Harassment' (Toronto: Law Society of Upper Canada: 24 Jan. 1992); 'The Adviser' (Law Society of Upper Canada: September 1992); and 'Discipline Digest' (Law Society of Upper Canada: November 1992). See also Commission on Women in the Legal Profession, 'Sexual Harassment Policies' (American Bar Association).

111 See Law Society of Upper Canada, 'Report of the Special Committee on Equity in Legal Education and Practice' (1991). See also the report on equity initiatives published in 1993 (Law Society of Upper Canada, *Benchers Bulletin*, January 1993).

112 For an overview of the process leading to the new rule, see Lynn Smith, 'Gender Equality: Professional and Ethical Issues' (CBA National Task Force on Gender Equality Conference: 1992), 26 ff. The Law Society of Upper Canada adopted a non-discrimination rule (rule 28) in 1994. See also Chris Tennant, 'Discrimination in the Legal Profession, Codes of Professional Conduct and the Duty of Non-Discrimination,' *Dalhousie Law Journal*, vol. 15 (1992), 463.

113 See CBA task force report, 220.

114 Ibid., chapter 13 (recommendations 13.1 to 13.31).

115 Ibid., 271.

116 For an analysis of the myth of effective 'choice,' see Mossman, 'Work and Family.'

117 See 'Equality in Legal Education,' 26.

118 Bruce Feldthusen, 'The Gender Wars: Where the Boys Are,' *Canadian Journal of Women and the Law*, vol. 4 (1990), 77. See also Rosalie Abella, 'Women in the Legal Profession,' *Law Society of Upper Canada Gazette*, vol. 12 (1983), 15, where the author suggests that the legal profession 'bends only creakingly to change.'

119 Mary Jane Mossman, 'Gender Bias and the Legal Profession: Challenges and Choices,' in *Investigating Gender Bias: Law, Courts, and the Legal Profession*, eds. Joan Brockman and Dorothy Chunn (Toronto: Thompson Educational Publishing Inc., 1993), 160 ff.

120 Reported in Cameron Harvey, 'Women in Law in Canada,' *Manitoba Law Journal*, vol. 4 (1970–1), 13. See also Marguerite Ritchie, 'Alice Through the Statutes,' *McGill Law Journal*, vol. 21 (1975), 685, and 'The Language of Oppression – Alice Talks Back,' *McGill Law Journal*, vol. 23 (1977), 535. The latter article was a reply to a critique of the former; see Elmer Driedger, 'Are Statutes Written for Men Only?' *McGill Law Journal*, vol. 22 (1976), 666. See also Mary Jane Mossman, 'Portia's Progress: Women as Lawyers; Reflections on Past and Future,' *Windsor Yearbook of Access to Justice*, vol. 8 (1988), 252.

121 Alan Watson, 'Legal Change: Sources of Law and Legal Culture,' in *Legal Origins and Legal Change*, ed. A. Watson (London: Hambleton Press 1991), 69.

122 Ibid., 84.

123 Ibid., 85; as the author states, 'the theory must not assume a simple mechanical and automatic relationship between law and society.'

124 Gwen Brodsky and Shelagh Day, *Canadian Charter Equality Rights for Women: One Step Forward or Two Steps Back?* (Ottawa: Canadian Advisory Council on the Status of Women 1989).

125 Although the Charter was not at issue in the Supreme Court of Canada decision in *Finlay v. Canada*, [1993] S.C.J. No. 39, the willingness of the majority to read the protections of the Canada Assistance Plan narrowly so as to support the province's right to collect overpayments suggests that the court may hesitate to make poverty an analogous ground of discrimination pursuant to section 15. By contrast, see *R. v. Rehberg* (NSSC: 1993).

126 CBA task force report, 268.

127 One 'cost' to the legal profession is the increasing rate of 'exits,' especially of women lawyers. See 'Transitions in the Legal Profession' (Toronto: Law Society of Upper Canada 1991) at 53–4 and table 41.

128 CBA task force report, 271.

129 Ibid., 272.

130 'Equality in Legal Education,' 41–2.

131 Ibid., 42.

10

The Charter and Mainstream Political Science: Waves of Practical Contestation and Changing Theoretical Currents*

ALEXANDRA DOBROWOLSKY

Alan Cairns, political scientist and committed chronicler of constitutionalism in Canada, argues that the Charter of Rights and Freedoms represents a 'profound, wrenching transformation'[1] of the Canadian constitutional order. Whether one subscribes to Cairnsiana or not, it is evident that, over the last two decades, the Charter has moved from the ideal to the real, from a political ploy stashed up Pierre Trudeau's nationalist sleeve[2] to a not always reliable, but nonetheless tangible, political stratagem in the hands of a wide array of socio-political actors.

In this process, the tried political proclivities for 'elite accommodation'[3] and 'executive federalism,'[4] whereby prime ministers and premiers engage in sequestered decision making and barter with the future of the country and its peoples, are no longer trusted. These old-style politics are challenged, in theory and in practice, by a variety of collective actors such as women's organizations, First Nations groups, and associations based on ethnicity, race, language, ability, and sexual orientation, among others. As a result, the citizenry effectively has de-legitimized the spectre of eleven white men in suits[5] monopolizing the 'roll of the [constitutional] dice.'[6]

It is crucial to clarify, however, that collective actors have not simply materialized out of the institution of the Charter. Social movements have struggled long and hard in Canada, engaging in politics in ways not restricted to 'civil society,' challenging both the state and political institutions as well.[7] The organization of some women to achieve enfranchisement at the turn of the century

* The author wishes to thank Richard Devlin, Jane Jenson, Radha Jhappan, David Schneiderman, and Denis St Martin for their words of encouragement as well as critical commentaries. Financial assistance was provided by the Centre for Constitutional Studies, University of Alberta, and the Social Sciences and Humanities Research Council. This paper is dedicated to my father, Justyn Dobrowolsky, who passed away on 1 Dec. 1993.

provides one well-known example.[8] The Charter, then, has not been the source of a participatory transformation, but rather, certain collective actors have identified the Charter as but one potential site of political innovation.[9] First Nations groups and individuals, for instance, as John Borrows and others attest, both work with and problematize the Charter[10]; at the same time, they have been and continue to be committed to seeking justice on issues such as land claims and/ or the promotion of Aboriginal women's concerns.[11] Didi Herman concurs: Pragmatic social movement activists, in general, and lesbians, gays, and bisexuals, in particular, 'fed up with political manoeuvrings and the slow pace of parliamentary reform, have turned to the Charter as another forum ... in which to make their case.'[12] The Charter has become an alternative terrain of political struggle.

In light of the foregoing, I pose the following question: Has mainstream[13] political science been moved by shifts wrought in the wake of the establishment of the Charter of Rights and Freedoms? Through a detailed examination of some prominent anglophone contributors to the political-science literature on federalism/constitutionalism, I will argue that engagement with the Charter has marked the intellectual face of the discipline. However, I also will demonstrate that traditional features persist and, as a result, that changes to the visage of political science have appeared only gradually and over time.

More specifically, in the English-language political-science literature on federalism/constitutionalism, there are two distinguishable categories of analysis: institutional/state-centric and societally based conceptualizations. I will elaborate upon this distinction and suggest that subscribers of both approaches have modified their formulations because of real-life contestation arising from the existence of the Charter as a site of struggle. In addition, I will examine how organizing for change via the Charter has instigated what may be termed as an 'academic backlash.' That is, I will expose the conservatism of a strain of Charter analysis which has developed in response to the strategic use of the Charter by activists.

To be clear, the intent is not to provide an exhaustive survey of Canadian political science literature. The discipline encompasses many intellectual currents, from behaviouralism to feminism and political economy. Rather, my aim is an appraisal of some significant anglo-Canadian contributions to the field in the area of federalism/constitutionalism and an identification of noteworthy trends in the era of Charter politics.[14] Given the implications of collective actors' Charter-based tactics, it will become apparent that the work of mainstream political scientists who study federalism/constitutionalism has had to evolve. For the most part, analytical modifications have occurred incrementally and have reflected a reactive theoretical justification that has developed as a response to real-life activism. Perhaps not surprisingly, the more institutionally retentive the interpretation, the more the Charter grows as an explanation of collective mobilization. The dilemma is not that the Charter becomes an object of analysis, or that we study the state, its institutions, norms, and actors, but that different forms of politics that are not necessarily and not always 'elite-driven' and institutionally tied are then objectified. This not only denies the history and character of identities that are not solely governmentally, or strictly territorially, situated, but it also ultimately serves to constrain their scope.

To map out this argument, a delineation of the work of specific scholars over time is useful. In the first section, I begin with a careful consideration of state-centred authors' writing prior to the Charter's entrenchment in order to sketch the parameters of the dominant debate. Then, in the second section, I outline innovations and limitations in the institutionalist schematic which have become manifest as the Charter has been used as a ground for political contestation. In the third section, I follow the same process for the society-centred category, which I proceed to subdivide into political-cultural and structural variants. The third section contains an assessment of one writer's political-cultural perspective and its progression, a critique of key structuralist contributions, and a discussion of post-Charter structuralist modifications. In the fourth section, I examine a new trend which, in my view, represents a concerted attempt to stem the tide of Charter-focused political activism. And finally, in the fifth section, I offer some concluding considerations on activist challenges, the Charter, and the study of Canadian politics.

State-centric Analyses

Prior to the Charter era, as Yves de Montigny acknowledges, the study of federalism occupied a central position in the field of Canadian politics.[15] Political science research developed from the legal-constitutional arguments of the 1940s and 1950s,[16] to the more institutionalist accounts of the 1960s,[17] then to a greater awareness of economic and societal forces in the 1970s,[18] and, finally, to a more acute understanding of the interaction of these forces with institutional forms in the 1980s and 1990s.[19] I will argue that the latter process was accelerated by the enactment of the Charter and its strategic manipulation by groups other than governmental elites that were based on various, often non-territorial, group-based identities.

Overall, the state-centred or institutionalist schematic, in its various permutations, has represented the dominant approach in the study of Canadian federalism. Institutionalist scholarship revolves around formal institutions, established political practices, and traditional power holders.[20] State-centric theorists hold that policy does not result because of the pressure from interested social groups; on the contrary, the state and its institutional networks are autonomous and, in the extreme, authoritarian.[21] Societal influences and economic forces tend to be minimized in this interpretation.

These assumptions are prevalent and prominent in the work of canon-building political scientists such as Donald Smiley, Richard Simeon, and Alan Cairns. Their studies, moreover, have underscored the research of most scholars of Canadian federalism. As a result, despite significant differences in tone and substance that will be examined below, one can advance the claim that state-centred theorization has been the central paradigm in explanations of the federal/constitutional process in Canada.

To begin with, in Donald Smiley's influential account, the institutions of federalism constitute the essential determinants of the behaviour of other institutions and actors.[22] Federalism influences three major axes: relations between the English and French, between the centre and the regions, and between Canada and the United States. The administration of these complex relations is confined to institutional actors – political elites – who either accommodate or conflict with respect to each plane.[23] Second, the territorial nature of these axes is evident. At least two of them are clearly spatially bound: regionally, in terms of core and periphery; and continentally, in terms of Canada and the United States. Furthermore, although the French and English aspect can be seen as a linguistic cleavage, Smiley and the institutionalists tend to consider it more in terms of the provincial government of Quebec versus the federal government, and so it too is spatially based. The institution of federalism feeds these spatial cleavages. Thus, Smiley's early work does not factor in socio-political influences beyond institutionally generated, spatially based, political elites.

Smiley's legacy is perhaps most evident in his elaboration of the notion of 'executive federalism.' The expression depicts the institutional outcome of Canada's hybrid constitution that combines both cabinet-influenced Parliament and federalism, resulting in the interdependence of federal and provincial levels of government as well as the tendency for them to engage in closed constitutional consultation and negotiation.[24] The concept derives from Smiley's long-standing view of contemporary federalism, that it is, above all, about governments.[25]

These formulations have proven to be a mainstay of the discipline, leading one political scientist to confess in the title of an article written after Smiley's death: 'We are all Smiley's people.'[26] To illustrate, Richard Simeon's now classic analysis, *Federal-Provincial Diplomacy*,[27] proceeds from Smiley's executive-federalist premise, providing 'empirical' support for the thesis and offering a prime example of an early and predominantly institutionalist understanding of federalism and intergovernmental relations.[28] In this work, Simeon limits his focus to direct and explicit negotiations between the executives of different governments.[29] The eleven governments are thus primary and pivotal actors, negotiating and engaging in diplomatic relations in a manner similar to that of European states. Other 'societal' influences, such as parties and/or interest groups, have little impact.[30] According to Simeon, institutional arrangements 'have a life of their own apart from social structures.'[31] As a result, there is little room for socio-political actors beyond unitary government ones.

In this branch of political science, the institutionalist assumptions of Smiley and Simeon have been, more often than not, developed rather than disputed. For J. Stefan Dupré, as an example, executive federalism and its inherent institutionalism are givens. The task he sets for himself is to determine how this situation can be most effective and workable.[32] While Richard Schultz sets out to challenge Simeon's model, acknowledging the relevance of interest groups, institutional actors are nonetheless the key, albeit intragovernmentally.[33] For Schultz, bureaucratic politics shapes interest-group activities. In general, then, students of Canadian federalism have worked within and built on each other's premises. The debate has tended to revolve around the internal workings of the institutions of governments and key concepts are shared and often become assumed, the invocation of Smiley's notion of executive federalism providing a prime example.

Granted, there are some points of divergence. There are political scientists who have criticized executive federalism from the outset. Cairns and Albert Breton take on executive federalism for different reasons.[34] In addition, it has been argued that the Cairnsian perspective is more socio-political than strictly institutional.[35] For example, Cairns's early position reflected sympathies towards provincialist, or territorially based, identities.[36] Yet, as with Smiley, Cairns's early work focused primarily on spatially based, provincial actors arising out of the institution of federalism, and, like Schultz's account of interest groups, his territorially based players are institutionally determined. For Cairns, the role played by non-institutional actors, and the reception they receive, result from the tension between controlling and manipulating governing elites. Identities, then, are shaped by institutions and institutional power holders.[37] The result, once again, is that the agency of societal actors is diminished as primacy is given to the institutional explanation.

In spite of different emphases – more 'conjectural' (Smiley) as opposed to more 'empirical' (Simeon) treatments, public-policy (Schultz and Dupré) versus rational-choice (Breton) and sociological (Cairns) influences – political-science analysts of federalism/constitutionalism have tended to be state-centred. Few of the scholars mentioned, in their early manifestations, concertedly focused on socio-economic themes or non-institutionally linked political identities. Clearly, federalism/constitutionalism is about governments, but in these studies the relations between governments are conceptualized in solely institutional terms. If, as with Smiley, Cairns, and Schultz, other actors are acknowledged, the causal arrow still runs from the state. It thus becomes apparent that the federal/constitutional conversation has been relatively closed, involving a limited number of speakers and digressing little from institutionalist imperatives. This, in turn, has meant that the potentialities, the history and struggles, of actors who are not necessarily institutionally or territorially based have been overlooked or underdeveloped and even constrained.

Charter-directed Challenges to State-centrism

Since the advent of the Charter, as Cairns has argued, Canadian federalism can no longer be described as an affair of governments in which political, bureaucratic, and judicial elites monopolize power. Moreover, in my view, the manifest activism leading up to and after the establishment of the Charter has highlighted the flaws in the state-centred schematic. In recent years, owing to the influence of actors that are not always governmentally or territorially based, such as women, First Nations peoples, groups mobilizing on the bases of ethnicity, race, sexual orientation, ability, and so on, the institutionalists have been compelled to reformulate their analyses to account for and accommodate the actions of a greater collection of group-based identities.[38]

In contrast to the institutionalist tendency to view the Charter as a causal force, the argument here is that the Charter has merely channelled certain social-movement activity rather than given rise to it. Women's groups, for instance, were established in Canada in the 1870s and by 1893 a federation of women's groups had been organized.[39] Nevertheless, as the contributions to this collection affirm, there is little doubt that collective actors have identified the Charter as a potential terrain of struggle. Feminist activists, for example, inspired mass mobilization to entrench sexual equality in the early 1980s.[40] In the case of both the Meech and Charlottetown accords, when this and other 'gains' were considered at risk, a wide array of equality-seeking groups worked, often in coalition, to jettison agreements which in their view highlighted old-style, exclusivist politics, jeopardized rights, and diminished federal powers. Equality-seekers have used Charter-based claims in the courts and have been making their voices heard in various constitutional commissions, committees, and conferences. They have assessed, criticized, and pushed for additions and deletions to constitutional proposals.[41] It is my contention that this real-life,

Charter-based activism, by actors not typically associated with 'governmental elite' circles, has tempered the institutionalists' appraisals.

In this section, I will limit my comments to the federal/constitutional oeuvres of Smiley, Simeon, and Cairns because of their sheer output, longevity, and legitimacy.[42] Arguably, Smiley remained the most committed statist; Simeon, perhaps, ventures the farthest from his institutional imperatives; and Cairns continues to refine his neo-institutionalism with a more expansive and nuanced notion of identity politics. The latter's work will be examined in the greatest detail since his commentary on identity politics with respect to the study of Canadian federalism/constitutionalism has been the most extensively articulated.[43]

In his last book, *The Federal Condition in Canada*, Smiley modified and supplemented his earlier analysis. To incorporate 'new' developments, which I take to mean the establishment of the Charter and the activism directed towards it, Smiley reconsidered the implications of executive federalism. In his earlier inquiries, Smiley had identified but did not criticize executive federalism. It was not considered to be a bad thing for political elites to be cooperatively governing, effectively communicating, and addressing regional concerns among themselves.[44] However, after Charter-based mobilization beyond the confines of governmental actors diverted the course of constitutional events, Smiley advanced a critique of executive federalism, describing it as a closed and ineffectual device.[45] Indeed, endorsing Breton's case for competitive federalism, Smiley wrote, 'Federal-provincial co-operation contributes to secrecy in the governmental process and to the frustration of public debate about important aspects of our common affairs.'[46]

A more telling shift occurred as Smiley suggested the possibility of incorporating a 'fourth' axis to his federalist framework. Beyond spatially based cleavages of region, language, and American/Canadian relations, Smiley conceded that non-spatially defined cleavages like those of gender may challenge the territorial aspects of federalism.[47] This admission was, no doubt, prompted by the need to account for the influential mobilization of women around the Charter. Through the efforts of key women's groups, a more carefully worded section 15 of the Charter became a reality, and, because of mass-based mobilization by women, a new equality rights section (28) free from any override, was included in the Charter.[48] The impact of the Charter and the women's movement are addressed specifically in the final pages of *The Federal Condition in Canada*, 'Retrospect and Prospect.' Here Smiley ventures: 'It is more probable that cleavages will emerge dividing Canadians along lines other than those of their residence in particular provinces. The Charter of Rights and

Freedoms and the women's movement have potentialities for such pan-Canadian mobilization.'[49]

In the end, however, Smiley staunchly defended his traditional, institutional perspective. Endorsing neo-statism over neo-Marxism, he wrote that political institutions have *real* as opposed to 'relative' autonomy in shaping both society and economics.[50] What is more, despite his concession to the contentiously termed 'new' cleavages, like those of gender, notions of race and/or class were not developed, and, at the same time, the dualism between English and French was still protrayed as the most significant division.[51] Therefore, while it is true that compromises were made, it is equally true that for Smiley identities remained, primarily, spatially based. In effect, federal institutions continued to shape identities, be they territorially delimited ones or others.

Simeon's scholarship provides more of a departure. In contrast to his initial, insular institutionalism, Simeon now demonstrates a greater commitment to explaining the interrelation between state and society. For example, after public protest influenced the outcome of the Meech Lake process, Simeon criticized executive federalism and elite accommodation more generally as 'increasingly at odds with the temper of modern democracy'[52] and, in another work, 'obsolete.'[53] In his research with Ian Robinson, moreover, Simeon advocates a theoretical position that blends the roles of 'economic and social forces, political institutions and political culture.'[54] Whereas he had previously examined hierarchically controlled, unitary institutional actors, he now takes account of multiple institutional and extra-institutional actors. Simeon claims that his current focus is the organization of collective interests and identities – parties, interest groups, as well as governments – and, in addition to territorial, socio-political forces, he also recognizes identities, such as those of class and gender, which transcend territorial lines.[55]

This is a far cry from *Federal-Provincial Diplomacy*. There is a greater awareness of the forces of globalization, the interrelation between state and society, and the presence of multiple institutional and extra-institutional actors. Nonetheless, some may counter that Simeon's analysis reflects the growing sophistication of a neo-institutionalist analysis,[56] with its appreciation of socio-economic and international, structural concerns, and, increasingly, its concession to collective identities.[57] While this may be the case, the development in Simeon's work has been marked. Again, while there are no doubt many explanations for this more diversified approach, I would posit that Simeon has had little choice but to modify his theorization in order to explain recent constitutional developments since the advent of the Charter. By integrating a neo-institutionalist analysis that not only considers socio-economic and international forces but also begins to grapple with collective mobilization, Simeon tries to accommodate pre- and post-Charter events that were inexplicable in his initial static, state-centrist formulations.

The evolution of political-science theorization on federalism/constitutionalism is commendable, and yet there are limits to its tendency to graft new considerations onto old frameworks. Although Smiley's and Simeon's work may be criticized on these grounds, Cairns's publications are particularly illustrative of the limitations of neo-institutionalism.

Over time, Cairns's sympathies towards provincial struggles have broadened to include non-spatially based identities. Thus, more expansively than Smiley, and more consistently and systematically than Simeon, Cairns has augmented the institutionalism of his earlier pieces to incorporate notions of 'identity politics.'[58] For example, he has begun to redress the poverty of the debate on Canadian constitutionalism which has tended to focus on formal institutions, established political practices, and traditional power holders, on 'governments' more than on 'societies.' In his oft-cited article 'Citizens (Outsiders) and Governments (Insiders) in Constitution-Making: The Case of Meech Lake,'[59] he highlights two competing perspectives: the government's constitution and the citizen's constitution. Proponents of the first, according to Cairns, promote the traditional discourse of federalism, division of powers, and amending formulae, while advocates of the second speak the language of 'national, ethnic and sexual identity, and of stigmatic exclusion versus honourable inclusion and recognition.'[60] The latter reflects Cairns's effort to add the notion of identity politics to the dominant institutional and executive-federalist views.

Cairns describes how the patriation of the constitution and a new Charter of Rights changed the face of constitutionalism in Canada by spurring the creation of new constitutional identities and new group elites.[61] These 'new' identities – women, Aboriginal peoples, ethnic communities, and others – provide an explanation for the failure of the Meech Lake Accord. According to Cairns, the emergent groups claimed 'niches' in the Charter and wished to defend them from the accord's encroachments. Here we observe the clash between citizens' and governments' constitutions referred to above. Thus, executive-federalist elite accommodation is injected with a dose of citizen activism. Unfortunately, the logic of Cairns's institutionalism precludes the forging of such connections. Despite important developments in his analysis, Cairns continues to subscribe to the dominant institutionalist discourse. True to this pattern, his interpretation ultimately rests more on elite 'insiders' than on citizen 'outsiders.' By fusing a notion of identity politics onto an institutional foundation, the former is adversely affected by the latter. The predicament is that the aforementioned identities, in Cairns's evaluation, appear to spring forth, full blown, out of institutions. For, at its core, his is an institutionalist understanding which is deficient in its account of the agency of actors outside the state and its network of institutions.

As a result, the mobilization of such collective actors as women and First Nations peoples is portrayed as a 'new' phenomenon, born out of the Charter. The Charter is reified and subjectified, and, identity-based groups, in turn, become objectified. This denies many years of prior activism on the part of these groups. For example, as Kathleen Mahoney and others point out, women's constitutional milestones were reached after centuries of legal and political battles.[62] Similarly, in the case of Aboriginal peoples, David Long comments that 'Indian leaders had begun ... organizing people as early as 1874.'[63]

Furthermore, because this form of identity politics is tied to institutionalism, it necessitates integration into Cairns's elite/mass schema. Group leaders become labelled 'elites.' Cairns claims that the Charter created a 'constitutional base for a counter-elite of group leaders'[64] and traditional elites are now 'joined by elites from the various groups that have received specific constitutional recognition.'[65] This elite designation is questionable. Feminist organizations, for example, tend to strive for 'internal egalitarianism.'[66] Organizational practices reflect an effort to 'empower the politically inexperienced'[67] by rotating both leadership and support roles, operating non-hierarchically, and making decisions on the basis of consensus.[68] In the words of one writer, this serves to deter the advancement of 'ego-tripping' leaders.[69] As another illustration, although Aboriginal groups have their own political organizations, their respective spokespersons and leaders,[70] it is dubious that they can be termed 'elites.' In fact, many Aboriginal communities promote consensual forms of decision making[71] which tend to militate against the emergence of an elite.

This loosely applied 'elite' label points to a more fundamental limitation. It is important to remember that the so-called 'elite' leaders often act as representatives of oppressed groups. Again, if we take as an example Canada's First Nations peoples, they experience systemic racism and are at the bottom rung of the socio-economic ladder. The fact that these issues are not a prime consideration in Cairns's notion of identity politics points to a broader failing in his analysis. That is, for Cairns, the struggles over power relations of race, gender, and class, among others, are peripheral. Yet it is typically these forms of oppression that provide the spark and galvanize many of the groups that Cairns includes in his analysis.[72] In short, it is the struggle against these long-standing forms of oppression that produces the catalyst for many groups, not the elite-led identities discursively constructed by an institution like the Charter.

Cairns's institutionalism focuses on governments despite his attempt to integrate the people. In fact, representatives of the people are re-encoded as elites and thereby become incorporated into the process. Cairns betrays his allegiance to the status quo in an article where he queries 'how good are the democratic and representative credentials of those who speak for women, aboriginals and others?'[73] This, to my mind, begs the question of how good are the democratic credentials of Canada's conventional, elected representatives? It is this paucity of 'representative' and 'democratic' qualities in institutional politics which has motivated many social movements and encouraged their mobilization outside traditional forums.

In most cases, the Charter has not 'generated' these groups. Nor can mobilization be limited to a 'new' participatory ethic stemming from post-material phenomena, as some critics of Cairns point out.[74] Socio-politico-economic mobilization is long-standing and complex. Its explanation cannot be confined to uni-dimensional and uni-directional determinants. However, I propose that the presence of activism directly focused on the Charter has spurred changes to Canada's conventional political-constitutional discourse. As Cairns himself admonishes (all the while exhibiting the limits of his identity-politics formulation): 'The student of constitutional politics of the future must examine and analyze the new constitutional actors generated by the Charter and aboriginal clauses with the same rigour that is applied to the study of governments. The constitutional politics of the Assembly of First Nations and the National Action Committee on the Status of Women deserve some of the attention we have previously devoted to executive federalism, courts, and amending formula.'[75]

Cairns perseveres in nuancing his position. In recent publications he is careful to classify identities promoted by groups based on gender, ethnicity, and ability not simply as 'new' but as 'reinvigorated old cleavages.'[76] Still, he continues to refine his state-centrism, drawing on a refurbished neo-institutionalism which incorporates the international context and supports a somewhat toned down 'limited autonomy' of the state.[77] Governments persist in 'seek[ing] to support cleavages most compatible with their own interests' and '[c]ontemporary Canadian citizens are still being drawn into provincial or national networks of policy and administration by old and new government programs shaped by a nineteenth-century division of powers.'[78] Cairns concedes that not all 'changes in how Canadians see themselves [are] results of explicit constitutional change,' but there are, nevertheless, definite 'state-sponsored cues' to this effect.[79] He still maintains, moreover, that the Charter begets 'a host of focused constitutional interest groups that identify with particular clauses, and see their task as the protection or strengthening of their niche in the Constitution.'[80] This is a familiar refrain.

On the surface, identity groups provide a challenge to executive federalism, but, because the core of Cairns's analysis is based on an elite/mass distinction, activism boils down to elite accommodation. Constitutional debates are basically depicted as an elite-driven and controlled process. This does not give enough opportunities for, nor credit to, the struggle of collective actors. To be clear, I am not suggesting that we have witnessed a giant leap forward in terms of the democratization of constitutional negotiations. I do argue, however, that neither have we simply a state-centric, executive-federalist process. Because of the persistent activism of collective actors, it has not been a case of, in Cairns's sense, politics as usual for elites.

In summary, since the advent of the Charter, Cairns's position, as well as those of Smiley and Simeon, have demonstrated an expanded awareness of societal influence. Simeon's work has changed the most, but then again, given, for example, his early disavowal of the impact of collective mobilization on federal/provincial relations, his position had the farthest to come in accounting for current constitutional events. As a result, Simeon's earlier uni-directional institutional framework has been substantially reworked to encompass a more complex matrix of socio-economico-political relations. Nonetheless, the institutionalist allegiance continues to be prominent, not only in Smiley's last piece but also in the recent work of Simeon and Cairns, albeit in a more contemporary, neo-institutionalist guise. This revitalized neo-institutionalism is still insufficiently attentive to the complexity of identity-based mobilization. As Cairns's work aptly illustrates, the 'add identities and stir approach' objectifies collective actors and fails to appreciate the history and character of old and new social, political, and economic struggles.

Society-centric Perspectives

The work of scholars included in the society-centred grouping does not exemplify the themes of this article as vividly as that of the state-centred political scientists. Analytical difficulties arise because society-centred explanations can be substantially different in their focus and content and because they tend to borrow generously from different approaches.[81] To assist in clarification, I will subdivide the societally based categorization into political-cultural and structural positions.[82] Here, too, it will become apparent that, despite the societal emphasis in both variants, the institutionalist inspiration remains discernible. This, in turn, results in a more complicated picture compared to the relatively straightforward state-centric account. What is more, tracing the progress of different authors in this category is difficult. General tendencies will be outlined and changes over time will be suggested, but the transformation is not as marked as with the institutionalists.

The institutionalists were bereft of a societal understanding and thus they were at a significant loss in accounting for collective mobilization directed towards the Charter. On the other hand, those who fit into the society-centred rubric start with the societal premise, for the explanatory weight in their interpretation is placed on social values and socio-economic determinants. Thus, presumably, the society-centric perspective would be able to accommodate the presence of socio-political, Charter-directed activism more easily than the institutionalist one. The society-centred analysis, then, has not been subject to the same fundamental challenge that was noted in the institutionalist schematic. Still, as we shall see, societally situated thinking has not been unmoved by shifts wrought by Charter-channelled activism. As a consequence, it, too, has had to develop further its theorizing, although in more subtle ways.

Pursuing Political Culture

Peter Russell, a political scientist and renowned court watcher, has straddled both institutionalist and political-cultural explanations.[83] This combination is indicative of inclinations in the Canadian political-culture approach more generally.[84] In Russell's case, scholarly attention is paid to the judiciary and constitutionalism in Canada, and thus his interests have been institutionally defined. However, somewhat secondarily, but nonetheless significantly, Russell also has noted the effects of political culture, the influence of values, and the sway of political socialization and/or behavioural norms on the institutions he studies. An examination of Russell's work over time provides a good measure of how the Charter has come to influence a political-cultural point of view.

Russell empirically examines legal institutions and uncovers the inherent values embedded within them. In his early pieces, he emphasized the values implicit in the courts, the impact of social attitudes on the judiciary, the socialization process for lawyers and judges, and the political nature of judicial decision making; the last factor, he argued, has been obscured in the Canadian context.[85] In addition, although an initial supporter of a repatriated constitution, Russell made explicit his concerns over judicial activism and any slide to an American-style separation of powers.[86] He stated his opposition to 'putting judicial institutions in general ... along side elected legislatures.'[87]

This critique was elaborated well before the entrenchment of the Charter[88] and lingered after the Charter became a reality as Russell expressed scepticism about the judiciary's capacity to engage in its new policy-making role in relation to criminal-justice policy and, more fundamentally, with regard to the equality guarantees in section 15. Currently, Russell's concern lies in the possible negative repercussions on the quality of Canadian political life stemming from the judicialization of the resolution of equality issues.[89] For Russell, the courts tend to be 'impersonal and formal, yielding winner-take all outcomes.'[90]

They translate issues of social and political justice into technocratic, legalistic responses.[91] Instead, Russell promotes less formal, more conciliatory mechanisms, deliberative and discursive forums – in short, legislatures.[92]

Charter Politics Changes

Russell's analysis is no doubt institutionally dependent[93]; however, his early political-cultural perspective, given the primacy he placed on political values, exhibited an affinity to behaviouralism. The years since the Charter have had an effect on Russell's position. First, his concerns over the detrimental impact of modifications to the institutional status quo have diminished somewhat, and second, his political-cultural perspective has been fleshed out further.

Increasingly, as Charter politics mature, Russell has expressed satisfaction with what he labels the 'moderate activism' which epitomized the early years of Supreme Court Charter decisions.[94] His initial dismay regarding the institutional consequences of appointed judges imposing their will on elected legislatures apparently has been allayed.[95] To be sure, Russell continues to display apprehension over the process whereby groups who are frustrated by the legislative process turn to the Charter to bring about change, compelling judges to engage in 'decision-making where politicians fear to tread.'[96] Yet Russell concedes that he finds the new 'constitutional ethos' compatible with the 'democratic ethos' of our time,[97] for the Charter is 'providing a new kind of opportunity for interest group activity'[98] and 'to a limited extent Charter litigation does "democratize" the law reform agenda.'[99] While he continues to assert that the courts should not serve as the sole method of resolving disputes, Russell also stresses that courts have provided an avenue for change. He admits: 'Some Charter critics ... have gone too far in denouncing judicial review under the Charter as excessively elitist and undemocratic. These critics tend to underestimate the extent to which legal aid and the organization of advocacy groups have made litigation much more accessible than in the past as well as the extent to which Charter litigation generates action on law reform issues which are neglected or ignored by legislatures. Also ... both the presentation of Charter issues before judges and the reasoned decisions of judges on Charter issues can contribute significantly to public understanding of rights issues.'[100]

At the same time, the political-cultural theme has become more prominent in Russell's work. First of all, many of his predictions about the effects of the Charter on the legal/political realms can now be borne out. He writes, 'Clearly, the judicialization of politics and the politicalization of the judiciary, which was predicted as a key consequence of the Charter, has begun.'[101] Second, Russell now draws more heavily on political-culture analysis to sketch out the societal repercussions of the Charter. In the mid-1980s he suggested that the

Charter may have the greatest bearing in terms of popular attitudes and civic consciousness and that this hypothesis had been insufficiently explored.[102] He has taken up the challenge and attempted to trace the political-cultural changes triggered by the Charter. Whereas before he concentrated on the institutional differences between Canada and the United States (the former's fusion of powers and the latter's separation of powers plus its dependence on a written constitution), Russell now expands on political-cultural divergences, setting out the evolution of federalism with respect to what he considers to be Canada's political values. Indeed, he structures recent books on the basis of Canada's shift from Burkean organic constitutionalism to American, Lockean liberalism as the result of the Charter. Russell suggests that Canada's constitutional future rests on the following quandary: 'Having become one of the world's oldest constitutional democracies largely on Burkean terms, Canadians must now find out whether they are capable of re-establishing their country on the basis of a Lockean social contract.'[103] For Russell, the 'Burkean' convention is the preferred alternative,[104] although he claims that the sharing of political-cultural values and shared social ideals provides some resonance.[105]

Russell's argument has remained fairly consistent over time. However, as Charter politics have transpired, some finely tuned changes in his work have become apparent. Primarily, his position on the political nature of the judiciary has been brought to the fore in the era of Charter politics. Second, his critique of an activist judiciary has moderated to a certain extent. Third, like the early institutionalists who had to expand their analytical purview, Russell has broadened the political-cultural implications of his work. By drawing on classical theorists, Russell attempts to move beyond institutional factors as explanations of our current constitutional environment.

At the same time, the institutionalist indebtedness persists. To illustrate, Russell makes the argument that executive federalism remains an important political instrument of constitutional reform.[106] More broadly, our purportedly changing political temper, from Burke to Locke, is traced, in a Cairnsian mode, to the Charter. The institution of the Charter becomes the causal determinant for change. What is more, Russell's longing for a Burkean status quo with its accompanying predilections for order and hierarchy,[107] and his continuing institutionalist sympathies, give liberal-sounding pronouncements about expanded opportunities for societally based activism a decidedly hollow ring.

The Structuralist Stream

In some respects, the structuralists' analyses of federalism provide more of a departure from the tenor of the institutionalist argument by criticizing federalism for its territorial boundedness. John Porter and Gad Horowitz, for instance, advocated the displacement of federal divisions with a more 'modern,' 'creative' politics of class.[108] Thus, for them, a non-territorially based identity was essential.

In contrast to the institutionalists, proponents of creative politics suggested that powerful economic interest groups act on provincial leaders: it is these interests that have an impact on ideology and thereby act *on* institutions. Porter wrote that 'a federal constitution, although purporting to prevent the centralization of political power, can become an instrument for the entrenchment of economic power.'[109] In fact, like Underhill before him,[110] Porter suggested that territorial divisions mystified other divisions, namely those of class.[111] Class is the focal point in this interpretation, and it is class that shapes institutions.

These ideas proved fertile for subsequent scholars who placed institutional-governmental relations in a socio-economic context. For Garth Stevenson, economic developments shape the federal system. Here, too, class analysis is central. In *Unfulfilled Union*,[112] Stevenson argues that, whether it is agrarian farmers versus capitalists or the new middle class in Quebec, class conflict fuels intergovernmental affairs. For him, the diplomatic relations outlined by Simeon are pivotal; however, the economic structure rather than the self-interest of governmental elites provides the explanatory factor.[113] Rather than transcending the regional dimension as the creative-politics school advocated, political economists have built on spatial *and* class analyses.[114] Stevenson, for instance, takes into consideration the spatial location of Canada next to the United States[115] along with economic motives and class conflict between capitalists and farmers to explain Confederation. The underlying logic of federalism, however, is the fulfilment of class interests, not any response to the people. As a result, Stevenson is critical of Canada's lack of participatory democracy, a shortcoming that he traces to the country's origins. This class emphasis and critique of democracy, however, denies the existence and/or agency of other collective identities beyond those of the ruling class and perhaps farmers involved in agrarian protest. Was there a relationship between, for example, ethnic and class conflict? What about the politics of gender and race? What was the role of the First Nations? These lines of inquiry are not pursued in a systematic way and thus a more complex understanding of social relations is not in evidence. To be sure, such omissions are not solely attributable to the structuralist perspective. Again, they are indicative of mainstream political science more generally, where, beyond the territorial and, in this case, singular class dimension, there is little concession given to other identities.

Reginald Whitaker develops an historical approach in which political economy, political culture, and institutionalism are interconnected.[116] Federalism, in Whitaker's estimation, provides a challenge to democratic theory since it serves to institutionalize 'the formal limitation of the national majority will as the legitimate ground for legislation.'[117] That is, federalism counters the concept of one sovereign power. The former is based on a notion of democratic sovereignty, for it renders the idea of a tyrannous majority doubtful; nevertheless, federalism also functions in such a way as to 'serialize' and 'atomize' the people into 'overlapping competitive and thus self-cancelling congeries of interests.'[118] With representative democracy, citizens are separated from decision-making political elites and federalism further dissipates linkages.[119] As a consequence, the democratic record in this area has been 'mixed to poor.'[120] Echoing the claims of the creative-politics school, Whitaker maintains that 'federalism as a system of representation remains formally silent about the economic and class content of the nation, but is predicated along the axis of space and its political organization.'[121]

The mystification of class-based identities is a familiar theme, but it is then tied to more of a Cairnsian approach. Whitaker speaks of the costs of territorial identities coexisting in the federal system and he describes federalism/constitutionalism since 1867 as an arrangement of elites. With federalism there are 'multiple, autonomously-based political elites,'[122] and so the problem is that whatever remnants of representative democracy do exist are further diminished by the federal arrangement and elite intergovernmental relations.

In light of this hybrid theoretical backdrop, Whitaker's assessment of the Charter is ambivalent. Just after the establishment of the Charter, Whitaker noted that it did serve a democratic purpose. In a less than enthusiastic conclusion, however, he maintained that 'even if [the Charter] actually will not change anything, it at least gives a constitutional sanction to the fundamentally democratic nature of the Canadian political system.'[123] Although groups gained formal rights in the Charter, Whitaker expressed his doubts as to the form these gains had taken – that is, the entrenchment of liberal as opposed to social-democratic rights. For Whitaker, 'social rights,' including the right to strike and the right to a job, were not in evidence.[124] These examples, of course, reflect his class-based affinities, his regard for worker's rights, and his support of social democracy.

Whitaker's historical treatment melds political economy and political-cultural influences; yet, for the most part, his understanding of democracy and federalism is institutionally based and elite-driven à la Cairns. Whitaker's early theorizing did not deal well with identities that were neither territorially tied nor predominantly non-class-identified. This criticism applies to the structuralists in general, who tended to place greater emphasis on class than on other identities such as those of gender and race. After the entrenchment of the Charter, however, the structuralist perspective began to change.

The Post-Charter Shift in Structuralist Theory

The Charter has not radically altered the structuralist account, but positions have gradually modified and trends perhaps not entirely, directly attributable to the Charter have nevertheless been reinforced by post-Charter activism. For example, soon after the early 1980s experience of mobilizing around the Charter, Whitaker toned down his Cairnsian-instigated reflections when he commented that the time had come 'for diverting some of the zero-sum rhetoric of competitive federalism, built up around governmental actors, into less territorially based forms of conflict.'[125]

What is more, whereas Stevenson's late 1970s account accepted Simeon's diplomacy model but placed it in a socio-economic context, towards the end of the 1980s, the work of later structuralists such as Keith Banting offered more of a critique of the institutionalists. Banting maintains that institutions do not determine the basic principles of his area of study, income security.[126] Contrary to Smiley and Cairns, he argues that institutions have not altered the redistributive goals of governments, and that, while federalism may slow the pace of change with respect to expansion and contraction of state activity, economic, social, and demographic factors are more revealing than institutional determinants. Banting resists the view that governing elites introduce programs without public input. Institutions have not frustrated public desires with regard to income security. Moreover, public attitudes are not regionally specific; there is more of a country-wide consensus on social programs. Here territorially based identities do not figure as prominently in the analysis, but, then again, neither do non-territorially based ones. By this I mean that, although Banting counters the institutionalists' elitism and discusses public input, what really affects relations in his final analysis is the broader political and economic structure. The role of human agency is therefore debatable.

Still, post-Charter politics have influenced Banting's structuralist leanings. For instance, while many left-leaning scholars discount the judicial realm as a site of struggle, Banting does suggest that the courts may open space for popular influence and that litigation 'might prove essential to the social responsiveness of the Canadian state.'[127] The latter concession towards considering the courts in the Charter era as a potential realm to bring about change raises an important point. In comparison to some of their institutionalist colleagues, the Charter has evoked more of a pragmatic response on the part of some political scientists with structuralist sympathies. This will be elaborated upon in more detail below.

More broadly, the left has had to reconsider its focus on class identity and its de-emphasis of human agency in favour of class and structural determinants. Charter activism highlights a multiplicity of identities that overlap and forge shifting alliances. Trade unionists are women and men and comprise different races and ethnic backgrounds, abilities, orientations, and so on. Feminist organizations have both created alliances and strained relations with the labour movement over constitutional matters. Similarly, Aboriginal mobilization around the Charter has been complicated by the politics of gender and vice versa. The multiplicity and interconnection of identity politics, the possibility of human agency despite structural constraints, are points of contention for the left in general,[128] but the presence of practical Charter-directed activism in Canada provides immediacy and relevancy to theoretical deliberation on these complex relations.

Not all of the left has taken up the foregoing challenges wholeheartedly. Stevenson's revised edition of *Unfulfilled Union*, for example, can still be criticized for its economic determinism and class reductionism.[129] His institutionalist proclivities are underscored as he argues that Canadian constitutional politics 'is managed and the outcomes determined by governments, not by academics, interest groups or opposition parties.'[130] However, there are some notable modifications in the tenor of his work since the Charter came into being.[131] For instance, in a move away from most political-economy analyses, Stevenson now maintains that the significance of the National Policy has diminished. He notes the altered emphases, from notions of duality to multiculturalism, and from 'Peace, Order, and Good Government' to Charterism. What then follows is Stevenson's recognition that there is a new momentum evident in the assertion of individual and some group rights against the state.[132] This demonstrates a greater awareness of multiple identities and strategies.

Marked change is apparent in structuralist analyses that focus predominantly on the contemporary Charter context.[133] For Whitaker, class and territorially based identities are no longer the primary considerations. Since the constitutional debates of 1980–1, Whitaker has come to admit the unique effects of more broadly based mobilization. He describes this popular influence at a particular point in the constitutional-negotiation process as follows: 'The conspiracy of first ministers to undermine rights provisions on women and native peoples, won earlier by popular representations, resulted in a massive grassroots lobbying campaign, which forced the heads of government to partially retreat. The women's and native people's causes were genuinely *national*, in the sense that they adhered to no regional power cluster, yet they were in no way seeking the aggrandizement of one level of government at the expense of others. Their partial victory should be taken as a heartening sign of the effect of popular mobilization on depolarizing federal-provincial conflict.'[134]

In a departure from his earlier formulations, Whitaker also accedes to a decline in elite accommodation. He discusses the role played by un- and underrepresented groups who seek 'direct public representation (women, gays, old age pensioners, etc.) outside the traditional elite structures, as well as the emergence of issue-oriented ... "public interest" groups (ecology, peace and pro- and anti-abortion, and so on).'[135] Of course, these groups are not 'new.' What is new is that structuralist theorists such as Whitaker have begun to recognize their influence and incorporate them more fully into their analyses.[136] Again, the Charter did not create these groups, but, because they have directed some of their collective energies towards it, both society-centred and state-centred analyses have had to reckon with them as never before.

What is more, I would venture that, in contrast to the legal left, which has tended to be critical of the Charter,[137] the political-science structuralists have shown more ambivalence. Banting alludes to this point, and in Whitaker's writings, more specifically, there has been a pragmatic response and a willingness to stray from anti-Charter dogmatism. As a result, the Charter is not categorically dismissed as a vehicle to bring about change.[138]

Here the nuancing of Whitaker's position comes to the fore. Like Russell, Whitaker notes a shift in political culture when equality-seekers question the representative and democratic capacity of Parliament and turn to 'nondemocratic' institutions, that is, the courts, in the post-Charter context. However, unlike Russell and the leading legal left academics who prefer legislative over litigative means, Whitaker emphasizes the failure of 'democratic' institutions to respond to the demands of women and other collective identities. Whitaker reminds the Charter skeptics that not only the courts but also traditional representative institutions have been elitist and unresponsive to the needs of 'minorities.'[139] Hence, the Charter and the courts provide another option; they are 'an avenue for previously marginal groups left out of the majoritarian institutions of representative democracy.'[140] Although he cautions that rights discourse may atomize social-movement politics, Whitaker maintains that the Charter, conceived as a means to seeking individual and group-rights claims, constitutes a 'flexible instrument for extending democratic equality.'[141] For Whitaker, the Charter has not 'displaced' politics but is rather 'helping to redefine politics.'[142]

Still, the change in Whitaker's analysis is not as great as it could be. Even though he finds the popular mobilization around the Charter 'heartening,'[143] he ultimately suggests that the democratization process 'has yet to find its appropriate institutional forms.'[144] Whitaker is concerned about 'the people' but he seeks an institutional mechanism for implementing their will.[145] This institutional element, as with Cairns, limits the full potential of identity politics. It does not recognize that popular mobilization need not have an institutional basis and/or institutional legitimacy. Whitaker does show some appreciation of democratization outside traditional elite structures in the direct participation of women, First Nations peoples, gays, and so on,[146] and he suggests that these 'fragmented democratic publics ... [are] able to improvise means to transform their diverse interests into coherent expressions.' That statement reflects the beginning of an appreciation of broader, collective mobilization which may or may not challenge conventional institutional forms. Unfortunately, this line of argumentation is not followed through.

More problematically, Whitaker shows some ambivalence with regard to these more expansive identity politics when he lapses into defining them as 'special interests.'[147] The emergence of such 'issue-oriented interest groups,' Whitaker claims, puts a strain on traditional forms of elite accommodation.[148] In other words, Whitaker does refer to 'populist' and women's movement mobilization as well as to various forms of coalitional politics in the era of the Charter, but he fears the dangers that could be unleashed as a result of 'special interests'' splintering effects. For example, with respect to mobilization around the Charter, Whitaker contends, 'While the Charter sparked significant popular mobilization, the truth of this mobilization was almost entirely around special interests and particularist identities. What *united* people about the Charter was what *divided* them as Canadians.'[149] In the end, Whitaker, like Cairns, seeks out an institutional way of making sense of and reigning in this broadly based mobilization, for he fears the consequences of excessive fragmentation. Consequently, here too there is a tendency that curtails the role of extra-institutional actors.

In sum, the structuralists, like the proponents of political- cultural and institutionalist theorization, have modified their position. Charter-directed activism has had an impact on these different approaches to the extent that they all have been forced to reassess their respective theoretical paradigms given real-life, practical contestation by non-territorial identities and non-governmental elites. What is more, those who espouse a society-centred viewpoint, from Banting to Whitaker, and, to a certain degree, Russell's political-culture perspective have noted collective actors' pragmatic approach to the Charter. Strategic use of the Charter has also been noticed by those who wish to stultify this type of popular mobilization. Their alarmist response to activism marks another change in the political-science literature since the age of Charter politics began, and it is to this subject that we now turn.

The Conservative Backlash

Whereas society-centred theorists have begun to appreciate the gains and losses of mobilized collective actors, any headway that takes place, in theory and in practice, is considered increasingly troublesome for those on the right. This reaction to the Charter and its strategic use is perhaps most aptly illustrated in Rainer Knopff's and F.L. Morton's *Charter Politics*.[150]

On the face of it, Knopff and Morton appear to concur with many students of contemporary constitutional politics, Russell among others, that there has been a merger of law and politics. However, in spite of giving the appearance of having conceded this much, Knopff and Morton subsequently advance an exclusivist, traditional understanding of the division of powers which serves to underscore their advocacy of judicial interpretivism. Thus, although they seemingly reject one constitutional dichotomy, they are defenders/promoters of the interpretivism/non-interpretivism divide.[151] What is more, Knopff and Morton suggest a rigid compartmentalization in other areas of institutional politics. Consequently, they uphold rather than reject many dualisms and ultimately seek a re-definition of the boundaries between politics and law, where politics may be judicialized but the judiciary de-politicized. This position, I will argue, stems from their concern that, as a result of the Charter, collective mobilization has made some progress on the judicial terrain. Knopff's and Morton's intent is to constrict the sites of political struggle for collective actors by rigidly defining political and judicial functions and thereby limiting access to these spheres.

There are three key elements to Knopff's and Morton's approach. First, they are interpretivists – they promote formal over substantive consideration of issues in the judicial realm; second, they seek a rigid separation of powers divorcing the judiciary from the legislature and the executive; third, once these institutions are separated, Knopff and Morton pit them against one another in an institutional tug of war. The motive behind this approach, I would argue, is not just to maintain the status quo but to constrain the strategies of extra-institutional actors.

To elaborate, Knopff and Morton label their version of constitutionalism as 'adjudicative.' By this they mean that the primary function of the courts is to resolve concrete disputes[152] and settle *factual* (my emphasis) discrepancies.[153] This can be understood as supporting legal interpretivism in that interpretivism demands that judges follow the letter of the law, focus on the rule of law, and not consider any 'abstract' tangents in the form of values or social issues. The politico-constitutional justification offered for interpretivism is founded on a conception of judicial legitimacy: that judges only apply the law, they do not make it; they are the conduits rather than the sources of law. It is not surprising, therefore, that Knopff and Morton favour judicial restraint or the limiting of judicial influence on public policy. This is never explicitly stated. However, their recurring criticism of so-called 'activist' judges, such as former Justice Bertha Wilson, points to their underlying assumption.

The judiciary, in Knopff's and Morton's estimation, is not solely responsible for constitutional law. They contend that legislators and executive officials can also interpret the constitution. Yet this can be done only in terms of their respective contexts. Consequently, with regard to the division of powers, the adjudicative position holds that 'each branch of government has a legitimate role in interpreting the constitution as a necessary part of carrying out its own distinct functions.'[154] Thus, the legislatures function in terms of assessing constitutional meaning so as to enact appropriate statutes, the executive 'conducts valid enforcement activities,'[155] and the judiciary determines the outcomes of constitutional disputes. Adjudicativism dictates that each branch acts 'within its own proper sphere of influence,'[156] thereby presuming that it has banished the spectre of 'illegitimacy.'

Knopff and Morton contrast this adjudicative position to the 'oracular' doctrine of judicial review in which the constitution is seen as the exclusive preserve of judges.[157] Here the constitutional interpretation by judges, alone, matters, and their decisions are binding on other branches. This, according to Knopff and Morton, has become the dominant view held by judges and by governments.[158] Wanting to nip oracularism in the bud, they revert to a more conventional adjudicative notion of the role of the courts.

In short, Knopff and Morton yearn for a traditional understanding of the political system. Through their schema, politics can be systematized and neutralized. Branches of government perform separate and distinct functions. The judiciary acts in a defined role as an unbiased arbiter judging on facts separated from values.

Knopff's and Morton's views of 'interest groups' underline these notions. They speak disparagingly of what they call the 'court party'[159] or those 'special interest groups'[160] who have brought their claims before the government, and, when this tactic was unsuccessful, redirected their claims to the courts. Because they are not in favour of the overlapping of law and politics, Knopff and Morton are critical of collective actors for blurring the distinctions between different realms. More precisely, they do not want to 'overload' the system with too many Charter equality-seekers. They write, 'If too many rivals enjoy an equal constitutional status, [its] advantage disappears. Simply put, the wide dispersion of constitutional status cheapens its value. Like all other resources, the value of legal resources is a function of their relative scarcity.'[161] By keeping their hands on the strings of the judicial purse, by seeking to enforce 'conditions of scarcity,' Knopff and Morton aim to end the equality-seekers' practice of hopping from one realm to another and also to limit the number of individuals and groups seeking redistributive justice.

Knopff and Morton, then, wish to de-politicize the judiciary and revert to a conservative, traditional, 'apolitical' realm where judges are neutral arbiters of factual disputes. Further, politics, for them, remain supreme if they are conducted in their distinctive sphere according to their particular functional requisites. For example, Knopff and Morton suggest that 'under the adjudicative version of the separation of powers, unpersuaded governments would be free to disregard ... judicial opinions and continue acting on their own views of constitutional requirements.'[162] In other words, if the courts did make the mistake of rendering a substantive decision, the government would still hold the power to disregard it. Finally, Knopff and Morton claim they would like to see a system of checks and balances where the legislatures can engage in something akin to a constitutional arm-wrestle with the judiciary. They contend that the embrace of their adjudicative view of the courts and the correlative enhancing of legislative capacity would engender a better system of checks and balances.

Knopff and Morton support a traditional conception of the judiciary and a clinical separation of powers. The consequence is that they, ultimately, limit the strategies of extra-institutional actors by divorcing institutional realms, promoting formal over substantive consideration of issues, and pitting institutions against one another. Thus, Knopff and Morton serve as spokes*men* of a more conservative turn in political-science commentaries since the enactment of the Charter.

Conclusion

The foregoing examination of key English-language contributions to the discipline indicates a clear advancement from unicausal argumentation and a growing awareness of the influences of multiple identity-based struggles in the realm of federalism/constitutionalism. At present, there is a greater appreciation of the interaction of state and society, an attempt to accommodate the interconnection of institutional and non-institutional actors, and a consideration of a network of determinants which include social, political, economic, and cultural conditions. Practical, collective mobilization directed towards the Charter has accelerated this process of theoretical maturation. The Charter itself has not caused this change, but the highly visible use of Charter-based tactics by social movements has meant that these kinds of political struggles can no longer be overlooked by mainstream political scientists.

In brief, as a result of Charter-based activism, the dominant institutionalist paradigm has shifted to incorporate more societal considerations. The change on the part of society-centred theorists, in both their political-cultural and structural streams, has been more incremental, and yet they also have been forced to respond to the complexities of social, economic, and political conditions. Another conclusion is that both political-cultural and structural theorists have considered the possibility that the courts may provide another site of struggle for collective actors. The right has responded to this theoretical and practical reality and in doing so has contributed a regressive analysis. Overall, there has been a change in the discipline and there is strong presumptive evidence to link this transformation back to the contingencies of Charter-directed mobilization.

For representatives of state and society-centred theorists, as well as for the defenders of the right, there has been, in every case, a move to examine the mobilization of actors that are not necessarily governmentally or territorially identified and/or defined. However, all the writers discussed above fumble with the categorization of these mobilized actors, awkwardly integrate identity-politics analyses, and often fall back on problematic categorizations such as 'special interest groups' to address social-movement gains and losses. This common difficulty in acknowledging multiple identities, and strategic, not essentially institutional, struggles underlines the fact that old habits, conventional paradigms, and traditional discourses die hard. It also reinforces the point that, for decades, research into Canadian federalism/constitutionalism has been led by a few venerable interpreters and fuelled by even fewer interpretations. As a result, although federal/constitutional scholars have worked to broaden their analyses and integrate more actors, they continue to fall short in understanding the history and character of sustained and pragmatic efforts at collective mobilization in Canada.

The discipline of political science requires an alternative approach that breaks through conventional strictures and considers more carefully the diversity of influences that work from the 'bottom up' to affect federalism/constitutionalism in Canada. Federal/constitutional politics do not merely consist of 'top down' processes that are elite-driven and solely institutionally or spatially determined. The time has come for a broader and deeper understanding of multiple actors and their political possibilities. To be sure, traditional political as well as socio-economic elites, institutions, and structures do generate significant constraints, but, as Charter-directed activism attests, there have been strategic openings.[163] Collective actors such as women's organizations, First Nations associations, and groups mobilizing around such issues as ethnicity, race, ability, and sexual orientation have seized these tactical opportunities and changed the course of contemporary constitutional events. Not only is a greater appreciation of the challenges posed and contributions made by these actors necessary, but also, a study of their struggles, foci, organizational premises, strengths, and weaknesses, as well as the promises and pitfalls of their mobilization, is essential to engaging in an integral, inclusive, and more realistic dialogue with respect to current theories and practices in Canadian politics.

Notes

1 Alan C. Cairns, *Disruptions: Constitutional Struggles from the Charter to Meech Lake* (Toronto: McClelland and Stewart 1991), 179. See also Cairns, 'Reflections on the Political Purposes of the Charter: The First Decade,' in *The Charter Ten Years Later*, ed. Gerald A. Beaudoin (Montreal: Les Éditions Yvon Blais 1993), 190.

2 It has been argued that Prime Minister Trudeau skilfully used his Charter card as a nationalizing impetus to counter the separatist sentiments in Quebec and growing provincializing tendencies beyond Quebec. See Rainer Knopff and F.L. Morton, 'Nation-Building and the Canadian Charter of Rights and Freedoms,' in *Constitutionalism, Citizenship and Society in Canada*, eds. Alan C. Cairns and Cynthia Williams (Toronto: University of Toronto Press 1985).

3 On elite accommodation, see Robert Presthus, *Elite Accommodation in Canadian Politics* (Toronto: Macmillan of Canada 1973).

4 Donald Smiley identified this process, which will be discussed in more detail later in the essay.

5 Rosemary McCarney's response to the Meech Lake Accord as quoted in 'Critics want chance to press for revisions,' *Globe and Mail*, Thursday, 4 June 1987, 11.

6 Brian Mulroney, of course, made this infamous quip. See *Globe and Mail*, 30 June 1990, 12, 23.

7 See, for example, Linda Cardinal, 'Les mouvements sociaux et la Charte canadienne des droits et libertés,' *International Journal of Canadian Studies*, vols. 7–8 (spring/fall 1993), 137–52.

8 See, for example, Catherine L. Cleverdon, *The Woman Suffrage Movement in Canada* (Toronto: University of Toronto Press 1974).

9 Ian Brodie and Neil Nevitte link the participatory revolution to Inglehart's post-materialist thesis and contemporary socio-structural changes. I would argue, however, that social-movement activism has a longer history, as the case of the women's movement attests. See Brodie and Nevitte, 'Evaluating the Citizen's Constitution Theory,' in *Canadian Journal of Political Science*, vol. 26, no. 2 (June 1993), passim.

10 See John Borrows, 'Contemporary Traditional Equality: The Effect of the Charter on First Nations Politics,' in this volume. See also Mary Ellen Turpel, 'Aboriginal Peoples and the Canadian Charter: Interpretive Monopolies, Cultural Differences,'

in *Canadian Perspectives on Legal Theory*, ed. Richard Devlin (Toronto: Emond Montgomery Publications 1991), 503–38.

11 Aboriginal women's activism, for instance, is reflected in the establishment of the Native Women's Association of Canada in 1974. See Lilianne E. Krosenbrink-Gelissen, 'The Canadian Constitution, the Charter, and Aboriginal Women's Rights: Conflicts and Dilemmas,' *International Journal of Canadian Studies*, vols. 7–8 (spring/fall 1993), 208–9.

12 See Didi Herman, 'The Good, the Bad, and the Smugly: Sexual Orientation and Perspectives on the Charter,' in this volume.

13 Not surprisingly, mainstream political science also reflects 'malestream' political science.

14 I am concerned with discussing the contributions of a number of established political scientists who have devoted most of their scholarship to issues of Canadian federalism and constitutionalism. My account is by no means intended to be an all-inclusive discussion of this area of study. For example, theorists such as Charles Taylor could have been incorporated, given his concern with the quest for identity and the contestation over the concepts of democracy, liberalism, nationalism, and federalism. See Charles Taylor, *Reconciling the Solitudes: Essays on Canadian Federalism and Nationalism* (Montreal: McGill-Queen's University Press 1992). However, because his work represents a more philosophical perspective, one that is primarily interested in issues of modernity and diversity and that crosses the disciplines of philosophy, social theory, and political science, I have chosen to focus on other contributors to the federal/constitutional political science canon.

15 See Yves de Montigny, 'The Impact (Real or Apprehended) of the Canadian Charter of Rights and Freedoms on the Legislative Authority of Quebec,' in this volume.

16 Here, the classical influences of F.R. Scott and Bora Laskin can be cited. See, for example, F.R. Scott 'Centralization and Decentralization in Canadian Federalism,' and Bora Laskin, 'Peace Order and Good Government Re-Examined,' both reprinted in *Federalism in Canada: Selected Readings*, ed. Garth Stevenson (Toronto: McClelland and Stewart 1989). By the 1960s and 1970s, political scientists were beginning to challenge the limitations of narrow legalism. See Alan C. Cairns, 'The Judicial Committee and its Critics,' *Canadian Journal of Political Science*, vol. 4 (1971) 301–45; and Edwin R. Black and Alan C. Cairns, 'A Different Perspective on Canadian Federalism,' *Canadian Public Administration*, vol. 9 (1966) 27–44, which offers an alternative to the conventional constitutional, legal, economic, and geographic interpretations of federalism. Some consider the Black/Cairns thesis influenced by behavioural trends and 'societal' influences, a position I counter below.

17 As we shall see, the Simeon, Smiley, and Cairns contributions are indicative of the trend.

18 This is evident in the more societal and structural analyses of Stevenson and Keith Banting. See Garth Stevenson, *Unfulfilled Union* (Toronto: Macmillan 1979), and Keith Banting, *The Welfare State and Canadian Federalism* (Montreal: McGill-Queen's University Press 1987).

19 See the discussion on neo-institutionalism in Gregory Albo and Jane Jenson, 'The Relative Autonomy of the State,' in *The New Canadian Political Economy*, eds. Wallace Clement and Glen Williams (Montreal: McGill-Queen's University Press 1989), 200–2.

20 Peter Hall, *Governing the Economy: The Politics of State Intervention in Britain and France* (Oxford, U.K.: Polity Press 1986), 20.

21 Ibid., 17. See also 'Bringing the State Back In: Strategies of Analysis in Current Research,' in Peter B. Evans, Dietrich Rueschemeyer, and Theda Skocpol, *Bringing the State Back In* (New York: Cambridge University Press 1986), 9–13, for examples of states as actors and of states as autonomous agents in constitutional polities.

22 For Smiley, the structures and processes of government and the ways public issues are raised are inextricably tied. See Donald V. Smiley, 'Federal-Provincial Conflict in Canada,' in *Canadian Federalism Myth or Reality*, ed. J. Peter Meekison (Toronto: Methuen 1977), 2. The attrition of federal power, for example, can be explained by the unresponsiveness of the federal government to provincial concerns. Smiley wrote: 'The centralizing and majoritarian structures of power in national government frustrate the territorial pluralism which made federalism necessary at the beginning and sustain federalism.' Donald V. Smiley, *The Federal Condition in Canada* (Toronto: McGraw-Hill Ryerson 1987), 60.

23 Janine Brodie describes how an institutional focus can overly simplify complex processes such as regionalism. In her account, regionalism 'loses its conceptual distinctiveness because it is forced into the conceptual strictures of federalism.' See Janine Brodie, 'The Concept of Region in Canadian Politics,' in *Federalism and Political Community*, eds. David Shugarman and Reginald Whitaker (Peterborough: Broadview Press 1987), 37.

24 Smiley's brief definition of executive federalism is as follows: 'The relations between elected and appointed officials of the two orders of government in federal-provincial interaction.' See Donald V. Smiley, *Canada in Question*, 3rd ed. (Toronto: McGraw-Hill Ryerson 1980), 91. On the centrality of this premise, see Ronald Watts, *Executive Federalism: A Comparative Analysis*, Research Paper 26. (Kingston: Institute of Intergovernmental Relations 1988).

25 Smiley, *The Federal Condition*, 9.

26 Richard Simeon, 'We Are All Smiley's People: Some observations on Donald Smiley and the Study of Federalism,' in Shugarman and Whitaker, *Federalism and Political Community*, 409–21.

27 Richard Simeon, *Federal-Provincial Diplomacy: The Making of Recent Policy in Canada* (Toronto: University of Toronto Press 1972).

28 To be sure, Simeon's other work reflected more of a societal and political-cultural analysis. See, for example, Richard Simeon and David Elkins, 'Regional Political Cultures in Canada,' *Canadian Journal of Political Science*, vol. 7, no 3 (1974), 397–437. However, even in this piece, Simeon suggests that his aim is to isolate regional political culture from socio-economic factors. Thus, the intent is to add historical, institutional considerations to the political-cultural methodology of Gabriel Almond and Sidney Verba. See Almond and Verba, *The Civic Culture* (Princeton, N.J.: Princeton University Press 1963). Indeed, Simeon is critical of Almond's and Verba's focus on 'extra-political' factors. As a result, what actually constitutes 'political culture' in this account is moot, even though Simeon tries to make use of the concept.

29 Simeon, *Federal Provincial Diplomacy*, 5.

30 Simeon argues that the party is the 'least important line of cleavage' (ibid., 194). With regard to interest groups, he writes that in his studies 'in no case did interest groups have a significant effect on the outcomes' (ibid.) He does concede the possibility of some societal interference in his examination of sociological interactions and the effects of attitudes and perspectives of leaders at each level. However, in the final analysis, Simeon contends that although the form of intergovernmental relations is affected by such considerations, the most important factor is the institutional one (ibid., 304).

31 Ibid., 25.

32 See J. Stefan Dupré, 'Reflections on the Workability of Executive Federalism,' in *Intergovernmental Relations*, ed. Richard Simeon (Toronto: University of Toronto Press 1985), 1.

33 Schultz disputes Simeon's focus on unitary intergovernmental actors and offers instead a bureaucratic-politics schema which integrates a conglomerate of organizations and actors engaging in conflictual relations. See Richard Schultz, *Federalism, Bureaucracy and Public Policy* (Montreal: McGill-Queen's University Press, 1980). For Schultz, power is more widely dispersed intragovernmentally, and he counters Simeon's marginalization of interest groups (ibid., 171). However, Schultz argues that the state acts upon these interest groups, using them for its own purposes. Thus, contrary to Grodzin's multiple-crack hypothesis which sees federalism as providing multiple openings for interest groups, Schultz maintains that federalism allows governments a 'crack at' interest groups (ibid., 172–3).

34 In Cairns's view, 'contemporary federalism makes a distinct contribution to the growth of governments whose competitive tendencies it cannot effectively restrain or control.' See Alan C. Cairns, 'The Other Crisis of Canadian Federalism,' *Canadian Public Administration*, vol. 22, no. 2 (summer 1979), 175–95. This combativeness is detrimental, for as governmental elites monopolize the debate and promote their own agenda, the gap between governmental politics and popular preference widens. In contrast, Breton argues for more conflict. He considers competition as an antidote to the collusion which would result from increased cooperation and which is indicative of the sort of executive federalism condoned in early Smiley, substantiated by Simeon, and advocated by Dupré. Breton, as a public-choice theorist, does not focus so much on institutions as on rational actors. However, he, too, sees governmental players as interacting within the confines of institutional structures and processes, that is, either cooperative or competitive federalism. Albert Breton, Supplementary Statement, in *Report of the Royal Commission on the Economic Union and Development Prospects for Canada*, vol. 3, (Ottawa: Minister of Supply and Services Canada 1985).

35 Robert Vipond suggests that Cairns typifies a 'sociological approach.' See Vipond, *Liberty and Community: Canadian Federalism and the Failure of the Constitution* (Albany, N.Y.: State University of New York Press 1991), 7. Knopff also suggests that Cairns's early critique of legal determinism 'was part of a much larger tendency to focus on the "societal" determinants of political behaviour.' See Rainer Knopff, 'The Charter of Rights and National Integration,' in *Canadian Political Life: An Alberta Perspective*, eds. Roger Gibbins, Keith Archer, and Stan Drabek (Dubuque, IA.: Kenall/Hunt 1990), 28.

36 For example, in an early piece, Cairns and Black criticize the BNA Act as too centralist a document and support the courts' tendency to give more leeway to the provinces. See Black and Cairns, 'Different Perspective,' passim.

37 According to Cairns, federal and provincial governmental elites and their advisers historically have structured the debate around federal/constitutional issues, from the BNA Act to the contemporary constitutional negotiations. See Cairns, *Disruptions*, 63.

38 Of course, First Nations activism has a territorial legitimacy and claims to self-government have an institutional basis. However, in my view, given the centuries of injustices perpetrated against them, the ongoing oppression they experience, and the historical and contemporary marginalization of their claims by the state, First Nations mobilization, in its multiple and diverse forms, shares a greater affinity to the activism of collective actors beyond governmental elite circles.

39 See Doris Anderson, *Unfinished Revolution: The Status of Women in Twelve Countries* (Toronto: Doubleday 1991), 200.

40 Jill Vickers, 'The Canadian Women's Movement and a Changing Constitutional Order,' *International Journal of Canadian Studies*, vols. 7–8 (spring/fall 1993), 275.

41 See Beverley Baines, 'Gender and the Meech Lake Committee,' *Queen's Quarterly*, vol. 94 (1987), 807–16. On mobilizing opposition to the Conservative government's 1991 *Shaping Canada's Future Together* proposals, see, for example, Radha Jhappan, 'Aboriginal Peoples' Right to Self Government,' and Alexandra Dobrowolsky, 'Women's Equality and the Constitutional Proposals,' in *Constitutional Politics*, eds. Duncan Cameron and Miriam Smith (Toronto: James Lorimer 1992). The role of activists in the call for a social charter is discussed in Joel Bakan and David Schneiderman, 'Introduction,' in *Social Justice and the Constitution*, eds. Joel Bakan and David Schneiderman (Ottawa: Carleton University Press 1992), 1–16.

42 Indeed, their work spans three and, in some cases, four decades and the authoritativeness attributed to them continues despite significant theoretical and practical developments over this period.

43 Charles Taylor's work in regard to identity politics and federalism has been long-standing as well. However, because Taylor's work is more interdisciplinary, I have chosen to examine writers such as Cairns who do not stray as far from the boundaries of mainstream political science.

44 See Watts's notation of Smiley's changed perspective on executive federalism: Watts, *Executive Federalism*, 3–4.

45 Simeon makes this assessment of Smiley's shift. See Simeon, 'We Are All Smiley's People,' 413.

46 Smiley, *The Federal Condition*, 98.

47 Ibid., 19.

48 See Penny Kome, *The Taking of 28: Women Challenge the Constitution* (Toronto: Women's Press 1983); Chaviva Hosek, 'Women in the Constitutional Process,' in *And No One Cheered*, eds. Keith Banting and Richard Simeon (Toronto: Methuen 1983); Chaviva Hosek, 'How Women Fought for Equality,' in *Women and Men: Interdisciplinary Readings on Gender*, ed. Greta Hoffman Nemiroff (Toronto: Fitzhenry and Whiteside 1987); Sandra Burt, 'The Charter of Rights and the Ad Hoc Lobby: The Limits of Success,' *Atlantis*, vol. 14, no. 1 (fall 1988); and Vickers, 'The Canadian Women's Movement and a Changing Constitutional Order.' For discussions on women and constitutional reform, see *Conversations: Among Friends/Entre Amies*, ed. David Schneiderman (Edmonton: Centre for Constitutional Studies, University of Alberta 1992).

49 Smiley, *The Federal Condition*, 194.

50 Ibid., 9.

51 Ibid., 164.
52 Richard Simeon, 'Meech Lake and Shifting Conceptions of Canadian Federalism,' in *Canadian Public Policy*, vol. 14, (1988), S7–24, S22.
53 Richard Simeon, 'Introduction: Setting Out the Framework,' in *Toolkits and Building Blocks*, eds. Richard Simeon and Mary Janigan (Toronto: C.D. Howe Trust 1991), 2.
54 See Richard Simeon and Ian Robinson, *State, Society and the Development of Canadian Federalism* (Toronto: University of Toronto Press 1990), xv. Departing from his earlier position, he concludes that 'societal forces, interacting with institutional forms, are chiefly responsible for the shifts in the division of powers, fluctuations in the nature and intensity of intergovernmental conflict and the changing character of the Canadian state' (ibid., 4).
55 Ibid., 126.
56 I am grateful to Denis St Martin for directing my attention to this point.
57 See the neo-institutionalist contributions made by Peter Hall, now incorporated by the formerly strict neo-statist Theda Skocpol in *Protecting Soldiers and Mothers* (Cambridge, Mass.: Harvard University Press 1992). J.G. March and J.P. Olsen also integrate identity-politics considerations with neo-institutionalism. See, for example, March and Olsen, *Rediscovering Institutions* (New York: Free Press 1989).
58 See, for instance, Alan C. Cairns, 'Governments and Societies of Canadian Federalism,' in *Constitution, Government and Society in Canada*, ed. Douglas Williams (Toronto: McClelland and Stewart 1988).
59 Allan C. Cairns, 'Citizens (Outsiders) and Governments (Insiders) in Constitution-Making: The Case of Meech Lake,' *Canadian Public Policy*, vol. 14 (supplement 1988), 121–45.
60 Ibid., S137.
61 He writes that the Charter 'brings new groups into the Canadian constitutional order and gives them constitutional identities,' (ibid., 179).
62 Kathleen Mahoney, 'Women's Rights,' in *Meech Lake and Canada: Perspectives from the West*, ed. Roger Gibbins (Edmonton: Academic Printing and Publishing 1988), 167. See also Mary Eberts, 'The Constitution, The Charter and the Distinct Society Clause: Why Are Women Being Ignored?' in *The Meech Lake Primer: Conflicting Views of the 1987 Constitutional Accord*, ed. Michael Behiels (Ottawa: University of Ottawa Press 1989), 302; and Beverley Baines, '"Consider, Sir, ... On What Does Your Constitution Rest?" Representational and Institutional Reform,' in Schneiderman, *Conversations Among Friends/Entre Amies*, 54.
63 David Long, 'Culture, Ideology, and Militancy: The Movement of Native Indians in Canada, 1969–1991)', in *Organizing Dissent: Contemporary Social Movements in Theory and Practice*, ed. William Carroll (Toronto: Garamond 1992), 119.

Indeed, Borrow notes opposition to the Indian Act's treatment of women in 1872. See Borrows, 'Contemporary Traditional Equality,' in this collection.

64 Cairns, *Disruptions*, 125.

65 Ibid., 134.

66 Jill Vickers, 'Bending the Iron Law of Oligarchy: Debates on the Feminization of Organization and Political Process in the English Canadian Women's Movement, 1970–1988,' in Jeri Dawn Wine and Janice L. Ristock, *Women and Social Change: Feminist Activism in Canada* (Toronto: James Lorimer 1991), 83.

67 Ibid.

68 Judy Rebick, past president of the National Action Committee on the Status of Women (NAC), stresses the importance and the centrality of the collective process in NAC and she claims that this process was crucial to developing the organization's stand in the referendum on the Charlottetown Accord: 'When we came out for the "No" [during the constitutional talks], it was not a question of this kind of phoney consensus ... but rather listening to all the points of view and developing a position based on as many points of view as could be incorporated.' See 'Interview with Judy Rebick,' *Studies in Political Economy*, vol. 44 (summer 1994), 47. According to Rebick, during the referendum debate, 'what the NAC did was stand up for equality-seeking groups: Native women, lesbians and gays, and people with disabilities, who were shoved aside. The other thing we did was create a progressive "No." If we had not come out for them, those people would not have had anyone to speak for them ... ' (ibid., 69). As the NAC case illustrates, feminist organizations have been working towards a politics of inclusion and away from practices of exclusion. See also Jill Vickers, Pauline Rankin, and Christine Appelle, *Politics As If Women Mattered: A Political Analysis of the National Action Committee on the Status of Women* (Toronto: University of Toronto Press 1993).

69 Juliet Mitchell, *Woman's Estate* (New York: Pantheon 1971), as quoted in Vickers, 'Bending the Iron Law,' 83.

70 Jennifer Smith, 'Representation and Constitutional Reform in Canada,' in *After Meech Lake: Lessons for the Future*, eds. David E. Smith, Peter MacKinnon, and John C. Courtney (Saskatoon: Fifth House Publishers 1991), 76.

71 Marie Smallface Marule discusses how this consensus approach to decision making works in practice in her article 'An Indian Perspective on Canadian Politics,' in *Politics in Canada* (7th ed.), eds. Paul Fox and Graham White (Toronto: McGraw 1991), 15–22. Further, Russell notes: 'Aboriginal peoples are committed to a highly consensual form of decision making that does not dovetail easily with the more top-down, tightly scheduled procedures of non-aboriginals.' See Peter H. Russell, *Constitutional Odyssey: Can Canadians Be A Sovereign People?* (Toronto: University of Toronto Press 1992), 170.

72 Indeed, Cairns succumbs to problematical stereotypes such as the following: 'The constitutional language of ethnicity wielded by ethnic elites is emotional and passionate – a Mediterranean language – rather than calculating and instrumental. Its affinities are with such concepts as shame, envy, resentment, honour and pride.' See Cairns, *Disruptions*, 169.

73 Cairns, 'The Charter, Interest Groups, Executive Federalism,' 28.

74 Brodie and Nevitte criticize Cairns for his attribution of a new participant ethic to the Charter. Instead, they make an argument for Ronald Inglehart's concept of post-industrial change or his 'New Politics' thesis, according to which 'the changing patterns of political participation are a consequence of the structural transformations common to all advanced industrial states.' See Brodie and Nevitte, 'Evaluating the Citizen's Constitutional Theory,' 241.

75 Cairns, 'The Charter, Interest Groups, Executive Federalism,' 29.

76 Alan C. Cairns, *Charter versus Federalism: The Dilemmas of Constitutional Reform* (Montreal: McGill-Queen's University Press 1992).

77 Ibid., 13–15.

78 Ibid., 55.

79 Ibid., 59.

80 Alan C. Cairns, 'Reflections on the Political Purposes of the Charter,' 173.

81 For instance, Garth Stevenson, a proponent of the socio-economic perspective, states: 'While the present writer finds them most persuasive, [these economic theories] are sometimes guilty of circular reasoning or of surreptitiously borrowing arguments from the other explanations.' See Stevenson, 'Federalism and Intergovernmental Relations,' 387.

82 Although I have grouped political culture and structural approaches in the same society-centric category, each is associated with a different school of thought: the former with a liberal perspective and the latter, marked as it is by a predominantly class-based analysis, with a more left-wing outlook. Indeed, David Bell notes that the genesis of political-culture analyses can be attributed to a liberal critique of the left's notion of ideology. See David Bell, *The Roots of Disunity: A Study of Canadian Political Culture* (Toronto: Oxford University Press 1992), 27.

83 David Bell discusses the meaning of political culture and suggests that it encompasses more than the psychological orientations studied by Almond and Verba; it also includes political discourse, metaphors, symbols, and myths. See Bell, 'The Political Culture of Problem Solving and Public Policy,' in Shugarman and Whitaker, *Federalism and Political Community*, 97. Also of interest are Almond's more recent views on political culture in *A Discipline Divided* (London: Sage 1990). For a more historical, political-cultural constitutional analysis, see Vipond, *Liberty and Community*, passim. In legal scholarship, Monahan provides another

example of the use of a political-culture analysis. See, for example, Patrick Monahan, *Politics and the Constitution: The Charter, Federalism and the Supreme Court of Canada* (Toronto: Carswell 1987).

84 In other words, the causal arrow tends to run from institutions to political culture as institutionalists grapple with the possible implications of political culture. See, for instance, Simeon and Elkins, 'Regional Political Cultures,' passim.

85 Peter H. Russell, 'The Supreme Court of Canada as a Bilingual and Bicultural Institution,' document prepared for the Royal Commission on Bilingualism and Biculturalism (Ottawa: Information Canada 1969), 57–8. See also Russell's 'Judicial Power in Canada's Political Culture,' in *Courts and Trials: A Multidisciplinary Approach*, ed. Martin L. Friedland (Toronto: University of Toronto Press 1975), 76–7, 84.

86 Peter Russell, 'Constitutional Reform of the Canadian Judiciary,' paper prepared for the Annual Meeting of Canadian Law Teachers Association, Calgary, 6 June 1968, 13–15.

87 Ibid., 19.

88 Peter H. Russell, 'The Political Role of the Supreme Court of Canada in Its First Century,' *Canadian Bar Review*, vol. 53 (1975), 576–96.

89 Peter H. Russell, 'The Effect of a Charter of Rights on the Policy-Making Role of Canadian Courts,' *Canadian Public Administration*, vol. 25, no. 1 (spring 1982), 26.

90 Ibid., 11.

91 See Peter H. Russell, 'The Anti-Inflation Case: The Anatomy of a Constitutional Decision,' *Canadian Public Administration*, vol. 20, no. 4 (winter 1977), 634.

92 Not surprisingly, then, he is clear about the need for judicial restraint. Peter H. Russell, 'The Political Purposes of the Canadian Charter of Rights and Freedoms,' *Canadian Bar Review*, vol. 61 (1983), 30–54.

93 For instance, Russell makes extensive use of Cairns's analysis. See, for instance, Peter H. Russell, 'Attempting Macro Constitutional Change in Australia and Canada: The Politics of Frustration,' *International Journal of Canadian Studies*, vols. 7–8 (spring/fall 1993), 44.

94 Peter H. Russell, 'The Supreme Court and the Charter: A Question of Legitimacy,' in Shugarman and Whitaker, *Federalism and Political Community*, 225.

95 Russell, 'The Political Purposes of the Canadian Charter.' See also Peter H. Russell, 'The First Three Years in Charterland,' *Canadian Public Administration*, vol. 28, no. 3 (fall 1985), 389, where, after reviewing of cases of so-called judicial activism, he writes: 'It would be unrealistic to view these "activist" court decisions on legal rights as imposing the views of appointed judges on elected legislators. In a number of instances, Charter decisions anticipate reforms whose time has come at the legislative level.'

96 Russell, 'The First Three Years,' 378.

97 Peter H.Russell, 'Commentary,' in *After Meech Lake: Lessons for the Future*, eds. David Smith *et al.* (Saskatoon: Fifth House 1991), 67.

98 Russell, 'The First Three Years,' 368–9.

99 Ibid., 390–1.

100 See Peter H. Russell, 'Standing Up for the Notwithstanding,' in *Law, Politics and Judicial Process in Canada*, (2nd ed.), ed. F.L. Morton (Calgary: University of Calgary Press 1992), 480–1.

101 Russell, 'The First Three Years,' 369.

102 Ibid., 369, 396.

103 Peter H. Russell, *Constitutional Odyssey: Can Canadians Become a Sovereign People?* 2nd ed. (Toronto: University of Toronto Press 1993), 11. See chapter 2 for the discussion of Hobbes versus Locke.

104 Russell concludes his book with the following wish: If Canadians can 'carry on together developing a common constitutional tradition, it will turn out that they are after all the people of Edmund Burke, not John Locke, and that their social contract is essentially organic, not covenantal. Some of us might settle for that' (ibid., 235).

105 Russell, 'Commentary,' 68.

106 Peter H. Russell, 'Meech Lake and the Supreme Court,' in *Competing Constitutional Visions*, eds. K.E. Swinton and C.J. Rogerson (Agincourt, Ont.: Carswell 1988), 100.

107 W.A. Bogart argues that Russell's embrace of Burke represents an explicit turn to the right. See Bogart, *Courts and Country: The Limits of Litigation and the Social and Political Life of Canada* (Toronto: Oxford University Press 1994), 63.

108 See John Porter, *The Vertical Mosaic* (Toronto: University of Toronto Press 1967) and Gad Horowitz, 'Toward the Democratic Class Struggle,' in *Agenda 1970: Proposals for a Creative Politics*, eds. T. Lloyd and J. McLeod (Toronto: University of Toronto Press 1958). Smiley's early work, discussed above, provided a direct contrast to this point of view. See Simeon, 'We Are All Smiley's People,' 417.

109 Porter, *Vertical Mosaic,* 381.

110 See Frank Underhill, 'The Canadian Party in Transition,' in his *In Search of Canadian Liberalism* (Toronto: Macmillan 1960).

111 Porter suggested that 'provincial political leaders ... have acquired vested interest in their own power, and the themes of their political rhetoric emphasize local and provincial differences.' See *Vertical Mosaic*, 381. This analysis has been developed further by Janine Brodie and Jane Jenson in *Crisis Challenge and Change* (Ottawa: Carleton University Press 1988).

112 Garth Stevenson, *Unfulfilled Union* (Toronto: Macmillan 1979).

113 Stevenson holds that it is the political economy of Canada which 'both produced conflicts between different classes and class fractions and at the same time caused these contending forces to identify their interests with different levels of government' (ibid., 82).

114 Stevenson writes that there are seven distinct although related topics with which old and new political economists are concerned: the nature of Confederation and the class forces involved in it; impact of staple commodities; external influences, particularly the United States; uneven development and regional underdevelopment; agrarian protest; Quebec nationalism and efforts to identify the class bases of its various forms; the consequences of having federal as opposed to unitary state structures. See Garth Stevenson, 'The Political Economy Tradition and Canadian Federalism,' *Studies in Political Economy*, vol. 6 (autumn 1991), 114.

115 As Brodie points out, Stevenson's analysis of federal-provincial relations indicates an indebtedness to the staple theory of the early political economist Harold Innis. See Janine Brodie, 'The Political Economy of Regionalism,' in Clement and Williams, *The New Canadian Political Economy*, 145.

116 Whitaker's political-economy perspective is pivotal since he maintains that the central role of the state is that of continental economic development. He supports the notion of a functional division of labour between the state and business, a relationship typified by John A. Macdonald's National Policy. For Whitaker, this is how Canadian nationalism becomes economic nationalism. Drawing on political-culture analyses, Whitaker goes on to explain the socio-economic repercussions of the replacement of nineteenth-century Toryism by a twentieth-century liberalism that is based on capitalism and lacks a viable national basis. (This liberalism is moderated, somewhat, by a slight socialist tinge.) Whitaker pursues his argument by studying the liberal ideas of Mackenzie King and Pierre Trudeau and raising the significance of our social-democratic heritage through an examination of the life and work of William Irvine. Both political-economy and political-cultural considerations, therefore, are influential determinants in Whitaker's work. See Reginald Whitaker, *A Sovereign Idea: Essays on Canada as a Democratic Community* (Montreal: McGill-Queen's University Press 1992), passim. This book collates over ten years of writing by Whitaker and thus I will draw on it extensively to suggest an evolution in his thought.

117 Ibid., 166.

118 Ibid., 180.

119 Ibid., 192–3.

120 Ibid., 228.

121 Ibid., 193.

122 Ibid.
123 Reginald Whitaker, 'Democracy and the Canadian Constitution,' in Banting and Simeon, *And No One Cheered*, 254.
124 Ibid., 255.
125 Ibid., 256.
126 See Keith Banting, *The Welfare State and Canadian Federalism* (Montreal: McGill-Queen's University Press 1987).
127 Keith Banting, 'Political Meaning and Social Reform,' in Swinton and Rogerson, *Competing Constitutional Visions*, 173.
128 Indeed, the contribution of Joel C. Bakan and Michael Smith to this volume, 'Rights, Nationalism, and Social Movements in Canadian Constitutional Politics,' highlights the fact that dominant ideological structures have 'absorbed' the constitutional efforts of collective actors, including the activists in NAC and NWAC. In my view, socio-economic, political, and ideological contexts as well as identity-politics constellations shift and change over time. As a result, there are potential 'tactical openings' which reflect the ongoing contestation between structure and agency. On 'tactical openings,' see 'Interview with Judy Rebick,' 44.
129 See the 3rd ed. of Stevenson's *Unfulfilled Union* (Toronto: Gage 1989).
130 Ibid., 262. What is more, in another article, he states that the most significant outcome of constitutional change has been the growth in size and strength of provincial governments, a development that in turn strengthens the executive-federalist impetus. See Garth Stevenson, 'Federalism and Intergovernmental Relations,' in *Canadian Politics in the 1990's* (3rd ed.), eds. Michael S. Whittington and Glen Williams (Scarborough: Nelson 1990), 387.
131 Stevenson now mentions that native and feminist groups 'lobbied strenuously' in the early 1980s. No further analysis is provided, however. See *Unfulfilled Union*, 3rd ed., 258.
132 Garth Stevenson, 'Commentary,' in *After Meech Lake*, 109.
133 Stevenson's brief assessment of the Charter is that it represents 'an untidy collection of miscellaneous provisions reflecting sordid and undignified compromises with a variety of provincial interests, and with no basis of legitimacy other than the bargains of politicians.' Stevenson, *Unfulfilled Union*, 3rd ed., 258.
134 Whitaker, *A Sovereign Idea*, 257–8.
135 Ibid., 278–9.
136 For Whitaker, as for Simeon and Cairns, Meech Lake highlighted the change. Whitaker suggests that, while elite accommodation has deteriorated since the 1960s, 'the Meech Lake fiasco was an exclamation point loudly marking the close of this phase' (ibid., 287).

137 Consider for a moment the claims of the legal left, represented by writers such as Michael Mandel, Andrew Petter and Allan Hutchinson, and Joel Bakan. See Mandel, *The Charter of Rights and the Legalization of Politics in Canada* (Toronto: Wall and Thompson 1989); Petter and Hutchinson, 'Rights in Conflict: The Dilemma of Charter Legitimacy,' *UBC Law Review*, vol. 23, no. 3 (1989), 531–48; and Bakan, 'Constitutional Interpretation and Social Change: You Can't Always Get What You Want (Nor What You Need),' in Devlin, *Canadian Perspectives on Legal Theory*. In recent years, some legal progressives, particularly those who have been influenced by feminist and new-social-movement analyses, have provided a more strategic assessment of the Charter and rights discourse. Consider Didi Herman's approach in 'The Good, the Bad, and the Smugly,' included in this volume. See also Bakan and Schneiderman, *Social Justice and the Constitution*, where progressive scholars argue the pros and cons of a social charter and some in fact counter the legal left's rights scepticism by arguing that the constitutional entrenchment of social rights would increase opportunities for the disadvantaged and oppressed. The following essays in the Schneiderman and Bakan volume are instructive in this regard: Martha Jackman, 'Constitutional Rhetoric and Social Justice: Reflections on the Justiciability Debate'; and Jennifer Nedelsky and Craig Scott, 'Constitutional Dialogue.' In another publication, Amy Bartholomew and Alan Hunt have incorporated a 'new social movement' analysis along the lines of Ernesto Laclau and Chantal Mouffe, bridging the critical legal studies versus 'minority critique' impasse with a more positive program for strategic-rights employment. See Bartholomew and Hunt, 'What's Wrong with Rights,' *Law and Inequality*, vol. 9, no. 1 (1990), 1–58. On this approach, see Laclau and Mouffe, *Hegemony and Socialist Strategy: Toward a Radical Democratic Politics* (London: Verso 1985). Nonetheless, it is equally evident that the more traditional legal left, and especially those inspired by Marxism, continue to dismiss any positive potentialities in the Charter. For example, Bakan extends his critique of the indeterminacy of rights to social-charter formulations, maintaining that positive as well as negative rights fail to provide substantive guarantees, and, what is more, both can be used by politically expedient actors for retrogressive ends. See Joel Bakan, 'What's Wrong with Social Rights,' in Bakan and Schneiderman, *Social Justice and the Constitution*, 86. The legal left persists with its oft-cited claim that Charter politics and rights create a diversion and undermine the class struggle. See Harry Glasbeek, 'The Social Charter: Poor Politics for the Poor,' in ibid. Further, the legal left has advanced new arguments to counter proponents of a pragmatic politics of rights. For a persuasive article along these lines, see Judy Fudge and Harry Glasbeek, 'The Politics of Rights: A Politics with Little Class,' *Social and Legal Studies*, vol. 1 (1992), 45–70.

138 This is an important nuance which has not been elaborated upon in an elucidation of the 'Charterphobia' of both left and right. See Richard Sigurdson, 'Left and Right-wing Charterphobia in Canada: A Critique of the Critics,' *International Journal of Canadian Studies*, vols. 7–8 (spring/fall 1993), 95–115.

139 Whitaker, *A Sovereign Idea*, 298.

140 Ibid.

141 Reginald Whitaker, 'Rights in a Free and Democratic Society: Abortion,' in Shugarman and Whitaker, *Federalism and Political Community*, 343.

142 Ibid., 337.

143 Whitaker, *A Sovereign Idea*, 255.

144 Ibid., see the opening of chapter 9 and also 286.

145 Ibid., 286.

146 Ibid., 278–9.

147 Ibid., 279.

148 Ibid.

149 Ibid., 299.

150 Rainer Knopff and F.L. Morton, *Charter Politics* (Calgary: Nelson 1992).

151 Interpretivists are those who believe that judges should make impartial decisions based solely and exclusively on the text of the law. Non-interpretivists hold the view that judging is a more subjective process in which judges can and in fact do draw upon 'non-legal' sources, such as politics, social values, or morality, in rendering their legal decisions and that, indeed, just as facts cannot be separated from values, politics cannot be separated from laws.

152 Knopff and Morton, *Charter Politics*, 195.

153 Ibid., 199.

154 Ibid., 171.

155 Ibid.

156 Ibid.

157 Ibid., 177.

158 For instance, they propose that governments have been reticent in using section 33 because they have succumbed to this oracular belief.

159 Ibid., 79.

160 Ibid.

161 Ibid., 82.

162 Ibid., 177.

163 On working through the structure/agency dilemma, see Jane Jenson, 'All the World's a Stage: Ideas, Spaces and Times in Canadian Political Economy,' *Studies in Political Economy*, vol. 36 (autumn 1991), 54.

Conclusion: Towards an Understanding of the Impact of the Charter of Rights on Canadian Law and Politics

DAVID SCHNEIDERMAN
and KATE SUTHERLAND

We ask our readers to return to Justice Bertha Wilson's last day on the bench, described in our introduction. In her speech on that occasion, Justice Wilson surmised that the Charter would continue to be 'a vital force in molding the lives of Canadians.' As the essays collected here suggest, her prognosis was correct. The Charter has had an impact that extends beyond individual litigants and individual rights-bearers to a multiplicity of social actors – many of whom have been canvassed in this collection: from governmental institutions and business firms to academic disciplines and social movements. The Charter's effect has been wide-ranging, albeit not uniform across these spectra of Canadian society.

In this conclusion, we attempt to draw together the varied strands of the discussion by examining the impact of the Charter on these diverse actors. We examine the Charter's impact in a dual sense – from the perspective of the Charter's effects on these social actors (how the Charter has shaped them) and from the perspective of the actors' effects on the Charter (how they have shaped Charter interpretation). These two perspectives are offered as lenses to understand better the impact of the Charter – they are heuristic devices and not rigid methodological demarcations. We suggest that the magnitude of social and political power held by each set of actors is an important variable in determining both the degree to which the Charter has shaped the actors' political, economic, and legal practices and the degree to which they, in turn, have shaped Charter jurisprudence. That is, we suggest that, in some respects, the most powerful actors in society have been more resistant to the influence of the Charter than those who are less powerful, while the most powerful may have been more successful in shaping Charter jurisprudence.

This suggestion may appear to be discordant with two strands of critical commentary on the Charter. The first strand contends that well-organized groups

– such as the women's movement – have used the Charter to advance specific legal and social agendas in the judicial arena that they could not attain in the legislative arena.[1] It is argued, for example, that a 'Court Party' has convinced a sympathetic judiciary to advance their special interests through Charter interpretation. A second strand identifies the more powerful and privileged actors in society as having benefited most from the Charter by assailing government laws and practices that restrict market-place activities: for example, laws that restrict commercial advertising or Sunday shopping. By invoking the classical liberal version of individual rights, it has been argued, the most privileged are able to maintain and reinforce their influence.[2]

It is not our intention here to take issue entirely with these critiques or to resolve their disagreements. Rather, we wish to readjust the focus of discussion by undertaking an analysis of the Charter's effects on law and politics from these dual perspectives. It is our view, in light of the evidence collected here, that the more privileged and powerful institutions and actors have been better able to resist or accommodate, to varying degrees, the influence of rights talk in their own institutional, political, and economic contexts. That is, the Charter's effect on these actors has been limited – powerful social actors have had success in shaping the discourse of rights, but they have not had to alter too significantly their own practices. The corollary is that less powerful social actors, who arguably have had less success in developing Charter jurisprudence to their benefit, nonetheless have had their internal practices more seriously disrupted in the attempt. The form that such disruption takes has varied. In some instances we note cleavages within and between equality-seeking groups. Others have noted that their agendas have had to conform to a more liberal, individualist path than they might otherwise have chosen to follow.

This is best explained by more clearly mapping out the Charter's influence on actors across socio-economic and political divides. We begin by discussing the Charter's impact on some of the more powerful actors in society, such as government and business, and then move to 'middle power' actors such as the courts and scholarly disciplines and afterwards to the least powerful actors, such as women, gays and lesbians, and Aboriginal peoples.

The Charter and Government

It is axiomatic that governmental power, both federal and provincial, has been curtailed by the Charter. Section 32 of the Charter directs courts to apply the Charter in respect of all matters 'within the authority' of Parliament and the legislatures. The legislative and regulatory schemes of publicly accountable officials and legislatures are the primary subject of Charter review. Governments at the federal and provincial levels invariably are parties to Charter litigation and thereby have had a vital role in influencing the development of Charter jurisprudence. Although further research into the pleadings of government in Charter litigation would be helpful, a preliminary observation suggests that governments have, for the most part, resisted Charter claims fervently. That resistance has focused oftentimes around the question of whether a governmental limitation is proportionate to the legislative goal. In addition, so as to help better defend against Charter challenges, governments have institutionalized processes for reviewing proposed legislative acts which might be subject to the Charter (what has been called 'Charter-proofing').[3] This also assists government in establishing a record for defending their actions as 'reasonable' limitations on Charter rights and freedoms. Some have lamented this relative decline in legislative power, as noted above, and suggest that there has been a concomitant rise of social movements and other 'special interests' which now are able to shift political debate from the legislatures to the courts.[4]

While legislative power can be subject to incessant Charter scrutiny, it may be that, in practice, the impact of the Charter on legislative powers has not been as profound as some critics have argued. Courts have shown a fair measure of deference to legislative schemes when it comes to certain social issues, such as the distribution of wealth through income taxation, as discussed by Kathleen Lahey in this volume.[5] Governments also have resisted Charter inroads into legislative jurisdiction. This has been particularly the case when these encroachments took the form of Charter decisions favourable to vulnerable minority groups, such as francophones in Alberta.[6] Legislatures also have been able to temper the impact of judicial rulings which were less politically popular than the status quo, such as the ruling that struck down the rape-shield law in the Criminal Code and the interpretation of the Charter that permitted self-induced intoxication as a defence in cases involving sexual assault and other crimes.[7] In each instance, the less popular judicial ruling led to a legislative response designed to temper or, as in the case of drunkenness as a defence, refute the Charter's effect.[8]

Substantively speaking, the Charter may not have intruded significantly into provincial legislative spheres. The potential intrusion has been of significant concern in the province of Quebec. As Yves de Montigny argues in this volume, while the courts have been active in striking down provincial laws, particularly when their subject matter concerned constitutionally guaranteed language rights,[9] the impact on the legislative scope available to provinces under the existing distribution of powers has not been profound.[10] Nonetheless, the enactment of the Charter over the objections of the Quebec National Assembly and its impact on provincial autonomy, however insignificant, continues to be a factor in debates within Quebec concerning provincial autonomy and the movement towards secession.[11] The appearance of a diminution in provincial power is exacerbated by the emergence of non-territorial Charter identities. It is argued that the Charter has generated a new form of pan-Canadian citizenship consisting of rights-bearing groups and individuals that subverts provincial identities and linguistic duality. The Charter's impact on Canadian federalism, then, continues to be profound, at least at the level of symbolic politics.

The Charter and Business

In our view, the impact of the Charter on the internal practices of business firms has been less than significant. Judicial interpretation has narrowed the scope of the Charter's application to governmental actors,[12] and hence there is little the Charter requires of business firms that would call for an alteration of business practices. Provincial human-rights codes, which target private marketplace activities, have been altered to accommodate many of the demands of the Charter's equality provisions. It is by the application of human-rights codes in the private sector that the terms and conditions of employment or of contracts of insurance may be affected indirectly by the Charter. To the extent, for example, that private insurance schemes and pension plans discriminate on the basis of sexual orientation, these plans may require some modification. But even here, the Charter's impact may be slight. The Supreme Court of Canada's decision in *Egan* suggests that employers may be permitted to discriminate on the basis of sexual orientation when their intention is to guard against contingencies which have a negative impact on the traditional nuclear family, focused around a male breadwinner and a female caregiver.[13]

Though the Charter has not had much of an effect on business practices, it has provided important opportunities to challenge all variety of legislative measures. Business exuberance has been limited, however, since not all Charter provisions have been available to business firms. The Supreme Court of Canada largely has, for example, kept the Charter out of the workplace,[14] limiting associative rights to the organization and constitution of associations, rather than extending such rights to the aims and objectives of associations of organized labour and, one assumes, business.[15] Freedom of association has had little impact where it could have had most – in the context of strikes and picketing. Nevertheless, the relationship between labour and business has not been symmetrical as far as the Charter is concerned. To return to our earlier point, business firms have been able to invoke the fundamental freedom of expression in order to attack a number of regulatory initiatives that negatively affect business practices, particularly where a concomitant consumer's 'right' to receive information has been threatened.[16] While business corporations have been denied the opportunity to claim the Charter guarantee of freedom of religion,[17] and the section 7 and 15 guarantees of liberty and equality, the courts have been open to corporate invocation of these sections as a shield against criminal or quasi-criminal prosecutions.[18] In addition to corporate 'persons,' individuals such as Merv Lavigne and associations of individuals such as the National Citizens Coalition have used Charter rights in order to assail limits on freedom of speech and association which operate to the disadvantage of corporate interests.[19]

The Charter and the Judiciary

The judiciary has been able to dodge the full impact of the Charter, in part by making much of its own activity largely immune to Charter review. The Supreme Court of Canada proclaimed early on that, where no government connection is present in a Charter challenge (courts being defined as outside the term 'government'), the Charter will not apply.[20] This immunity to Charter review has been diluted somewhat by the application of Charter 'values' to assist courts in the development of common-law rules. In the few cases where the Supreme Court has allowed the common law to be tested against Charter values, it has suggested a measure of deference to the common law that is not usually shown in Charter challenges.[21] In struggling with the coherence of this doctrine, the Court appears to have arrived at the position that a rather low level of scrutiny is required in such circumstances. Nonetheless, judges also have reserved to themselves the right to invoke the Charter to test the actions of private actors that have a negative impact on the courts – such as picketing at Vancouver courthouses.[22] In sum, the judiciary continues to reserve the right to control its own process when it comes to Charter review. Aside from the few provisions of the Charter that apply directly to the judicial process (such as the right to an interpreter in criminal proceedings), the impact of the Charter on the practices of the judiciary perhaps may be limited to the broader range of political questions which now are the subject of judicial review and the corresponding increase in the use of social-science evidence in the Charter adjudication process.[23]

The Charter and Universities

A variety of academic disciplines and academic institutions have been affected by the Charter. With regard to academic vocations, the interdisciplinary nature of Charter review has given rise to the teaching of law cases at an unprecedented level in political-science departments. There also has been a tremendous outpouring of periodical literature and books on the Charter authored by political scientists or aimed at political-science audiences.[24] Perhaps no less surprising is the appearance of political scientists as expert witnesses in Charter cases. Both governments and private parties have called on political scientists to provide expert evidence at trial regarding whether governmental limitations on rights and freedoms are reasonable in light of available, less restrictive, alternatives.[25] The Charter's impact on the discipline of political science, however, may be more limited. As academicians, political scientists have successfully assimilated the Charter into the dominant theoretical discourses of political science, as Alexandra Dobrowolsky argues in this volume.[26]

The environment for legal education has changed as well. To incorporate the changes the Charter has wrought, law school curricula have been modified by expanding the domains of traditional constitutional-law courses and by including new courses in women and the law, gay and lesbian rights, and theories of the Charter. Just as other academic disciplines have begun incorporating law cases into their teaching material, legal-teaching material has grown to include more interdisciplinary sources by which to make sense of Charter rulings and to train better Charter advocates. Hirings and admission goals also have changed, to some extent, with a view to Charter values, as Mary Jane Mossman writes in this volume.[27] Recognizing the multiplicity of social actors with an interest in Charter rights, both hiring and admissions policies have been altered to accommodate the representation of more segments of Canadian society in the legal academy. This, in turn, may have some impact on the make-up of the legal profession. However, the long-term impact of these changes has yet to be felt, with both law faculties and students exhibiting some resistance to change.

The Charter and Social Movements

Social movements, perhaps, have been most profoundly affected by the Charter. The women's movement, for example, has played an important role in shaping the development of Charter jurisprudence in the realm of equality rights, particularly through the efforts of the Women's Legal Education and Action Fund.[28] Notably, most of these cases involved challenges to gains that the women's movement wished to preserve (as in *Butler*, concerning a Charter challenge to the obscenity provisions of the Criminal Code)[29] – that is, most of the 'victories' involved the preservation of laws and regulations that would not have been vulnerable to legal attack were it not for the Charter. The victories here may have been of a more discursive nature: advancing understandings about equality theory and the use of those understandings in non-constitutional litigation, political lobbying, and the mobilization of women's groups more generally.

Internally, the women's movement has been divided by the discursive impact of the Charter. Most pertinent in this regard is the debate over whether rights discourse can be used to advance the goal of not just procedural but also substantive equality. This debate has pitched feminists who see Charter rights as a useful tool to advance women's equality against those who fear the Charter's retrenchment of the public/private divide and potential setbacks in social-equality gains.[30] Divisions also emerged during the Meech and Charlottetown Accord debates between and among Québécois, anglophone, and Aboriginal women. These divisions intersected over such matters as the impact of Quebec's 'distinct society' clause in equality litigation and the impact of both the distinct society clause and the Charter in the establishment of a framework for Aboriginal self-government.[31] A different schism emerged over the pornography issue, between 'anti-pornography' feminists and lesbian activists.[32]

Gays and lesbians have been less influential in Charter outcomes but they have been no less transformed in their political struggle by Charter discourse. For example, the fact that the decision in *Butler* expressed little concern about the use of the Criminal Code's obscenity provisions to prohibit gay and lesbian literature and erotica amounted to a serious setback for the movement.[33] Gay and lesbian activists have been somewhat more successful when it comes to the recognition of their rights under section 15 of the Charter. As a consequence of the decision in *Egan and Nesbit*,[34] discrimination on the basis of sexual orientation will now be prohibited by the Charter. The likely result is that gays and lesbians will obtain the usual protections afforded by human rights regimes where this protection has been resisted. It is less likely, however, that litigation in this area will have any impact beyond the formal recognition of sexual orientation as a prohibited ground of discrimination, a recognition that can be overcome in the interests of preserving and promoting the traditional family structure. More controversial rulings, such as recognition of marriage rights or access to pension rights, may remain elusive. The judicial and the public mood are likely to intersect, consistent with Didi Herman's observation that support for lesbian and gay rights 'erodes as specific demands are formulated.'[35]

Cleavages have occurred in the gay and lesbian movements, too, over a number of strategic questions. Litigating Charter equality rights bears a number of risks, including the possibility that the 'oppositional discourse' of the gay and lesbian movement will be 'structured out of the legal process.'[36] That is, fitting gay and lesbian equality claims within paradigmatic liberal-rights discourse may require those claims to be structured in ways that resemble the heterosexual norm.[37] Lesbian and gay Charter ligation has had the potential effect of obfuscating divisions between and within the lesbian and gay communities as well as potentially marginalizing oppositional strategies in the interests of a strategic uniformity.[38]

Aboriginal peoples also have been affected by the Charter. With respect to the impact of the Charter on Aboriginal rights, Aboriginal peoples have arguably seen their constitutionally entrenched rights in section 35 limited as a result of the Charter's influence. Aboriginal and treaty rights, following the decision of the Supreme Court of Canada in *Sparrow*, are subject to legislative limitations when courts are satisfied that governments have met a standard of justification resembling that required under section 1 of the Charter. Aboriginal rights may be infringed where, among other things, there is a valid legislative objective, the rights limitations are as consistent as possible with their recognition and affirmation in the constitution, and the rights are infringed as little as possible.[39] The Charter's constitutional architecture and its implicit preservation of parliamentary sovereignty holds sway over the recognition of Aboriginal and treaty rights. This is so even though section 35 is found in a part of the constitution different from that of the Charter and no qualifying language exists in section 35 similar to that found in the Charter's section 1. To a significant extent, then, the culture of the Charter has shaped limits, albeit unarticulated ones, to the constitutional recognition of Aboriginal rights.

The Charter also has had a significant impact on the politics of Aboriginal peoples. As John Borrows contends, the conflict within First Nations over the application of the Charter 'has provoked severe internal contention.'[40] The relevance of the Charter's equality rights to the improvement of Aboriginal women, for example, has been a source of intense division.[41] Similarly, disputes over the application of the Charter to Aboriginal criminal-justice systems remains a significant factor, perhaps an impediment, to their ultimate realization.[42] As Joel Bakan and Michael Smith demonstrate in this volume, the Aboriginal self-determination movement was divided, at least partially, along gender lines during the Charlottetown Accord debates over whether institutions of Aboriginal self-government should be subject to Charter review. This had important consequences for the way in which the movement towards self-government was portrayed in popular media and opposed in public discourse.[43]

The Future

Paradoxically, the social actors who, in 1982, were thought to have had the most to gain from the Charter in fact may have gained the least and, perhaps, lost the most. Judging by the essays in this collection, many of the same social actors are also the least willing to give up rights discourse and litigation strategies as a tool, albeit not the only one, in their social struggles.

What happens next? At this point in Charter temperature-taking, the wide-ranging impact of the Charter beyond discrete constitutional cases is clear. As the evolution of Charter jurisprudence continues at a slower pace than in the early, heady days of Charter interpretation, will the Charter's impact diminish? Although we can answer this question in only a preliminary way, we suggest not. Indeed, it may be that we are witnessing a shift in the battleground from the courts to the legislatures: a primary site for the impact of court rulings. Further research into these changes would be worthwhile.

While those we have identified as the most powerful actors continue to fight one another in the courts (for example, in recent litigation between the government of Canada and the tobacco industry), the least powerful actors may be looking elsewhere for their victories though with one foot still in the realm of rights discourse. Adopting a cautious approach (akin to what Didi Herman in her essay identifies as the 'critical pragmatist' approach), equality-seeking groups will continue to use the Charter but with a view that extends beyond the specific outcome of a given case to its potential impact on the wider political context within which they operate. As some commentators have noted, even perceived negative outcomes in litigation can have a positive impact in the broader scheme of things; for example, the striking down of rape-shield laws in *Seaboyer* giving rise to new and improved legislation.[44] And so the dance continues, with the Charter transforming a multiplicity of social actors and they, in turn, transforming the Charter.

Notes

1 See, for example, F.L. Morton, 'The Charter Revolution and the Court Party,' *Osgoode Hall Law Journal*, vol. 30 (1992), 627.

2 See, for example, Joel C. Bakan, *Just Words: Constitutional Rights and Social Wrongs* (Toronto: University of Toronto Press 1997).

3 See Patrick Monahan and Marie Finkelstein, 'The Charter of Rights and Public Policy in Canada,' *Osgoode Hall Law Journal*, vol. 30 (1992), 501, and Julie Jai, 'Policy, Politics and Law: Changing Relationships in Light of the Charter' (unpublished ms.).

4 See, for example, Rainer Knopff and F.L. Morton, *Charter Politics* (Scarborough: Nelson Canada 1992).

5 Kathleen A. Lahey, 'The Impact of the Canadian Charter of Rights and Freedoms on Income Tax Law and Policy,' in this volume.

6 See Ian Urquhart 'Infertile Soil? Sowing the Charter in Alberta,' in this volume.
7 On the dialogic relationship between courts and legislatures as a result of the Charter, see Brian Slattery, 'A Theory of the Charter,' *Osgoode Hall Law Journal*, vol. 25 (1987), 701.
8 See Janet Hiebert, 'Debating Policy: The Effect of Rights Talk,' in *Equity and Community: The Charter, Interest Advocacy and Representation*, ed. F. Leslie Seidle (Montreal: Institute for Research on Public Policy 1993) on the rape-shield law, and Martha Shaffer, '*R. v. Daviault:* A Principled Approach to Drunkenness or a Lapse of Common Sense?' *Review of Constitutional Studies*, vol. 3 (1996), 311, on drunkenness as a defence.
9 F.L. Morton, G. Solomon, I. McNish, and D.W. Poulton, 'Judicial Nullification of Statutes under the Charter of Rights and Freedoms, 1982–88,' *Alberta Law Review*, vol. 29 (1990), 396.
10 Yves de Montigny, 'The Impact (Real or Apprehended) of the Canadian Charter of Rights and Freedoms on the Legislative Authority of Quebec,' in this volume.
11 See Guy Laforest, *Trudeau and the End of the Canadian Dream* (Montreal: McGill-Queen's University Press 1995), chapter 6, and Alan C. Cairns, *Charter Versus Federalism: The Dilemmas of Constitutional Reform* (Montreal: McGill-Queen's University Press 1992), chapter 4.
12 *Retail, Wholesale and Department Store Union, Local 580 v. Dolphin Delivery Ltd.*, [1986] 2 S.C.R. 573.
13 See *Egan and Nesbit v. The Queen*, [1995] S.C.R. and, for further commentary, Hester Lessard, Bruce Ryder, David Schneiderman, and Margot Young, 'Developments in Constitutional Law: The 1994–95 Term,' *Supreme Court Law Review*, vol. 7 (1996) 81–156 (2d).
14 Paul Weiler, 'Labouring under the Charter,' *University of Toronto Law Journal*, vol. 40 (1990), 117.
15 See *Reference Re Public Service Employee Relations Act (Alta.)*, [1987] 1 S.C.R. 313 and *Professional Institute of the Public Service of Canada v. Northwest Territories*, [1990] 2 S.C.R. 367. For commentary, see Patrick Macklem, 'Developments in Employment Law: The 1990–91 Term,' *Supreme Court Law Review*, vol. 3 (1992), (2d) 227.
16 This occurred, for example, in *RJR-MacDonald v. Canada*, (1995) 27 D.L.R. (4th) 1 (S.C.C.).
17 But see the dissent of Justice L'Heureux-Dubé in *Hy and Zel's Inc. v. Ontario (Attorney General)*, [1993] 3 S.C.R. 675.
18 See *R. v. Wholesale Travel Group Inc.*, [1993] 3 S.C.R. 154.
19 Lavigne's constitutional challenge to mandatory union dues was directed largely at halting the labour movement's financial support for the federal New Democratic Party. *Lavigne v. Ontario Public Service Employees Union*, [1991] 2 S.C.R.

211; *National Citizen's Coalition Inc. and Brown v. Canada (A.G.)*, [1984] 5 W.W.R. 436 (Alta. Q.B.); *Somerville v. Canada*, (1994) (Alta. C.A.).
20 *Retail, Wholesale and Department Store Union, Local 580 v. Dolphin Delivery Ltd.*, [1986] 2 S.C.R. 573.
21 See *Hill v. Church of Scientology* (1995), 126 D.L.R. (4th) 129 (S.C.C.) In *Dagenais v. C.B.C.*, [1994] 1 S.C.R. 835 the Court strictly applied the Charter to the common-law rule permitting the issuance of publication bans in criminal trials. In *Scientology*, the Court explained the result in *Dagenais*. The measure of deference to Charter values was due to the fact that the case concerned a criminal trial – the quintessential form of government action.
22 *B.C.G.E.U. v. British Columbia (A.G.)*, [1988] 2 S.C.R. 214.
23 See G.V. La Forest, 'The Balancing of Interests Under the Charter,' *National Journal of Constitutional Law*, vol. 2 (1992), 133 at 135.
24 These works include Knopff and Morton, *Charter Politics*; Peter McCormick, *Canada's Courts* (Toronto: James Lorimer 1994); Ian Greene, *The Charter of Rights* (Toronto: James Lorimer 1989); Christopher Manfredi, *Judicial Power and the Charter: Canada and the Paradox of Liberal Constitutionalism* (Toronto: McClelland and Stewart 1992). Among the legal academics who have written books on this subject are Michael Mandel, *The Charter of Rights and the Legalization of Politics*, rev. ed. (Toronto: Thompson Educational Publishing 1994); David Beatty, *Constitutional Law in Theory and Practice* (Toronto: University of Toronto Press 1995); and Allan C. Hutchinson, *Waiting for Coraf: a Critique of Law and Rights* (Toronto: University of Toronto Press 1995).
25 Consider, for example, Neil Nevitte of the University of Calgary and Janet Hiebert of Queen's University, who appeared on behalf of the National Citizen's Coalition and the Government of Canada, respectively, in *Somerville*; Fred Fletcher of York University and David Bercuson (an historian) of the University of Calgary, who appeared on behalf of the Reform Party and the attorney general of Canada, respectively, in *Reform Party of Canada v. Canada (A.G.)*, (1992) 7 Alta. L.R. (3d) 1 (Q.B.); and Thomas Pangle of the University of Toronto and Christopher Manfredi of McGill University, who appeared on behalf of the chief electoral officer of Canada in *Sauvé v. Canada (Chief Electoral Officer)*, [1995] F.C.J. No. 1735.
26 Alexandra Dobrowolsky, 'The Charter and Mainstream Political Science: Waves of Practical Contestation and Changing Theoretical Currents,' in this volume.
27 Mary Jane Mossman, 'The Charter and Access to Justice in Canada,' in this volume.
28 As in *Law Society of British Columbia v. Andrews*, [1989] 1 S.C.R. 143; *R. v. Keegstra*, [1990] 3 S.C.R. 697; and *R. v. Butler*, [1992] 1 S.C.R. 452. See Sherene Razack, *Canadian Feminism and the Law* (Toronto: Second Story Press 1991).

29 *R. v. Butler*, [1992] 1 S.C.R. 452.
30 For an optimistic interpretation, see Lorenne M.G. Clarke, 'Liberalism and the Living Tree: Women, Equality and the Charter,' *Alberta Law Review*, vol. 28 (1990), 384, and, for a pessimistic account, see Judy Fudge, 'The Public/Private Distinction: The Possibilities of and the Limits to the Use of Charter Litigation to Further Feminist Struggles,' *Osgoode Hall Law Journal*, vol. 25 (1987), 485.
31 See Joel Bakan and Michael Smith, 'Rights, Nationalism, and Social Movements in Canadian Constitutional Politics,' in this volume; Ginette Busque, 'Why Women Should Care about Constitutional Reform,' in *Conversations among Friends: Proceedings of an Interdisciplinary Conference on Women and Constitutional Reform*, ed. David Schneiderman (Edmonton: Centre for Constitutional Studies, University of Alberta, 1992); Jill Vickers, 'The Canadian Women's Movement and a Changing Constitutional Order,' *International Journal of Canadian Studies*, vol. 7–8 (1993), 261.
32 See Ann Scales, 'Avoiding Constitutional Depression: Bad Attitudes and the Fate of *Butler*,' *Canadian Journal of Women and the Law*, vol. 7 (1994), 349.
33 See Carl F. Stychin, *Law's Desire: Sexuality and the Limits of Justice* (London: Routledge 1995) chapters 3–4, and Karen Busby, 'LEAF and Pornography: Litigating on Equality and Sexual Representations,' *Canadian Journal of Law and Society*, vol. 9 (1994), 165; and Brenda Cossman, Shannon Bell, Lise Gotell, and Becki L. Ross, *Bad Attitude/s on Trial: Pornography, Feminism, and the Butler Decision* (Toronto: University of Toronto Press 1997).
34 [1995] 2 S.C.R. 513.
35 Didi Herman, *Rights of Passage: Struggles for Lesbian and Gay Legal Equality* (Toronto: University of Toronto Press 1994), 75.
36 Ibid., 49.
37 See Carl F. Stychin, 'Essential Rights and Contested Identities: Sexual Orientation and Equality Rights Jurisprudence in Canada,' *Canadian Journal of Law and Jurisprudence*, vol. 8 (1995), 64, and Brenda Cossman, 'Family Inside/Out,' *University of Toronto Law Journal*, vol. 44 (1994), 1.
38 Herman, *Rights of Passage*, 44.
39 See Kent McNeil, 'Envisaging Constitutional Space for Aboriginal Governments,' *Queen's Law Journal*, vol. 19 (1993), 103, 105.
40 John Borrows, 'Contemporary Traditional Equality: The Effect of The Charter on First Nations Politics,' in this volume.
41 See Mary Ellen Turpel, 'Aboriginal Peoples and the Charter: Interpretive Monopolies, Cultural Differences,' *Canadian Human Rights Yearbook*, 1989, 3; Joyce Green, 'Constitutionalising the Patriarchy: Aboriginal Women and Aboriginal Government,' *Constitutional Forum*, vol. 4 (1993), 110.

42 See Mary Ellen Turpel, 'On the Question of Adapting the Canadian Criminal
    Justice System for Aboriginal Peoples: Don't Fence Me In,' and Teressa Nahanee,
    'Dancing with a Gorilla: Aboriginal Women, Justice and the Charter,' both in the
    Royal Commission on Aboriginal Peoples, *Aboriginal Peoples and the Justice
    System* (Ottawa: Supply and Services 1993).
43 Bakan and Smith, 'Rights, Nationalism, and Social Movements,' in this volume.
44 See Catherine Dauvergne, 'A Reassessment of the Effects of a Constitutional
    Charter of Rights on the Discourse of Sexual Violence in Canada,' *International
    Journal of Sociology*, vol. 27 (1994), 291.